Pete Boettke

MICROECONOMIC ANALYSIS

Second Edition

MICROECONOMIC ANALYSIS

Second Edition

Hal R. Varian UNIVERSITY OF MICHIGAN

W · W · NORTON & COMPANY
New York · London

Published simultaneously in Canada by Stoddart Publishing.

PRINTED IN THE UNITED STATES OF AMERICA.

The text of this book is composed in Times Roman, with display type set in Janson. Manufacturing by The Maple-Vail Book Manufacturing Group.

ISBN 0-393-95282-7

W. W. Norton & Company, Inc., 500 Fifth Avenue, New York, N. Y. 10110
W. W. Norton & Company Ltd., 37 Great Russell Street, London WC1B 3NU

1 2 3 4 5 6 7 8 9 0

To my parents

Contents

Preface

I have been pleased with the positive reception of the first edition of *Microeconomic Analysis* and am grateful for the opportunity to prepare this new edition. This edition contains about 60 pages of new material. Some of this material, such as the treatment of classical comparative statics techniques, corrects omissions in the first edition. Other additions arose from my teaching experience and the suggestions of colleagues concerning their experience in the classroom. Yet other new topics reflect my research interests in recent years.

Many of my friends, colleagues, and students have contributed valuable comments and suggestions on the first edition which I have incorporated into this new edition. Unfortunately, a fire in the Economics Building at the University of Michigan destroyed my list of the sources of many of these suggestions, so I am unable to thank all those who contributed comments.

However, I can offer a special thanks to Mark Machina of the University of California at San Diego, who undertook a detailed reading of the manuscript for the second edition and suggested many improvements.

• • •

As before, this textbook is intended for a course in microeconomics theory for beginning graduate students and advanced undergraduates with a sound mathematical preparation. A good understanding of calculus and a familiarity with elementary linear algebra is necessary to understand this text. Some elementary analysis is used in a few sections, but these sections are for the most part optional. (Optional advanced material is denoted by an (M) at the beginning of the section.)

To make full use of this text, students need to have or to develop a certain amount of mathematical sophistication; that is, they need to understand the concept of a proof and to be able to construct simple proofs themselves. For this reason, a number of examples and exercises have been included. In several cases the exercises contain important results that were excluded from the text due to limitations of space.

The exercises are graded according to difficulty. They range from 5-point problems, which should take only a few minutes to do, to 30-point problems which could easily take an hour or so. Selected answers and hints have been provided at the end of the book.

The core material of the book is contained in Chapters 1, 2, 3, and 5. These chapters cover the theory of the producer, the single market, the consumer, and general equilibrium theory and welfare economics. Most of this basic material is approached from the dual point of view, which in my opinion is not only more powerful but is also simpler than the traditional approach. The methods of analysis developed in these chapters are then applied to specific problems in Chapter 4 (econometrics), Chapter 6 (topics in general equilibrium), and Chapter 7 (welfare economics). Chapter 8 surveys some recent developments in the economics of information.

I have attempted to acknowledge the sources used in writing this text in notes and references listed at the end of each chapter. Original sources, at least for the most important topics, are also acknowledged. Undoubtedly, the references are not complete, for which I apologize to any slighted authors.

Since the exercises were developed during several years of teaching it is impossible to acknowledge each of their originators. In cases where exercises have been taken from recently published works, at least the author's name, if not the exact citation, is indicated.

Several of my teachers, friends, students, and colleagues have contributed valuable suggestions concerning the material treated in this text. Perhaps my greatest debt is to Daniel McFadden, from whom I learned much of the material presented in this book. The unpublished lecture noted of McFadden and Winter had a direct influence on this work, especially on Chapters 1, 3, and 5. Robert Hall's lecture notes and problem sets were also quite helpful.

Several students and colleagues read parts of the text and provided useful comments. Among them were Leonard Chang, Vincent Crawford, Franklin Fisher, Jan Kmenta, Edmund Phelps, Michael Rothschild, Carl Shapiro, and Robert Willig. Had I had the patience to follow all of their suggestions, I am certain I would have written a better book.

Finally, I have to thank several years of students at MIT who suffered through the many earlier versions of this text and corrected the many errors, typographical and otherwise. I hope the iterations have finally converged.

MICROECONOMIC ANALYSIS

Second Edition

Chapter 0

Introduction

0.1 DESCRIPTION OF MICROECONOMICS

Microeconomics is concerned with the behavior of individual economic units and their interactions. The two types of economic units typically considered are *firms* and *consumers*. The major type of interaction that is usually analyzed is that of *market interaction*. These concepts will be the primary focus of this book.

In pursuing this study of economic units and their interactions we will utilize two major analytic techniques. The first technique involves the analysis of *optimization*. We will model the behavior of economic units as optimizing behavior. In doing this we need to specify the *objectives* of the unit and the *constraints* which it faces.

For example, when we model the behavior of firms, we will want to describe the objective as profit maximization and the constraints as technological constraints and market constraints. When we model the behavior of consumers we will describe the objective as utility maximization and the constraints as budget constraints.

The second analytic technique that we will use in our study of microeconomic behavior involves the study of *equilibrium*. At its broadest level, equilibrium analysis can be viewed as the analysis of what happens to an economic system when all of the unit's behavior is *compatible*. Thus we will typically not be concerned with the analysis of an economic system when some firms or consumers find their actions thwarted.

This focus on equilibrium analysis is not due to the belief that equilibrium is necessarily more important than disequilibrium, but rather that the analysis of behavior in disequilibrium is substantially more difficult.

If we accept the model of optimizing behavior and restrict ourselves to the examination of equilibrium states, then the focus of microeconomics becomes the examination of situations in which no economic unit can further its objectives through feasible changes in its behavior. In other words, in an economic equilibrium, each unit is choosing an action which, given the choices of the other agents, it perceives as optimal, and the resulting behavior of the system as a whole is feasible.

0.2 OPTIMIZING BEHAVIOR

A specification of optimizing behavior involves a description of the *actions* a unit can undertake, the *constraints* on those actions, and an *objective function* that evaluates the actions. For example, the actions involved in specifying firm behavior are the choices of the way in which products will be produced, how much of the products will be produced, and what prices will be charged for the products. The constraints in this process are the physical and engineering constraints that describe physically possible production plans and the market constraints that describe possible combinations of prices and quantities of output that can be sold.

In many situations we will not be able to observe both the objectives and the constraints involved in an optimization problem. In the case of firm behavior, we may believe that we accurately model the objective of the firm as profit maximization, but we may feel that we do not have an adequate a priori description of the technological constraints the firm faces. The situation is precisely the reverse in the case of consumer behavior: there we feel that we have an accurate description of the constraint the consumer faces—the budget constraint—but we do not have an adequate a priori description of the objectives of a given consumer.

It might be thought that this lack of information would preclude any serious investigation of behavior, but this is not the case. As long as we have an understanding of the *form* of the optimization problem involved, we can investigate the kind of behavior that it might generate.

This is well illustrated by the development of the material in Chapter 1, where we investigate the consequences of profit-maximizing and cost-minimizing behavior. We will show that the observed demand behavior of such a firm must obey certain nonobvious restrictions which follow solely as a consequence of the hypothesized model. Similarly, in Chapter 3 we show that the theory of utility maximization implies certain testable restrictions on the observed choices of consumers.

Such restrictions have several sorts of uses. For example, one can use these observed restrictions to test the model against actual behavior of economic units. Given some data, one can ask if it could have been generated by a maximizing unit of the sort investigated in Chapters 1 and 3.

Another sort of use of these restrictions is to predict the response of some economic unit to a change in its economic environment. This sort of exercise is known in the economics literature as *comparative statics* and in the operations research literature as *sensitivity analysis* or *perturbation analysis*. We will encounter many examples of this analysis in our studies of consumer and firm behavior.

Given that the behavior of an economic agent is *consistent* with a particular maximizing model, we might go on to ask what sort of behavior is implied by objective functions or constraints of certain specialized *forms*.

These special cases of the general model are often of considerable interest because they may allow us to make more predictions than would otherwise be possible.

When we have found some restrictions on observed behavior that are implied by a model, we might well ask whether we have in fact discovered *all* such restrictions. One way to answer this question involving the *sufficiency* of restrictions is to ask wether data satisfying our list of observable restrictions can be used to construct a hypothetical objective function or constraint set that would in fact generate the data under examination.

Suppose, for example, that we consider the model of profit maximization. The observable consequence of such a model is the demand-and-supply behavior of a firm. We hypothesize that this behavior is generated in an attempt to maximize profits subject to the technological possibilities. When we examine the theory, we conclude that the observed behavior must satisfy conditions A, B, and C.

Suppose now that we are given some observed behavior that satisfies conditions A, B, and C. Can we find a technology that would generate this behavior as profit-maximizing behavior? If so, we know that A, B, and C are in fact a *complete* list of the restrictions imposed by the maximizing model in that they exhaust the observable implications of the model.

This question of *recoverability* has been motivated by consideration of the sufficiency of maximization restrictions. But it may often be of considerable interest in its own right. In the case of production analysis, an important result of Chapter 1 will show us how to recover an estimate of the underlying technological opportunities of a firm solely by examining its market choices at various prices. Similarly, in the case of a consumer, we will describe methods to recover estimates of the underlying utility function or preferences solely by examining *observable* market behavior.

Such methods have many applications in economics in the areas of cost benefit analysis, policy analysis, econometric estimation, and the like.

0.3 EQUILIBRIUM ANALYSIS

As mentioned above, an economic equilibrium is usually considered to be a situation where economic agents' behavior—typically maximizing behavior—is compatible. A common way to model this is through *systems of equations*.

For example, we may consider demand and supply behavior. Here one group of economic agents determines how much they wish to supply of some good as a function of its price. This determination of demand is presumably the result of some underlying maximization, or at least can be modeled as such. We let the function $D(p)$ be the function that relates the possible prices to the desired choices; $D(p)$ may, of course, depend on many other variable which for the moment we take to be fixed. Similarly, another group of economic agents determines by some maximization process their desired supply of the good in question. We denote this desired supply by $S(p)$ and make the same caveat about the other arguments of this function.

At an arbitrary price p, it is unlikely that the amount of the good demanded, $D(p)$, will be compatible with the amount supplied, $S(p)$. In this case we say that the market is in *disequilibrium*.

It may well be of interest to examine how markets may behave in such events. In certain cases it may be that some trades will be made at the price p and some of the agents will simply find their desires thwarted. In other cases it may be that no trades will be made at the prices p, and instead some agents will modify the prices at which they are willing to trade. In this book, we will typically not examine such disequilibrium situations; instead we will focus on the situation where the agents' trades are compatible. In the above case this means that we will examine situations where the amount demanded in fact equals the amount supplied.

In the case given above we often say that the price "adjusts" to equilibrate the market. This terminology assumes a kind of dynamic process which seems plausible but is often difficult to model in a satisfactory way. (Some attempts will be described in Section 6.8.)

Recall that in the description of the simple supply-and-demand framework given above we have assumed that some variables have been exogenously fixed at predetermined levels. Thus we say that we are considering the market behavior in a *partial equilibrium* framework.

We might continue to specify equilibrium conditions for these other variables. For example, suppose that the other variables are themselves prices of other goods that may serve as substitutes or complements for the good in question. Then we might represent the state of the system of demands by the *vector* of prices of the various goods, $\mathbf{p}=(p_1, \cdots, p_k)$. In this case, the demands and the supplies of each of the k goods will depend on the entire vector of prices, and equilibrium price vectors will be determined by the condition that *all* of the agents' behavior is in fact compatible:

$$D_i(\mathbf{p}) = S_i(\mathbf{p}) \text{ for } i=1, \cdots, k$$

There are many interesting questions that one can ask about such equilibrium systems. First, one may be interested in the question as to whether the equilibrium conditions can in fact be satisfied. If one proposes an equilibrium theory as a description of reality, then we would hope that the equilibrium concept can in fact be realized in many circumstances of interest. This is the question of the *existence* of an equilibrium; it serves as a necessary prior question to any further analysis.

Given that an equilibrium exists, we may well ask how it responds to changes in the economic environment. As in the case of maximization, we refer to this as the study of *comparative statics*. Here the terminology makes more sense: "comparative" refers to the fact that we are comparing two states, and "statics" refers to the fact that they are equilibrium states—i.e., we are not concerned with the adjustment mechanism that takes us from one to the other.

As an an example of a comparative-statics question, we may consider the imposition of a specific tax in a single market. If we let p be the price payed by the demanders of a good, then $p-t$ will be the price received by the suppliers of a good. If the price p is to be an equilibrium price, it must satisfy:

$$D(p)=S(p-t)$$

Given this equilibrium model, we note that we have implicitly determined an equilibrium price p as a function of the tax t. We might ask how p will change as t changes. The interest of this question is obvious for policy purposes.

Another aspect of equilibrium analysis is the attempt to characterize equilibria. Sometimes this takes the form of showing that an equilibrium that appears to be complex can in fact be seen as being very simple, once its underlying structure is exposed. (Sometimes it takes the form of showing the reverse: that an apparently simple equilibrium may actually be quite complex!)

One interesting way in which equilibria can be characterized is by examining how well they succeed in furthering the individual agents' objectives. For example, we say that a situation is *Pareto efficient* if there is no other situation that is unanimously preferred by all agents. It is obviously of interest to ask how well various economic institutions perform with respect to this criterion. We will see that in some circumstances, markets such as those described above will in fact have equilibria that are Pareto efficient. In other circumstances we may not expect the outcome of similar sorts of market institutions to be satisfactory.

This is perhaps one of the most important questions one can ask in an economic investigation: How well does the institution being examined perform in satisfying human wants and needs? Ultimately the techniques examined in this book should be directed toward such questions.

Chapter 1

Theory of the Firm

1.1 PROFIT MAXIMIZATION

Economic *profit* is defined to be the difference between the revenue a firm receives and the costs that it incurs. It is important to understand that *all* costs must be included in the calculation of profit. If a small businessman owns a grocery store and he also works in the grocery, his salary as an employee should be counted as a cost. If a group of individuals loans a firm money in return for a monthly payment, these interest payments must be counted as a cost of production.

Both revenues and costs of a firm depend on the actions taken by the firm. These actions may take many forms: actual production activities, purchases of factors, and purchases of advertising are all examples of actions undertaken by a firm. At a rather abstract level, we can imagine that a firm can engage in a large variety of actions such as those listed above, "operating" each action at some appropriate level. Thus we can write revenue as a function of the level of operations of some n actions, $R(a_1, \cdots, a_n)$, and costs as a function of these same n activity levels, $C(a_1, \cdots, a_n)$.

The basic assumption of most economic analysis is that the firm acts so as to maximize its profits; that is, a firm chooses actions $(a_1, \cdots, a_n)$ so as to maximize $R(a_1, \cdots, a_n) - C(a_1, \cdots, a_n)$. This is the behavioral assumption that will be used throughout this book.

Yet even at this broad level of generality, two basic principles of profit maximization emerge. The first follows from a simple application of calculus. The problem facing the firm can be written as:

$$\max_{a_1, \cdots, a_n} R(a_1, \cdots, a_n) - C(a_1, \cdots, a_n)$$

A simple application of calculus (Section A. 10 of the Mathematical Appendix) shows that an optimal set of actions, $\mathbf{a}^* = (a_1^*, \cdots, a_n^*)$, is characterized by the conditions:

$$\frac{\partial R(\mathbf{a}^*)}{\partial a_i} = \frac{\partial C(\mathbf{a}^*)}{\partial a_i} \qquad i = 1, \cdots, n$$

The intuition behind these conditions should be clear: if marginal revenue were greater than marginal cost it would pay to increase the level of the activity; if marginal revenue were less than marginal cost, it would pay to decrease the level of the activity.

This fundamental condition characterizing profit maximization has several concrete interpretations. For example, one decision the firm makes is to choose its level of output. The fundamental condition for profit maximization tells us that the level of output should be chosen so that the production of one more unit of output should produce a marginal revenue exactly equal to its marginal cost of production. Another decision of the firm is to determine how much of a specific factor—say labor—to hire. The fundamental condition for profit maximization tells us that the firm should hire an amount of labor such that the marginal revenue from employing one more unit of labor should be equal to the marginal cost of hiring that additional unit of labor.

factor inputs

The second fundamental condition of profit maximization is the condition of equal long-run profits. Suppose that two firms have identical revenue functions and cost functions. Then it is clear that in the long run the two firms cannot have unequal profits—since each firm could imitate the actions of the other. This condition is very simple, but its implications are often surprisingly powerful.

In order to apply these conditions in a more concrete way, we need to break up the revenue and cost functions into more basic parts. Revenue is composed of two parts: how much a firm sells of various outputs times the price of each output. Costs are also composed of two parts: how much a firm uses of each input times the price of each input.

The firm's profit maximization problem therefore reduces to the problem of determining what prices it wishes to charge for its outputs or pay for its inputs and what levels of output and inputs it wishes to use. Of course, it cannot set prices and activity levels unilaterally. In determining its optimal policy the firm faces two kinds of constraints: technological constraints and market constraints.

Technological constraints are simply those constraints that concern the feasibility of the production plan. We will discuss how one can describe technological constraints in the following sections of this chapter.

Market constraints are those constraints that concern the effect of actions of other agents on the firm. For example, the consumers who buy output from the firm may only be willing to pay a certain price for a certain amount of output; similarly, the suppliers of a firm may accept only certain prices for their supplies of inputs.

When the firm determines its optimal actions, it must take into account both sorts of constraints. In this chapter the primary focus will be on the technological constraints. For this reason the firms described in the following sections will exhibit the simplest kind of market behavior, namely that of *price-taking* behavior. Each firm will be assumed to take prices as given, exogenous variables to the profit-maximizing problem. Thus, the firm will be concerned only with determining the profit-maximizing levels of outputs and inputs. Such a price-taking firm is often referred to as a *competitive* firm; the reason for this terminology will be discussed in the next chapter. However, we can briefly indicate here the kind of situation where price-taking behavior might be an appropriate model. Suppose we have a collection of well-informed consumers who are buying a homogeneous product that is produced by a large number of firms. Then it is fairly clear that all firms must charge the same price for their product—any firm that charged more than the going market price for its product would immediately lose all of its customers. Hence, each firm must take the market price as given when it determines its optimal policy. In this chapter we will study the optimal choice of production plans, given a configuration of market prices.

1.2 DESCRIPTION OF TECHNOLOGY

A firm produces outputs from various combinations of inputs. We need a convenient way to summarize the production possibilities of the firm, i.e., which combinations of inputs and outputs are feasible.

It is usually most satisfactory to think of the inputs and outputs as being measured in terms of *flows:* so many units per time period. We can also think of the inputs as being distinguished by the calendar time in which they are available, the location in which they are available, and even the circumstances in which they are available.

Suppose the firm has n possible goods to serve as inputs and/or outputs. We can represent a specific production plan by a vector $\mathbf{y}$ in R^n where y_i is negative if the ith good serves as a net input and positive if the ith good serves as a net output. Such a vector is called a *net output* vector, or simply a *netput* vector. The set of all feasible production plans—netput vectors—is called the firm's *production possibilities* set and will be denoted by Y, a subset of R^n.

The set Y is supposed to describe all patterns of inputs and outputs that are feasible. Thus, it gives us a complete description of the technological possibilities facing the firm. When we study the behavior of a firm in its economic environment we may want to distinguish between production plans that are "immediately feasible" and those that are "eventually" feasible. For example, in the short run, some inputs of the firm are fixed so that only production plans compatible with these fixed factors are possible. In the long run, such factors may be variable, so that the firm's technological possibilities may well change.

We will generally assume that such restrictions can be represented parametrically by some vector $\mathbf{z}$ in R^n. The *restricted* or *short-run production possibilities set* will then be denoted by $Y(\mathbf{z})$; this consists of all feasible netput bundles compatible with the constraint level $\mathbf{z}$.

Example 1.1 Suppose we are considering a firm that produces only one output. In this case, we write the netput bundle as $(y, -\mathbf{x})$ where $\mathbf{x}$ is a vector of inputs that can produce y. We can then define a special case of a restricted production possibilities set, the *input requirement set:*

$$V(y) = \{\mathbf{x} \text{ in } R^n_+\text{: } (y, -\mathbf{x}) \text{ is in } Y\}$$

The input requirement set gives all input bundles that produce at least y.

Example 1.2 In the case above we can also define an *isoquant:*

$$Q(y) = \{\mathbf{x} \text{ in } R^n_+\text{: } \mathbf{x} \text{ is in } V(y), \mathbf{x} \text{ is not in } V(y') \text{ for } y' > y.\}$$

The isoquant gives all input bundles that produce exactly y.

Example 1.3 Suppose a firm produces some output from labor and some kind of machine which we will vaguely refer to as capital. Production plans then look like $(y, -q, -k)$ where y is the level of output, q the level of labor input, and k the level of capital input. We imagine that labor can be varied immediately but that capital is fixed at the level z in the short run. Then

$$Y(z) = \{(y, -q, -k) \text{ in } Y\text{: } k = z\}$$

is an example of a short-run production possibilities set.

Example 1.4 If the firm has only one output we can define the production function:

$$f(\mathbf{x}) = \{y \text{ in } R\text{: } y \text{ is the maximum output associated with } -\mathbf{x} \text{ in } Y\}$$

Example 1.5 There is an n-dimensional analog of a production function that is often useful. A production plan $\mathbf{y}$ in Y is called *efficient* if there is no $\mathbf{y}'$ in Y such that $\mathbf{y}' \geqq \mathbf{y}$; that is, a production plan is efficient if there is no way to produce more output with the same inputs or to produce the same output with less inputs. We often assume that we can describe the set of *efficient* production plans by some function $T: R^n \rightarrow R$ where $T(\mathbf{y}) = 0$ if and only if $\mathbf{y}$ is efficient. Just as a production function picks out the maximum *scalar* output as a function of the inputs, the transformation function picks out the maximum *vector* "netputs."

Example 1.6   The Cobb-Douglas technology is defined in the following manner (see also Figure 1.1):

$$Y = \{(y, -x_1, -x_2) \text{ in } R^3 : y \leq x_1^a x_2^{1-a}\} \qquad 0 < a < 1$$

$$V(y) = \{(x_1, x_2) \text{ in } R^2_+ : y \leq x_1^a x_2^{1-a}\}$$

$$Q(y) = \{(x_1, x_2) \text{ in } R^2_+ : y = x_1^a x_2^{1-a}\}$$

$$Y(z) = \{(y, -x_1, -x_2) \text{ in } R^3 : y \leq x_1^a x_2^{1-a}, x_2 = z\}$$

$$T(y, x_1, x_2) = y - x_1^a x_2^{1-a}$$

$$f(x_1, x_2) = x_1^a x_2^{1-a}$$

(handwritten margin notes:) Cobb-Douglas production function the exponents add up to 1. for example, $f(x_1, x_2) = x_1^a x_2^{1-a}$ where $a + 1 - a = 1$

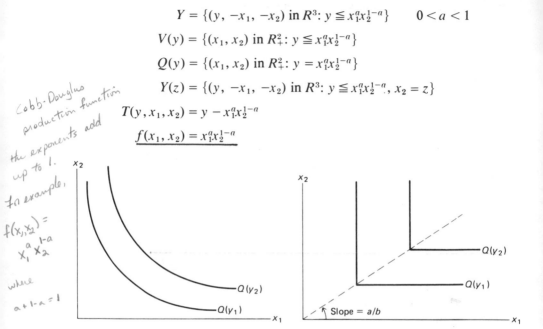

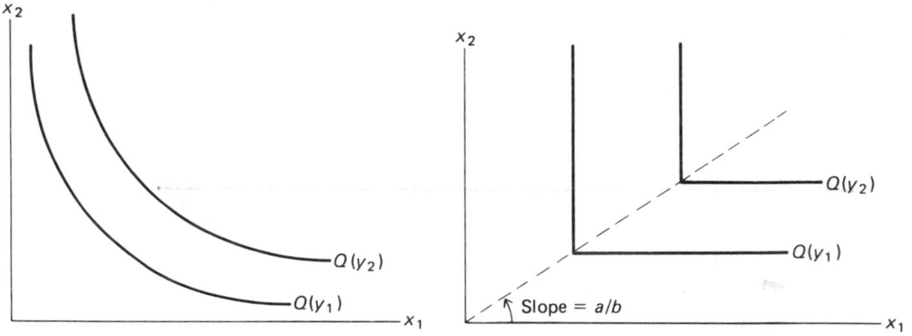

Fig. 1.1   *Cobb-Douglas and Leontief Technologies*

Example 1.7   The Leontief technology is defined in the following manner (see also Figure 1.1):

$$Y = \{(y, -x_1, -x_2) \text{ in } R^3 : y \leq \min (ax_1, bx_2)\}$$

$$V(y) = \{(x_1, x_2) \text{ in } R^2_+ : y \leq \min (ax_1, bx_2)\}$$

$$Q(y) = \{(x_1, x_2) \text{ in } R^2_+ : y = \min (ax_1, bx_2)\}$$

$$T(y, x_1, x_2) = y - \min (ax_1, bx_2)$$

$$f(x_1, x_2) = \min (ax_1, bx_2)$$

(handwritten margin notes:) Leontief production function is a fixed proportion production function. For example, H_2O. No matter how many Os you have if you have only 2 H's then you only get 1 unit of H_2O.

In this chapter we will deal primarily with firms that produce only one output; we will therefore describe their technology by input requirement sets or production functions. In order to avoid sign confusion as much as possible, we generally denote inputs by positive numbers rather than by using the sign convention of the netput vector.

1.3 DESCRIPTION OF PRODUCTION SETS AND INPUT REQUIREMENT SETS

The most straightforward way of describing production sets or input requirement sets is simply to list the possible production plans. For example, suppose that we are thinking about producing some output of a good using inputs 1 and 2. There are two different techniques by which this can be done:

Technique A—1 unit of good 1 and 2 units of good 2 produces 1 unit of output.
Technique B—2 units of good 1 and 1 unit of good 2 produces 1 unit of output.

This list summarize the engineering data about the available technology. It is represented as an input requirement set by the simple finite set:

$$V(1)=\{(1, 2), (2, 1)\}$$

This input requirement set is depicted in Figure 1.2. We may also suppose that to produce y units of output we could just use y times as much of everything for $y=1, 2, \cdots$. In this case we might summarize $V(y)$ by the set:

$$V(y)=\{(y_A, 2y_A), (2y_B, y_B): y_A=1, 2, \cdots, y_B=1, 2, \cdots\}$$

Here y_A is the amount of output produced by technique A and y_B is the amount of output produced by technique B, so that $y=y_A+y_B$.

This set is depicted in Figure 1.3 for $y=2$. (Note that (3, 3) can produce two units of y by producing one unit using activity A and one unit using activity B.) Of course, there is no particular reason to limit ourselves to integer levels of output; we could easily generalize the picture of $V(y)$ in Figure 1.2 to describe arbitrary levels of output y.

Suppose that we had an input vector (3, 2). Is this sufficient to produce 1 unit of output? We may argue that since we could dispose of 2 units of good 1 and be left with (1, 2), it would indeed be possible to produce 1 unit of output from the inputs (3, 2). Thus, if such *free disposal* is possible, it is reasonable to argue that if $\mathbf{x}$ is a feasible way to produce y units of output and $\mathbf{x}'$ is a input vector with at least as much of each input, then $\mathbf{x}'$ should be a feasible way to produce y. Thus the input sets should be *monotonic* in the following sense:

MONOTONICITY If $\mathbf{x}$ is in $V(y)$ and $\mathbf{x}' \geq \mathbf{x}$, then $\mathbf{x}'$ is in $V(y)$.

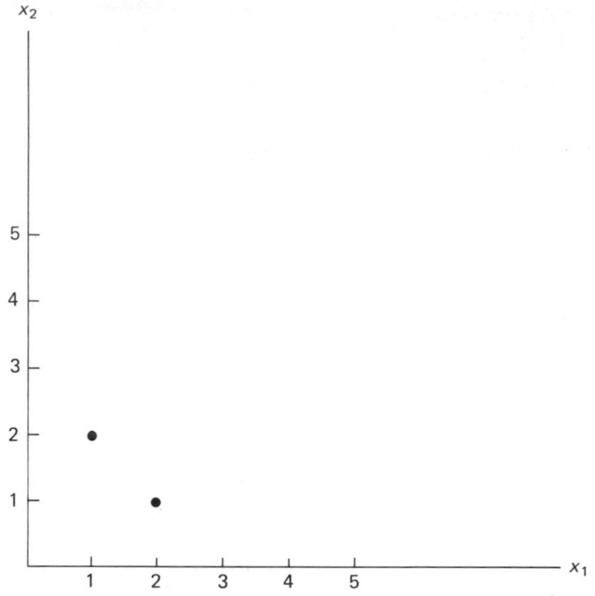

Fig. 1.2 V(*1*)

If we assume free disposal—monotonicity—then the input requirement set depicted in Figure 1.3 becomes the set depicted in Figure 1.4.

Let us now consider what the input requirement set looks like if we want to produce 100 units of output. As a first step, we might argue that if we multiply the vectors (1, 2) and (2, 1) by 100, we should be able just to *replicate* what we were doing before and thereby produce 100 times as much. It is clear that not all production processes will necessarily allow for this kind of replication, but it seems to be plausible in many circumstances.

If such replication is possible, then we can conclude that (100, 200) and (200, 100) are in $V(100)$. Are there any other possible ways to produce 100 units of output? Well, we could operate 50 processes of type 1 and 50 processes of type 2. This would use 150 units of good 1 and 150 units of good 2 to produce 100 units of output; hence, (150, 150) should be in the input requirement set. Similarly we could operate 25 processes of type A and 75 processes of type B. This would imply that $(.25 \cdot 100 + .75 \cdot 200, .25 \cdot 200 + .75 \cdot 100) = (175, 125)$ should be in V (100). More generally, $(t100 + (1-t)200, t200 + (1-t)100)$ should be in $V(100)$ for $t = 0, .01, .02, \cdots, 1$.

We might as well make the obvious approximation here and let t take on any fractional value between 0 and 1. This leads to a production set

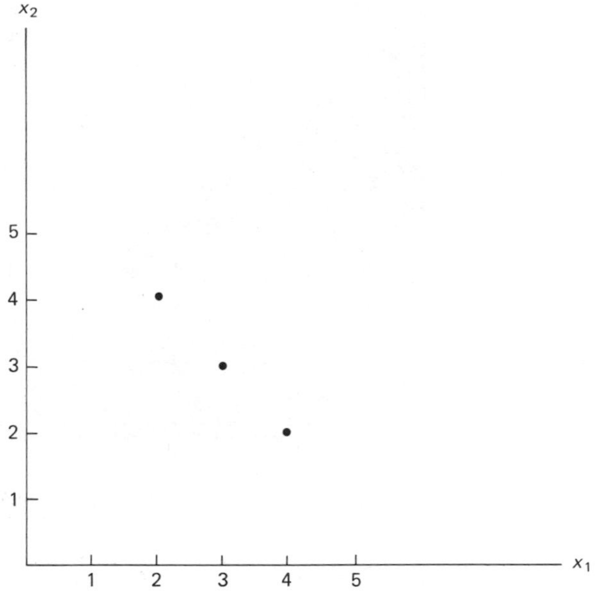

Fig. 1.3 V(*2*)

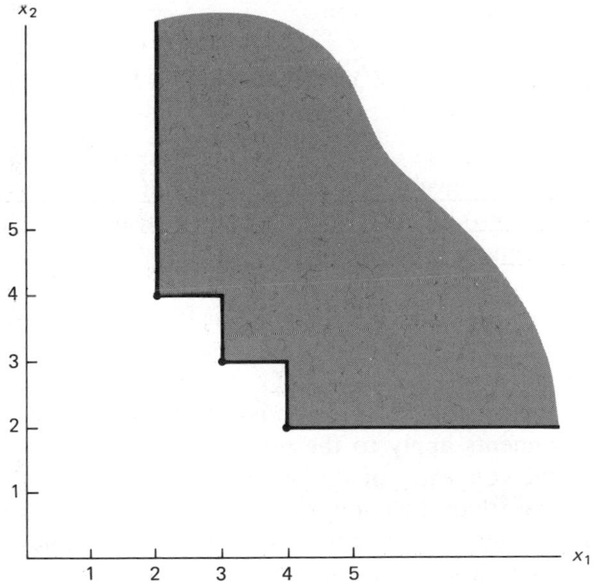

Fig. 1.4 *Monotonic* V(y)

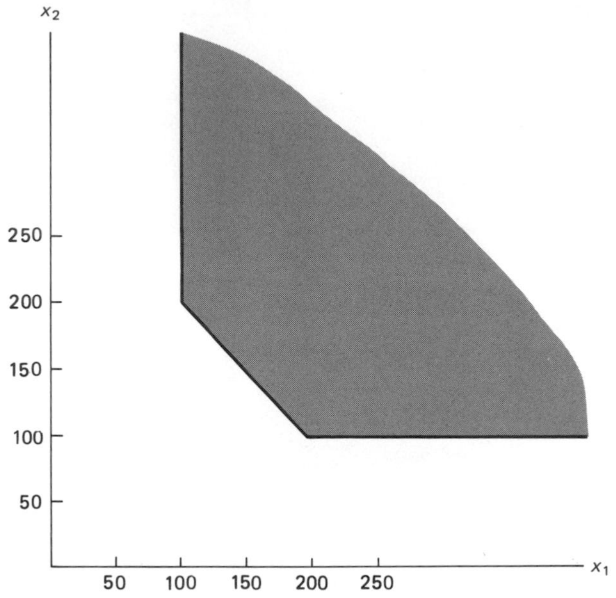

Fig. 1.5 *Convex* V(y)

of the form depicted in Figure 1.5. The precise statement of this property is given in the next definition.

CONVEXITY If **x** is in $V(y)$ and $\mathbf{x}'$ is in $V(y)$ then $t\mathbf{x}+(1-t)\mathbf{x}'$ is in $V(y)$ for all $0 \le t \le 1$. That is, $V(y)$ is a convex set.

We have motivated the convexity assumption by a replication argument. If we want to produce a "large" amount of output and we can replicate "small" production processes, then it appears that the technology should be modeled as being convex. However, if the scale of the production process is large relative to the desired amount of output, convexity may not be a reasonable hypothesis. If we have only 1½ units of good 1 and 1 ½ units of good 2, it simply may not be possible to produce 1 unit of output.

We applied the arguments given above to the input requirement sets, but similar arguments apply to the production set. However, it should be noted that the convexity of the production set is a much more problematic hypothesis than the convexity of the input requirement set. This will be discussed further in Section 1.6 on returns to scale.

For now we will describe a few of the relationships between the convexity of $V(y)$, the curvature of the production function and the convexity of Y.

(1) *If* Y *is a convex set, then* V(y) *is a convex set.*

PROOF. If $t(y, -\mathbf{x}) + (1-t)\ (y', -\mathbf{x}')$ is in Y for all $0 \leq t \leq 1$ and $(y, -\mathbf{x})$, $(y', -\mathbf{x}')$ in Y, then certainly this is true for $y = y'$. □

(2) V(y) *is a convex set if and only if* $f(\mathrm{x})$ *is a quasiconcave function.*

PROOF. By definition $V(y) = \{\mathbf{x}: f(\mathbf{x}) \geq y\}$, which is just the upper contour set of $f(\mathbf{x})$. But the definition of a quasiconcave function is that it have convex upper contour sets. (See Section A.6 of the Mathematical Appendix.) □

(3) *If* V(y) *is a convex set, then* Y *need not be convex.*

PROOF. Consider the technology generated by the production function $f(x) = x^2$. □

Finally, we consider a weak regularity condition concerning $V(y)$.

REGULAR V(y) *is a closed nonempty set for all* y.

This assumption requires that there is some way to produce any given level of output, and if we have a sequence $(\mathbf{x}^i)$ of input bundles that can each produce y and this sequence converges to an input bundle $(\mathbf{x}^0)$, then $\mathbf{x}^0$ can produce y. Loosely speaking, we require that $V(y)$ "contains its own boundary"—i.e., that it is a closed set.

1.4 PARAMETRIC REPRESENTATION OF TECHNOLOGY

Suppose that we have many possible ways to produce some given level of output as in Figure 1.6. Then it might be reasonable to summarize this input set by a "smoothed" input set as in Figure 1.7. That is, we may want to fit a nice curve through the possible production points. Such a smoothing process should not involve any great problems, if there are indeed many slightly different ways to produce a given level of output.

If we do make such an approximation to "smooth out" the input requirement set, it is natural to look further for a convenient way to represent the technology by a parametric function involving a few unknown parameters. For example, the Cobb-Douglas technology mentioned earlier assumes that any input bundle (x_1, x_2) that satisfies $x_1^a x_2^b \geq 1$ can produce at least 1 unit of output, where a and b are given parameters. These parametric technological representations should not necessarily be thought of as a literal depiction of production possibilities. The production pos-

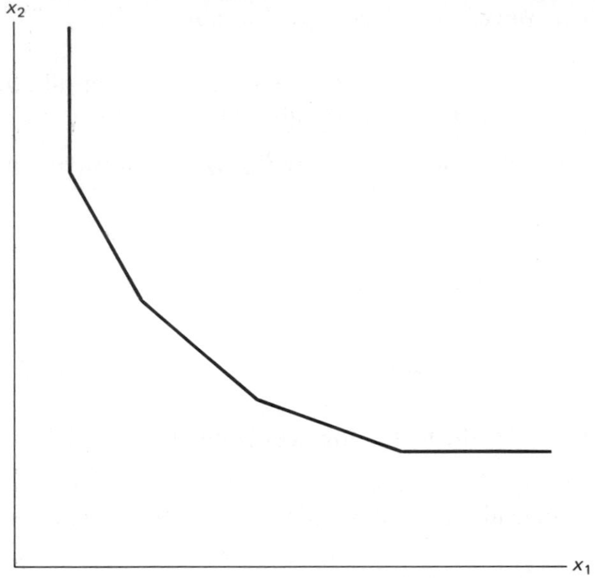

Fig. 1.6 *Many Slightly Different Activities*

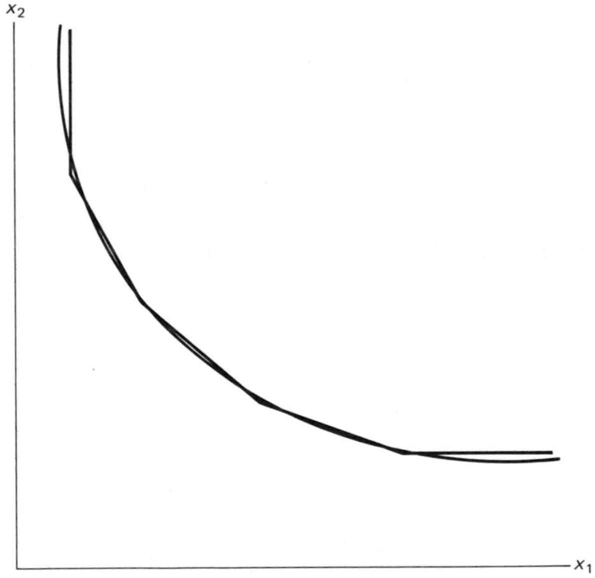

Fig. 1.7 *Smoothed Input Requirement Set*

sibilities are literally a list of the engineering data describing physically possible production plans. It may well happen that this engineering data can be simply described by a convenient functional form such as the Cobb-Douglas function, but this is only accidental.

However, these parametric representations are very convenient as pedagogic tools, and we will often take our technologies to have such a representation. We can then bring the tools of calculus and algebra to investigate the production choices of the firm.

1.5 THE TECHNICAL RATE OF SUBSTITUTION

Suppose that we have some technology summarized by a smooth production function and that we are currently producing at $y^* = f(x_1^*, \cdots, x_n^*)$. Imagine that we want to increase the amount of input 1 and decrease the amount of input n so as to maintain a constant level of output. How can we determine this *technical rate of substitution* between these two factors?

Following the discussion in Section A.7 of the Mathematical Appendix we let $x_n (x_1, \cdots, x_{n-1})$ be the (implicit) function that tells us how much of x_n it takes to produce y if we are using $x_1 \cdots x_{n-1}$ of the other factors. Then the function $x_n (x_1, \cdots, x_{n-1})$ has to satisfy the identity:

$$f(x_1, \cdots, x_{n-1}, x_n(x_1, \cdots, x_{n-1})) \equiv y$$

We are after an expression for $\partial x_n(x_1^*, \cdots, x_{n-1}^*)/\partial x_1$. Differentiating the above identity we find:

$$\frac{\partial f(\mathbf{x}^*)}{\partial x_1} + \frac{\partial f(\mathbf{x}^*)}{\partial x_n} \frac{\partial x_n(x_1^*, \cdots, x_{n-1}^*)}{\partial x_1} = 0$$

or

$$\frac{\partial x_n(x_1^*, \cdots, x_{n-1}^*)}{\partial x_1} = - \frac{\partial f(\mathbf{x}^*)/\partial x_1}{\partial f(\mathbf{x}^*)/\partial x_n}$$

Example 1.8 Technical Rate of Substitution in a Cobb-Douglas Technology   Since $f(x_1, x_2) = x_1^a x_2^{1-a}$

$$\frac{\partial f(x)}{\partial x_1} = ax_1^{a-1}x_2^{1-a}$$

$$\frac{\partial f(x)}{\partial x_2} = (1 - a)x_1^a x_2^{-a}$$

$f(x_1, x_2)$

$\dfrac{\partial f(x)}{\partial x_1} = a x_1^{a-1} x_2^{1-a} = 0$

$\dfrac{\partial f(x)}{\partial x_2} = 1 - a x_1^a x_2^{1-a-1} = 0$

we have

$$\frac{\partial x_2(x_1)}{\partial x_1} = -\frac{a x_1^{a-1} x_2^{1-a}}{(1-a) x_1^a x_2^{-a}} = -\frac{a}{(1-a)} \frac{x_2}{x_1}$$

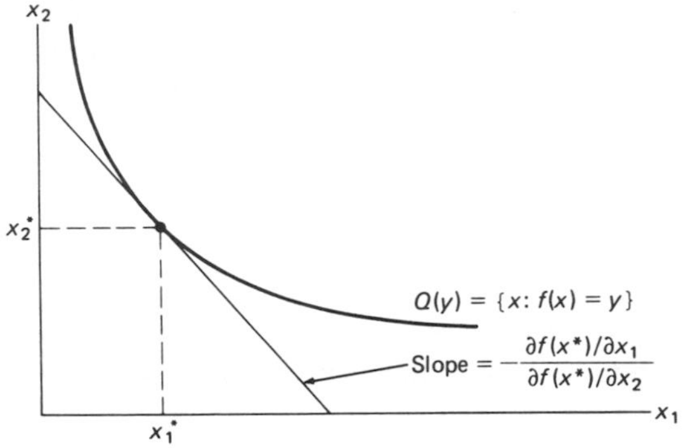

Fig. 1.8 *The Technical Rate of Substitution*

1.6 RETURNS TO SCALE

Suppose that we are using some vector of inputs **x** to produce some output y and we decide to scale all inputs up or down by some amount $t > 0$. What will happen to the level of output?

In the cases we described earlier, where we wanted only to scale output *up* by some amount, we typically assumed that we could simply replicate what we were doing before and thereby produce t times as much output as before. If this sort of scaling is always possible, we will say that the technology exhibits *constant returns to scale*. More formally,

CONSTANT RETURNS TO SCALE A technology exhibits constant returns to scale if any of the following are satisfied:

(1) **y** in Y implies t**y** is in Y, for all $t > 0$;
(2) **x** in $V(y)$ implies t**x** is in $V(ty)$ for all $t > 0$;
(3) $f(t\mathbf{x}) = tf(\mathbf{x})$ for all $t > 0$; i.e., $f(\mathbf{x})$ is homogeneous of degree 1.

The replication argument given above indicates that constant returns to scale is often a reasonable assumption to make about technological structures. However, it is not always satisfied.

One circumstance where constant returns to scale may be violated is when we try to "subdivide" a production process. Even if it is always possible to replicate so that we can scale operations up by integer amounts, it may not be possible to scale operations *down* in the same way. For example, there may be some minimal scale of operation so that producing output below this scale involves different techniques. Once the minimal scale of operation is reached, larger levels of output can be produced by replication.

Another circumstance where constant returns to scale may be violated is when we want to scale operations up by noninteger amounts. Certainly, replicating what we did before is simple enough, but how do we do one and one half times what we were doing before?

These two situations where constant returns to scale is not satisfied are only important when the scale of production is small relative to the minimum scale of output. This, of course, depends on the technology and production decisions actually being made.

A third circumstance where constant returns to scale is inappropriate is when doubling all inputs allows for a *more* efficient means of production to be used. Replication says that doubling our output by doubling our inputs is feasible, but there may be a better way to produce output. Consider, for example, a firm that builds an oil pipeline between two points and uses as inputs labor, machines, and steel to construct the pipeline. We may take the relevant measure of output for this firm to be the capacity of the resulting line. Then it is clear that if we double all inputs to the production process, the output may more than double since increasing the surface area of a pipe by 2 will increase the volume by a factor of 4. (Of course, a larger pipe may be more difficult to handle, so we may not think of output necessarily increasing exactly by a factor of 4. But it may very well increase by more than a factor of 2.) In this case, when output increases by more than the scale of the inputs, we say the technology exhibits *increasing returns to scale*.

INCREASING RETURNS TO SCALE A technology exhibits increasing returns to scale if $f(t\mathbf{x}) > tf(\mathbf{x})$ for all $t > 1$.

A fourth way that constant returns to scale may be violated is by being *unable* to replicate some input. Consider, for example, a 100-acre farm. If we wanted to produce twice as much output, we could use twice as much of each input. But this would imply using twice as much land as well. It may be that this is impossible to do for some reason or other. Even though the technology exhibits constant returns to scale if we increase *all* inputs, it may be convenient to think of it as exhibiting *decreasing returns to scale* with respect to the inputs under our control. More precisely, we have:

DECREASING RETURNS TO SCALE A technology exhibits decreasing returns to scale if $f(t\mathbf{x}) < tf(\mathbf{x})$ for all $t > 1$.

The most natural case of decreasing returns to scale is the case where we are unable to replicate some inputs. Thus we should expect that most *restricted production possibility sets* would exhibit decreasing returns to scale. In a formal sense, it can always be assumed that decreasing returns to scale is due to the presence of some fixed input. Suppose that $f(\mathbf{x})$ is a production function for some k inputs that exhibits decreasing returns to scale. Then construct a new "pseudoinput" and measure its level by z; let this input enter the production function in the following way:

$$F(z, \mathbf{x}) = zf(\mathbf{x}/z)$$

Then if we multiply all inputs—the $\mathbf{x}$ inputs and the z input—by some $t > 0$, we have output going up by t. And if z is fixed at 1, we have exactly the same technology that we had before. Hence, the original decreasing returns technology $f(\mathbf{x})$ can be thought of as a restriction of the constant returns technology $F(z, \mathbf{x})$ for $z = 1$.

Finally, let us note that the various kinds of returns to scale defined above are global in nature. It may well happen that a technology exhibits increasing returns to scale for some values of $\mathbf{x}$ and decreasing returns to scale for other values. Thus in many circumstances a local measure of returns to scale is useful. We can define the *elasticity of scale* in the following way. Consider what happens to output if we increase all inputs by some small amount t. This is given by:

$$\frac{df(t\mathbf{x})}{dt}$$

Now we convert this into an elasticity measure to find:

$$\frac{df(t\mathbf{x})}{dt} \frac{t}{f(\mathbf{x})}$$

Finally, we evaluate this measure at $t = 1$ to see what the elasticity of scale is at $\mathbf{x}$:

$$e(\mathbf{x}) = \frac{df(t\mathbf{x})}{dt} \frac{t}{f(\mathbf{x})}\bigg|_{t=1}$$

The elasticity of scale, $e(\mathbf{x})$, measures the percent increase in output due to a percent increase in scale. We say that the technology exhibits locally increasing, constant, or decreasing returns to scale as $e(\mathbf{x})$ is greater, equal, or less than 1.

1.7 THE COMPETITIVE FIRM

Now that we have considered ways to describe a firm's technological possibilities, we can begin to discuss its economic behavior.

Let us consider the problem of a firm that takes prices as given in both its output and its factor markets. Let **p** be a vector of prices for inputs and outputs of the firm. The profit maximization problem of the firm can be stated as:

$$\pi(\mathbf{p}) = \max \ \mathbf{p}\cdot\mathbf{y} \quad \text{s.t.} \ \mathbf{y} \text{ is in } Y$$

Since outputs are positive numbers and inputs are negative numbers, this problem does indeed give us the maximum of revenue minus costs. The function $\pi(\mathbf{p})$, which gives us the maximum profits as a function of the prices, is called the *profit function* of the firm.

Several variants of the profit function arise. For example, if we are considering a short-run maximization problem, we might define the *short-run* or *restricted profit function:*

$$\pi(\mathbf{p}, \mathbf{z}) = \max \ \mathbf{p}\cdot\mathbf{y} \quad \text{s.t.} \ \mathbf{y} \text{ is in } Y(\mathbf{z})$$

If the firm produces only one output the profit function can be written as:

$$\pi(p, \mathbf{w}) = \max \ pf(\mathbf{x}) - \mathbf{w}\cdot\mathbf{x}$$

where p is now the (scalar) price of output and **w** is the vector of factor prices. In such a case, we can also define a variant of the restricted profit function, the *cost function:*

$$c(\mathbf{w}, y) = \min \ \mathbf{w}\cdot\mathbf{x} \quad \text{s.t.} \ \mathbf{x} \text{ is in } V(y)$$

In the short run, we may want to consider the restricted or short-run cost function:

$$c(\mathbf{w}, y, \mathbf{z}) = \min \ \mathbf{w}\cdot\mathbf{x} \quad \text{s.t.} \ (y, -\mathbf{x}) \text{ is in } Y(\mathbf{z})$$

The cost function gives the minimum cost of producing a level of output y when factor prices are **w**. Since only the factor prices are taken as exogenous in this problem, the cost function can be used to describe firms that are price takers in factor markets but do not take prices as given in the output markets. This observation will prove useful in our study of monopoly.

Profit-maximizing and cost-minimizing behavior can be characterized by calculus. For example, the first-order conditions for the single output profit maximization problem are:

$$p\mathbf{D}f(\mathbf{x}^*) = \mathbf{w}$$

or

$$p\,\frac{\partial f(\mathbf{x}^*)}{\partial x_i} = w_i \qquad i = 1, \cdots, n$$

These conditions say that the "value marginal product of each factor must be equal to its price." This is just a special case of the optimization rule we stated earlier: that the marginal revenue of each action be equal to its marginal cost.

This condition can also be exhibited graphically. Suppose the production possibilities set is as given in Figure 1.9. In this two-dimensional case, profits are given by $P = p \cdot y - w \cdot x$. The level sets of this function for fixed p and w are straight lines which can be represented as functions

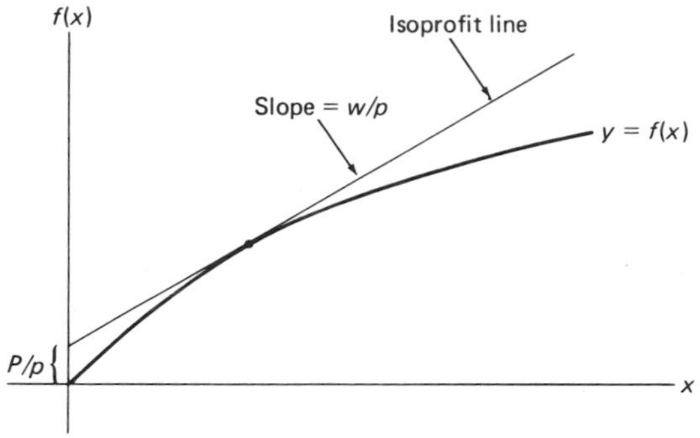

Fig. 1.9 *Profit Maximization*

of the form: $y = P/p + (w/p)\,x$. Thus the slope of the isoprofit line gives the real wage, and the vertical intercept gives the real level of profits.

A profit-maximizing firm wants to find a point on the production set with the maximal level of profits—this is a point where the vertical axis intercept of the associated isoprofit line is maximal. By inspection it can be seen that such an optimal point can be characterized by the tangency condition $\frac{df(x^*)}{dx} = w/p$.

The second-order condition for profit maximization is that the matrix of second derivatives of the production function must be negative semidefinite at the optimum point; that is, the second-order conditions require that the matrix

$$\mathbf{D}^2 f(\mathbf{x}^*) = \left(\frac{\partial^2 f(\mathbf{x}^*)}{\partial x_i \partial x_j} \right)$$

satisfy the condition that $\mathbf{h}\mathbf{D}^2 f(\mathbf{x}^*)\mathbf{h} \leqq 0$ for all vectors $\mathbf{h}$. Geometrically, this means that the production function must be locally concave in the neighborhood of an optimum.

For each vector of prices $(p, \mathbf{w})$ there will in general be some optimal choice of factors $\mathbf{x}^*$. The function $\mathbf{x}(p, \mathbf{w})$, that gives us this optimal choice of inputs as a function of the prices, is called the *demand function* of the firm. Similarly $y(p, \mathbf{w}) = f(\mathbf{x}(p, \mathbf{w}))$ is called the *supply function* of the firm. For the moment we will simply assume that these functions are well defined and nicely behaved.

In many situations it is not reasonable to model a firm as taking its output price as given. For example, if the firm is the sole supplier of some product we would expect that it would take into account its influence on the market price when it determined its supply of output. However, regardless of how the firm determines its supply of output, it is clear that it would like to produce this supply of output in the cheapest possible manner. We therefore consider the problem of finding a cost-minimizing way to produce a given level of output:

$$\begin{aligned} \min \quad & \mathbf{w} \cdot \mathbf{x} \\ \text{s.t.} \quad & f(\mathbf{x}) = y \end{aligned}$$

The first-order conditions characterizing an interior solution to this problem are:

$\mathbf{w} = \lambda \mathbf{D} f(\mathbf{x}^*)$ where λ is the Lagrange multiplier of the constraint (see Section A.10 of the Mathematical Appendix)

or

$$\frac{w_i}{w_j} = \frac{\dfrac{\partial f(\mathbf{x}^*)}{\partial x_i}}{\dfrac{\partial f(\mathbf{x}^*)}{\partial x_j}} \qquad i, j = 1, \cdots, n$$

The term $\dfrac{\partial f(\mathbf{x}^*)}{\partial x_i} \Big/ \dfrac{\partial f(\mathbf{x}^*)}{\partial x_j}$ represents the technical rate of substitution—at what rate factor j can be substituted for factor i while maintaining a constant level of output. The term w_i/w_j represents the economic rate of substitution—at what rate factor j can be substituted for factor i while maintaining a constant cost. The conditions given above require that the technical rate of substitution be equal to the economic rate of substitution. If this were not so, there would be some kind of arbitrage that would result in a lower cost way of producing the same output.

For example, suppose

$$\frac{w_i}{w_j} = \frac{2}{1} \neq \frac{1}{1} = \frac{\dfrac{\partial f(\mathbf{x}^*)}{\partial x_i}}{\dfrac{\partial f(\mathbf{x}^*)}{\partial x_j}}$$

Then if we use one unit less of factor i and one unit more of factor j, output remains essentially unchanged but costs have gone down. For we have saved two dollars by hiring one unit less of factor i and incurred an additional cost of only one dollar by hiring more of factor j.

This condition can also be represented graphically. In Figure 1.10, the curved lines represent isoquants and the straight lines represent constant cost curves. When y is fixed, the problem of the firm is to find a cost-minimizing point on the isoquant $Q(y)$. The equation of a constant cost curve, $C = w_1x_1 + w_2x_2$, can be written as $x_2 = C/w_2 - (w_1/w_2)x_1$. For fixed w_1 and w_2 the firm wants to find a point on $Q(y)$ where the associated constant cost curve has minimal vertical intercept. It is geometrically clear that such a point will be characterized by the tangency condition that the slope of the constant cost curve must be equal to the slope of the isoquant. Substituting the algebraic expressions for these slopes gives the mathematical result described above.

The second-order conditions for cost minimization can be found by

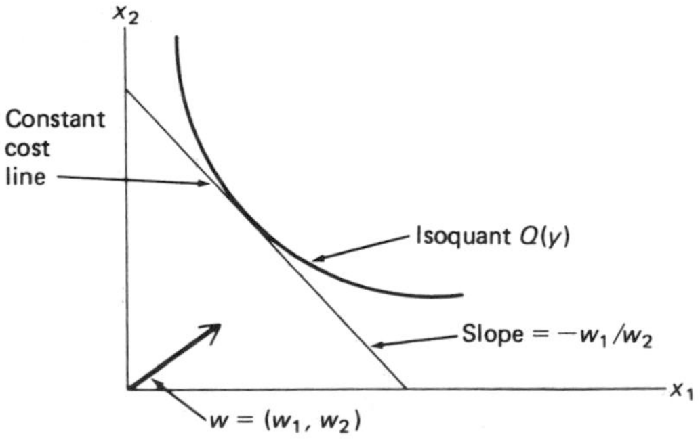

Fig. 1.10 *Cost Minimization*

applying Fact A.12 of the Mathematical Appendix. The Lagrangian expression is:

$$L(\mathbf{x}, t) = \mathbf{w}\cdot\mathbf{x} - t(f(\mathbf{x}) - y)$$

so

$$\frac{\partial^2 L(\mathbf{x}^*, t)}{\partial x_i \partial x_j} = -t\,\frac{\partial^2 f(\mathbf{x}^*)}{\partial x_i \partial x_j}$$

The second-order conditions can therefore be written as:

$$\mathbf{h}\mathbf{D}^2 f(\mathbf{x}^*)\mathbf{h} \leqq 0 \text{ for all } \mathbf{h} \text{ satisfying } \mathbf{w}\cdot\mathbf{h} = 0$$

Algebraically, this means that $\mathbf{D}^2 f(\mathbf{x}^*)$ must be negative semidefinite for all directions $\mathbf{h}$ orthogonal to $\mathbf{w}$. Geometrically, this essentially requires that the production function be locally quasiconcave, which is just another way of saying that the input requirement set must be locally convex. (See Section A.6 of the Mathematical Appendix.) In other words, the isoquant surface must lie above the isocost surface, as depicted in Figure 1.10.

For each choice of $\mathbf{w}$ and y there will be some choice of $\mathbf{x}^*$ that minimizes the cost of producing y units of output. We will call the function that gives us this optimal choice the *conditional factor demand function* and write it as $\mathbf{x}(\mathbf{w}, y)$. Note that conditional factor demands depend on the level of output produced as well as on the factor prices.

We can combine the problems of cost minimization and profit maximization for a price-taking firm by writing the profit maximization problem in the following way:

$$\max \quad p\cdot y - c(\mathbf{w}, y)$$

Here the first term gives revenue and the second term gives the minimum cost of achieving that revenue. Then the first-order conditions for profit maximization are:

$$p = \frac{\partial c(\mathbf{w}, y^*)}{\partial y}$$

or price equals marginal cost. Again, this condition is a special case of the fundamental marginal condition discussed earlier. The second-order condition for profit maximization is that $\partial^2 c(\mathbf{w}, y^*)/\partial y^2 \geqq 0$, or that marginal cost must be increasing at the optimal level of output.

The conditions characterizing profit maximization and cost minimization are intuitive, but they can sometimes lead one astray. There are four possible pitfalls.

First, the technology in question may not be representable by a differentiable production function, so the calculus techniques cannot be applied. The Leontief technology is a good example of this problem. We will calculate its cost function directly in Example 1.14.

Second, the calculus conditions make sense only when the choice variables can be varied in an open neighborhood of the optimal choice. In many economic problems the variables are naturally nonnegative; so if some variables have a value of zero at the optimal choice, the calculus conditions described above may be inappropriate. The above conditions are valid only for *interior solutions*—where none of the variables is zero.

The necessary modifications of the conditions to handle *boundary solutions* are not difficult to state. For example, if we constrain $\mathbf{x}$ to be nonnegative in the cost minimization case, the relevant first-order conditions turn out to be:

$$p\frac{\partial f(\mathbf{x})}{\partial x_i} - w_i \leq 0 \quad \text{for } x_i \geq 0$$

$$p\frac{\partial f(\mathbf{x})}{\partial x_i} - w_i = 0 \quad \text{for } x_i > 0$$

Thus the marginal profit from increasing x_i must be nonpositive, otherwise the firm would increase x_i. If $x_i = 0$, the marginal profit from increasing x_i may be negative—which is to say, the firm would like to decrease x_i. But since x_i is already zero, this is impossible. Finally, if $x_i > 0$ so that the nonnegatively constraint is not binding, we will have the usual conditions for an interior solution.

Cases involving nonnegativity constraints or other sorts of inequality constraints can be handled formally by meqns of the Kuhn-Tucker Theorem described in Appendix A.9. An illustrative example of its application is given in Example 1.15.

The third problem in applying these conditions is that they may not determine a unique operating position for the firm. The calculus conditions are, after all, only necessary conditions. Although they are usually sufficient for the existence of *local* optimum, they will uniquely describe a global optimum only under certain convexity conditions—i.e., requiring $V(y)$ to be convex for cost minimization problems and requiring Y to be convex for profit maximization problems.

The fourth problem in naïvely applying first-order conditions is that they only make sense when an optimal choice actually exists. Let us consider the case where the production function is $f(x) = x$ so that one unit of x produces one unit of output. It is not hard to see that for $p > w$ no profit maximizing plan will exist. If you want to maximize $px - wx$ for $p > w$, you would want to choose an indefinitely large value of x.

Let us consider further when this sort of problem might arise.

There is not much problem with the cost function's being well defined. The set $V(y)$ has been assumed to be closed, and costs are certainly bounded from below since the least it can cost to produce y is zero. Hence, a minimum cost production plan will always exist.

The situation is not so nice for the profit function. There is at least one important case where the profit function is not well defined. It turns out that profits may be unbounded when the technology exhibits constant or increasing returns to scale.

To see that profits may be unbounded in these circumstances, we hypothesize that we can find some $(p, \mathbf{w})$ where optimal profits are strictly positive:

$$pf(\mathbf{x}^*) - \mathbf{w} \cdot \mathbf{x}^* = \pi^* > 0$$

Suppose that we scaled up production by a factor $t > 1$; our profits would then be:

$$pf(t\mathbf{x}^*) - \mathbf{w} \cdot (t\mathbf{x}^*) \geq tpf(\mathbf{x}^*) - t\mathbf{w} \cdot \mathbf{x}^* = t\pi^* > \pi^*$$

This means that, if profits are ever positive, they can be made bigger—hence, profits are unbounded. No maximal profit point may exist.

It is clear from this demonstration that the only meaningful profit-maximizing position for a constant-returns-to-scale firm is that of zero profits. If the firm is operating at a zero profit point, it is indifferent about the level of output at which it produces. However, once this level of output has been determined by other considerations, the firm can be viewed as a cost minimizer with respect to its choice of inputs, so that the *conditional* factor demand functions will be well defined.

In what follows we will usually consider the long-run constant-returns-to-scale situation to be the "standard" situation, but we will also consider the other possibilities. As far as the profit function goes, we have the following general principle: if the technology exhibits constant or increasing returns to scale, the profit function may often not be well defined. However, in the short run, when some factors are fixed, the firm is likely to exhibit decreasing returns to scale with respect to the variable inputs so that the short-run or restricted profit function almost always makes sense.

Example 1.9 Constant Returns to Scale and the Cost Function If the production function exhibits constant returns to scale then it is intuitively clear that the cost function should exhibit costs that are linear in the level of output: if you want to produce twice as much output it will cost you twice as much. This intuition is verified in the following proposition:

PROPOSITION *If the production function exhibits constant returns to scale, the cost function may be written as* $c(\mathbf{w}, y) = yc(\mathbf{w}, 1)$.

PROOF. Let $\mathbf{x}^*$ be a cheapest way to produce one unit of output at prices $\mathbf{w}$ so that $c(\mathbf{w}, 1) = \mathbf{w} \cdot \mathbf{x}^*$. Then I claim that $c(\mathbf{w}, y) = \mathbf{w} \cdot y\mathbf{x}^* = yc(\mathbf{w}, 1)$. Notice first that $y\mathbf{x}^*$ is feasible to produce y since the technology is constant returns to scale. Suppose that it does not minimize cost; instead let $\mathbf{x}'$ be the cost-minimizing bundle to produce y at prices $\mathbf{w}$ so that $\mathbf{w} \cdot \mathbf{x}' < \mathbf{w} \cdot y\mathbf{x}^*$. Then $\mathbf{w} \cdot \mathbf{x}'/y < \mathbf{w} \cdot \mathbf{x}^*$ and $\mathbf{x}'/y$ can produce 1 since the economy is constant returns to scale. This contradicts the definition of $\mathbf{x}^*$. □

Example 1.10 Cost Function of the Generalized Cobb-Douglas Technology

$$c(\mathbf{w}, y) = \min_{x_1, x_2} w_1 x_1 + w_2 x_2 \quad \text{s.t.} \quad A x_1^a x_2^b = y$$

This is equivalent to:

$$\min_{x_1} \quad w_1 x_1 + w_2 A^{-\frac{1}{b}} y^{\frac{1}{b}} x_1^{-\frac{a}{b}}$$

The first-order condition is:

$$w_1 - \frac{a}{b} w_2 A^{-\frac{1}{b}} y^{\frac{1}{b}} x_1^{-\frac{a+b}{b}} = 0$$

which gives us the conditional demand function for factor 1:

$$x_1(w_1, w_2, y) = A^{-\frac{1}{a+b}} \left[\frac{a w_2}{b w_1} \right]^{\frac{b}{a+b}} y^{\frac{1}{a+b}}$$

The other conditional demand function is:

$$x_2(w_1, w_2, y) = A^{-\frac{1}{a+b}} \left[\frac{a w_2}{b w_1} \right]^{-\frac{a}{a+b}} y^{\frac{1}{a+b}}$$

The cost function is:

$$c(w_1, w_2, y) = w_1 x_1(w_1, w_2, y) + w_2 x_2(w_1, w_2, y) = A^{-\frac{1}{a+b}} \left[\left(\frac{a}{b}\right)^{\frac{b}{a+b}} + \left(\frac{a}{b}\right)^{-\frac{a}{a+b}} \right] w_1^{\frac{a}{a+b}} w_2^{\frac{b}{a+b}} y^{\frac{1}{a+b}}$$

When we use the Cobb-Douglas technology for examples we will usually measure units so that A = 1 and use the constant-returns-to-scale assumption that $a + b = 1$. In this case the cost function reduces to:

$$c(w_1, w_2, y) = K w_1^a w_2^{1-a} y$$

where $K = a^{-a}(1 - a)^{a-1}$.

Example 1.11 The Profit Function for the Restricted Cobb-Douglas Technology Suppose that, in the short run, factor 2 is constrained to be operated at the level k. Then the restricted profit function can be found by solving:

$$\begin{aligned} \max \quad & py - (w_1 x_1 + w_2 k) \\ \text{s.t.} \quad & x_1^a k^{1-a} = y \end{aligned}$$

This is equivalent to:

$$\max \quad p x_1^a k^{1-a} - w_1 x_1 - w_2 k$$

The first-order condition is:

$$p a x_1^{a-1} k^{1-a} - w_1 = 0$$

This can be rearranged to get the demand function for good 1:

$$x_1 = \left[\frac{w_1}{ap}\right]^{\frac{1}{a-1}} k$$

The restricted profit function can be found by substitution.

Example 1.12 The Profit Function for the Generalized Cobb-Douglas Technology Let us write the cost function for the generalized Cobb-Douglas technology as:

$$c(\mathbf{w}, y) = Kc(\mathbf{w}) y^{\frac{1}{a+b}}$$

Then the profit maximization problem of the firm is:

$$\max \quad py - Kc(\mathbf{w}) y^{\frac{1}{a+b}}$$

The first-order condition is:

$$p - \frac{K}{a+b} c(\mathbf{w}) y^{\frac{1-a-b}{a+b}} = 0$$

The supply function is therefore:

$$y = \left[p \frac{(a+b)}{Kc(\mathbf{w})}\right]^{\frac{a+b}{1-a-b}}$$

Notice that the supply function will be well defined only when $a + b < 1$, that is, when the technology exhibits decreasing returns to scale. The profit function is:

$$\pi(p, \mathbf{w}) = p\left[\frac{p(a+b)}{Kc(\mathbf{w})}\right]^{\frac{a+b}{1-a-b}} - Kc(\mathbf{w})\left[\frac{p(a+b)}{Kc(\mathbf{w})}\right]^{\frac{1}{1-a-b}}$$

Example 1.13 The CES Production Function The *constant elasticity of substitution* or CES production function has the form:

$$y = [a_0 + a_1x_1^\rho + a_2x_2^\rho]^{\frac{1}{\rho}}$$

If $a_0 = 0$, it is easy to verify that the CES function exhibits constant returns to scale. The CES function contains several other well-known production functions as special cases. These are detailed below and illustrated in Figure 1.11.

(1) The Linear Production Function ($\rho = 1$). Simple substitution yields

$$y = a_0 + a_1x_1 + a_2x_2$$

(2) The Cobb-Douglas Production Function ($\rho = 0$). Let us measure units of the goods so that $a_1 + a_2 = 1$. We assume constant returns to scale so that $a_0 = 0$. Consider the behavior of the logarithm of the CES production function:

$$ln\ y = \frac{1}{\rho}\ ln\ [a_1x_1^\rho + a_2x_2^\rho]$$

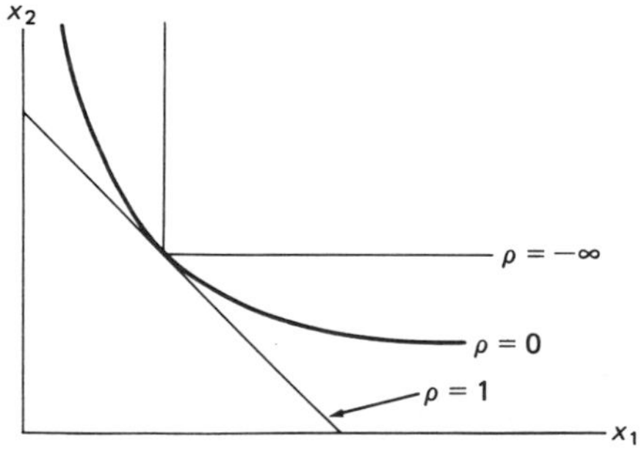

Fig. 1.11 *Isoquants for the CES Production Function*

as $\rho \to 0$. At $\rho = 0$, the value of the function is indeterminate, but $\lim_{\rho \to 0} \ln y$ can be calculated by L'Hòpital's rule:

$$\lim_{\rho \to 0} \ln y = \frac{a_1 x_1^\rho \ln x_1 + a_2 x_2^\rho \ln x_2}{[a_1 x_1^\rho + a_2 x_2^\rho]}$$

Evaluate this expression at $\rho = 0$ to get the Cobb-Douglas form:

$$\lim_{\rho \to 0} \ln y = (a_1 \ln x_1 + a_2 \ln x_2)/(a_1 + a_2)$$

(3) The Leontief Production Function ($\rho = -\infty$). Let us measure units so that $a_1 = a_2$ and assume $a_0 = 0$. Then the CES function has the form:

$$y = [x_1^\rho + x_2^\rho]^{\frac{1}{\rho}}$$

Let us suppose that $x_1 = \min(x_1, x_2)$. We want to show that

$$x_1 = \lim_{\rho \to -\infty} [x_1^\rho + x_2^\rho]^{\frac{1}{\rho}}$$

First of all, we note that

$$x_1^\rho \leqq x_1^\rho + x_2^\rho$$

so

$$x_1 \geqq (x_1^\rho + x_2^\rho)^{\frac{1}{\rho}}$$

On the other hand since $\rho < 0$ and $x_1 = \min(x_1, x_2)$ we have:

$$x_1^\rho + x_2^\rho \leqq x_1^\rho + x_1^\rho = 2x_1^\rho$$
$$(x_1^\rho + x_2^\rho)^{\frac{1}{\rho}} \geqq 2^{\frac{1}{\rho}} x_1$$

Combining this inequality with the preceding inequality and letting $\rho \to -\infty$ completes the proof.

Next we will derive the cost function for the CES technology. In order to avoid excessive notation, we first consider the case where $a_0 = 0$, $a_1 = a_2 = 1$. The cost minimization problem is:

$$\begin{aligned} \min \quad & w_1 x_1 + w_2 x_2 \\ \text{s.t.} \quad & x_1^\rho + x_2^\rho = y^\rho \end{aligned}$$

The first-order conditions are:

$$\frac{w_1}{w_2} = \frac{x_1^{\rho-1}}{x_2^{\rho-1}}$$

or

$$\frac{w_1 x_1}{w_2 x_2} = \frac{x_1^{\rho}}{x_2^{\rho}}$$

Add one to both sides:

$$\frac{w_1 x_1 + w_2 x_2}{w_2 x_2} = \frac{x_1^{\rho} + x_2^{\rho}}{x_2^{\rho}}$$

or

$$\frac{c(\mathbf{w}, y)}{w_2 x_2} = \frac{y^{\rho}}{x_2^{\rho}}$$

Solving for x gives:

$$x_2 = c(\mathbf{w}, y)^{1/1-\rho} y^{\rho/\rho-1} w_2^{1/\rho-1}$$

so

$$w_2 x_2 = c(\mathbf{w}, y)^{1/1-\rho} y^{\rho/\rho-1} w_2^{\rho/\rho-1}$$

By symmetry

$$w_1 x_1 = c(\mathbf{w}, y)^{1/1-\rho} y^{\rho/\rho-1} w_1^{\rho/\rho-1}$$

Thus

$$c(\mathbf{w}, y) = w_1 x_1 + w_2 x_2 = c(\mathbf{w}, y)^{1/1-\rho} y^{\rho/\rho-1} [w_1^{\rho/\rho-1} + w_2^{\rho/\rho-1}]$$

Solving for $c(\mathbf{w}, y)$, we get:

$$c(\mathbf{w}, y)^{-\rho/1-\rho} = y^{\rho/\rho-1} [w_1^{\rho/\rho-1} + w_2^{\rho/\rho-1}]$$

so

$$c(\mathbf{w}, y) = y \left[w_1^{\frac{\rho}{\rho-1}} + w_2^{\frac{\rho}{\rho-1}} \right]^{\frac{\rho-1}{\rho}}$$

Note that this has the same form as the CES production function with $\rho/(\rho-1)$ playing the role of ρ. In the general case where

$$f(x_1, x_2) = [(a_1x_1)^\rho + (a_2x_2)^\rho]^{1/\rho}$$

similar computations can be done to show that

$$c(w_1, w_2, y) = [(w_1/a_1)^r + (w_2/a_2)^r]^{1/r}y$$

where $r = \rho/(\rho-1)$.

Example 1.14 The Cost Functions for the Leontief Technology
Suppose $f(x_1, x_2) = \min\{ax_1, bx_2\}$. What is the associated cost function? Clearly, if the firm wants to produce y units of output, it must use y/a units of good 1 and y/b units of good 2 no matter what the input prices are. Hence, the cost function is given by:

$$c(w_1, w_2, y) = w_1y/a + w_2y/b = (w_1/a + w_2/b)y$$

Example 1.15 The Cost Function for the Linear Technology
Suppose that $f(x_1, x_2) = ax_1 + bx_2$, so that factors 1 and 2 are perfect substitutes. What will the cost function look like? Since the two goods are perfect substitutes, the firm will use whichever is cheaper. Hence, the cost function will have the form $c(w_1, w_2, y) = \min\{w_1/a, w_2/b\}y$.

In this case the answer to the minimization problem is a boundary solution: one of the two factors will be used in a zero amount. Although it is easy to see the answer to this particular problem, it is worthwhile presenting a more formal solution since it serves as a nice example of the Kuhn-Tucker theorem in action. For notational convenience we consider the special case where $a = b = 1$. We pose the minimization problem as:

$$\begin{aligned} \min \quad & w_1x_1 + w_2x_2 \\ \text{s.t.} \quad & x_1 + x_2 = y \\ & x_1 \geq 0 \\ & x_2 \geq 0 \end{aligned}$$

The Lagrangean for this problem can be written as:

$$L = w_1x_1 + w_2x_2 - \lambda(x_1 + x_2 - y) - \mu_1x_1 - \mu_2x_2$$

The first-order conditions become:

$$\begin{aligned} w_1 - \lambda - \mu_1 &= 0 \\ w_2 - \lambda - \mu_2 &= 0 \\ x_1 + x_2 &= y \\ x_1 &\geq 0 \\ x_2 &\geq 0 \end{aligned}$$

The complementary slackness conditions are:

$$\mu_1 \geq 0, \ \mu_1 = 0 \text{ if } x_1 > 0$$

$$\mu_2 \geq 0, \ \mu_2 = 0 \text{ if } x_2 > 0$$

In order to determine the solution to this minimization problem, we have to examine each of the possible cases where the inequality constraints are binding or not binding. Since there are two constraints and each can be binding or not binding, we have four cases to consider.

(1) $x_1 = 0, x_2 = 0$

In this case, we cannot satisfy the condition that $x_1 + x_2 = y$ unless $y = 0$.

(2) $x_1 = 0, x_2 > 0$

In this case, we know that $\mu_2 = 0$. Hence, the first two first-order conditions give us:

$$w_1 = \lambda + \mu_1$$
$$w_2 = \lambda$$

Since $\mu_1 \geq 0$, this case can only arise when $w_1 \geq w_2$. Since $x_1 = 0$, it follows that $x_2 = y$.

(3) $x_2 = 0, x_1 > 0$

Reasoning similar to that in the above case shows that $x_1 = y$ and that this case can only occur when $w_2 \geq w_1$.

(4) $x_1 > 0, x_2 > 0$

In this case, complementary slackness implies that $\mu_1 = 0$, $\mu_2 = 0$. Thus, the first-order conditions imply that $w_1 = w_2$.

The above problem, though somewhat trivial, is typical of the methods used in applying the Kuhn-Tucker theorem. If there are k constraints that can be binding or not binding, there will be 2^k configurations possible at the optimum. Each of these must be examined to see if it is actually compatible with all of the required conditions and thus represents a possibly optimal solution.

1.8 AVERAGE AND MARGINAL COSTS

Just as the production function is our production primary means of describing the technological possibilities of production, the cost function will be our primary means of describing the economic possibilities of a firm. In the next two sections we will investigate the behavior of the cost function $c(\mathbf{w},y)$ with respect to its price and quantity arguments. Before undertaking that study we need to define a few related functions, namely the average and the marginal cost functions.

Let us consider the structure of the cost function. In general, the cost function can always be expressed simply as the value of the conditional factor demands:

$$c(\mathbf{w}, y) \equiv \mathbf{w} \cdot \mathbf{x}(\mathbf{w}, y)$$

This just says that the minimum cost of producing y is the cost of the cheapest way to produce y.

In the short run, some of the factors of production are fixed at predetermined levels. Let $\mathbf{x}_f$ be the vector of fixed factors, and break up $\mathbf{w}$ into $\mathbf{w} = (\mathbf{w}_v, \mathbf{w}_f)$, the vectors of prices of the variable and the fixed factors. The short-run conditional factor demand functions will generally depend on $\mathbf{x}_f$, so we write them as $\mathbf{x}_v(\mathbf{w}, y, \mathbf{x}_f)$. Then the short-run cost function can be written as:

$$c(\mathbf{w}, y, \mathbf{x}_f) = \mathbf{w}_v \cdot \mathbf{x}_v(\mathbf{w}, y, \mathbf{x}_f) + \mathbf{w}_f \cdot \mathbf{x}_f$$

The term $\mathbf{w}_v \cdot \mathbf{x}(\mathbf{w}, y, \mathbf{x}_f)$ is called *short-run variable costs* (SVC), and the term $\mathbf{w}_f \cdot \mathbf{x}_f$ is *fixed costs* (FC). We can define various derived cost concepts from these basic units:

$$\text{short-run average cost} = \text{SAC} = \frac{c(\mathbf{w}, y, \mathbf{x}_f)}{y}$$

$$\text{short-run average variable cost} = \text{SAVC} = \frac{\mathbf{w}_v \cdot \mathbf{x}_v (\mathbf{w}, y, \mathbf{x}_f)}{y}$$

$$\text{short-run average fixed cost} = \text{SAFC} = \frac{\mathbf{w}_f \cdot \mathbf{x}_f}{y}$$

$$\text{short-run total cost} = \text{STC} = \mathbf{w}_v \cdot \mathbf{x}(\mathbf{w}, y, \mathbf{x}_f) + \mathbf{w}_f \cdot \mathbf{x}_f = c(\mathbf{w}, y, \mathbf{x}_f)$$

$$\text{short-run marginal cost} = \text{SMC} = \frac{\partial c(\mathbf{w}, y, \mathbf{x}_f)}{\partial y}$$

When all factors are variable, the firm will optimize in the choice of $\mathbf{x}_f$. Hence, the long-run cost function only depends on the factor prices and the level of output as indicated earlier.

We can express this long-run function in terms of the short-run cost function in the following way. Let $\mathbf{x}_f(\mathbf{w}, y)$ be the optimal choice of the fixed factors and let $\mathbf{x}_v(\mathbf{w}, y) = \mathbf{x}_v(\mathbf{w}, y, \mathbf{x}_f(\mathbf{w}, y))$ be the optimal choice of the variable factors. Then the long-run cost function can be written as:

$$c(\mathbf{w}, y) = \mathbf{w}_v \cdot \mathbf{x}_v(\mathbf{w}, y) + \mathbf{w}_f \cdot \mathbf{x}_f(\mathbf{w}, y) = c(\mathbf{w}, y, \mathbf{x}_f(\mathbf{w}, y))$$

The long-run cost function can be used to define cost concepts similar to those defined above:

$$\text{long-run average cost} = \text{LAC} = \frac{c(\mathbf{w}, y)}{y}$$

$$\text{long-run marginal cost} = \text{LMC} = \frac{\partial c(\mathbf{w}, y)}{\partial y}$$

Notice that "long-run average cost" equals "long-run average variable cost" since all costs are variable in the long-run; "long-run fixed costs" are zero for the same reason.

Long run and short run are of course relative concepts. Which factors are considered variable and which are considered fixed depends on the particular problem being analyzed. The important questions to ask are: (1) over what time period do we wish to analyze the firm's behavior, and (2) what factors can the firm adjust during that time period?

Example 1.16. The Short-Run Cobb-Douglas Cost Functions Suppose the second factor in a Cobb-Douglas technology is restricted to operate at a level k. Then the cost-minimizing problem is:

$$\begin{aligned} \min \quad & w_1 x_1 + w_2 k \\ \text{s.t.} \quad & y = x_1^a k^{1-a} \end{aligned}$$

Inversion of the constraint gives:

$$x_1 = (yk^{a-1})^{\frac{1}{a}}$$

Thus

$$c(y, w_1, w_2, k) = w_1 (yk^{a-1})^{\frac{1}{a}} + w_2 k$$

The following variations can also be calculated:

$$\text{short-run average cost} = w_1 (y/k)^{\frac{1-a}{a}} + w_2 k/y$$

$$\text{short-run average variable cost} = w_1 (y/k)^{\frac{1-a}{a}}$$

$$\text{short-run average fixed cost} = w_2 k/y$$

$$\text{short-run marginal cost} = \frac{w_1}{a} (y/k)^{\frac{1-a}{a}}$$

1.9 THE GEOMETRY OF COSTS

The cost function is the single most useful tool for studying the economic behavior of a firm. In a sense to be made clear later, the cost function summarizes all economically relevant information about the technology of the firm. In the following sections we will examine some of the properties of the cost function. This is most conveniently done in two stages: first, we examine the properties of the cost function under the assumption of fixed factor prices. In this case, we will write the cost function simply as $c(y)$. Second, we will examine the properties of the cost function when factor prices are free to vary.

Since we have taken factor prices to be fixed, costs depend only on the level of output of a firm, and useful graphs can be drawn that relate output and costs. The total cost curve is always assumed to be monotonic in output: the more you produce, the more it costs. The average cost curve, however, can exhibit a variety of shapes. Several possibilities are depicted in Figure 1.12. The last case is often thought to be the most realistic, at least in the short run. The reason for this is as follows.

In the short run the cost function has two components: fixed costs and variable costs. We can therefore write short-run average cost as:

$$\text{SAC} = \frac{c(\mathbf{w}, y, \mathbf{x}_f)}{y} = \frac{\mathbf{w}_f \cdot \mathbf{x}_f}{y} + \frac{\mathbf{w}_v \cdot \mathbf{x}_v(\mathbf{w}, y, \mathbf{x}_f)}{y}$$
$$= \text{SAFC} + \text{SAVC}$$

In most applications, the short-run fixed factors will be such things as machines, buildings, and other types of capital equipment while the variable factors will be labor and raw materials. As we increase output it seems reasonable to suppose that the variable factors required will increase more or less proportionally until we approach some capacity level of output determined by the amounts of the fixed factors. When we are

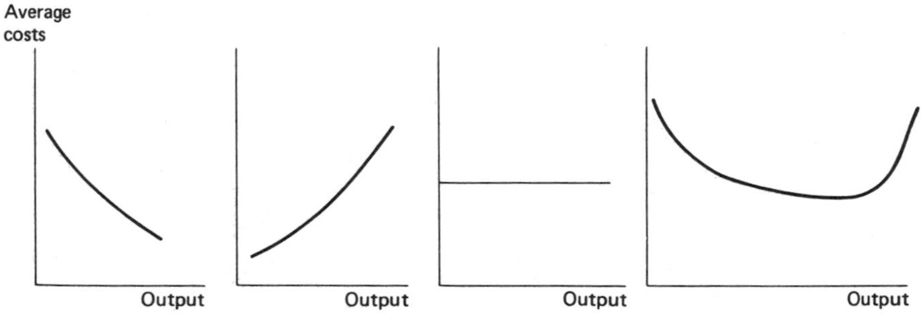

Fig. 1.12 *Average Cost Curves*

near to capacity, we need to use more than a proportional amount of the variable inputs to increase output. Thus, the *variable* cost function should have the form shown in Figure 1.13. This means that average variable costs will have the form shown in Figure 1.14.

Fixed costs and average fixed costs have the shapes depicted in Figure 1.15. Finally, adding together average variable costs and average fixed costs, we get a U-shaped average curve in Figure 1.16.

Note that fixed and variable costs have interacted so as to produce a unique minimal average cost level of output; i.e., there is an optimal scale of production.

In the long run all costs are variable costs; in such circumstances increasing average costs seems unreasonable since a firm could always replicate its production process. Hence the reasonable long-run possibilities should be either constant or decreasing average costs. On the other hand, as we mentioned earlier, certain kinds of firms may not exhibit a long-run constant-returns-to-scale technology because of long-run fixed factors. If some factors do remain fixed even in the long run, the appropri-

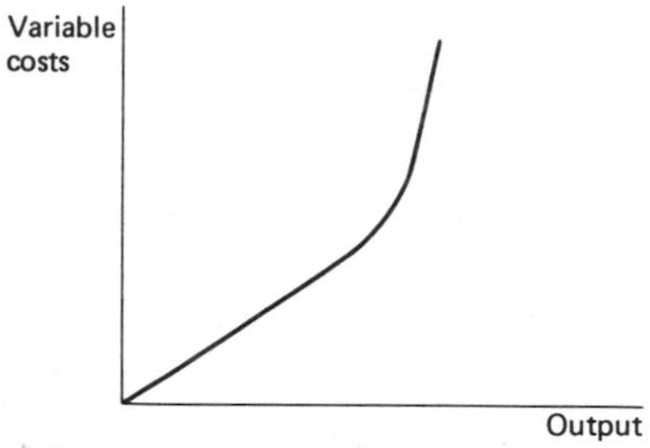

Fig. 1.13 *Variable Cost Function*

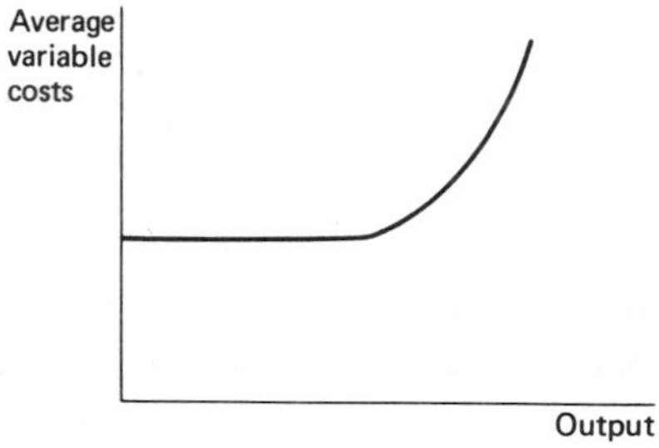

Fig. 1.14 *Average Variable Costs*

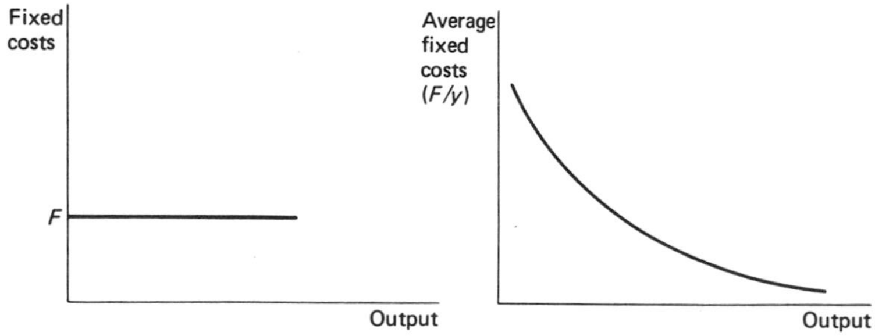

Fig. 1.15 *Fixed Cost and Average Fixed Costs*

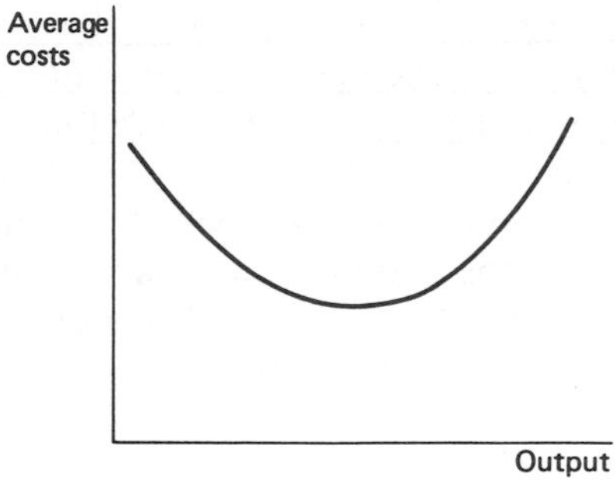

Fig. 1.16 *U-shaped Average Cost Curve*

ate long-run average cost curve should presumably be U-shaped, for essentially the same reasons as given above.

Let us now consider the marginal cost curve. What is its relationship to the average cost curve? Let y^* denote the point of minimum average cost; then to the left of y^* average costs are declining so that $\frac{d}{dy}\left(\frac{c(y)}{y}\right) \leqq 0$ for $y \leqq y^*$. Taking the derivative gives:

$$\frac{yc'(y) - c(y)}{y^2} \leqq 0 \qquad \text{for } y \leqq y^*$$

which implies

$$c'(y) \leqq \frac{c(y)}{y} \qquad \text{for } y \leqq y^*$$

This says that marginal cost is less than average cost to the left of the minimum average cost point. A similar analysis gives us

$$c'(y) \geqq \frac{c(y)}{y} \qquad \text{for } y \geqq y^*$$

And combining the two inequalities gives us:

$$c'(y^*) = \frac{c(y^*)}{y^*}$$

that is, marginal costs equal average costs at the point of minimum average costs.

What is the relationship of the marginal cost curve to the variable cost curve? Simply by changing the notation in the above argument we can show that the marginal cost curve lies below the average variable cost curve when the average variable cost curve is decreasing, above it when it is decreasing, and, therefore, passes through the minimum point.

It is also not hard to show that the marginal cost curve must equal the average variable costs at one unit of output. After all, if only one unit of output is produced, then the marginal costs of that unit must be equal to the average variable costs. A more formal demonstration is also possible. Average variable cost is defined by:

$$\mathrm{AVC}(y) = c_v(y)/y$$

If $y = 0$, this expression reduces to 0/0, which is indeterminate. However, the limit of $c_v(y)/y$ can be calculated using L'Hòpital's rule:

$$\lim_{y \to 0} c_v(y)/y = c_v'(0)/1$$

So average variable cost at zero output is just marginal cost.

All of the analysis just discussed holds in both the long and the short run. However, if production exhibits constant returns to scale in the long run, so that the cost function is linear in the level of output, the picture becomes degenerate as depicted in Figure 1.18.

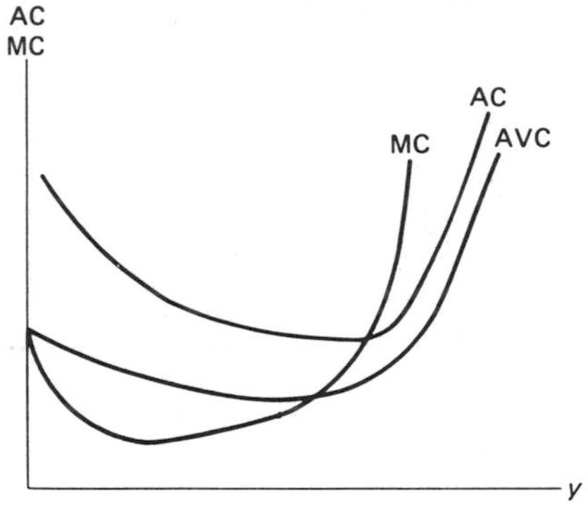

Fig. 1.17 *Average, Average Variable, and Marginal Cost Curves*

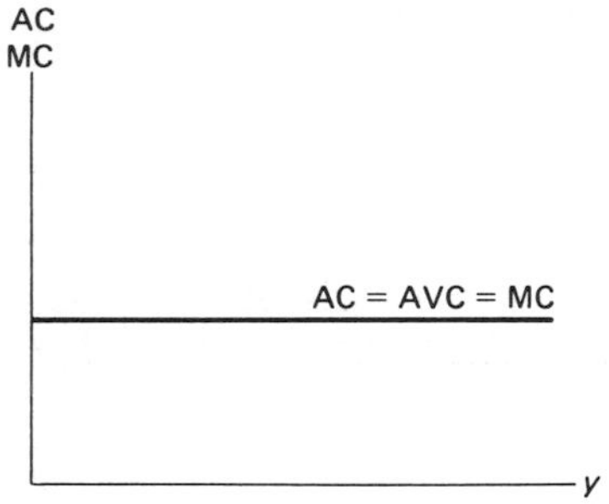

Fig. 1.18 *Cost Curves with Constant Returns to Scale*

Example 1.17 The Cobb-Douglas Cost Curves As shown in Example 1.10, the generalized Cobb-Douglas technology has a cost function of the form:

$$c(y) = Ky^{\frac{1}{a+b}} \qquad a + b \leqq 1$$

where K is a function of prices and parameters.

Thus

$$AC(y) = \frac{c(y)}{y} = Ky^{\frac{1-a-b}{a+b}}$$

$$MC(y) = c'(y) = \frac{K}{a+b}y^{\frac{1-a-b}{a+b}}$$

If $a + b < 1$ the cost curves exhibit increasing AC as in Figure 1.19; if $a + b = 1$, the cost curves have the shape depicted in Figure 1.20.

The short-run generalized Cobb-Douglas technology has the form:

$$c(y) = Ky^{\frac{1}{r}} + F$$

Thus

$$AC(y) = \frac{c(y)}{y} = Ky^{\frac{1-r}{r}} + \frac{F}{y}$$

The point of minimum average cost is where $AC(y) = MC(y)$, or

$$Ky^{\frac{1-r}{r}} + \frac{F}{y} = \frac{Ky^{\frac{1-r}{r}}}{r}$$

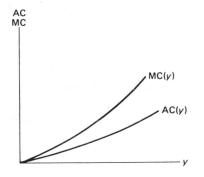

Fig. 1.19 *Average Cost and Marginal Cost in Cobb-Douglas Case*

Fig. 1.20 *Average Cost and Marginal Cost with Constant Returns to Scale*

This can be solved for the point of minimum average cost (Figure 1.21):

$$y^* = \left[\frac{rF}{(1-r)K}\right]^r$$

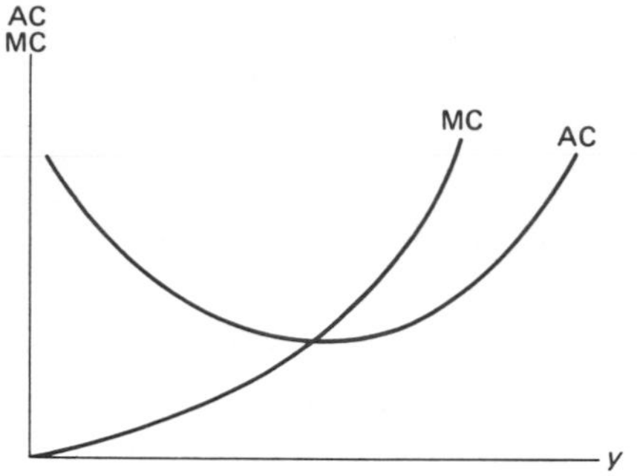

Fig. 1.21 *Short-Run Cobb-Douglas Cost Curves*

1.10 LONG- AND SHORT-RUN COST CURVES

Let us now consider the relationship between the long-run cost curves and the short-run cost curves. It is clear that the long-run cost curve must never lie above any short-run cost curve since the short-run cost minimization problem is just a constrained version of the long-run cost minimization problem.

Let us write the long-run cost function as $c(y) = c(y, \mathbf{z}(y))$. Here we have omitted the factor prices since they are assumed fixed, and we let $\mathbf{z}(y)$ be the cost-minimizing demand for the fixed factors. Let y^* be some level of output, and let $\mathbf{z}^* = \mathbf{z}(y^*)$ be the associated long-run demand for the fixed factors. The short-run costs, $c(y, \mathbf{z}^*)$, must be at least as great as the long-run cost, $c(y, \mathbf{z}(y))$, for all levels of output, and the short-run cost will equal the long-run costs at output y^*: $c(y^*, \mathbf{z}^*) = c(y^*, \mathbf{z}(y^*))$. Hence, the long- and the short-run cost curves must be tangent at y^*.

This is just a geometrical restatement of the envelope theorem (Section A.11 of the Mathematical Appendix). The slope of the long-run cost curve at y^* is:

$$\frac{dc(y^*, \mathbf{z}(y^*))}{dy} = \frac{\partial c(y^*, \mathbf{z}^*)}{\partial y} + \sum_i \frac{\partial c(y^*, \mathbf{z}^*)}{\partial z_i} \frac{\partial z_i(y^*)}{\partial y}$$

But since $\mathbf{z}^*$ is the *optimal* choice of the fixed factors at the output level y^*, we must have:

$$\frac{\partial c(y^*, \mathbf{z}^*)}{\partial z_i} = 0 \qquad \text{all } i$$

Thus, long-run marginal costs at y^* equal short-run marginal costs at $(y^*, \mathbf{z}^*)$.

Finally, we note that if the long- and short-run cost curves are tangent, the long- and short-run *average* cost curves must also be tangent. Some typical configurations are illustrated in Figure 1.22.

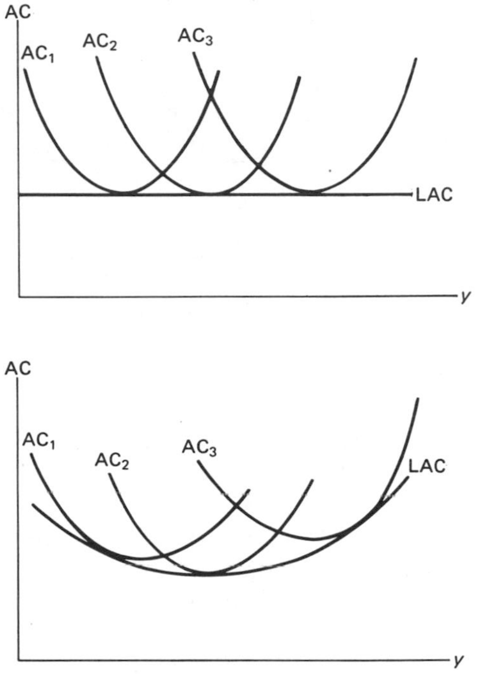

Fig. 1.22 *Long-Run and Short-Run Average Cost Curves*

Another way to see the relationship between the long-run and the short-run average cost curves is to start with the family of short-run average cost curves. If, for example, we had a fixed factor that could be used at only three levels of output—z_1, z_2, z_3—we could illustrate this family of curves in Figure 1.23. What would be the long-run cost curve? Simply the lower envelope of these short-run curves since the optimal choice of z will simply be the one that has minimum average costs. This envelope operation generates a "scalloped"-shaped long-run average cost curve. If there are many possible values of the fixed factor, these scallops become a smooth curve.

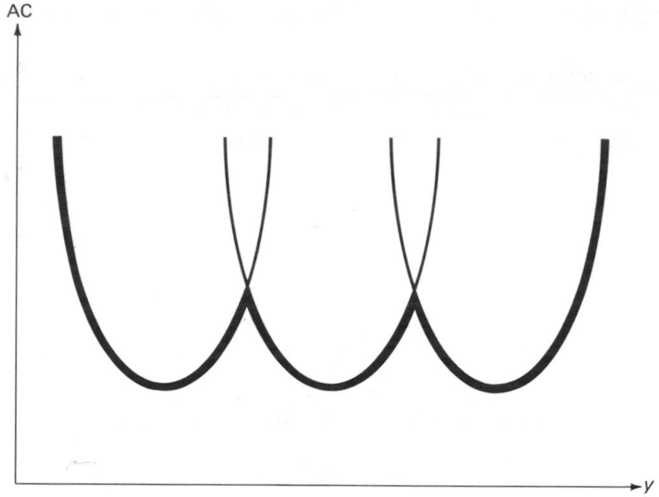

Fig. 1.23 *Long-Run AC Curve Is Lower Envelope*

1.11 COST AND PROFIT FUNCTIONS WITH VARIABLE FACTOR PRICES

We turn now to the study of the price behavior of cost and profit functions. Several interesting properties follow directly from the definition of the functions. These are summarized in the following remarks.

PROPERTIES OF THE COST FUNCTION

(1) (*nondecreasing in* $\mathbf{w}$) *If* $\mathbf{w}' \geqq \mathbf{w}$, *then* $c(\mathbf{w}', y) \geqq c(\mathbf{w}, y)$.
(2) (*homogeneous of degree 1 in* $\mathbf{w}$) $c(t\mathbf{w}, y) = tc(\mathbf{w}, y)$ *for* $t > 0$.
(3) (*concave in* $\mathbf{w}$) $c(t\mathbf{w} + (1 - t)\mathbf{w}', y) \geqq tc(\mathbf{w}, y) + (1 - t)c(\mathbf{w}', y)$ *for* $0 \leqq t \leqq 1$.
(4) (*continuous in* $\mathbf{w}$) c *is continuous as a function of* $\mathbf{w}$, *for* $\mathbf{w} \gg 0$.

PROOF.

(1) This is obvious, but a formal proof may be instructive. Let $\mathbf{x}$ and $\mathbf{x}'$ be cost-minimizing bundles associated with $\mathbf{w}$ and $\mathbf{w}'$. Then $\mathbf{w}\,\mathbf{x} \leq \mathbf{w}\,\mathbf{x}'$ by minimization and $\mathbf{w}\,\mathbf{x}' \leq \mathbf{w}'\mathbf{x}'$ since $\mathbf{w} \leq \mathbf{w}'$. Putting these inequalities together gives $\mathbf{w}\mathbf{x} \leqq \mathbf{w}'\mathbf{x}'$ as required.

(2) We show that if $\mathbf{x}$ is the cost-minimizing bundle at prices $\mathbf{w}$, then $\mathbf{x}$ also minimizes costs at prices $t\mathbf{w}$. Suppose not, and let $\mathbf{x}'$ be a cost-minimizing bundle at $t\mathbf{w}$ so that $t\mathbf{w}\,\mathbf{x}' < t\mathbf{w}\,\mathbf{x}$. But this inequality implies $\mathbf{w}\,\mathbf{x}' < \mathbf{w}\mathbf{x}$, which contradicts the definition of $\mathbf{x}$.

Hence, multiplying factory prices by a positive scalar t does not change the composition of a cost-minimizing bundle, and, thus, costs must rise by exactly a factor of t: $c(t\mathbf{w}, y) = t\mathbf{w}\,\mathbf{x} = tc(\mathbf{w}, y)$.

(3) Let $(\mathbf{w}, \mathbf{x})$ and $(\mathbf{w}', \mathbf{x}')$ be two cost-minimizing price-factor combinations and let $\mathbf{w}'' = t\mathbf{w} + (1-t)\mathbf{w}'$ for any $0 \leq t \leq 1$.

Now,

$$c(\mathbf{w}'', y) = \mathbf{w}'' \cdot \mathbf{x}'' = t\mathbf{w} \cdot \mathbf{x}'' + (1-t)\mathbf{w}' \cdot \mathbf{x}''$$

Since $\mathbf{x}''$ is not necessarily the cheapest way to produce y at prices $\mathbf{w}'$ or $\mathbf{w}$, we have $\mathbf{w} \cdot \mathbf{x}'' \geqq c(\mathbf{w}, y)$ and $\mathbf{w}' \cdot \mathbf{x}'' \geqq c(\mathbf{w}', y)$. Thus,

$$c(\mathbf{w}'', y) \geqq tc(\mathbf{w}, y) + (1-t)\, c(\mathbf{w}', y)$$

(4) The continuity of c follows from the fact that it is concave. (See Section A.6 of the Mathematical Appendix.) □

The only property that is surprising here is the concavity. Suppose we graph cost as a function of the price of a single input, with all other prices held constant. If the price of a factor rises, costs will never go down (property 1), but they will go up at decreasing rate (property 3). Why? Because as this one factor becomes more expensive and other prices stay the same, the cost-minimizing firm will shift away from it to use other inputs.

This is made more clear by considering Figure 1.24 below. Let $\mathbf{x}^*$ be a cost-minimizing bundle at prices $\mathbf{w}^*$. Suppose the price of factor 1 changes from w_1^* to w_1. If we just behave passively and continue to use $\mathbf{x}^*$, our costs will be $c = w_1 x_1^* + \sum_{i=2}^{n} w_i^* x_i^*$. The minimal cost of production $c(\mathbf{w}, y)$ must be less than this "passive" cost function; thus, the graph

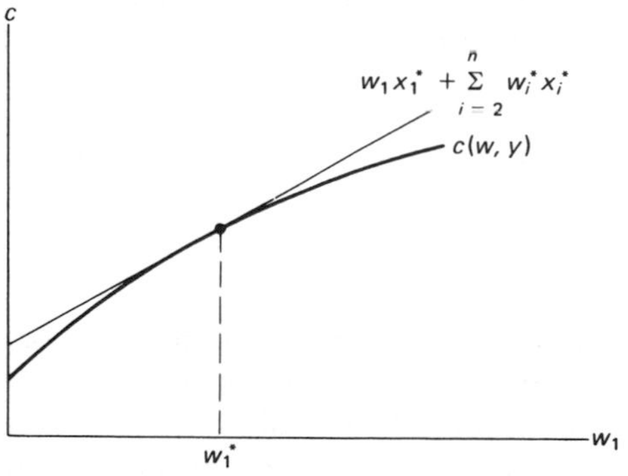

Fig. 1.24 *The Cost Function and the "Passive" Cost Function*

of $c(\mathbf{w}, y)$ must lie below the graph of the passive cost function, with both curves coinciding at w_1^*. It is not hard to see that this implies $c(\mathbf{w}, y)$ is concave with respect to w_1.

The analogous properties of the profit function are listed below. The proofs are essentially the same, but the careful reader should be sure to work them out to be certain he or she understands the arguments. Two remarks are in order: (1) the conditions only make sense when the profit function is well defined, and (2) if suitably interpreted these properties hold for the restricted profit function as well.

PROPERTIES OF THE PROFIT FUNCTION

(1) (*nondecreasing in* p, *nonincreasing in* $\mathbf{w}$) *If* $p' \geqq p$ *and* $\mathbf{w}' \leqq \mathbf{w}$, *then* $\pi(p', \mathbf{w}') \geqq \pi(p, \mathbf{w})$.

(2) (*homogeneous of degree 1 in* $(p, \mathbf{w})$) $\pi(tp, t\mathbf{w}) = t\pi(p, \mathbf{w})$ *for all* $t > 0$.

(3) (*convex in* p, $\mathbf{w}$) *Let* $(p'', \mathbf{w}'') = (tp + (1-t)\,p',\ t\cdot\mathbf{w} + (1-t)\,\mathbf{w}')$. *Then*

$$\pi(p'', \mathbf{w}'') \leqq t\pi(p, \mathbf{w}) + (1-t)\,\pi(p', \mathbf{w}') \text{ for } 0 \leqq t \leqq 1$$

(4) *continuous in* $(p, \mathbf{w})$, *at least when* $p > 0$, $\mathbf{w} \gg 0$.

1.12 PROPERTIES OF DEMAND AND SUPPLY FUNCTIONS

The functions that give the optimal choices of inputs and outputs as a function of the prices are known as the demand and supply functions. The fact that these functions are the solutions to a maximization problem of a specific form—the profit-maximization problem—will imply certain restrictions on the nature of the demand and supply functions.

For example, it is easy to see that if we multiply all of the prices by some positive number t, the levels of factor inputs that maximize profits will not change. (Can you prove this rigorously?) Hence, the factor demand functions $x_i(\mathbf{p}, \mathbf{w})$, $i = 1, \cdots, n$ must satisfy the restriction that:

$$x_i(t\mathbf{p}, t\mathbf{w}) = x_i(\mathbf{p}, \mathbf{w})$$

In other words the factor demand functions must be homogeneous of degree zero. (For the definition of this concept, see Section A.14.) This property is fairly important: an immediate way to check whether some observed behavior could come from the profit-maximizing model is to see if the demand functions are homogeneous of degree zero. If they aren't, the firm in question couldn't possibly be maximizing profits.

We would like to find other such restrictions on demand functions. In fact, we would like to find a *complete* list of such restrictions. We could use such a list in two ways. First, we could use it to examine theoretical statements about how a profit-maximizing firm would respond to changes in its economic environment. An example of such a statement would be: "If all prices are doubled, the levels of goods demanded and supplied by a profit-maximizing firm will not change." Second, we could use such restrictions empirically to decide whether a particular firm's observed behavior is consistent with the profit-maximization model. If we observed that some firm's demands and supplies changed when all prices doubled and nothing else changed, we would have to (reluctantly) conclude that this firm was not a profit maximizer.

Thus both theoretical and empirical considerations suggest the importance of determining the properties that demand and supply functions possess. We will attack this problem in three ways. The first, and most traditional way is by examining the first-order conditions that characterize the optimal choices. The second, somewhat newer, way is to examine the properties of the profit and cost functions and relate these properties to the demand functions. This approach is sometimes referred to as the "dual approach." The third approach is to examine the maximizing properties of the demand and supply functions directly. We will proceed with each of these approaches examining the behavior of both the profit-maximizing and the cost-minimizing firm.

1.13 COMPARATIVE STATICS FROM THE FIRST-ORDER CONDITIONS FOR PROFIT MAXIMIZATION

Let us first consider the simple example of a firm maximizing profits with one output and one input. The problem facing the firm is, therefore:

$$\max pf(x) - wx$$

The demand function—the x that maximizes profits—is denoted by $x(p, w)$. If $f(x)$ is differentiable, $x(p, w)$ must satisfy the necessary first-order condition:

$$pf'(x(p, w)) - w \equiv 0$$

Notice that this condition is an *identity* in p and w—that is, it must be satisfied by all values of p and w. Since this expression is an identity, we can differentiate it with respect to w, say, to get:

$$pf''(x(p, w))dx(p, w)/dw - 1 \equiv 0$$

Assuming that $f''(x)$ is not zero, we have:

$$dx(p, w)/dw \equiv 1/pf''(x(p, w))$$

This identity gives us some interesting facts about how the optimal choice $x(p, w)$ responds to changes in w. First, it gives us an explicit expression for dx/dw in terms of the production function. If the production function is very curved in a neighborhood of the optimum—so that the second derivative is large in magnitude—then the change in x as w changes will be small. (You may draw a diagram similar to Figure 1.9 and experiment a bit to verify this fact.) Second, it gives us important information about the *sign* of the effect: since the second-order condition for maximization implies that $f''(x(p, w))$ is negative, this immediately implies that $dx(p, w)/dw$ is negative. That is, the factor demand curve slopes downward.

The same procedure of differentiating the first-order conditions can be used to examine profit-maximizing behavior when there are many inputs. For notational convenience we will fix the level of the output price and denote the vector of demanded factors by $\mathbf{x}(\mathbf{w})$. This vector of demands must satisfy the first-order conditions:

$$p\mathbf{D}f(\mathbf{x}(\mathbf{w})) - \mathbf{w} = \mathbf{0}$$

If we differentiate with respect to $\mathbf{w}$, we get:

$$p\mathbf{D}^2 f(\mathbf{x}(\mathbf{w}))\mathbf{D}\mathbf{x}(\mathbf{w}) - \mathbf{I} = \mathbf{0}$$

Here $\mathbf{I}$ is the n by n identity matrix. You may like to work a two-good example to see what these matrix equations look like.

Solving for the derivatives of the x's:

$$\mathbf{D}\,\mathbf{x}(\mathbf{w}) = [p\mathbf{D}^2 f(\mathbf{x}(\mathbf{w}))]^{-1}$$

Here we assume that the Hessian matrix is nonsingular—a natural generalization of our earlier assumption that the second derivative was nonzero.

The matrix of partial derivatives of the factor demands with respect to the factor prices—the matrix $\mathbf{Dx}(\mathbf{w})$—is called the *substitution matrix* since it measures how raising the price of factor i induces the firm to "substitute" some of factor j for factor i.

This formula is, of course, a natural analog of the one good case described above. However, we now have extracted more information than we had before. First, we note that the matrix of derivatives of factor demands with respect to factor prices—the substitution matrix—must be a negative semidefinite matrix. The substitution matrix is just the inverse of the Hessian of the production function (times the price of output), and the second-order conditions for maximization imply that this matrix must be negative semidefinite at the profit-maximizing levels of factor demands. Second, we note that the substitution matrix must be a symmetric matrix since it is the inverse of a symmetric matrix. (The Hessian matrix must be symmetric since $\partial^2 f(\mathbf{x})/\partial x_i \partial x_j$ must equal $\partial^2 f(\mathbf{x})/\partial x_j \partial x_i$ by the ordinary rules of calculus.)

This result is unintuitive. Why should the change in a firm's demand for good i when price j changes necessarily be equal to the change in the firm's demand for good j when price i changes? There is no obvious reason—but it is implied by the model of profit-maximizing behavior!

What is the empirical content of the statement that the substitution matrix is negative semidefinite? We can provide the following interpretation.

Suppose that the factor prices change from $\mathbf{w}$ to $\mathbf{w}+\mathbf{dw}$. Then the associated change in the factor demands is:

$$\mathbf{dx} = \mathbf{Dx}(\mathbf{w}) \cdot \mathbf{dw}$$

Multiplying both sides of this equation by **dw:**

$$\mathbf{dwdx} = \mathbf{dw} \cdot \mathbf{Dx}(\mathbf{w}) \cdot \mathbf{dw} \leq 0$$

The inequality follows from the definition of a negative semidefinite matrix. We see that negative semidefiniteness of the substitution matrix means that the product of the change in factor prices and the change in factor demands must always be negative, at least for infinitesimal changes in factor prices. If, for example, only the price of the ith factor changes, then the change in demand for the ith factor must be negative.

1.14 PROPERTIES OF CONDITIONAL FACTOR DEMAND FUNCTIONS

Let us now turn to the cost-minimization problem and the conditional factor demands. Applying the usual arguments, the conditional factor demand functions $\mathbf{x}(\mathbf{w}, y)$ must satisfy the first-order conditions

$$\begin{aligned} \mathbf{w} - \lambda \mathbf{Df}(\mathbf{x}(\mathbf{w}, y)) &= 0 \\ f(\mathbf{x}(\mathbf{w}, y)) &= y \end{aligned}$$

It is easy to get lost in matrix algebra in the following calculations, so we will consider a simple two-good example. In this case the first-order conditions look like:

$$w_1 - \lambda \partial f(x_1(w_1, w_2, y), x_2(w_1, w_2, y))/\partial x_1 \equiv 0$$
$$w_2 - \lambda \partial f(x_1(w_1, w_2, y), x_2(w_1, w_2, y))/\partial x_2 \equiv 0$$
$$f(x_1(w_1, w_2, y), x_2(w_1, w_2, y)) \equiv y$$

Just as before, these first-order conditions are *identities*—they are true for all values of w_1, w_2, and y. Let us, therefore, differentiate them with respect to w_1.

We find:

$$1 - \lambda\left[\frac{\partial^2 f}{\partial x_1^2}\frac{\partial x_1}{\partial w_1} + \frac{\partial^2 f}{\partial x_1 \partial x_2}\frac{\partial x_2}{\partial w_1}\right] - \frac{\partial f}{\partial x_1}\frac{\partial \lambda}{\partial w_1} \equiv 0$$

$$0 - \lambda\left[\frac{\partial^2 f}{\partial x_2 \partial x_1}\frac{\partial x_1}{\partial w_1} + \frac{\partial^2 f}{\partial x_2^2}\frac{\partial x_2}{\partial w_1}\right] - \frac{\partial f}{\partial x_2}\frac{\partial \lambda}{\partial w_1} \equiv 0$$

$$\frac{\partial f}{\partial x_1}\frac{\partial x_1}{\partial w_1} + \frac{\partial f}{\partial x_2}\frac{\partial x_2}{\partial w_1} \equiv 0$$

These equations can be written in matrix form as:

$$\begin{bmatrix} \lambda\dfrac{\partial^2 f}{\partial x_1^2} & \lambda\dfrac{\partial^2 f}{\partial x_1 \partial x_2} & \dfrac{\partial f}{\partial x_1} \\ \lambda\dfrac{\partial^2 f}{\partial x_2 \partial x_1} & \lambda\dfrac{\partial^2 f}{\partial x_2^2} & \dfrac{\partial f}{\partial x_2} \\ \dfrac{\partial f}{\partial x_1} & \dfrac{\partial f}{\partial x_2} & 0 \end{bmatrix} \begin{bmatrix} \dfrac{\partial x_1}{\partial w_1} \\ \dfrac{\partial x_2}{\partial w_1} \\ \dfrac{\partial \lambda}{\partial w_1} \end{bmatrix} \equiv \begin{bmatrix} 1 \\ 0 \\ 0 \end{bmatrix}$$

Note the important fact that the matrix on the left-hand side is precisely the bordered Hessian involved in the second-order conditions for maximization (Section A.11). We can use a standard technique from matrix algebra, Cramer's rule, which is discussed in Section A.3, to solve for $\partial x_1/\partial w_1$:

$$\frac{\partial x_1}{\partial w_1} = \frac{\begin{vmatrix} 1 & \lambda\dfrac{\partial^2 f}{\partial x_1 \partial x_2} & \dfrac{\partial f}{\partial x_1} \\ 0 & \lambda\dfrac{\partial^2 f}{\partial x_2^2} & \dfrac{\partial f}{\partial x_2} \\ 0 & \dfrac{\partial f}{\partial x_2} & 0 \end{vmatrix}}{H}$$

$$= -\left[\frac{\partial f}{\partial x_2}\right]^2 \frac{1}{H}$$

where H is the determinant of the bordered Hessian.

Just as before, we find an expression for how the optimal choice responds to the change in a parameter to involve a ratio of two terms. The denominator automatically has a positive sign by the second-order conditions for maximization. The sign of the numerator is easily seen to be negative. Hence, the sign of $\partial x_1/\partial w_1$ is negative: factor demand curves slope downward.

Similarly, we can derive the expression for $\partial x_2(\mathbf{w}, y)/\partial w_1$. Proceeding as before, we find:

$$\frac{\partial x_2}{\partial w_1} = \frac{\begin{vmatrix} \lambda \dfrac{\partial^2 f}{\partial x_1^2} & 1 & \dfrac{\partial f}{\partial x_1} \\ \lambda \dfrac{\partial^2 f}{\partial x_2 \partial x_1} & 0 & \dfrac{\partial f}{\partial x_2} \\ \dfrac{\partial f}{\partial x_1} & 0 & 0 \end{vmatrix}}{H}$$

$$= \left(\frac{\partial f}{\partial x_1}\right)\left(\frac{\partial f}{\partial x_2}\right) \Big/ H$$

By symmetry, we can also calculate the expression for $\partial x_1(\mathbf{w}, y)/\partial w_2$.

$$\frac{\partial x_1}{\partial w_2} = \frac{\begin{vmatrix} 0 & \lambda \dfrac{\partial^2 f}{\partial x_1 \partial x_2} & \dfrac{\partial f}{\partial x_1} \\ 1 & \lambda \dfrac{\partial^2 f}{\partial x_2^2} & \dfrac{\partial f}{\partial x_2} \\ 0 & \dfrac{\partial f}{\partial x_2} & 0 \end{vmatrix}}{H}$$

$$= \left(\frac{\partial f}{\partial x_2}\right)\left(\frac{\partial f}{\partial x_1}\right) \Big/ H$$

Comparing the last two expressions, we note that they are identical. Thus $\partial x_1(w_1, w_2, y)/\partial w_2$ equals $\partial x_2(w_1, w_2, y)/\partial w_1$. Just as in the case of profit maximization, we find a symmetry condition: the "cross price effects must be equal" as a consequence of the model of cost minimization.

We now proceed to rephrase the above calculations in terms of matrix algebra. The first-order conditions for cost minimization are:

$$\begin{aligned} \mathbf{w} - \lambda \mathbf{D} f(\mathbf{x}(\mathbf{w})) &\equiv \mathbf{0} \\ f(\mathbf{x}(\mathbf{w})) &\equiv y \end{aligned}$$

Differentiating these identities with respect to **w** we find:

$$\mathbf{I} - \lambda \mathbf{D}^2 f(\mathbf{x}(\mathbf{w}))\mathbf{D}\mathbf{x}(\mathbf{w}) - \mathbf{D}f(\mathbf{x}(\mathbf{w})) \cdot \mathbf{D}\lambda(\mathbf{w}) = 0$$
$$\mathbf{D}f(\mathbf{x}(\mathbf{w}))\mathbf{D}\mathbf{x}(\mathbf{w}) = 0$$

Rearranging slightly:

$$\begin{bmatrix} \lambda \mathbf{D}^2 f(\mathbf{x}) & -\mathbf{D}f(\mathbf{x}) \\ -\mathbf{D}f(\mathbf{x}) & 0 \end{bmatrix} \begin{bmatrix} \mathbf{D}\mathbf{x}(\mathbf{w}) \\ \mathbf{D}\lambda(\mathbf{w}) \end{bmatrix} = \begin{bmatrix} -\mathbf{I} \\ 0 \end{bmatrix}$$

Note that the matrix is simply the bordered Hessian matrix—i.e., the second derivative matrix of the Lagrangean. We can solve for the substitution matrix **Dx(w)** by taking the inverse of this matrix:

$$\begin{bmatrix} \mathbf{D}\mathbf{x}(\mathbf{w}) \\ \mathbf{D}\lambda(\mathbf{w}) \end{bmatrix} = \begin{bmatrix} \lambda \mathbf{D}^2 \mathbf{f}(\mathbf{x}) & -\mathbf{D}\mathbf{f}(\mathbf{x}) \\ -\mathbf{D}\mathbf{f}(\mathbf{x}) & 0 \end{bmatrix}^{-1} \begin{bmatrix} -I \\ 0 \end{bmatrix}$$

Since the bordered Hessian is symmetric, its inverse is symmetric, which shows that the cross-price effects are symmetric. It can also be shown that the substitution matrix is negative semidefinite. Since we will present a simple proof of this below using other methods, we will omit this demonstration here.

1.15 THE RELATONSHIP BETWEEN DEMAND FUNCTIONS AND PROFIT FUNCTIONS

Here we will describe a much nicer way to develop the properties of demand functions by relating demand functions to profit functions. The key to accomplishing this is the following fundamental result.

PROPOSITION *(Hotelling's lemma; the derivative property) Let* y(p, **w**) *be the firm's supply function and let* x_i (p, **w**) *be the firm's demand function for factor* i. *Then*

$$y(p, \mathbf{w}) = \frac{\partial \pi(p, \mathbf{w})}{\partial p}$$

$$x_i(p, \mathbf{w}) = -\frac{\partial \pi(p, \mathbf{w})}{\partial w_i} \qquad i = 1, \cdots, n$$

when the derivatives exist, and when $\mathbf{w} \gg 0$, $p > 0$.

PROOF Suppose $(y^*, \mathbf{x}^*)$ is a profit-maximizing supply-demand plan at prices $(p^*, \mathbf{w}^*)$. Then define the function:

$$g(p, \mathbf{w}) = \pi(p, \mathbf{w}) - (p \cdot y^* - \mathbf{w} \cdot \mathbf{x}^*)$$

Clearly, the profit maximizing production plan at prices $(p, \mathbf{w})$ will always be at least as profitable as the production plan $(y^*, \mathbf{x}^*)$. However, the plan $(y^*, \mathbf{x}^*)$ will be a best plan at prices $(p^*, \mathbf{w}^*)$, so the function g reaches a minimum value of 0 at $(p^*, \mathbf{w}^*)$. The assumptions on prices imply this is an interior minimum.

The first-order conditions for a minimum then imply that

$$0 = \frac{\partial g(p^*, \mathbf{w}^*)}{\partial p} = \frac{\partial \pi(p^*, \mathbf{w}^*)}{\partial p} - y^*$$

$$0 = \frac{\partial g(p^*, \mathbf{w}^*)}{\partial w_i} = \frac{\partial \pi(p^*, \mathbf{w}^*)}{\partial w_i} + x_i^* \quad \text{for} \quad i = 1, \cdots, n$$

Since this is true for all $\mathbf{w}^*$ and p^* we have

$$y(p, \mathbf{w}) = \frac{\partial \pi(p, \mathbf{w})}{\partial p}$$

$$x_i(p, \mathbf{w}) = \frac{-\partial \pi(p, \mathbf{w})}{\partial w_i} \qquad i = 1, \cdots, n \; \square$$

Here is a second, more direct but less elegant, proof.

PROOF By definition the profit function is simply the profits the firm gets by choosing the profit-maximizing inputs. Hence:

$$\pi(p, \mathbf{w}) = pf(\mathbf{x}(p, \mathbf{w})) - w\mathbf{x}(p, \mathbf{w})$$

Differentiating with respect to w_i:

$$\frac{\partial \pi}{\partial w_i} = p \sum_{j=1}^{n} \frac{\partial f}{\partial x_j} \frac{\partial x_j}{\partial w_i} - \sum_{j=1}^{n} w_j \frac{\partial x_j}{\partial w_i} - x_i(p, \mathbf{w})$$

$$= \sum_{j=1}^{n} \left[p \frac{\partial f}{\partial x_j} - w_j \right] \frac{\partial x_j}{\partial w_i} - x_i(p, \mathbf{w})$$

But the bracketed expression is zero by the first-order conditions for profit maximization, and thus the result is established. $\square$

What does this say in plain English? When the price of a factor changes infinitesimally, there will be two effects. First, there is a direct effect on profits of $d\pi = -dw_i x_i(p, \mathbf{w})$ because if the price of a factor changes by ten cents and the firm is employing 100 units of that factor, the profits will go down by ten dollars. Second, there is an indirect effect in that the firm will find it in its interest to change its production plans. But the impact on profits of any infinitesimal change in the production plan must be zero since we are already at the optimum production plan. Hence, the total impact of the indirect effect is zero, and we are left only with the direct effect.

From these proofs it should be clear that an analogous property holds for the cost function. This time, though, the demand functions for the inputs are *conditional factor demands* since they depend on the level of output.

PROPOSITION *(Shephard's lemma; the derivative property) Let* $x_i(\mathbf{w}, y)$ *be the firm's conditional factor demand for input* i. *Then if* c *is differentiable at* $(\mathbf{w}, y)$, *and* $\mathbf{w} \gg 0$

$$x_i(\mathbf{w}, y) = \frac{\partial c(\mathbf{w}, y)}{\partial w_i} \qquad i = 1, \cdots, n.$$

PROOF The proof is very similar to the proof of the last proposition. Let $\mathbf{x}^*$ be a cost-minimizing bundle that produces y at prices $\mathbf{w}^*$. Then define the function

$$g(\mathbf{w}) = c(\mathbf{w}, y) - \mathbf{w} \cdot \mathbf{x}^*$$

Since $c(\mathbf{w}, y)$ is the cheapest way to produce y, this function is always nonpositive. At $\mathbf{w} = \mathbf{w}^*$, $g(\mathbf{w}^*) = 0$. Since this is a maximum value of $g(\mathbf{w})$, its derivative must vanish:

$$\frac{\partial g(\mathbf{w}^*)}{\partial w_i} = \frac{\partial c(\mathbf{w}^*, y)}{\partial w_i} - x_i^* = 0 \qquad i = 1, \cdots, n$$

Hence the cost-minimizing input vector is just given by the vector of price derivatives of the cost function. □

Since this proposition is important, we will suggest *four* different ways of proving it. First, the cost function is by definition equal to $c(\mathbf{w}, y)) \equiv \mathbf{wx}(\mathbf{w}, y)$. Differentiating this expression with respect to w_i and using the first-order conditions give us the result. (Hint: $\mathbf{x}(\mathbf{w}, y)$ also satisfies the identity $f(\mathbf{x}(\mathbf{w}, y)) \equiv y$. You will need to differentiate this with respect to w_i.)

Second, the above calculations are really just repeating the derivation of the Envelope theorem described in Section A.12 of the Mathematical Appendix. This theorem can be applied directly to give the desired result.

Third, there is a nice geometrical argument that uses the same Figure 1.24 we used in arguing for concavity of the cost function. Recall in Figure 1.24 that the line $c = w_1 x_1^* + \sum_{i=2}^{n} w_i x_i^*$ lay above $c = c(\mathbf{w}, y)$ and both curves coincided at $w_1 = w_1^*$. Thus, the curves must be tangent, so that $x_1^* = \partial c(\mathbf{w}^*, y)/\partial w_1$.

Finally, we consider the basic economic intuition behind the proposition. If we are operating at a cost-minimizing point and the price w_1 increases, there will be a direct effect, in that the expenditure on the first factor will increase. There will also be an indirect effect, in that we will want to change the factor mix. But since we are operating at a cost-minimizing point, any such infinitesimal change must yield zero additional profits.

We have shown earlier that cost functions have certain properties that follow from the structure of the cost minimization problem; we have shown above that demand and supply functions are simply the derivatives of the cost functions. Hence, the properties we have found concerning the cost function will translate into certain restrictions on its derivatives, the factor demand functions. These restrictions will be the same sort of restrictions we found earlier using other methods, but their development via the cost function is quite nice.

Let us go through these restrictions one by one.

(1) *The cost function is increasing in factor prices*. Therefore, $\partial c(\mathbf{w}, y)/\partial w_i = x_i(\mathbf{w}, y) \geq 0$.

(2) *The cost function is homogeneous of degree 1 in* **w**. Therefore, the derivatives of the cost function, the factor demands, are homogeneous of degree 0 in **w** (Fact A.17 of the Mathematical Appendix).

(3) *The cost function is concave in* w. Therefore, the matrix of second derivatives of the cost function—the matrix of first derivatives of the factor demand functions—is a symmetric negative semidefinite matrix. This is not an obvious outcome of cost-minimizing behavior. It has several implications.

(a) the cross-price effects are symmetric—that is,
$\partial x_i(\mathbf{w}, y)/\partial \mathbf{w}_j = \partial^2 c(\mathbf{w}, y)/\partial \mathbf{w}_j \partial \mathbf{w}_i = \partial^2 c(\mathbf{w}, y)/\partial \mathbf{w}_i \partial \mathbf{w}_j = \partial x_j(\mathbf{w}, y)/\partial \mathbf{w}_i$

(b) the own price effects are negative—since $\partial x_i(w, y)/\partial w_i = \partial^2 c(w, y)/\partial w_i^2 \leq 0$ since the diagonal terms of a negative semidefinite matrix must be nonpositive.

(c) $\mathbf{dwdx} \leq 0$ by the argument given in Section 1.13.

Note that since the concavity of the cost function followed solely from the hypothesis of cost minimization, the symmetry and negative semidefinitness of the first derivative matrix of the factor demand functions follow solely from the hypothesis of cost minimization and do not involve any restrictions on the structure of the technology.

Similar exercises can be carried out concerning the profit function. Since $\pi(\mathbf{p})$ is a convex function, the matrix $\mathbf{D}^2\pi(\mathbf{p}) = \mathbf{Dy}(\mathbf{p})$ is a symmetric *positive* semidefinite matrix. In the case where we have only one output, this matrix can be written as:

$$\mathbf{D}^2\pi(p,\mathbf{w}) = \begin{bmatrix} \frac{\partial y}{\partial p} & \frac{\partial y}{\partial w_1} & \cdots & \frac{\partial y}{\partial w_n} \\ \cdot & \cdot & & \\ \cdot & & \cdot & \\ \cdot & & & \cdot \\ -\frac{\partial x_n}{\partial p} & \cdots & & -\frac{\partial x_n}{\partial w_n} \end{bmatrix}.$$

Hence, by the properties of positive semidefinite matrices we find that:

(a) the own supply effect is positive—$\partial y(p, \mathbf{w})/\partial p > 0$.
(b) the own demand effect is negative—$\partial x_i(p, \mathbf{w})/\partial w_i \leq 0$.
(c) the cross-price effects are symmetric—$\partial x_i/\partial w_j = \partial x_j/\partial w_i$

As above, the positive semidefiniteness of the above matrix can be translated into a more concrete statement concerning the net supply response to a price change $\mathbf{dp}$—namely, $\mathbf{dpdy} \geq 0$. Of course, suitably interpreted, these results hold in the multiple-output case as well.

Example 1.18 The LeChatelier Principle Let us consider the short-run response of a firm's supply behavior as compared to the long-run response. It seems plausible that the firm will respond more to a price change in the long run since, by definition, it has more factors to adjust in the long run than in the short run.

This intuitive proposition can be proved rigorously. Consider the short-run profit function $\pi(\mathbf{p},\mathbf{z})$ where $\mathbf{z}$ is the vector of factors that are fixed in the short run. Let the long-run profit-maximizing demand for these factors be given by $\mathbf{z}(\mathbf{p})$ so that the long-run profit function is given by $\pi(\mathbf{p}) = \pi(\mathbf{p}, \mathbf{z}(\mathbf{p}))$. Finally, let $\mathbf{p}^*$ be some given price vector, and let $\mathbf{z}^* = \mathbf{z}(\mathbf{p}^*)$ be the optimal long-run demand for the z factors at $\mathbf{p}^*$.

Now the long-run profits are always at least as large as the short-run profits since the firm has more factors to adjust. So:

$$g(\mathbf{p}) = \pi(\mathbf{p}, \mathbf{z}(\mathbf{p})) - \pi(\mathbf{p}, \mathbf{z}^*) \geq 0$$

for all prices $\mathbf{p}$. At the prices $\mathbf{p}^*$ the difference between the short- and long-run profits is zero, so that $g(\mathbf{p})$ reaches a minimum at $\mathbf{p} = \mathbf{p}^*$. Hence, the first derivative must vanish at $\mathbf{p}^*$. By Hotelling's principle, we see that the short-run and the long-run net supplies for each good must be equal at $\mathbf{p}^*$.

Since $\mathbf{p}^*$ is in fact a *minimum* of $g(\mathbf{p})$, the second-order conditions imply that the matrix of second derivatives of $g(\mathbf{p})$ is positive semidefinite. But this matrix is simply the *difference* of the two substitution matrices for the long- and short-run net supplies.

Since the diagonal terms of a positive semidefinite matrix must be nonnegative, we have:

$$\partial y_i(\mathbf{p}^*)/\partial p_i \geq \partial y_i(\mathbf{p}^*, z^*)/\partial p_i$$

Hence, the long-run response of net supply to a change in price is larger than the short-run response at any fixed price vector $\mathbf{p}^*$. This analysis thus confirms the intuition given above.

Example 1.19 The Effects of Price Stabilization Suppose that an industry faces a randomly fluctuating price for its output. For simplicity we imagine that the price of output will be p_1 with probability q and p_2 with probability $(1 - q)$.

It has been suggested that it may be socially desirable to stabilize the price of output at the average price $p = qp_1 + (1 - q)p_2$. How would this affect profits in the industry?

We have to compare average profits when p fluctuates to the profits at the average p. Since the profit function is convex:

$$q\pi(p_1, \mathbf{w}) + (1 - q)\,\pi(p_2, \mathbf{w}) \geqq \pi(qp_1 + (1 - q)\,p_2, \mathbf{w})$$

Thus, average profits with a fluctuating price are greater than with a stabilized price.

At first this result seems nonintuitive, but when we remember the economic reason for the convexity of the profit function it becomes clear. The industry will produce more output when the price is high and less when the price is low. The profit from doing this will exceed the profits from producing a fixed amount of output at the average price.

1.16 THE ALGEBRAIC APPROACH TO PROFIT MAXIMIZATION

In this section we will continue to examine the consequences of profit-maximizing behavior that follow *directly* from the definition of maximization itself. We will do this in a slightly different setting than before.

Instead of taking the behavior of the firm as being given by its demand and supply functions, we will think of just having a finite number of observations on a firm's behavior. This allows us to avoid some tedious details involved in taking limits and gives us a more realistic setting for empirical analysis. (Who has ever had an infinite amount of data anyway?)

Thus, we take our given to be a list of observed price vectors $\mathbf{p}^i$, and the associated net output vectors $\mathbf{y}^i$, for $i = 1, \cdots, n$. We refer to this collection as the *data*. In terms of the net supply functions we described before, the data are just $(\mathbf{p}^i, \mathbf{y}(\mathbf{p}^i))$ for $i = 1, \cdots, n$.

The first question we will ask is what the model of profit maximization implies about the set of data. If the firm is profit-maximizing, then the observed net output choice at price $\mathbf{p}^i$ must have a level of profit at least as great as the profit at any other net output the firm could have chosen. We don't know *all* the other choices that are feasible in this situation, but we do know some of them—namely, the other choices $\mathbf{y}^j$, $j = 1, \cdots, n$ that we have observed. Hence, a *necessary* condition for profit maximization is that:

$$\mathbf{p}^i\mathbf{y}^i \geq \mathbf{p}^i\mathbf{y}^j \qquad \text{for all } i \text{ and } j = 1, \cdots, n$$

We will refer to this condition as the Weak Axiom of Profit Maximization (WAPM).

This simple condition is actually very powerful. Let us derive some of its consequences. Fix two observations *i* and *j*, and write WAPM for each one. We have:

$$\mathbf{p}^i\,(\mathbf{y}^i - \mathbf{y}^j) \geq 0$$
$$-\mathbf{p}^j\,(\mathbf{y}^i - \mathbf{y}^j) \geq 0$$

Adding these two inequalities:

$$(\mathbf{p}^i - \mathbf{p}^j)\,(\mathbf{y}^i - \mathbf{y}^j) \geq 0$$

Letting $\Delta\mathbf{p}^i = (\mathbf{p}^i - \mathbf{p}^j)$ and $\Delta\mathbf{y}^i = (\mathbf{y}^i - \mathbf{y}^j)$, we can rewrite this as:

$$\Delta\mathbf{p}\Delta\mathbf{y} \geq 0$$

For example, if $\Delta\mathbf{p}$ is the vector $(1, 0, \cdots, 0)$, then this inequality implies that Δy_1 must be positive. If the first good is in net supply, it must increase when its price rises; if it is in net demand, then the magnitude of the demand must decrease. (Remember, demands are *negative* numbers in this notation.)

Of course, $\Delta\mathbf{p}\ \Delta\mathbf{y} \geq 0$ is simply a "delta" version of the infinitesimal inequality derived in Section 1.13. But it is much stronger in that it applies for *all* changes in prices, not just for infinitesimal ones.

The question immediately arises: Are there more such conditions available? Does WAPM exhaust all of the implications of profit-maximizing behavior, or are there other conditions yet to be found?

One way to answer this question is to try to construct a technology that generates the observed behavior $(\mathbf{p}^i, \mathbf{y}^i)$ $i = 1, \cdots, n$ as profit maximizing behavior. If we can find such a technology for any data that satisfy WAPM, then WAPM must indeed exhaust the implications of cost profit-maximizing behavior. Of course, we would like to construct the nicest possible technology compatible with $(\mathbf{p}^i, \mathbf{y}^i)$ $i = 1, \cdots, n$. We might even try for a closed convex production possibilities set. Since we know that the underlying production possibilities set (if it exists) must contain $\mathbf{y}^i$ for $i = 1, \cdots, n$, it is natural to take an "inner approximation" to this set by:

$$YI = \text{convex hull of } \{\mathbf{y}^i\text{: } i = 1, \cdots, n\}$$

It turns out that this construction will lead to a possible technology that could have generated the observed behavior. All we have to do is to check that:

$$\mathbf{p}^i\mathbf{y}^i \geq \mathbf{p}^i\mathbf{y} \qquad \text{for any } \mathbf{y} \text{ in } YI$$

Suppose that this is not the case. That is, for some observation i, $\mathbf{p}^i\mathbf{y}^i < \mathbf{p}^i\mathbf{y}$ for some $\mathbf{y}$ in YI. Then it must be the case that $\mathbf{p}^i\mathbf{y}^i < \mathbf{p}^i\mathbf{y}^j$ for some j. (Draw a picture to convince yourself of this fact about convex sets whose vertices are the given by the $\mathbf{y}^j$'s.) But this inequality violates WAPM.

Thus the set YI "rationalizes" the observed behavior in the sense that it is one possible technology that could have generated that behavior. It is not hard to see that YI must be contained in any convex technology that generated the observed behavior: if Y generated the observed behavior and it is convex, then it must contain the observed choices $\mathbf{y}^i$ for $i = 1, \cdots, n$, and the convex hull of these points is the smallest such set. In this sense, YI gives us an "inner bound" to the true technology that generated the data.

The question naturally arises: Can we find an outer bound to this "true" technology? Can we find a set YO that is guaranteed to *contain* any technology that is consistent with the observed behavior?

The trick to answering this question is to rule out all of the points that couldn't possibly be in the true technology and then take everything that is left over. More precisely, let us define NOTY by:

$$NOTY = \{\mathbf{y}\text{: } \mathbf{p}^i\mathbf{y} > \mathbf{p}^i\mathbf{y}^i \text{ for some } i = 1, \cdots, n\}$$

NOTY consists of all those net output bundles that yield higher profits than some observed choice. If the firm is a profit maximizer, such bundles couldn't be technologically feasible; otherwise they would have been chosen. Now as our outer bound to Y we just take the complement of this set:

$$YO = \{\mathbf{y}: \mathbf{p}^i\mathbf{y} \leq \mathbf{p}^i\mathbf{y}^i \text{ for all } i = 1, \cdots, n\}$$

It is left as an exercise for the reader to verify that YO does rationalize the data in the sense described above. (Show that the profits of the observed choices are at least as great as the profits at any other $\mathbf{y}$ in YO.)

1.17 THE ALGEBRAIC APPROACH TO COST MINIMIZATION

We can apply the algebraic techniques of the last section to the problem of cost minimization in a similar manner. We take as our data some observed choices by a firm of output levels y^i, factor prices $\mathbf{w}^i$, and factor levels $\mathbf{x}^i$, for $i = 1, \cdots, n$. When will these data be consistent with the model of cost minimization?

An obvious necessary condition is that the cost of the observed choice of inputs is no greater than the cost of any other level of inputs that would produce at least as much output. Translated into symbols, this says:

$$\mathbf{w}^i\mathbf{x}^i \leq \mathbf{w}^i\mathbf{x}^j \text{ for all } y^j \geq y^i$$

We will refer to this condition as the *Weak Axiom of Cost Minimization* or WACM.

As in the case of profit maximization, WACM can be used to derive the delta version of downward-sloping demands: $\Delta\mathbf{w} \cdot \Delta\mathbf{x} \leq 0$. This calculation is left for the reader.

One can also construct inner and outer bounds to the true input requirement set that generated the data. We will state the bounds here and leave it to the reader to verify that they are correct. The arguments are similar to those of the last section.

The inner bound is given by:

$$VI(y) = \text{convex monotonic hull of } \{\mathbf{x}^i: y^i \geq y\}$$

That is, the inner bound is simply the convex monotonic hull of all observations that can produce at least y amount of output. The outer bound is given by:

$$VO(y) = \{\mathbf{x}: \mathbf{w}^i\mathbf{x} \geq \mathbf{w}^i\mathbf{x}^i \text{ for all } i \text{ such that } y^i \leq y\}$$

These constructions are analogous to the earlier constructions of *YO* and *YI*. A picture of *VO* and *VI* is given in Figures 1.25 and 1.26.

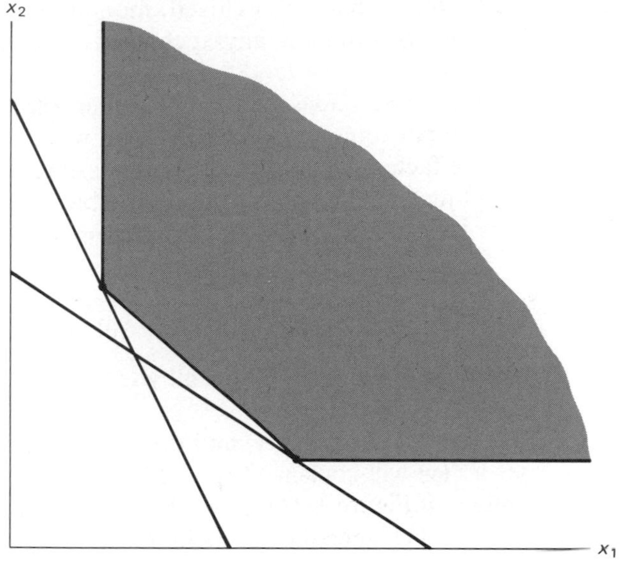

Fig. 1.25 *Inner-bound to* V(y)

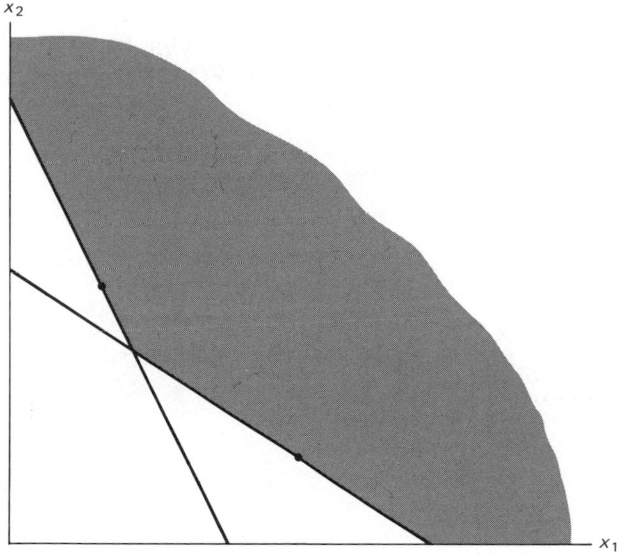

Fig. 1.26 *Outer-bound to* V(y)

1.18 DUALITY

Let us consider some properties of $VO(y)$ which we have defined above. It is straightforward to verify that it is a closed, monotonic, and convex technology. Furthermore, it contains any technology that could have generated the data $(\mathbf{w}_i, \mathbf{x}_i, y_i)$ for $i = 1, \cdots, n$.

If we let the number of observations increase, it appears clear that $VO(y)$ will approach the true input requirement set in some way. Suppose, for example, that we let the factor prices vary over all possible price vectors $\mathbf{w} \geq \mathbf{0}$, and thus the optimal choice will range all possible factor demands $\mathbf{x}(\mathbf{w}, y)$. We will refer to this "limiting" input requirement set as $V^*(y)$; it is given by:

$$V^*(y) = \{\mathbf{x}\colon \mathbf{wx} \geq \mathbf{wx}(\mathbf{w}, y) \text{ for all } \mathbf{w} \geq 0\} \text{ or}$$

$$V^*(y); = \{\mathbf{x}\colon \mathbf{wx} \geq c(\mathbf{w}, y) \quad \text{for all } \mathbf{w} \geq 0\}$$

What is the relationship between $V^*(y)$ and the true input requirement set $V(y)$? Of course, $V^*(y)$ will contain $V(y)$, and in general it will strictly contain it. For example, in Figure 1.27 we see that the crosshatched area cannot be ruled out of $V^*(y)$ since the points in this area satisfy the condition that $\mathbf{wx} \geq c(\mathbf{w}, y)$.

The same is true in the second figure for the hatched points. The cost function can only contain information about the *economically relevant* sections of $V(y)$, namely, those factor bundles that could actually be the solution to a cost minimization problem, i.e., that could actually be conditional factor demands.

However, suppose that our original technology is convex and monotonic. In this case $V^*(y)$ will equal $V(y)$. This is because, in the convex, monotonic case, each point on the boundary of $V(y)$ is a cost-

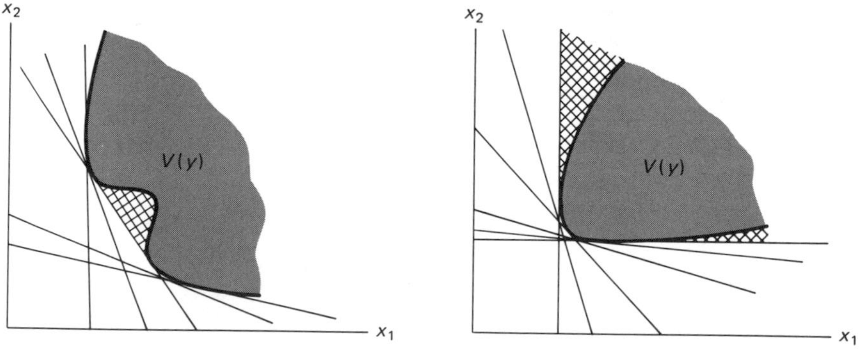

Fig. 1.27 *Relationship between* V(y) *and* V*(y)

minimizing factor demand for *some* price vector $\mathbf{w} \geqq 0$. Thus, the set of points where $\mathbf{w} \cdot \mathbf{x} \geqq c(\mathbf{w}, y)$ for all $\mathbf{w} \geqq 0$ will precisely describe the input requirement set. More formally:

PROPOSITION *Suppose* V(y) *is a regular, convex, monotonic technology. Then* V*(y) = V(y).

PROOF (Sketch) We already know that $V^*(y)$ contains $V(y)$, so we only have to show that if $\mathbf{x}$ is in $V^*(y)$ then $\mathbf{x}$ must be in $V(y)$. Suppose it is not. Then since $V(y)$ is a closed convex set satisfying the monotonicity hypothesis, we can apply a version of the separating hyperplane theorem (see Section A.6 of the Mathematical Appendix) to find a vector $\mathbf{w}^* \geqq 0$. such that $\mathbf{w}^* \cdot \mathbf{x} < \mathbf{w}^* \cdot \mathbf{z}$ for all $\mathbf{z}$ in $V(y)$. (See Figure 1.28.) Let $\mathbf{z}^*$ be a cost-minimizing bundle at prices $\mathbf{w}^*$; then in particular we have $\mathbf{w}^* \cdot \mathbf{x} < \mathbf{w}^* \cdot \mathbf{z}^* = c(\mathbf{w}^*, y)$. But then $\mathbf{x}$ cannot be in $V^*(y)$, a contradiction. □

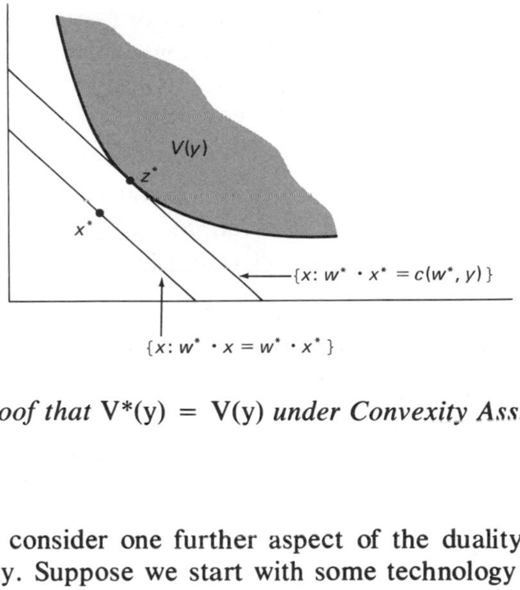

Fig. 1.28 *Proof that* V*(y) = V(y) *under Convexity Assumption*

Finally, we consider one further aspect of the duality between cost and technology. Suppose we start with some technology $V(y)$, possibly nonconvex. We find its cost function $c(\mathbf{w}, y)$ and then generate $V^*(y)$. We know from the above results that $V^*(y)$ will not necessarily be equal to $V(y)$, unless $V(y)$ happens to have the convexity and monotonicity properties. However, suppose we define

$$c^*(\mathbf{w}, y) = \min \mathbf{w} \cdot \mathbf{x}$$
$$\text{s.t. } \mathbf{x} \text{ is in } V^*(y)$$

What is the relationship between $c^*(\mathbf{w}, y)$ and $c(\mathbf{w}, y)$?

PROPOSITION $c^*(\mathbf{w}, y) = c(\mathbf{w}, y)$.

PROOF It is easy to see that $c^*(\mathbf{w}, y) \leqq c(\mathbf{w}, y)$; since $V^*(y)$ always contains $V(y)$, the minimal cost bundle in $V^*(y)$ must be at least as small as the minimal cost bundle in $V(y)$. Suppose that for some prices $\mathbf{w}'$, the cost minimizing bundle $\mathbf{x}'$ in $V^*(y)$ has the property that $\mathbf{w}' \cdot \mathbf{x}' = c^*(\mathbf{w}', y) < c(\mathbf{w}', y)$. But this can't happen, since by definition of $V^*(y)$, $\mathbf{w}' \cdot \mathbf{x}' \geqq c(\mathbf{w}', y)$. □

This proposition shows that the cost function for the technology $V(y)$ is the same as the cost function for its convexification $V^*(y)$. In this sense, the assumption of convex input requirement sets is not very restrictive from an economic point of view.

Let us summarize the discussion to date:

(1) Given a cost function we can define an input requirement set $V^*(y)$.
(2) If the original technology is convex and monotonic, the constructed technology will be identical with the original technology.
(3) If the original technology is nonconvex or nonmonotonic, the constructed input requirement will be a convexified, monotonized version of the original set, and, most importantly, the constructed technology will have the same cost function as the original technology.

We can summarize the above three points succinctly with the fundamental principle of duality in production: *the cost function of a firm summarizes all of the economically relevant aspects of its technology*.

(M)* *1.19 SUFFICIENT CONDITIONS FOR COST FUNCTIONS*

We have seen in the last section that the cost function summarizes all of the economically relevant information about a technology. We have seen in Section 1.11 that all cost functions are nondecreasing, homogeneous, concave, continuous function of prices. The question arises: suppose that you are given a nondecreasing, homogeneous, concave, continuous function of prices—is it necessarily the cost function of some technology?

Another way to phrase this question is: are the properties described in Section 1.11 a *complete* list of the implications of cost-minimizing behavior? Given a function that has those properties, must it necessarily arise from some technology? The answer is yes, and the following proposition shows how to construct such a technology.

* (M) indicates optional advanced material.

PROPOSITION *Let $\phi(\mathbf{w}, y)$ be a differentiable function satisfying:*

(1) $\phi(t\mathbf{w}, y) = t\phi(\mathbf{w}, y)$ *for all* $t \geqq 0$
(2) $\phi(\mathbf{w}, y) > 0$ *for* $\mathbf{w} \geqq 0$, $y > 0$
(3) $\phi(\mathbf{w}', y) \geqq \phi(\mathbf{w}, y)$ *for* $\mathbf{w}' \geqq \mathbf{w}$
(4) $\phi(\mathbf{w}, y)$ *is concave in* $\mathbf{w}$

Then $\phi(\mathbf{w}, y)$ is the cost function for the technology defined by $V^*(y) = \{\mathbf{x} \geqq 0: \mathbf{w} \cdot \mathbf{x} \geqq \phi(\mathbf{w}, y),$ *all* $\mathbf{w} \geqq 0\}$.

PROOF Given a $\mathbf{w} \geqq 0$ we define

$$\mathbf{x}(\mathbf{w}, y) = \left(\frac{\partial \phi(\mathbf{w}, y)}{\partial w_1}, \ldots, \frac{\partial \phi(\mathbf{w}, y)}{\partial w_n}\right)$$

and note that since $\phi(\mathbf{w}, y)$ is homogeneous of degree 1 in w, Euler's Law (Section A.14 of the Mathematical Appendix) implies that $\phi(\mathbf{w}, y)$ can be written as:

$$\phi(\mathbf{w}, y) = \sum_{i=1}^{n} w_i \frac{\partial \phi(\mathbf{w}, y)}{\partial w_i} = \mathbf{w} \cdot \mathbf{x}(\mathbf{w}, y)$$

Note that the monotonicity of $\phi(\mathbf{w}, y)$ implies $\mathbf{x}(\mathbf{w}, y) \geqq 0$.

What we need to show is that for any given $\mathbf{w}' \geqq 0$, $\mathbf{x}(\mathbf{w}', y)$ actually minimizes $\mathbf{w} \cdot \mathbf{x}$ over all $\mathbf{x}$ in $V^*(y)$:

$$\phi(\mathbf{w}', y) = \mathbf{w}' \cdot \mathbf{x}(\mathbf{w}', y) \leqq \mathbf{w}' \cdot \mathbf{x} \text{ for all } \mathbf{x} \text{ in } V^*(y)$$

First, we show that $\mathbf{x}(\mathbf{w}', y)$ is feasible; that is, $\mathbf{x}(\mathbf{w}', y)$ is in $V^*(y)$. By the concavity of $\phi(\mathbf{w}, y)$ in $\mathbf{w}$ we have:

$$\phi(\mathbf{w}', y) \leq \phi(\mathbf{w}, y) + \mathbf{D}\phi(\mathbf{w}, y)(\mathbf{w}' - \mathbf{w})$$

for all $\mathbf{w} \geq 0$. (Fact A.3 of the Mathematical Appendix.)

Using Euler's law as above, this reduces to:

$$\phi(\mathbf{w}', y) \leq \mathbf{w}' \, \mathbf{x}(\mathbf{w}, y) \text{ for all } \mathbf{w} \geq 0$$

Hence $\mathbf{x}(\mathbf{w}', y)$ is in $V^*(y)$.

Next we show that $\mathbf{x}(\mathbf{w}, y)$ actually minimizes $\mathbf{wx}$ over all $\mathbf{x}$ in $V^*(y)$. If $\mathbf{x}$ is in $V^*(y)$, then by definition it must satisfy:

$$\mathbf{wx} \geq \phi(\mathbf{w}, y)$$

But by Euler's law:

$$\phi(\mathbf{w}, y) = \mathbf{w}\mathbf{x}(\mathbf{w}, y)$$

The above two expressions imply:

$$\mathbf{w}\mathbf{x} \geq \mathbf{w}\mathbf{x}(\mathbf{w}, y)$$

for all $\mathbf{x}$ in $V^*(y)$ as required. □

This proposition raises another interesting question. Suppose you are given a set of functions $(g_i(\mathbf{w}, y))$ that satisfy the properties of conditional factor demand functions described in Section 1.15, namely, that they are homogeneous of degree 0 in prices and that

$$\left(\frac{\partial g_j(\mathbf{w}, y)}{\partial w_j}\right)$$

is a symmetric negative semidefinite matrix. Are these functions necessarily factor demand functions for some technology?

Let us try to apply the above proposition. First we construct a candidate for a cost function:

$$\phi(\mathbf{w}, y) = \sum_{i=1}^{n} w_i g_i(\mathbf{w}, y).$$

Next we check whether it satisfies the properties required for the proposition just proved.

(1) Is $\phi(\mathbf{w}, y)$ homogeneous of degree 1 in $\mathbf{w}$? To check this we look at $\phi(t\mathbf{w}, y) = \sum_i tw_i g_i(t\mathbf{w}, y)$. Since the functions $g_i(\mathbf{w}, y)$ are by assumption homogeneous of degree 0, $g_i(t\mathbf{w}, y) = g_i(\mathbf{w}, y)$ so that

$$\phi(t\mathbf{w}, y) = t\Sigma\ wg_i(\mathbf{w}, y) = t\phi(\mathbf{w}, y).$$

(2) Is $\phi(\mathbf{w}, y) \geqq 0$ for $\mathbf{w} \geqq 0$, $y > 0$? Since $g_i(\mathbf{w}, y) \geqq 0$, the answer is clearly yes.

(3) Is $\phi(\mathbf{w}, y)$ nondecreasing in w_i? We compute

$$\frac{\partial \phi(\mathbf{w}, y)}{\partial w_i} = g_i(\mathbf{w}, y) + \sum_{j=1}^{n} w_j \frac{\partial g_j(\mathbf{w}, y)}{\partial \mathbf{w}_i} = g_i(\mathbf{w}, y) + \sum_{j=1}^{n} w_j \frac{\partial g_i(\mathbf{w}, y)}{\partial w_j}$$

Since $f_i(\mathbf{w}, y)$ is homogeneous of degree 0 the last term vanishes and $f_i(\mathbf{w}, y)$ is clearly greater than or equal to 0.

(4) Finally is $\phi(\mathbf{w}, y)$ concave in $\mathbf{w}$? To check this we differentiate $\phi(\mathbf{w}, y)$ twice to get

$$\left(\frac{\partial^2 \phi}{\partial w_i \partial w_j}\right) = \left(\frac{\partial g_i(\mathbf{w}, y)}{\partial w_j}\right)$$

For concavity we want these matrices to be symmetric and negative semidefinite, which they are by hypothesis.

Hence the proposition proved in this section applies and there is a technology $V^*(y)$ that yields $(g_i(\mathbf{w}, y))$ as its conditional factor demands. This means that the properties of homogeneity and negative semidefiniteness form a complete list of the restrictions on demand functions imposed by the model of cost-minimizing behavior.

Of course, essentially the same results hold for profit functions and (unconditional) demand and supply functions. If the profit function obeys the restrictions described in Section 1.11 or, equivalently, if the demand and supply functions obey the restrictions in Section 1.15, then there must exist a technology that generates this profit function or these demand and supply functions.

Example 1.20 Applying the Duality Mapping Suppose we are given a specific cost function $c(\mathbf{w}, y) = y w_1^a w_2^{1-a}$. How can we solve for its associated technology? According to the derivative property:

$$x_1(\mathbf{w}, y) = a y w_1^{a-1} w_2^{1-a} = a y \left(\frac{w_2}{w_1}\right)^{1-a}$$

$$x_2(\mathbf{w}, y) = (1-a) y w_1^a w_2^{-a} = (1-a) y \left(\frac{w_2}{w_1}\right)^{-a}$$

We want to eliminate w_2/w_1 from these two equations and get an equation for y in terms of x_1 and x_2. Rearranging each equation gives:

$$\frac{w_2}{w_1} = \left(\frac{x_1}{ay}\right)^{\frac{1}{1-a}}$$

$$\frac{w_2}{w_1} = \left(\frac{x_2}{(1-a)y}\right)^{-\frac{1}{a}}$$

Setting these equal to each other and raising both sides to the $-a(1-a)$ power,

$$\frac{x_1^{-a}}{a^{-a} y^{-a}} = \frac{x_2^{1-a}}{(1-a)^{(1-a)} y^{1-a}}$$

or

$$[a^a (1-a)^{1-a}] y = x_1^a x_2^{1-a}$$

This is just the Cobb-Douglas technology.

Example 1.21 Constant Returns to Scale and the Cost Function Since the cost function tells us all of the economically relevant information about the technology, we can try to interpret various restrictions on costs in terms of restrictions on technology. Compare the following proposition to the one in Example 1.21.

PROPOSITION *Let* V(y) *be convex and monotonic; then if* c(**w**, y) *can be written as* yc(**w**), V(y) *must exhibit constant returns to scale.*

PROOF Under the convexity and monotonicity assumptions we know that

$$V(y) = V^*(y) = \{\mathbf{x}\text{: } \mathbf{w}\cdot\mathbf{x} \geqq yc(\mathbf{w}) \text{ for all } \mathbf{w} \geqq 0\}$$

We want to show that, if **x** is in $V^*(y)$, then t**x** is in $V^*(ty)$. If **x** is in $V^*(y)$ we know that $\mathbf{w}\cdot\mathbf{x} \geqq yc(\mathbf{w})$ for all $\mathbf{w} \geqq 0$. Multiplying both sides of this equation by t we get: $\mathbf{w}\cdot t\mathbf{x} \geqq tyc(\mathbf{w})$ for all $\mathbf{w} \geqq 0$. But this says $t\mathbf{x}$ is in $V^*(ty)$. □

Example 1.22 Returns to Scale and the Cost Function The results of Examples 1.9 and 1.21 can be generalized in the following manner. Given a production function $f(\mathbf{x})$ we can consider the local measure of returns to scale known as the *elasticity of scale:*

$$e(\mathbf{x}) = \frac{df(t\mathbf{x})}{dt}\frac{t}{f(\mathbf{x})} \quad \text{evaluated at } t = 1$$

which was defined in Section 1.6. The technology exhibits locally decreasing, constant, or increasing returns to scale as $e(\mathbf{x})$ is less than, equal to, or greater than one.

Given some vector of factor prices we can compute the cost function of the firm $c(\mathbf{w}, y)$. Let $\mathbf{x}^*$ be the cost-minimizing bundle at $(\mathbf{w}, y)$. Then I claim:

$$e(\mathbf{x}^*) = \frac{c(\mathbf{w}, y)/y}{\partial c(\mathbf{w}, y)/\partial y} = \frac{\mathrm{AC}(y)}{\mathrm{MC}(y)}$$

To see this, we perform the differentiation indicated in the definition of $e(\mathbf{x})$:

$$e(\mathbf{x}^*) = \frac{\sum_{i=1}^{n} \frac{\partial f(\mathbf{x}^*)}{\partial x_i} x_i^*}{f(x^*)}$$

Since $\mathbf{x}^*$ minimizes costs it satisfies the first order conditions that

$w_i = \lambda \dfrac{\partial f(x^*)}{\partial x_i}$. Furthermore, by exercise 1.14, $\lambda = \partial c(\mathbf{w}, y)/\partial y$. Thus

$$e(\mathbf{x}^*) = \frac{\sum_{i=1}^{n} w_i \cdot x_i^*}{tf(\mathbf{x}^*)} = \frac{c(\mathbf{w}, y)/y}{\partial c(\mathbf{w}, y)/\partial y} = \frac{\mathrm{AC}(y)}{\mathrm{MC}(y)}$$

1.20 GEOMETRY OF DUALITY

Using the idea of the duality mapping, we can examine geometrically the relationship between a firm's technology as summarized by its production function and its economic behavior as summarized by its cost function.

In Figure 1.29 we have illustrated the isoquant of a firm and an isocost curve for the same level of output y. The slope at a point (w_1^*, w_2^*) on this isocost curve is given by:

$$\frac{dw_2(w_1^*)}{dw_1} = -\frac{\dfrac{\partial c(\mathbf{w}^*, y)}{\partial w_1}}{\dfrac{\partial c(\mathbf{w}^*, y)}{\partial w_2}} = -\frac{x_1(\mathbf{w}^*, y)}{x_2(\mathbf{w}^*, y)}$$

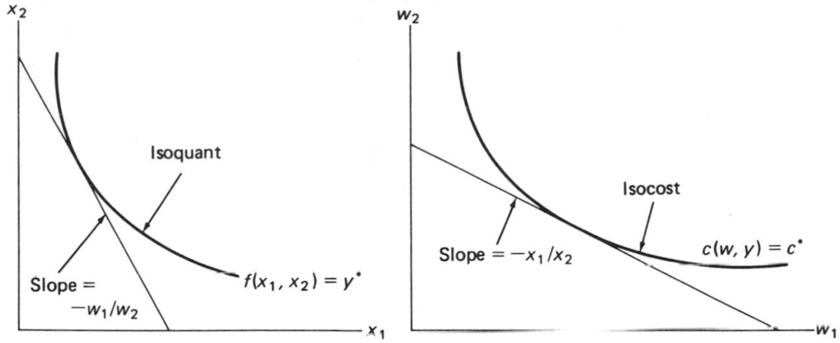

Fig. 1.29 *Curvature of Isoquants and Isocosts*

On the other hand, an isoquant is defined by:

$$f(\mathbf{x}) \equiv y$$

The slope of an isoquant at a point $\mathbf{x}^*$ is given by:

$$\frac{dx_2(x_1^*)}{dx_1} = -\frac{\dfrac{\partial f(\mathbf{x}^*)}{\partial x_1}}{\dfrac{\partial f(\mathbf{x}^*)}{\partial x_2}}$$

Now if (x_1^*, x_2^*) is a cost-minimizing point at prices (w_1^*, w_2^*) we know it fulfills the first-order conditions

$$\frac{w_1^*}{w_2^*} = \frac{\dfrac{\partial f(\mathbf{x}^*)}{\partial x_1}}{\dfrac{\partial f(\mathbf{x}^*)}{\partial x_2}}$$

Notice the nice duality: the slope of the isoquant curve gives the ratio of the factor prices while the slope of the isocost curve gives the ratio of the factor levels.

What about the *curvature* of the isoquant and the isocost curves? It turns out that their curvatures are inversely related: if the isocost curve is very curved, the isoquant will be rather flat and vice versa. We can see this by considering some specific (w_1, w_2) on the isocost curve and then moving to some (w_1', w_2') on the isocost curve that is fairly far away. Suppose we find that the slope of the isocost curve doesn't change very much—i.e., the isocost curve has little curvature. Since the slope of the isocost curve gives us this factor demand, this means that the cost-minimizing bundles must be rather similar. Referring to Figure 1.29 we see that this means that the isoquant must be very curved.

Similarly if we start at (w_1, w_2) and move to a nearby (w_1', w_2') and find that the slope of the isocost curve has changed a lot, then we know that the cost-minimizing bundles must be rather far apart. Thus, we have an inverse relationship between the curvature of the isoquant and the isocost curves. In the extreme case we find that cost function of the Leontief technology is a linear function and that the "Leontief cost function" corresponds to a linear technology, as in Figure 1.30.

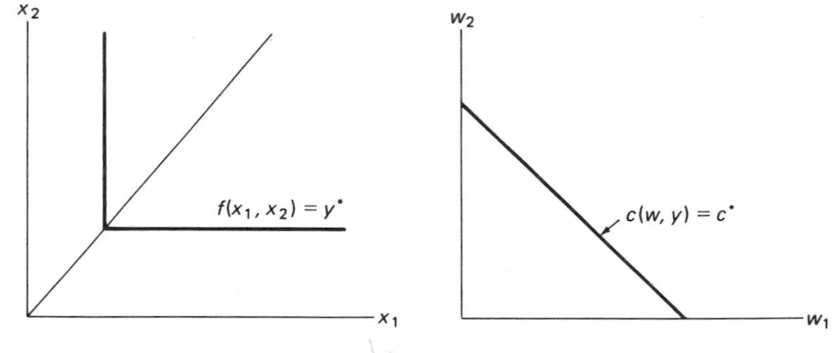

Fig. 1.30 *Leontief Technology and Isocost Curves*

Example 1.23 The Elasticity of Substitution It is often convenient to have a measure of how "substitutable" one input is for another. Perhaps the most natural measure would just be the cross-elasticity of factor demands: $(\partial x_1(\mathbf{w}, y)/\partial w_2)\,(w_2/x_1)$. However, most economists instead use a related measure known as the *elasticity of substitution*.

Let us describe this measure in the simple case where we have a two input constant returns to scale technology. First, we note that, as above, the natural measure of substitutability would be $\partial x_1(\mathbf{w}, y)/\partial w_2$. Second, we note that $\partial x_1(\mathbf{w}, y)/\partial w_1$ would serve just as well. This follows easily from Euler's law for homogeneous functions: since $x_1(\mathbf{w}, y)$ is homogeneous of degree 0 in (w_1, w_2), we have:

$$\frac{\partial x_1(\mathbf{w}, y)}{\partial w_1} w_1 + \frac{\partial x_1(\mathbf{w}, y)}{\partial w_2} w_2 = 0$$

so

$$\frac{\partial x_1(\mathbf{w}, y)}{\partial w_1} = \frac{-\partial x_1(\mathbf{w}, y)}{\partial w_2}\frac{w_2}{w_1}$$

This says $\partial x_1/\partial w_1$, is strictly proportional to $\partial x_1/\partial w_2$, with a change of sign. Third, we note that since the factor demands are homogeneous of degree 0, only relative prices matter, so we might as well consider: $\partial x_1(\mathbf{w}, y)/\partial(w_1/w_2)$ and just take the derivative with respect to the relative price of the factors. Fourth, since output is constant, we know that if we use more of x_1 we have to use less of x_2 so that it is the *relative* factor mix that is important. Therefore, we might as well consider:

$$\frac{\partial \dfrac{x_1(\mathbf{w}, y)}{x_2(\mathbf{w}, y)}}{\partial(w_1/w_2)}$$

Fifth, we want to convert this into an elasticity, so we have:

$$\sigma = \frac{\partial \dfrac{x_1(\mathbf{w}, y)}{x_2(\mathbf{w}, y)}}{\partial(w_1/w_2)} \frac{\dfrac{w_1}{w_2}}{\dfrac{x_1}{x_2}}$$

You can verify that if x_1/x_2 responds greatly to changes in w_1/w_2 then σ will be large and vice versa.

Although the theoretical expression is rather forboding, in practice things usually work out neatly. Let us calculate σ for the Cobb-Douglas production function, $f(x_1, x_2) = x_1^a x_2^{1-a}$. The first order conditions take the form:

$$\frac{w_1}{w_2} = \frac{a x_1^{a-1} x_2^{1-a}}{(1-a) x_1^a x_2^{-a}} = \frac{a}{(1-a)}\left[\frac{x_1}{x_2}\right]^{-1}$$

Thus

$$\frac{x_1}{x_2} = \frac{a}{(1-a)} \left[\frac{w_1}{w_2}\right]^{-1}$$

so

$$\frac{\partial(x_1/x_2)}{\partial(w_1/w_2)} \frac{(w_1/w_2)}{(x_1/x_2)} = \frac{-a}{(1-a)} \left[\frac{w_1}{w_2}\right]^{-2} \left[\frac{w_1}{w_2}\right] \frac{(1-a)}{a} \left[\frac{w_1}{w_2}\right]$$

$$\sigma = -1$$

Now, let's try the CES production function, $f(x_1, x_2) = (x_1^\rho + x_2^\rho)^{1/\rho}$. As in Example 1.13, the first-order conditions have the form:

$$\frac{w_1}{w_2} = \frac{x_1^{\rho-1}}{x_2^{\rho-1}} = \left[\frac{x_1}{x_2}\right]^{\rho-1}$$

Thus

$$\frac{x_1}{x_2} = \left[\frac{w_1}{w_2}\right]^{\frac{1}{(\rho-1)}}$$

so

$$\frac{\partial(x_1/x_2)}{\partial(w_1/w_2)} \frac{(w_1/w_2)}{(x_1/x_2)} = \frac{1}{(\rho-1)} \left[\frac{w_1}{w_2}\right]^{\frac{(2-\rho)}{(\rho-1)}} \left[\frac{w_1}{w_2}\right] \left[\frac{w_1}{w_2}\right]^{\frac{-1}{(\rho-1)}}$$

$$\sigma = \frac{1}{(\rho-1)}$$

When there are more than two factors of production, the definition of the elasticity of substitution is somewhat problematic. We still want to measure how the ratio of inputs i and j responds to a change in the relative price of i and j, but we have to ask what happens to the other variables in the system. If we consider holding the other factor prices fixed during the experiment, then the other quantities will adjust optimally and we will have a measure known as the *Allen elasticity of substitution*. If instead we hold the other quantities fixed, thus implicitly allowing the other factor prices to vary, we will have a measure known as the *elasticity of complementarity*.

Example 1.24 Production Functions, Cost Functions, and Conditional Factor Demands Suppose we have a nice smooth convex isoquant. Then the isocost curve is also convex and smooth and the conditional factor demand curves are well behaved as in Figure 1.31.

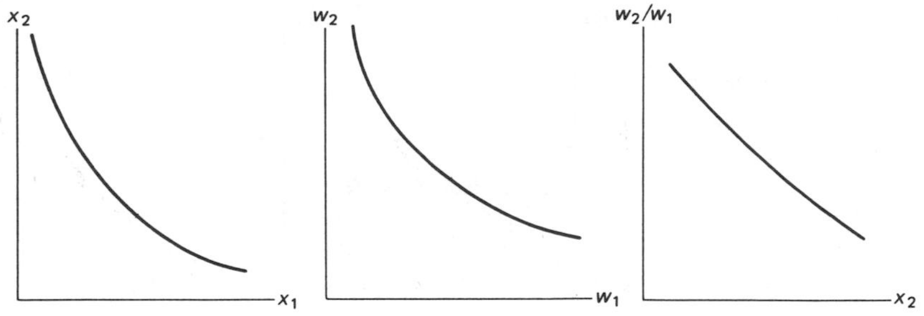

Fig. 1.31 *Technology, Costs, and Demand*

Suppose that the isoquant has a flat spot, so that at some combination of factor prices there is no unique bundle of factor demands. Then the isocost curve must be nondifferentiable at this level of factor prices, and the conditional factor demand functions are multivalued as in Figure 1.32.

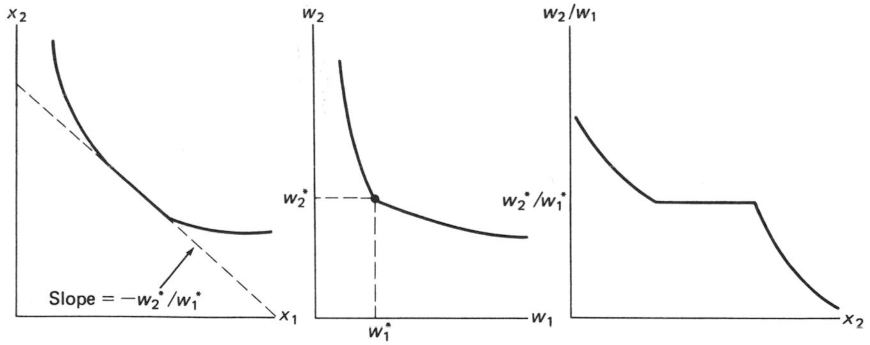

Fig. 1.32 *Technology, Costs, and Demand*

Suppose that the isoquant has a kink at some point. Then for some *range* of prices, a fixed bundle of inputs will be demanded. This means that the isocost curve must have a flat spot as in Figure 1.33.

Suppose the isoquant is nonconvex over some range. Then the isocost curve has a kink at some point and the conditional factor demands are discontinuous and multivalued. Notice how the cost function for this technology is indistinguishable from the cost function for the convexification of this technology by comparing Figures 1.32 and 1.34.

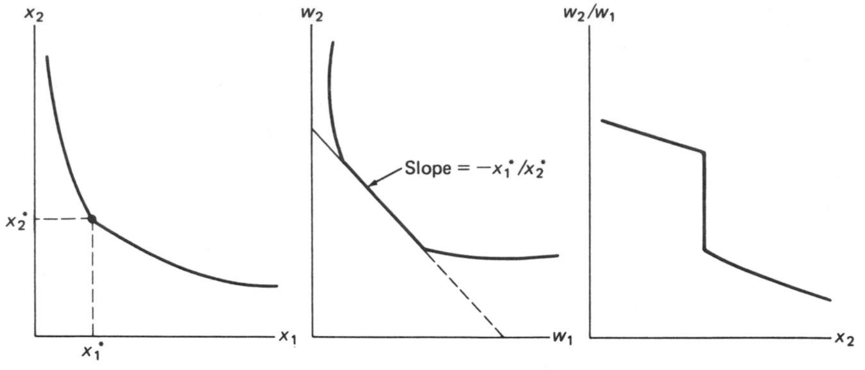

Fig. 1.33 *Technology, Costs, and Demand*

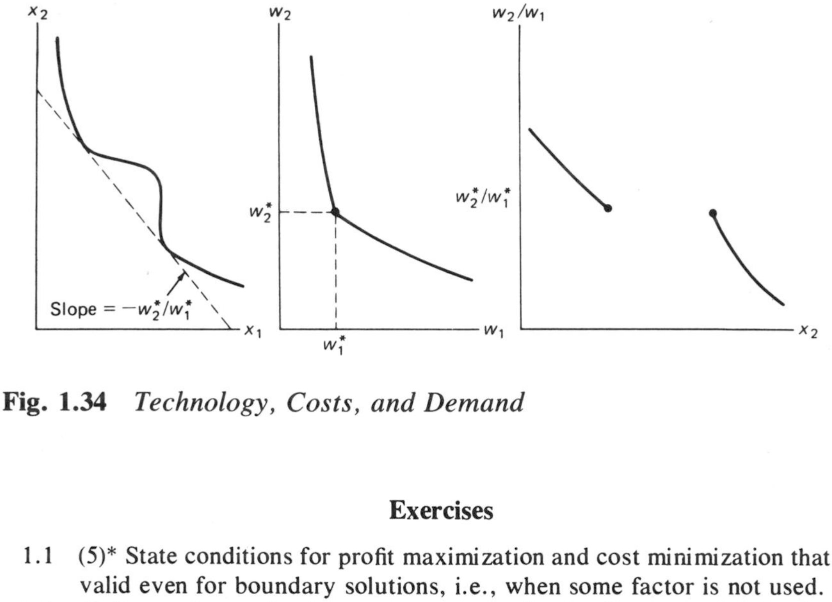

Fig. 1.34 *Technology, Costs, and Demand*

Exercises

1.1 (5)* State conditions for profit maximization and cost minimization that are valid even for boundary solutions, i.e., when some factor is not used.

1.2 (5) Prove rigorously that profit maximization implies cost minimization.

1.3 Prove that a solution to the cost-minimization problem exists as long as $V(y)$ is a closed subset of the nonnegative orthant and $w \gg 0$.

1.4 (10) One can argue that the supply and demand functions have the proper slopes by a finite argument. Let $\mathbf{y}$ be an optimal netput vector at prices $\mathbf{p}$ and let $\mathbf{y}'$ be an optimal netput vector at prices $\mathbf{p}'$. By definition $\mathbf{p}\cdot\mathbf{y} \geqq \mathbf{p}\cdot\mathbf{y}'$

* The numbers in parentheses indicate the difficulty of the exercise; 5-point problems should take only a few minutes to work, while 30-point problems could easily take an hour.

and $\mathbf{p}' \cdot \mathbf{y}' \geqq \mathbf{p}' \cdot \mathbf{y}$. Manipulate these inequalities to get an expression involving $\Delta \mathbf{p} = (\mathbf{p} - \mathbf{p}')$ and $\Delta \mathbf{y} = (\mathbf{y} - \mathbf{y}')$ and take limits.

1.5 (30) For each of the following input requirement sets, determine whether the given technology is: regular, monotonic, convex. Where possible draw a representative isoquant, and derive the production function, cost function, and conditional factor demands: $P = \{\mathbf{x} \text{ in } R^n: \mathbf{x} \geqq 0\}$.
(a) $V(y) = \{\mathbf{x} \text{ in } P: ax_1 \geqq \log y,\ bx_2 \geqq \log y\}$
(b) $V(y) = \{\mathbf{x} \text{ in } P: ax_1 + bx_2 \geqq y,\ x_1 > 0\}$
(c) $V(y) = \{\mathbf{x} \text{ in } P: ax_1 + \sqrt{x_1x_2} + bx_2 \geqq y\}$
(d) $V(y) = \{\mathbf{x} \text{ in } P: ax_1 + bx_2 \leqq y\}$
(e) $V(y) = \{\mathbf{x} \text{ in } P: x_1(1 - y) \geqq a;\ x_2(1 - y) \geqq b\}$
(f) $V(y) = \{\mathbf{x} \text{ in } P: ax_1 - \sqrt{x_1x_2} + bx_2 \geqq y\}$
(g) $V(y) = \{\mathbf{x} \text{ in } P: x_1 + \min(x_2, x_3) \geqq 3y\}$.

1.6 (30) For the following "cost functions" indicate which if any of properties of the cost function fails; e.g., homogeneity, concavity, monotonicity, or continuity. Where possible derive a production function.
(a) $C(y, \mathbf{w}) = y^{1/2}(w_1w_2)^{3/4}$
(b) $C(y, \mathbf{w}) = \sqrt{y}(2w_1^{1/2}w_2^{1/2})$.
(c) $C(y, \mathbf{w}) = y(w_1 + \sqrt{w_1w_2} + w_2)$
(d) $C(y, \mathbf{w}) = y(w_1e^{-w_1} + w_2)$
(e) $C(y, \mathbf{w}) = y(w_1 - \sqrt{w_1w_2} + w_2)$
(f) $C(y, \mathbf{w}) = (y + 1/y)\sqrt{w_1w_2}$

1.7 (20) Suppose a firm has an input requirement set given by:

$$V(y) = \{\mathbf{x} \text{ in } P: ax_1 + bx_2 \geqq y^2\}$$

(a) What is the production function?
(b) What is the cost function?
(c) What are the conditional factor demands?

1.8 (20) For what parameters $(a, b, c, d, \alpha, \beta, \gamma, \delta)$ are the following equations a valid system of factor demands?

$$x_1(w_1, w_2, y) = (a + bw_1^\alpha w_2^\beta)y$$

$$x_2(w_1, w_2, y) = (c + dw_1^\gamma w_2^\delta)y$$

1.9 (10) Let $f(x_1, x_2)$ be a homogeneous (of degree 1) production function. Then an increasing average product for one input implies that the marginal product of the other input must be negative.

1.10 (15) Let $f(\mathbf{x})$ be the production function for a firm with a constant-returns-to-scale technology. Suppose each factor x_i is payed its *value marginal product* $w_i = p\partial f(\mathbf{x})/\partial x_i$. Show that profits must be 0.

1.11 (15) Show that if the production set is convex, the technology cannot exhibit increasing returns to scale. However, a convex input requirement set is perfectly compatible with increasing return.

1.12 (10) Show that if $f(\mathbf{x})$ represents a monotonic convex technology, then $F(z, \mathbf{x}) = zf(\mathbf{x}/z)$ will also be a convex monotonic technology.

1.13 (20) Suppose that the technology is *additive* in the sense that $f(\mathbf{x}+\mathbf{z}) = f(\mathbf{x}) + f(\mathbf{z})$ and that the inputs are infinitely divisible. Show that the technology must be convex.

1.14 (25) Show that the derivative of the cost function gives the conditional factor demands by using the envelope theorem directly.

1.15 (12) A production function is said to be *homothetic* if $f(\mathbf{x})$ can be written as $h(g(\mathbf{x}))$ where h is monotonic and g is homogeneous of degree 1. Show that, under suitable hypotheses, $f(\mathbf{x})$ is homothetic if and only if the cost function can be written as $c(\mathbf{w}, y) = k(y)c(\mathbf{w})$.

1.16 (10) Suppose $f(\mathbf{x})$ is a homothetic production function. Show that the technical rate of substitution at $t\mathbf{x}$ is independent of t.

1.17 (25) A factor of production is called inferior if the conditional demand for that factor falls as output is increased, i.e., one for which $\partial x_i(\mathbf{w}, y)/\partial y < 0$.

(a) Show by a geometrical example that such things exist.

(b) Show that if the technology is homothetic then no factors can be inferior.

(c) Show that, if marginal cost decreases as the price of some factor increases, then that factor must be inferior.

1.18 (10) Suppose we have a convex, monotonic technology. Suppose average cost is increasing at all levels of output and at all factor prices. Show that the elasticity of scale must be everywhere less than one.

1.19 (10) The first-order conditions for cost minimization are $w_i = t\,\partial f(\mathbf{x}^*)/\partial x_i$. Use the envelope theorem to relate t to the cost function $c(\mathbf{w}, y)$.

1.20 (15) Derive a profit function for the technology

$$\begin{aligned} f(x) &= \ln x \qquad x \geqq 1 \\ &= 0 \qquad\quad x < 1 \end{aligned}$$

Verify that it obeys the restrictions on profit functions described in the text.

1.21 (30) Given the following production function:

$$Y = 100\, x_1^{1/2} x_2^{1/4}$$

(a) Find $c(w_1, w_2, y)$.

(b) Find the effect of an increase in output on marginal cost, and verify that λ = marginal cost.

(c) Given p = price of output, find $x_1(w, p)$, $x_2(w, p)$ and $\pi(w, p)$. Use Hotelling's lemma to derive the supply function $y(w, p)$.

(d) Verify that the production function is homothetic.

1.22 (10) Let $c(\mathbf{w}, y) = (aw_1 + bw_2)y^{1/2}$ be a cost function. Derive its production function and draw a representative family of isoquants.

1.23 (10) (Producer's surplus) Show that the integral of the supply function between the p° and p' gives the change in profits when price changes from p° to p'.

1.24 (20) Suppose a firm has a marginal cost curve with the following shape:

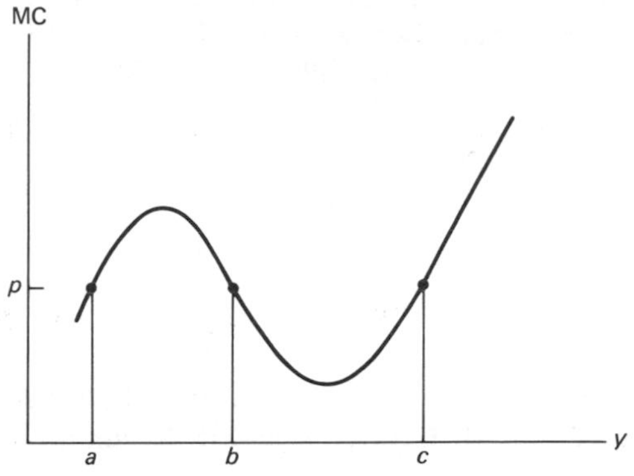

(a) At price p at what levels of output might a competitive firm produce?
(b) Of the choices mentioned in part a, how would you determine geometrically at which point the firm would operate?
(c) Construct the firm's supply curve.

1.25 (10) Suppose $f(\mathbf{x})$ is homogeneous of degree k so that $f(t\mathbf{x}) = t^k f(\mathbf{x})$ for all $t > 0$. Show that the elasticity of scale, $e(\mathbf{x})$, is precisely k.

1.26 (30) (Diewert) Suppose we have two groups of inputs to production, $x_1, \ldots, x_n$ and $x_1', \ldots, x_m'$. Let $V(y)$ be the input requirement set. Suppose that the vectors of prices for these inputs $\mathbf{w}$ and $\mathbf{w}'$ always move proportionally so that $\mathbf{w} = \alpha\mathbf{w}_0$ and $\mathbf{w}' = \beta\mathbf{w}_0'$. Show that there exist aggregate inputs $X = \mathbf{w}_0 \cdot \mathbf{x}$ and $X' = \mathbf{w}_0' \cdot \mathbf{x}'$ and an aggregate input requirement set $V'(y)$ such that $(\mathbf{x}, \mathbf{x}')$ is in $V(y)$ if and only if (X, X') is in $V'(y)$. (Hint: define $c(\alpha, \beta, y) = \min \alpha X + \beta X'$ such that $(\mathbf{x}, \mathbf{x}')$ is in $V(y)$. Show that this is a legitimate cost function and consider the $V^*(y)$ associated with it.)

1.27 (20) Suppose we have a single output and many inputs. Suppose that all input prices increase by $d\mathbf{w} = (dw_1, \ldots, dw_n)$, where $dw_i > 0$. Under what conditions will output decline?

Notes

The dual approach to production theory was developed by several authors. The first complete, rigorous development of the properties of the cost function is Shephard (1953), (1970). However, some of the properties of cost and profit function had been stated earlier by Hotelling (1932), Hicks (1946), and Samuelson (1947).

The basic duality between cost and production functions was first shown by Shephard (1953). Since then many other authors have contributed to the theory; a comprehensive survey and historical notes is available in Diewert (1974). The treatment of this material here owes most to McFadden (1978). Several of the examples were taken from McFadden (1978) and Hall (1972).

References

DIEWERT, E. 1974. "Applications of Duality Theory." In *Frontiers of Quantitative Economics*, vol. 2, ed. M. Intriligator and D. Kendrick. Amsterdam: North Holland.

HALL, R. 1972. "Lecture Notes in Microeconomics." Unpublished.

HICKS, J. 1946. *Value and Capital*. 2d ed. Oxford, Eng.: Clarendon Press.

HOTELLING, H. 1932. "Edgeworth's Taxation Paradox and the Nature of Demand and Supply Function." *Journal of Political Economy* 40:577–616.

MCFADDEN, D. 1978. "Cost, Revenue, and Profit Functions." In *Production Economics: A Dual Approach to Theory and Applications*, ed. M. Fuss and D. McFadden. Amsterdam: North Holland.

SAMUELSON, P. 1947. *Foundations of Economic Analysis*. Cambridge, Mass.: Harvard University Press.

SHEPHARD, R. 1953. *Cost and Production Functions*. Princeton, N.J.: Princeton University Press.

———. 1970. *Theory of Cost and Production Functions*. Princeton, N.J.: Princeton University Press.

Chapter 2

Theory of the Market

In the introduction to Chapter 1 we indicated that the firm faces two kinds of constraints which influence its profit-maximizing behavior. The first type of constraint is technological. These technological constraints simply indicate that not all production plans are physically possible, and the search for a maximal profit plan must necessarily be limited only to the technologically feasible plans. A main theme of Chapter 1 was the fact that the technological possibilities of a firm, as indicated by its production function, bore an important relationship to the economic behavior of the firm, as indicated by its cost function.

The second type of constraint that affects firm behavior are the market constraints. Market constraints relate to the interactions of the economic agents. For example, a firm cannot unilaterally decide how much output to produce *and* at what price to sell this output. Rather, the firm has to take account of demand behavior in determining its pricing and production policies. In Chapter 1 the market constraints facing a firm were largely ignored. In that chapter, firms were modeled as taking prices as given, exogenous variables. Thus, the profit maximization problem of the firm could be reduced to examining only the choice of the best output for a given price configuration.

In this chapter we will concentrate on modeling the market behavior of the firm. How do firms determine the price at which they will sell their output or the prices at which they are willing to purchase inputs? We will see that in certain situations the "price-taking behavior" described in Chapter 1 might be a reasonable approximation to optimal behavior, but in other situations we will have to explore models of the price-setting process. The first model we examine will be concerned with a pure case of such price-setting behavior.

2.1 PURE MONOPOLY

Let us consider the case of a market dominated by a single firm that sells a single output good. Such a *monopolistic* firm must make two sorts of decisions: how much output it should produce, and at what price it should sell this output. Of course, it cannot make these decisions unilaterally. The amount of output that the firm is able to sell will depend on the price that it sets. We summarize this relationship between demand and price in a *demand function* for output, $y(p)$. In Chapter 3 we will investigate the derivation of this function, but for now we will take it as a primitive concept. The demand function tells how much output consumers will demand as a function of the price that the monopolist charges. It is often more convenient to consider the *inverse* demand function $p(y)$, which indicates the price that consumers are willing to pay for y amount of output. The inverse demand function is simply the mathematical inverse of the usual demand function. The revenue that the firm receives will depend on the amount of output it chooses to supply. We write this revenue function as $R(y) = p(y)y$.

The cost function of the firm also depends on the amount of output produced. This relationship was extensively studied in Chapter 1. Here we take the factor prices as constant so that the conditional cost function can be written only as a function of the level of output of the firm.

The profit maximization problem of the firm can then be written as:

$$\max R(y) - c(y) = \max p(y)y - c(y)$$

The first-order conditions for profit maximization are that marginal revenue equals marginal cost, or

$$p(y^*) + p'(y^*)y^* = c'(y^*)$$

The intuition behind this condition is fairly clear. If the monopolist considers producing one extra unit of output dy, he will increase his revenue by $p(y^*)dy$ dollars in the first instance. But in order to sell the increased level of output the monopolist will have to reduce his price by $p'(y^*)dy$, and he will lose this revenue on each of the y^* units he is selling. The sum of these two effects gives the marginal revenue. If the marginal revenu exceeds the marginal cost of production the monopolist will expand output. The expansion stops when the marginal revenue and the marginal cost balance out.

The first-order conditions for profit maximization can be expressed in a slightly different manner through the use of the *price elasticity of demand*. The price elasticity of demand is given by:

$$\epsilon(y) = \frac{p}{y(p)} \frac{dy(p)}{dp}$$

Note that this is always a negative number since $dy(p)/dp$ is negative.

Simple algebra shows that the marginal revenue equals marginal cost condition can be written as:

$$p(y^*)\left[1+\frac{y^*}{p(y^*)}\frac{dp(y^*)}{dy}\right]=p(y^*)\left[1+\frac{1}{\epsilon(y^*)}\right]=c'(y^*)$$

that is, the price charged by a monopolist is a markup over marginal cost, with the level of the markup being given as a function of the price elasticity of demand.

There is also a nice graphical illustration of the profit maximization condition. Suppose for simplicity that we have a linear inverse demand curve: $p(y) = a - by$. Then the revenue function is $R(y) = ay - by^2$, and the marginal revenue function is just $R'(y) = a - 2by$. The marginal revenue curve has the same vertical intercept as the demand curve but is twice as steep. We have illustrated these two curves in Figure 2.1, along with the average cost and marginal cost curves of the firm in question.

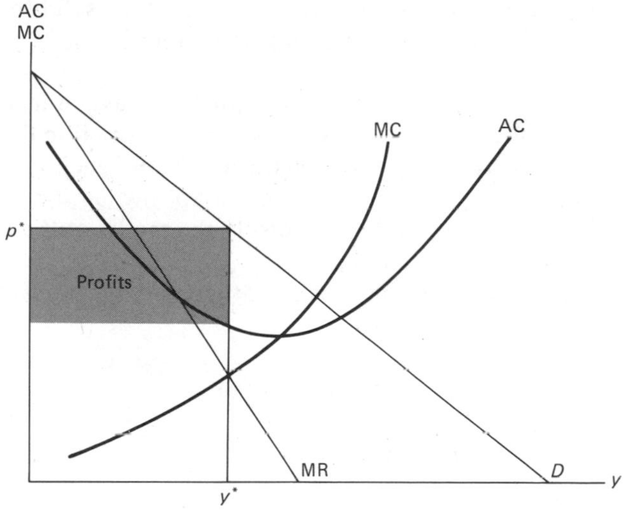

Fig. 2.1 *Determination of Profit-Maximizing Monopolist's Price and Output*

The optimal level of output is located where the marginal revenue and the marginal cost curves intersect. This optimal level of output sells at a price $p(y^*)$ so the monopolist gets an optimal revenue of $p(y^*)y^*$. The cost of producing y^* is just y^* times the average cost of production at that level of output. The difference between these two areas gives us a measure of the monopolist's profits.

2.2 *PURE COMPETITION*

At the opposite pole from pure monopoly we have the case of pure competition. Here instead of one seller, we have a large number of independent sellers of some uniform product. In this situation, when each firm sets the price at which it sells its output, it will have to take into account not only the behavior of the consumers but also the behavior of the other producers.

Let us first consider the behavior of the consumers. As long as there is perfect information about the prices being charged, and as long as the product really is identical across firms, it is clear that each firm that sells the product must sell it for the same price; for if any firm attempted to set its price at a level greater than the market price, it would immediately lose all of its customers. If any firm set its price at a level below the market price, all of the consumers would immediately come to it so that the other firms would have to match its price if they wanted to stay in business.

Of course in the real world demand is not so responsive to price as this simple model would suggest. Nevertheless, this competitive story represents a limiting case of market behavior that is very useful for economic analysis, just as the study of a frictionless system is useful for a physicist.

In a world with many such competing firms we have argued that there can be only one price for output: the market price. Any firm that wishes to sell any output at all must do so at this price. Thus, each firm must take the market price as a given, exogenous variable when it determines its supply decision. Of course, this is precisely the model of the price-taking firm that we discussed in Chapter 1.

We saw there that the profit maximization problem for such a price-taking firm could be written as:

$$\max py - c(y)$$

The first-order condition for this problem is:

$$p = c'(y^*) \qquad \text{for } y^* > 0$$

This first-order condition is really the same as the condition of *marginal revenue equals marginal cost* associated with the monopolist, but now the marginal revenue from selling one more unit of output is just the market price, since the competitive firm by definition ignores the impact of its output decision on the level of the market price.

The second-order condition for profit maximization is that $c''(y^*) \geqq 0$, or that marginal cost at y^* is increasing. Taken together, these two conditions determine the supply function of a competitive firm: at any price p, the firm will supply an amount of output $y(p)$ such that $p = c'(y(p))$ and

$c''(y(p)) > 0$. Conversely, in order to induce a competitive firm to supply an amount of output y, the market price must be $p = c'(y)$, and furthermore $c''(y) > 0$.

Recall that $p = c'(y^*)$ is the first-order condition characterizing the optimum only if $y^* > 0$, that is, only if y^* is an interior optimum. It could happen that at a low price a firm might very well decide to go out of business. Let us write the cost function as the sum of variable costs plus fixed costs: $c(y) = c_v(y) + F$. If the firm produces at $y = 0$, it still has to pay fixed costs F. On the other hand if it does produce where $y > 0$, y must satisfy $p = c'(y) = c_v'(y)$. Thus, the supply curve for the competitive firm is in general given by:

$$\begin{aligned} p &= c'(y) \quad &&\text{if } py - c_v(y) - F \geqq -F \\ y &= 0 &&py - c_v(y) - F < -F \end{aligned}$$

The nonnegative profit condition can be written as $p \geqq c_v(y)/y$. Thus, the firm will operate at a positive level of output as long as it can cover variable costs. Geometrically, we have the situation depicted in Figure 2.2. The supply curve coincides with the upward sloping portion of the marginal cost curve as long as the price covers average variable cost, and the supply curve is zero if price is less than average variable cost.

Suppose that we have n firms in the market. (For the competitive model to make sense, n should be rather large.) Then if $y_i(p)$ is the supply function of the ith firm, we can denote the *aggregate supply function* by $Y(p) = \sum_{i=1}^{n} y_i(p)$. The aggregate supply function just gives us the total amount of the good supplied to the market by the n firms for each value of the market price.

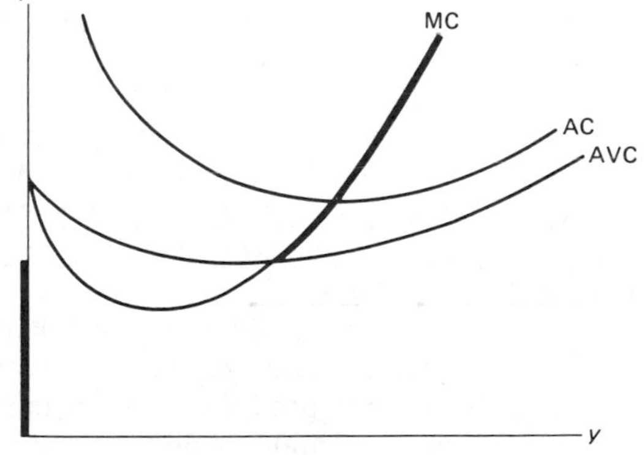

Fig. 2.2 *The Supply Curve of a Competitive Firm*

But how is the market price determined? It is determined by the requirement that the firms be able to sell their entire amount of output; that is, the *equilibrium* market price will be that price such that the total amount of output that the firms wish to supply will be equal to the total amount of output that the consumers wish to demand.

Once this equilibrium price is determined, we can go back to look at the individual supply schedules of each firm and determine the firm's level of output, its revenue, and its profits just as in the monopolistic case. In Figure 2.3 we have depicted cost curves for three firms. The first has

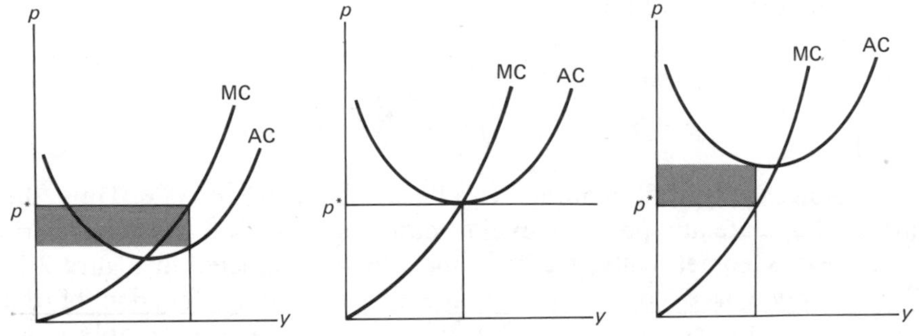

Fig. 2.3 *Positive, Zero, and Negative Profits*

positive profits, the second has zero profits, and the third has negative profits. Even though the third firm has negative profits, it may make sense for it to continue to produce as long as its revenues cover its variable costs. However, in the long run we would expect such a firm to go out of business. This would affect the amount of goods supplied in the industry, which would in turn affect the market price. The determination of the long-run equilibrium price will be discussed in the next section.

Example 2.1 Monopoly, Competition, and Efficiency We say that a situation is *Pareto efficient* if there is no way to make everyone better off. Pareto efficiency will be a major theme in our discussion of welfare economics, but we can give a nice illustration of the concept here.

Let us consider the typical monopolistic configuration illustrated in Figure 2.4. It turns out a monopolist always operates in a Pareto inefficient manner. This means that there is some way to make everyone—both the monopolist and his customers—better off.

To see this let us think of the monopolist in Figure 2.4 after he has sold y_m units of output at the price p_m and received his monopoly profits. Suppose that the monopolist were to produce one more unit of output and offer it to the public. How much would people be willing to pay for this extra output? Clearly they would be willing to pay p_m dollars. How much would it cost to produce this extra output? Clearly, just the marginal cost,

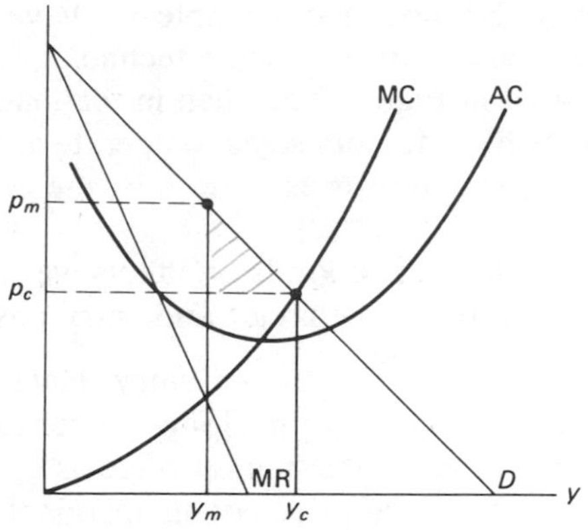

Fig. 2.4 *Pareto Efficiency, Monopoly, and Competition*

MC(y_m). Under this rearrangement the consumers are better off since they are freely purchasing the extra unit of output, and the monopolist is better off since he can sell the extra unit at a price that exceeds the cost of its production. These extra monopoly profits can be distributed so as to make everyone better off. Here we are allowing the monopolist to *discriminate* in his pricing: he first sells y_m units at p_m, then sells more output at some other price.

How long can this process be continued? Clearly as long as the amount that people are willing to pay for each extra unit of the good exceeds the marginal cost of producing that good, that is, as long as the demand curve for the good lies above the marginal cost curve. Once the competitive level of output is reached, no further improvements are possible.

The competitive level of price and output is Pareto efficient for this industry. In Chapter 4 we will investigate the concept of Pareto efficiency as applied to the whole economy.

2.3 COMPETITION IN THE LONG RUN

The long-run behavior of a competitive industry is determined by two sorts of effects. The first effect is the entry and exit phenomena mentioned in the last section. If some firm is making negative profits, we would expect that it would eventually have to change its behavior. Conversely, if a firm is making positive profits we would expect that this would eventually encourage entry to the industry. If we have an industry characterized by free entry and exit, it is clear that in the long run all firms must make the same level of profits.

The second influence on the long-run behavior of a competitive industry is that of technological adjustment. In the long run, firms will attempt to adjust their fixed factors so as to produce the equilibrium level of output in the cheapest way. Suppose for example we have a competitive firm with a long-run constant-returns-to-scale technology that is operating at the position illustrated in Figure 2.5. Then in the long run it clearly pays the firm to change its fixed factors so as to operate at a point of minimum average cost. But if every firm tries to do this, the equilibrium price will certainly change.

In order to sort out these two kinds of effects we will consider various combinations of long-run cost behavior and entry possibilities.

(1) Constant average costs, restricted entry. Here there is some fixed number of firms, each operating with a long-run constant-returns-to-scale technology. If each firm takes the market price as given and is willing to supply a level of output where price equals marginal cost, the aggregate supply curve will be flat at the point where price equals (constant) average cost. If the market price is greater than this average cost of production, the industry will be willing in the long run to supply an infinite amount of output. If the market price is less than this average cost of production, the industry will not be willing to supply any output. Thus, in the long-run equilibrium, price must equal average cost, and profits will therefore be zero.

(2) Constant average costs, free entry. Here we have a constant returns technology, but the number of firms in the market is variable. In this situation the number of firms is indeterminate. We could have a thousand firms producing one unit of output apiece, or a hundred firms, each producing ten units of output. Since the technology is constant returns to scale, any number of firms is possible, but, since average costs are constant, the market price is determined by the condition that price equals average cost.

(3) Increasing average costs, restricted entry. If average costs are increasing, marginal costs will be greater than average costs, and a competi-

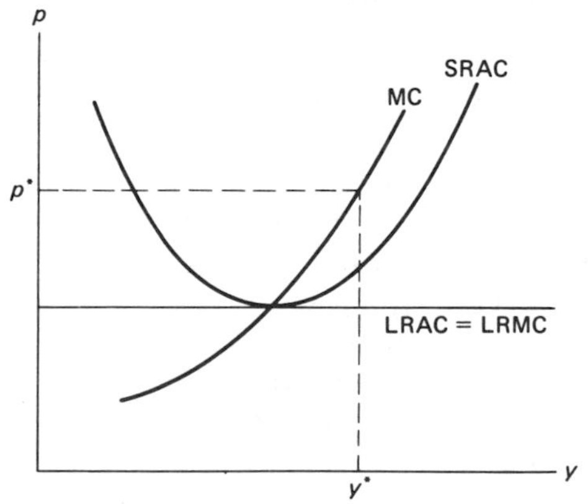

Fig. 2.5 *Long-Run Adjustment with Constant Costs*

tive firm will make positive profits. If there is some sort of restriction to entry in this industry, such a situation could well persist in the long run.

A good example of such an industry might be the farming industry. Suppose we have a number of competitive farmers, each owning a small farm. The average costs of producing output rise as output increases since more intensive farming methods must be used—i.e., the average variable costs are increasing. Since all arable land is owned by the existing farmers so that entry cannot occur, each farmer will be making positive profits, even in the long run.

However, if we look at things a bit more closely, we might want to describe this situation rather differently. The problem comes in how we measure profits. Each farmer is actually playing two roles: first, each farmer is playing a role as the *owner* of his land, and, secondly, each farmer plays a role as a *producer*. It is often convenient to think of the farmer's behavior in two stages: first, in his role as an owner of a factor of production he considers selling or renting his land to a producer. Then, in his role as a producer he determines his optimal supply of output, and thus his optimal profits, now counting the rent on the land *as a (fixed) cost of production*. The total profit to the farmer is the sum of his *rent* as the supplier of the land and of his profits on farming the land as a supplier of the output.

Now what proportion of his profits are attributable to each sort of activity? Well, how much will the rent on his land be?

If the price of output is p^* and the optimal supply of output is y^*, then the most anyone would be willing to pay to rent the farmer's land would be $p^*y^* - c(y^*)$, where $c(y^*)$ is the costs of producing y^* units of output exclusive of rent. If there are many farmers competing for the right to rent this land, this is exactly how much they would be willing to pay: the rent will be $p^*y^* - c(y^*)$. But then the profit attributable to the activity of *operating* the farm will be zero. The "profits" in the industry are due entirely to the rent on the scarce factor. Thus, properly measured, long-run profits in the industry will still be zero.

The same sort of phenomenon arises in many industries. A common reason to experience increasing average costs is that there is some fixed factor present. In such situations one can interpret equilibrium profits as rent due to the fixed factor.

(4) Increasing average costs, free entry. This combination is rather paradoxical. With increasing average costs, the smaller the scale of production the lower the average costs. Hence the long-run equilibrium should exhibit an infinite number of firms, each supplying an infinitesimal amount of output. This seems rather implausible. An increasing-cost industry without some sort of fixed factor seems rather peculiar, since replication would always be possible.

(5) Decreasing average costs, restricted entry. Here we have a fairly unstable market structure. If firms really behave competitively and price

at marginal cost they will all lose money since marginal cost is always less than average cost. What seems more likely is that some firm will hold out until other firms leave the industry and then start to behave as a monopolist.

(6) Decreasing average costs, free entry. In this case we have the same problem as above, but now there is no easy solution. Any firm who behaves as a monopolist will immediately invite imitators. Presumably some sort of oligopolistic outcome will result.

(7) U-shaped average costs, restricted entry. Here the long-run situation is essentially the same as the short-run situation. Presumably firms with negative profits drop out, and we are left with however many firms are necessary to maintain nonnegative profits.

(8) U-shaped average costs, free entry. In general entry will occur whenever it is profitable so that profits will be driven down. In equilibrium we would expect to see each firm making nonnegative profits, but any new firm would make negative profits. The exact outcome depends on the relationship between the optimal scale of the firm and the size of the market.

For example, let us think of an industry which has firms characterized by U-shaped average cost curves. Let y^* be the minimum average cost level of output and let $c^* = c(y^*)/y^*$ be this minimal average cost. If the demand for the output of this industry is some integral multiple of y^*, then each firm will produce at y^*, and the equilibrium price will be $p^* = c^*$. Thus profits will be zero.

If the demand for the output of the industry were not an integral multiple of y^*, we would have essentially the same situation, at least if demand were large relative to y^*. For we would just see each firm produce slightly more than y^* and charge slightly more than p^*. Profits would be positive but not sufficiently high to encourage successful entry.

Recall the basic argument for constant returns to scale that was put forward in Chapter 1: firms could always replicate their existing technology. The above argument shows that, even if firms have some optimal size in the long run, the market itself can serve as a device for replication.

Let us summarize our discussion of the long-run behavior of a competitive industry. We list the cases below.

(1) Constant average costs, with or without free entry. The long-run supply curve is flat. Profits are zero. The number of firms is indeterminate.

(2) Increasing average costs.
   - (a) restricted entry—long-run supply curve slopes up, positive "accounting" profits, but zero "economic" profits;
   - (b) free entry—an infinite number of firms each producing an infinitesimal level of output. Implausible.

(3) Decreasing average costs. Incompatible with pure competition.

(4) U-shaped average costs.
   (a) restricted entry—essentially the same as the short-run situation;
   (b) free entry—profits are driven down to a minimal level. If the size of the market is large relative to the size of a firm, profits are essentially zero and the long-run industry supply curve is essentially flat.

Example 2.2 The Long-Run Supply Curve of an Industry with U-shaped Average Costs Suppose the long-run cost function for a firm is $c(y) = y^2 + 1$. The optimal scale of the firm is at $y^* = 1$ and this incurs a minimal cost of $c^* = 2$. The supply curve of such a firm is:

$$p = c'(y) = 2y$$

or

$$y(p) = p/2.$$

If there are n identical firms then the aggregate supply will be:

$$Y(p) = np/2$$

In Figure 2.6 we have illustrated the industry supply curves for $n = 1, 2, 3 \cdots$. We have also illustrated the demand curve for the industry's product. For any fixed number of firms, the short-run equilibrium price is given by the intersection of the demand curve and the relevant supply curve.

If the number of firms is variable, the long-run equilibrium price will be the lowest short-run equilibrium price that is compatible with nonnegative profits. It is easy to see that, the larger the equilibrium demand, the

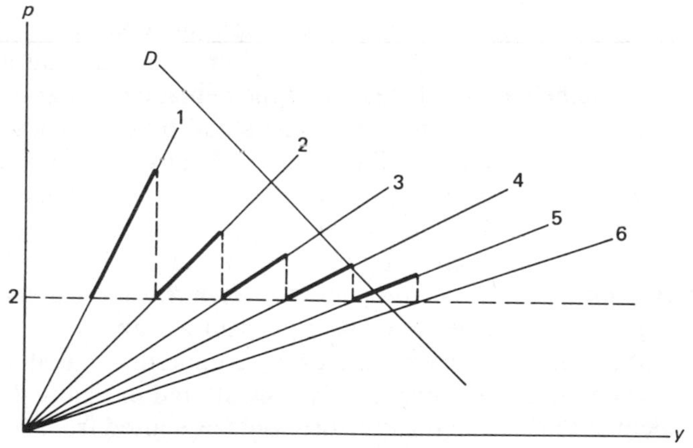

Fig. 2.6 *Industry Supply Curve with U-Shaped Average Costs*

closer the long-run equilibrium price is to the level of minimum average cost. The relevant portions of the family of supply curves—the "long-run industry supply curve"—is represented as a heavy line. If the number of firms is large relative to the optimal scale of operation of the firm, it is reasonable to think of this industry supply curve as being a flat line at the point where price equals minimum average cost.

Example 2.3 Taxation in the Short and Long Run When studying the effect of some new policy one must be sure to work out both the short-run and the long-run responses of the industry. For example, let us consider what happens when we tax the output of an industry that has long-run constant average costs.

Let $P_d(q)$ be the inverse demand curve for the consumers and $P_s(q)$ be the inverse supply curve for the producers. The before-tax equilibrium condition is that $P_d(q^*) = P_s(q^*)$: i.e., the price that consumers are willing to pay for q^* units of output is equal to the price at which producers are willing to supply q^* units of output.

Let us suppose that we impose a tax of t dollars per unit output on the *suppliers* of a good. Then if the price paid by the demanders is P_d (the demand price), the price received by the suppliers (the supply price) is $P_s = P_d - t$. The condition for equilibrium is therefore:

$$P_s(q) = P_d(q) - t$$

What happens if we impose the tax on the *demanders* of the good? Then if the supply price is P_s dollars, the demand price will be $P_d = P_s + t$ dollars. The equilibrium condition is that:

$$P_d(q) = P_s(q) + t$$

Note the important fact that the two equilibrium conditions are the same. Thus, the equilibrium demand price, supply price, and quantity are independent of whether the tax is levied on the demanders or suppliers of the good—a fact that is apparently not understood by most legislators.

The geometry of the tax is illustrated in Figure 2.7. Suppose that we impose the tax on the suppliers of the good and measure the demand price on the vertical axis. Then the demand curve is just as it always was, but the supply curve is now given by $P_s(q) + t$; that is, to induce the suppliers to supply q units of output, they must receive $P_s(q) + t$ dollars per unit, output, since t dollars per unit must be paid as tax. Geometrically this means that the supply curve shifts up by an amount t, as illustrated.

The new equilibrium configuration is illustrated in Figure 2.7: the equilibrium demand price and the quantity sold has shifted from (p_1, q_1) to (p_2, q_2). Notice an interesting fact: the price to the consumers has risen by less than the amount of the tax; that is, p_2 is less than $p_1 + t$. This happens because the increase in the net price has induced consumers to demand less, and the lower amount of output can be produced at a lower marginal cost. However, at this new lower price, firms are making negative profits (Figure 2.7). Thus, firms will either exit from the market or change their technology so as to better produce this smaller amount of output. In the long run the supply curve of the industry is flat at the point where price equals long-run average cost. Thus, shifting the demand curve will not change the long-run equilibrium price to the producer at all. This means that the price to the consumer will have to rise by exactly the amount of the tax, as depicted in Figure 2.8.

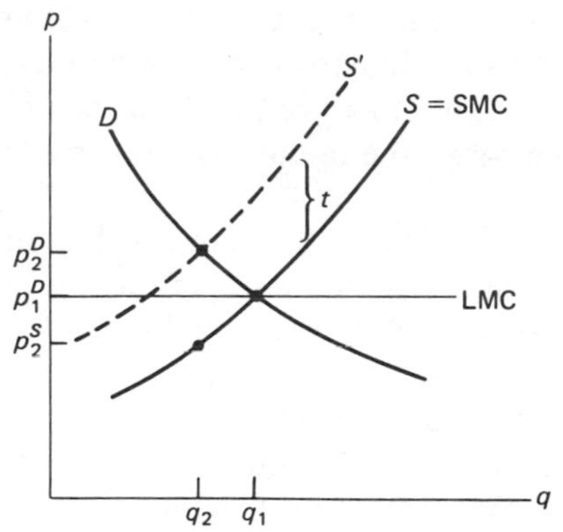

Fig. 2.7 *Short-Run Effect of a Tax on a Competitive Industry*

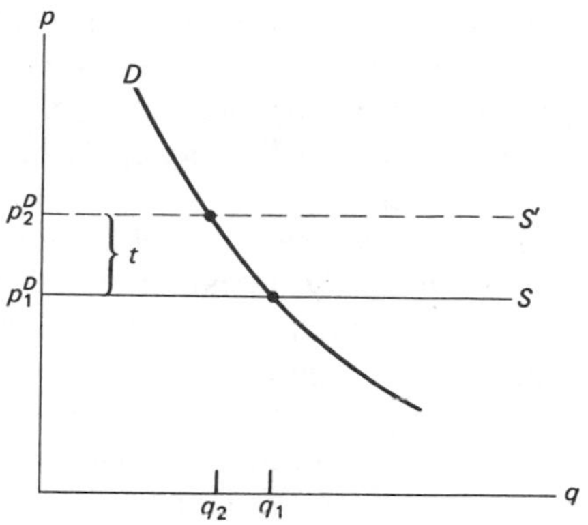

Fig. 2.8 *Long-Run Effect of a Tax on a Competitive Industry with Constant Average Costs*

2.4 *MONOPOLY IN THE LONG RUN*

We have seen how the long-run and the short-run behavior of a competitive industry may differ because of changes in technology and entry. There are similar effects in a monopolized industry. The technological effect is the simplest: the monopolist will choose the level of his fixed factors so as to maximize his long-run profits. Thus, he will operate where marginal revenue equals long-run marginal cost, and that is all that needs to be said.

The entry effect is a bit more subtle. Presumably, if the monopolist is earning positive profits, other firms would like to enter the industry. *If the monopolist is to remain a monopolist, there must be some sort of barrier to entry.*

These barriers to entry may be of a legal sort, but often they are due to the fact that the monopolist owns some unique factor of production. For example, a firm might own a patent on a certain product, or it might own a certain secret process for producing some item. If the monopoly power of the firm is due to a unique factor we have to be careful about how we measure profits.

Just as is the case in the increasing-cost industry described in Section 2.3, the monopolist is playing two roles: first, he is the owner of a factor of production, and, secondly, he is the operator of some productive process. We could think of the monopolist's offering to sell his patent or secret process to the highest bidder; the most that anyone would be willing to pay would be the amount of the monopoly profits that this resource would enable the buyer to obtain. When the monopolist actually engages in production we can think of his profits as actually being "rents" for this scarce factor. For this reason, some economists like to describe monopoly profits as *monopoly rent*. The "rent" is thought of as a return to the scarce factor that makes the monopoly possible—i.e., the factor that serves as a barrier to entry.

The long-run behavior of a monopolistic industry does not involve entry, virtually by definition. But entry might nevertheless play a role in affecting the monopolist's behavior. Even though the monopolist by definition has no direct competitors, he may have indirect competitors. High monopoly profits may encourage firms to produce products that can *substitute* for the product of monopolist. Thus, we might think of an industry structure with many monopolists, each producing similar but not identical products. This kind of market structure is a kind of intermediate case between pure competition and pure monopoly and as such shares elements of both theories.

For this reason, such industries are referred to as *monopolistically competitive* industries. They will be discussed in the next section.

2.5 *MONOPOLISTIC COMPETITION*

Recall that we assumed that the demand curve for the monopolist's product depended only on the price set by the monopolist; in other words the monopolist took the prices of all other goods as given. We pointed out in the last section that this assumption is an extreme one. Most commodities have some substitutes, and the prices of those substitutes will affect the demand for the original commodity. The monopolist sets his price assuming all the producers of other commodities will maintain their prices, but of course, this will not be true. The prices set by other firms will respond—perhaps indirectly—to the price set by the monopolist in question.

The analysis of the pure monopolist is only a partial equilibrium analysis; in this section we will consider what happens when several monopolists "compete" in setting their prices and output levels.

We imagine a group of n "monopolists" who sell similar, but not identical, products. The price that consumers are willing to pay for the output of firm i depends on the level of output of firm i but also on the levels of output of the other firms; we write this inverse demand function as $p_i(y_i; \mathbf{y}_{-i})$ where $\mathbf{y}_{-i}$ is the $n-1$ vector consisting of the outputs of all forms except firm i.

Each firm is interested in maximizing its profits; that is, each firm i wants to choose its level of output y_i so as to maximize:

$$p_i(y_i; \mathbf{y}_{-i})y_i - c_i(y_i)$$

Unfortunately, the demand facing the ith firm depends on what the other firms do. How is firm i supposed to forecast the other firms' behavior?

We will adopt a very simple behavioral hypothesis: namely, that firm i assumes the other firms' behavior will be constant. Thus, each firm i will choose its level of output y_i^* so as to satisfy:

$$p_i(y_i^*; \mathbf{y}_{-i}) + \frac{\partial p_i(y_i^*; \mathbf{y}_{-i})}{\partial y_i} y_i^* - c_i'(y_i^*) = 0$$

For each combination of operating levels for the firms $\mathbf{y}_{-i}$, there will be some optimal operating level for firm i. We will denote this optimal choice of output by $Y_i(\mathbf{y}_{-i})$.

In order for the market to be in equilibrium, each firm's forecast about the behavior of the other firms must be compatible with what the other firms actually do. Thus, if $(y_1^*, \cdots, y_n^*)$ is to be an equilibrium, it must satisfy:

$$\begin{aligned} y_1^* &- Y_1(y_2^*, \cdots, y_n^*) \\ &\cdot \\ &\cdot \\ &\cdot \\ y_n^* &= Y_n(y_1^*, \cdots, y_{n-1}^*) \end{aligned}$$

that is, y_1^* must be the optimal choice for firm 1 if it assumes the other firms are going to produce $y_2^*, \cdots, y_n^*$, and so on. Thus a *monopolistic competition equilibrium* $(y_1^*, \cdots, y_n^*)$ must satisfy:

$$p_i(y_i^*; \mathbf{y}_{-i}^*) + \frac{\partial p_i(y_i^*; \mathbf{y}_{-i}^*)}{\partial y_i} y_i^* - c_i'(y_i^*) = 0 \qquad i = 1, \cdots, n$$

For each firm, its marginal revenue equals its marginal cost, given the actions of all the other firms. This is illustrated in Figure 2.9.

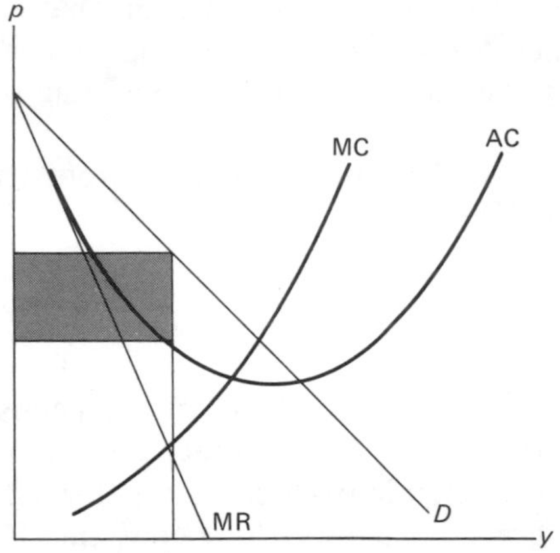

Fig. 2.9 *Monopolistic Competition Equilibrium (Short Run)*

Now at the monopolistic competition equilibrium depicted in Figure 2.9, firm i is making positive profits. We would therefore expect other firms to enter the industry. If a new firm enters and begins to produce a product that is a close substitute for the product of firm i, firm i would find that the demand for its product would change. In particular, firm i would find that at each price it would not be able to sell as much as it did before: its demand curve would shift inward.

In the long run, firms would enter the industry until the profits of each firm were driven to zero. This means that each firm i must charge a price p_i^* and produce an output y_i^* such that:

$$p_i^* y_i^* - c_i(y_i^*) = 0$$

or

$$p_i^* = \frac{c_i(y_i^*)}{y_i^*} \qquad i = 1, \cdots, n$$

This last equation just says that price must equal average cost for each firm. In addition, each firm must be operating at the maximal profit point on its demand curve; that is, there can be no points (p, y) on its demand curve where the firm would experience *positive* profits. But positive profit points are just those where price is greater than average cost, i.e., points above the average cost curve. Putting these facts together we see that the demand curve facing firm i must be *tangent* to its average cost curve as depicted in Figure 2.10.

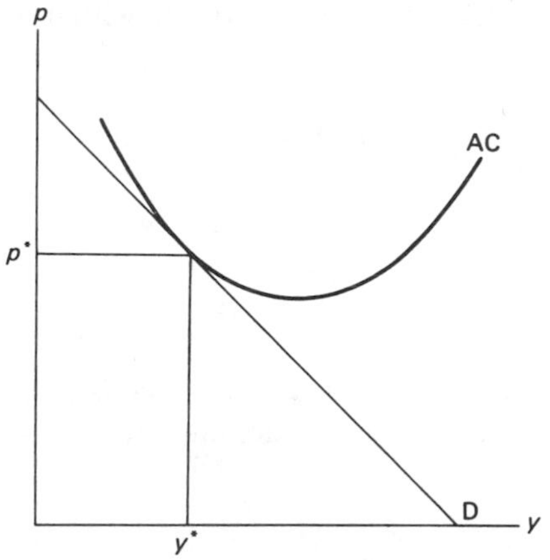

Fig. 2.10 *Monopolistic Competition Equilibrium (Long Run)*

We can now see an important fact: as long as the demand curve facing each firm still has some negative slope, each firm will produce at a point where average costs are greater than the minimum average costs. The monopolistic competition equilibrium reveals "excess capacity."

The monopolistic competition model is nice in that it represents an intermediate case between competition and monopoly. If there is only one firm in the industry and there is some sort of barrier to entry, then the monopolistic competition equilibrium is just the monopoly equilibrium. On the other hand, suppose that there are several firms and that the goods produced are all *very* close substitutes so that the demand curve facing each firm is almost flat. Then the long-run monopolistic competition equilibrium is very nearly the competitive equilibrium. In the limit, when the goods produced are perfect substitutes, the demand curve facing each firm is flat, and we have exactly the competitive solution.

Example 2.4 Monopolistic Competition in Location Let us consider a model where identical consumers reside along a circle of unit circumference. The total number of consumers is L, so an interval of length $0 \leqq t \leqq 1$ contains Lt consumers. We imagine that each consumer wants to buy one and only one unit of some output good and that the most that each consumer is willing to pay is v.

There are n identical firms located discretely along the circle, so that the distance between each firm will therefore be $1/n$. Each consumer will have to travel some distance, d, to reach a firm. We suppose the cost of such travel is $c \cdot d$. Thus, the potential market of a firm which charges a price p will consist of all consumers who are willing to make the trip to buy the good, that is, all consumers who live within d^* of the firm, where d^* is defined by:

$$cd^* + p = v$$

or

$$d^* = \frac{v - p}{c}$$

If the firm sets a price p, it will get $2Ld^*$ consumers, half coming from each side. Therefore, the potential demand curve facing each firm is

$$Q^m(p) = \frac{2L}{c}(v - p) \quad \text{for} \quad p < v$$
$$= 0 \qquad\qquad\qquad\qquad p \geqq v$$

Of course this is just the potential demand since it ignores the behavior of competing firms. If some consumers lie in the market area of two firms, they will go to whichever has the best total cost—i.e., price plus travel cost.

Let p be the price charged by one firm and $\bar{p}$ be the price charged by its competitors on each side. Then the location x of the consumer who is just indifferent to coming to the original firm is given by:

$$\begin{matrix}\text{cost of going to}\\ \text{original firm}\end{matrix} = p + cx = \bar{p} + c\left(\frac{1}{n} - x\right) = \begin{matrix}\text{cost of going to}\\ \text{competitor}\end{matrix}$$

or

$$x = \frac{\bar{p} - p + c/n}{2c}$$

(See Figure 2.11.)

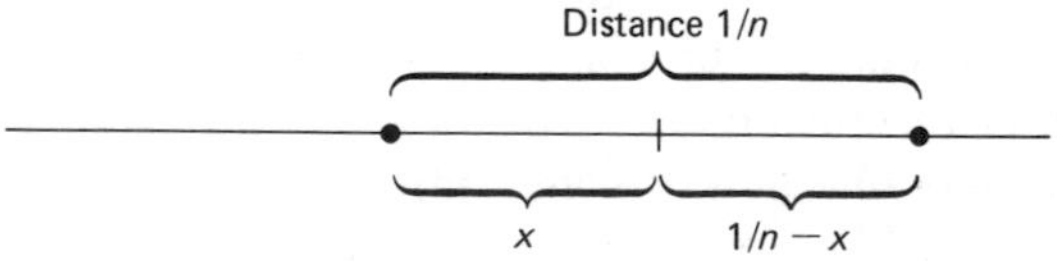

Fig. 2.11 *Potential Market Areas of Firms*

Therefore, the number of consumers from this region who would come to the firm charging p would be

$$Q^c(p) = 2L_x = \frac{L}{c}(\bar{p} + c/n - p)$$

The final demand curve facing the firm will therefore be:

$$Q(p) = \min\,[Q^c(p),\, Q^m(p)].$$

This curve is illustrated in Figure 2.12 for various values of n.

The actual demand facing the firm depends on what the other firms do. If $\bar{p}$ is very large, or n is very small, the firm will have a monopoly on all of its neighboring customers. If $\bar{p}$ is small, or n is large, firms will be crowded closely together and will have to compete for most of their customers. (See Figure 2.12.)

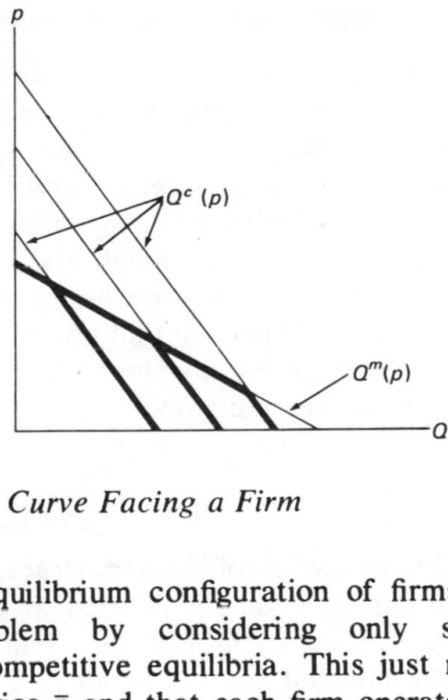

Fig. 2.12 *Demand Curve Facing a Firm*

What will the equilibrium configuration of firms look like? Let us simplify the problem by considering only symmetric long-run monopolistically competitive equilibria. This just means that all firms charge the same price $\bar{p}$ and that each firm operates somewhere on its average cost curve, so that it makes zero profits. To find such an equilibrium, we just superimpose the average cost curve on Figure 2.12 and look at the configurations where the demand curve could be tangent to the average cost curve. There are three possible outcomes, depicted in Figure 2.13.

(1) Pure monopoly—Here each firm operates at a point inside its own market area. The consumers living between the market areas of the firms are not served.

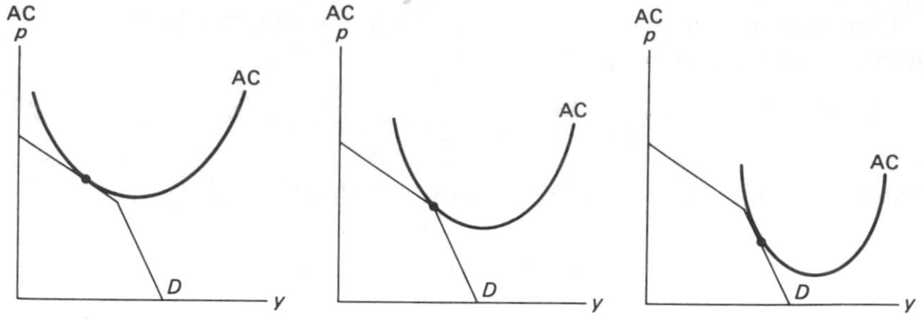

Fig. 2.13 *Monopolistic Competition Equilibria*

(2) Kinked equilibrium—Here the market areas of the firms just meet. Each firm has essentially a monopoly on its own customers, but all customers are served.

(3) Competing equilibrium—Here the market areas overlap so that each firm has to compete for some of its customers.

There are many interesting comparative statics and welfare statements one can make about this model; for details, the reader should consult the reference listed at the end of this chapter.

We note that the model can also be interpreted as a "product choice" model: consumers' tastes are distributed along a line, and each consumer chooses a product that is closest to his ideal. For example suppose the circle represents time and the products are airline flights that depart at various times. Then it seems reasonable that consumers' optimal departure times might be distributed uniformly along a line, and each would use the flight that was closest to his optimum.

2.6 *OLIGOPOLY*

We have considered three models of industry structure: pure monopoly, pure competition, and monopolistic competition. In the latter two cases we had to face the problem that each firm's possibilities depended on the other firms' actions. We modeled this interaction in a rather naive way by simply assuming that each firm would take the other firms' behavior as fixed when it decided its own policies. The implicit justification for this model is the assumption that each firm is a relatively small part of the industry so that it is justified in ignoring its own impact on the other firms' behavior, though not so small as to ignore the impact of its actions on its own demand.

On the other hand, there are some market structures characterized by there being only a few firms in the industry, so that each one constitutes a fairly substantial share of the market. Such an industry is called an *oligopoly*.

In the next sections we will describe three models of oligopolistic behavior. The essence of the models comes across even when there are only two firms, so we will limit ourselves to this case, the case of *duopoly*.

2.7 THE COURNOT-NASH EQUILIBRIUM

Suppose we have a market with only two firms; let us denote firm 1's output by y_1 and firm 2's output by y_2. Then the price consumers are willing to pay depends on the aggregate supply to the market, $p(y_1 + y_2)$.

Let us make the assumption that each firm takes its competitor's supply as fixed and then ask what level of output each firm will choose. Firm 1 wishes to maximize profits taking firm 2's level of output as fixed:

$$\max_{y_1} p(y_1 + \bar{y}_2)y_1 - c(y_1)$$

The solution to this problem y_1^* must satisfy:

$$p'(y_1^* + \bar{y}_2)y_1^* + p(y_1^* + \bar{y}_2) - c'(y_1^*) = 0$$

or

$$p(y_1^* + \bar{y}_2) = c'(y_1^*) - p'(y_1^* + \bar{y}_2)y_1^*$$

Of course, the analogous condition must hold for firm 2:

$$p(\bar{y}_1 + y_2^*) = c'(y_2^*) - p'(\bar{y}_1 + y_2^*)y_2^*$$

Under what circumstances will the actions of the two firms be consistent? Clearly, they will be consistent when the choices each firm makes are compatable with the other firm's expectations, that is, when $\bar{y}_1 = y_1^*$ and $\bar{y}_2 = y_2^*$.

Mathematically speaking, we are just asking for the solution of two nonlinear equations in two unknowns, y_1 and y_2. Let $Y_1(y_2)$ be the function describing firm 1's optimal choice of output given firm 2's output, and let $Y_2(y_1)$ be the analogous function for firm 2. We can plot these "reaction" curves in (y_1, y_2) space, as in Figure 2.14; a Cournot-Nash equilibrium is simply a combination (y_1^*, y_2^*) that lies on both firms' reaction curves.

At a Cournot-Nash equilibrium, each firm is behaving optimally given the other firm's actions. This solution concept is exactly the behavior we postulated in our analysis of competition and monopolistic competition.

We have assumed above that each firm takes the other firm's supply

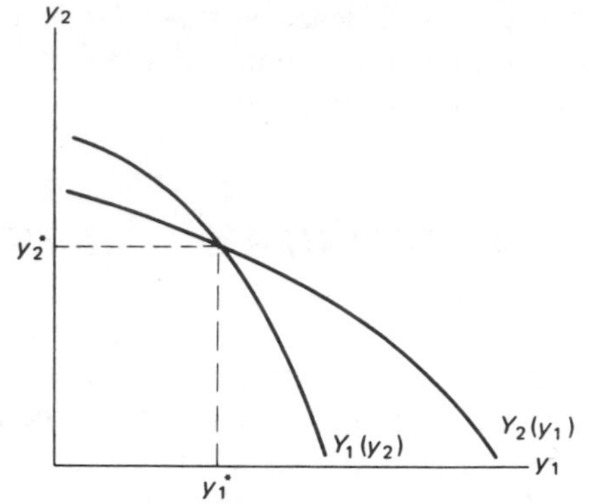

Fig. 2.14 *A Cournot-Nash Equilibrium*

of output to be fixed. An alternative assumption is that each firm may take the other firm's *price* of output to be fixed. Let us explore this hypothesis.

What is the nature of the demand curve facing firm 1? If the product is really homogeneous, as we have assumed, then presumably if firm 1 raises its price above its rival's price, it will lose all of its customers to its rival. If it lowers its price slightly below its rival's price then it will get all of the customers. It is, therefore, clear that if both firms actually operate in equilibrium, they will both have to charge the same price, say p^*.

Suppose that p^* is above marginal cost. Then firm 1 can steal all of firm 2's customers by charging $p^* - \epsilon$ and still make a profit—at least on some of the extra customers. More precisely, let us suppose that (p^*, y_1^*, y_2^*) is a Cournot equilibrium with fixed price strategies and that $p^* > c_1'(y_1^*)$. Then if firm 1 charges $p^* - \epsilon$, it will get all of the demand $D(p^* - \epsilon)$. Before, it was getting only a fraction of this demand. Since it has achieved a finite increase in demand for an arbitrarily small decrease in price, there is an ϵ small enough so that its profits will increase.

Hence a Nash equilibrium in price strategies is in fact a competitive equilibrium, in which price equals marginal cost.

2.8 COLLUSION

It is presumably in the interest of firms to collude in setting their output levels. Since the Cournot-Nash outcome is always a possible collusive choice, firms can always do at least as well by colluding as by acting independently.

Suppose each firm desires to maximize total industry profit:

$$\max_{y_1,y_2} p(y_1 + y_2)(y_1 + y_2) - c_1(y_1) - c_2(y_2)$$

The first-order conditions are

$$p'(y_1^* + y_2^*)(y_1^* + y_2^*) + p(y_1^* + y_2^*) - c_1'(y_1^*) = 0$$
$$p'(y_1^* + y_2^*)(y_1^* + y_2^*) + p(y_1^* + y_2^*) - c_2'(y_1^*) = 0$$

This problem is clearly the same as the problem of a single monopolist who has two different plants with possibly different cost functions. It is easy to see from the above first-order conditions that profit maximization implies $c_1'(y_1^*) = c_2'(y_2^*)$. If the cost functions are identical, we must have a symmetric solution where $y_1^* = y_2^*$. If cost functions differ between the two firms, the firm with the cost advantage will produce more.

At the collusive solution it will always be in the interest of one firm to increase its own production if it believes the other firm will hold its production constant. To see this, we rearrange the first-order condition of firm 1:

$$p'(y_1^* + y_2^*)y_1^* + p(y_1^* + y_2^*) - c_1'(y_1^*) = -p'(y_1^* + y_2^*)y_2^*$$

The left-hand side is the marginal increase in firm 1's profits if it increases its output a small amount. This marginal increase is a positive number since $p'(y_1^* + y_2^*)$ will generally be negative. Hence, profits of firm 1 can be increased by increasing production if firm 2's production stays constant. It is this type of instability that tends to disrupt collusive solutions in the real world. If there are only a few firms in an industry, they may be able to police each other's behavior well enough to prevent serious cheating of this sort. If there are many firms, enforcing the collusive outcome may become quite difficult.

2.9 *STACKELBERG BEHAVIOR*

In the Cournot model each firm takes the other's *actions* as given; in the Stackelberg model, one firm takes the other firm's *reactions* as given. Let $Y_1(y_2)$ be the reaction function for firm 1; it gives the level of output firm 1 would choose if it expected firm 2 to produce y_2.

Suppose firm 2 believes that firm 1 will behave this way. Then it should incorporate this information into its profit maximization problem and choose y_2 so as to maximize its profits:

$$\max_{y_2} p(Y_1(y_2) + y_2)y_2 - c_2(y_2)$$

Firm 2 "leads" the way by setting its level of output and firm 1 "follows" by choosing a profit maximizing level of output given firm 2's behavior. Does it pay more to be a follower or a leader? The answer depends on the relationship between the two cost functions. Each firm can do the calculations indicated and determine its profits under the various combinations of follower-leader. If one firm decides to be a follower and the other a leader, fine. This outcome is called a *Stackelberg equilibrium*. If each wants to be a follower, and each assumes the other will be a follower, the Cournot-Nash solution will be the outcome. If each desires to be a leader, the situation is indeterminate; this situation is called *Stackelberg warfare*.

2.10 CONJECTURAL VARIATIONS

There is a nice way to relate the three sorts of oligopoly models described in the last three sections by the use of a concept known as the *conjectural variation*. When a firm makes a decision about how much output to produce, it has to make a guess about how the other firms in the industry will respond to its choice. If it assumes that they will not respond at all, then the firm is behaving as a Cournot maximizer. If it assumes that they will adjust their output so as to keep the market price constant, then the firm will behave as a competitive firm. We will describe these hypotheses about the other firms' behavior by the concept of a *conjectural variation*.

Let us write the profit maximization problem of a given firm as:

$$\max p(Y)y - c(y)$$

Here we let Y be the total industry output and y the output of the firm in question. Differentiating with respect to y, we find:

$$p(Y) + (dp(Y)/dy)\, y - c'(y) = 0$$

The term $dp(Y)/dy$ measures how the given firm assumes that the price will respond to its change in output. We may call it the firm's *conjectural price variation*. This conjectural price variation can be written as:

$$dp(Y)/dy = dp(Y)/dY \cdot dY/dy$$

That is, the assumption as to how the price will change as output changes is composed of two effects: how price changes as total industry output changes, and how industry output changes as the individual firm's output changes. Let us denote this second effect by $k = dY/dy$ and call it the *conjectural industry output variation*, or simply the conjectural variation for short.

Then we can write the first-order condition for profit maximization as:

$$p(Y) + p'(Y)ky - c'(y) = 0$$

Comparing this equation to the models of market structure described earlier, we can classify the various cases:

(1) $k = 0$ implies competitive behavior. In this case the firm believes that the price will not change with respect to a change in its output.

(2) $k = 1$ implies Cournot behavior. Here the firm believes that the other firms will not change their output decisions, so that a change in its output of 1 unit will lead to a change in industry output of 1 unit.

(3) $k = Y/y$ implies collusive behavior. Substituting into the first-order condition, we get $p(Y) + p'(Y)Y - c'(y) = 0$ which is the first-order condition for a monopoly.

(4) $k = dY(y)/dy$ implies Stackelberg behavior, where $Y(y)$ gives the true reactions of the rest of the industry to the given firm's output choice.

Thus the conjectural variation provides a unified framework for describing firm behavior in an oligopoly model.

If we think of the firm as choosing price rather than output, we can consider a slightly different sort of conjectural variation. Suppose, for example, that we have an industry where firms produce similar but not necessarily identical products. The demand for the output of industry 1 will, therefore, depend on all of the prices being offered; so we write $D_1(p_1, \cdots, p_n)$. The profit maximization problem for firm 1 can be written as:

$$\max p_1 D_1 (p_1, \cdots, p_n) - c_1(D_1(p_1, \cdots, p_n))$$

Taking the derivative with respect to p_1:

$$\left(p_1 - \frac{dc_1}{dy}\right)\left(\frac{\partial D_1}{\partial p_1} + \frac{\partial D_1}{\partial p_2}\frac{dp_2}{dp_1} + \cdots + \frac{\partial D_1}{\partial p_n}\frac{dp_n}{dp_1}\right) + D_1(p_1, \cdots, p_n) = 0$$

Here the terms of the form dp_i/dp_1 represent firm 1's conjectural about how the other firms will change their price in response to firm 1's price change. As above, specific assumptions about these conjectures lead to specific models of market behavior.

2.11 *MONOPSONY*

In this chapter we have seen several models of industry behavior. The two paradigm cases of industry behavior are the *competitive model,* which seems to be relevant when there are a large number of independent producers, and the *monopoly model,* which seems to be relevant when there is only one producer in a market.

In our discussion up until now we have generally assumed that we have been dealing with the market for an output good and that all firms have behaved as price takers in the factor markets. Output markets can be classified as "competitive" or "monopolistic" depending on whether firms take the market price as given or whether firms take the demand behavior of consumers as given.

There is similar classification for the market for factors of production. If firms take the factor prices as given, then we have competitive factor markets. If instead there is only one firm which demands some factor of production and it takes the supply behavior of its suppliers into account, then we say we have a *monopsonistic* factor market. The behavior of a monopsonist is analogous to that of a monopolist. Let us consider a simple example of a firm that is a competitor in its output market but is the sole purchaser of some input good x. Let $w(x)$ be the (inverse) supply curve of this factor of production. Then the profit maximization problem is:

$$\max pf(x) - w(x)x$$

The first-order condition is:

$$pf'(x^*) - w(x^*) - w'(x^*)x^* = 0$$

This just says that the marginal revenue product of an additional unit of the input good should be equal to its marginal cost. Another way to write the condition is:

$$p \frac{\partial f(x^*)}{\partial x} = w(x^*)[1 + 1/\epsilon]$$

where ϵ is the price elasticity of supply. As ϵ goes to infinity the behavior of a monopsonist approaches that of a pure competitor.

Recall that in Chapter 1, where we defined the cost function of a firm, we considered only the behavior of a firm with competitive factor markets. However, it is certainly possible to define a cost function for a monopsonistic firm. Suppose for example that $x_i(\mathbf{w})$ is the supply curve for factor i. Then we can define:

$$\begin{aligned} c(y) = \min \quad & \Sigma w_i x_i(\mathbf{w}) \\ \text{s.t.} \quad & f(x(\mathbf{w})) = y \end{aligned}$$

This just gives us the minimum cost of producing y. Notice that the monopsonist cost function does not depend on $\mathbf{w}$. Why? Because the monopsonist *chooses* **w** in order to maximize his profits—he does not take it as an exogenously given variable. In other words the factor price **w** has been "maximized out" of the cost function.

However, as far as the output behavior is concerned, $c(y)$ is a perfectly good cost function and can be used in exactly the same way as the competitive cost function.

Exercises

2.1 (10) Show that a monopolist will never operate at an inelastic portion of his demand curve.

2.2 (20) An industry consists of a large number of firms, each of which has a cost function of the form:

$$c(w_1, w_2, y) = (y^2 + 1)w_1 + (y^2 + 2)w_2$$

(a) Find the average cost curve of a firm and describe how it shifts as the factor price ratio w_1/w_2 changes.
(b) Find the short-run supply curve of an individual firm.
(c) Find the long-run industry supply curve.
(d) Describe an input requirement set for an individual firm.

2.3 (20) A firm faces the following demand function for its output:

$$D(p) = \begin{cases} 12 - p & \text{for } 0 \leqq p \leqq 8 \\ 20 - 2p & \text{for } 8 \leqq p \leqq 10 \\ 0 & \text{for } p \geqq 10 \end{cases}$$

(a) Graph this demand function. For what value of output y^* does this function have a kink?
(b) What is the firm's revenue function?
(c) What is the firm's marginal revenue function? Graph this function.
(d) Can you think of a plausible reason why a firm's demand function might look like this? (Hint? Think of the firm's competitors' behavior.)

2.4 (20) Assume the firm in 2.3 above produces according to a constant-returns-to-scale production function with c the cost of producing one unit of output.
(a) For what values of c will the firm not produce?
(b) For what values of c will the firm produce at the kink y^*?
(c) For what values of c will the firm produce output less than y^*?
(d) For what values of c will the firm produce output greater than y^*?
(e) If $c = 0$ how much output will the firm produce? Will the firm ever produce output greater than this amount?

2.5 (20) Assume the firm described in 2.3 has a production function $y = q^{1/2}$ where q is the amount of labor input and w is the wage rate.
(a) Find the firm's total, average, and marginal cost functions.
(b) For what values of w will the firm not produce?
(c) For what values of w will the firm produce output less than y^*?

(d) For what values of w will the firm produce at the kink y^*?
(e) For what values of w will the firm produce more than y^*?
(f) At $w = 0$ what level of output will be produced?

2.6 (20) A farm produces yams (Y) using capital (K), labor (L), and land (T) according to the production technology described by:

$$Y = 3K^{1/3}L^{1/3}T^{1/3}$$

The firm faces prices (p, q, w, r) for (Y, K, L, T).

(a) Suppose that in the short run K and T are fixed at $K = T = 1$. Derive the short-run supply function of the firm, when $w = 1$.
(b) Suppose that, in the long run, competitive conditions ensure zero excess profits and further assume that $w = q = 1$. Furthermore, suppose labor and capital are sold on markets but land is not marketable. Derive the long-run supply function of the firm with T acres of land.
(c) If $p = 2$, what is the equilibrium size of the firm?
(d) If there were a market for land, how much would the firm be willing to pay for more land if it is currently operating at $p = w = r = 1, T = 3$?
(e) Does this production function exhibit diminishing, constant, or increasing returns to scale?

2.7 (15) Consider an industry composed of many firms that have the following technological characteristics. Each firm can produce either: one or zero apples, one or zero bananas, or one or zero coconuts. So for each firm i the supplied amount of apples $a_i(p_a, p_b, p_c) = 1$ or 0; and similarly for bananas and coconuts $b_i(p_a,p_b,p_c) = 1$ or 0, $c_i(p_a,p_b,p_c) = 1$ or 0.

The firms have different costs of producing oranges, apples, and pears so that each firm produces only that good which is most profitable for it.

The aggregate amount of apples, bananas and coconuts produced is:

$$A(p_a, p_b, p_c) = \sum_{i=1}^{n} a_i(p_a, p_b, p_c)$$

$$B(p_a, p_b, p_c) = \sum_{i=1}^{n} b_i(p_a, p_b, p_c)$$

$$C(p_a, p_b, p_c) = \sum_{i=1}^{n} c_i(p_a, p_b, p_c)$$

Suppose now that the price of apples increases. Show that

$$\frac{\Delta A}{\Delta p_a} \geqq 0$$

$$\frac{\Delta B}{\Delta p_a} \leqq 0$$

$$\frac{\Delta C}{\Delta p_a} \leqq 0$$

2.8 (20) A competitive industry is in long-run equilibrium with an output of 2,400 units being produced at a price of 12 per unit. The wage rate is

\$1/hour, and the cost of machine hours is \$1/hour. There are 300 firms in the industry described as follows:

number	*technology*	*output and factor demands*
100	$y = 1/2(K + L)$	$L = 8$, $K = 8$
100	$y = K^{1/2}L^{1/2}$	$L = 8$, $K = 8$
100	$y = \min(K, L)$	$L = 8$, $K = 8$

(a) Plot the short-run industry supply curve when machine hours are fixed at $K = 8$.

(b) Suppose that demand shifts and that the new demand curve for the industry is $Q = 1{,}300 - 200p$. What is the short-run equilibrium industry output and price? What are the outputs of each firm?

2.9 (20) A salmon cannery produces Q 1-lb. cans of salmon according to a technology given by $Q = 18K^{1/4}L^{2/3}$. In addition it purchases inputs of salmon and cans at a cost of 35¢ per can of final output. It has fixed costs of \$192/day for overhead.

(a) If the market price for cans of salmon is \$1.35 and $K = 16$, what is the short-run demand for labor?

(b) If $K = 16$ and $w = 3$, what is the firm's short-run supply curve of canned salmon?

(c) If $K = 16$, $w = 3$, and $p = \$1.35$, what would the firm be willing to pay to rent a unit of capital?

(d) If $w = 3$ and capital rents for \$36/day, what will be the long-run price of a can of salmon? Assume the long-run equilibrium profit level is zero.

2.10 (20) A firm has the following technology: there are two techniques to produce output. Technique A uses 2 men and 1 acre of land to produce 1 unit of output per day. Technique B uses 1 man and 3 acres of land to produce 1 unit of output per day.

(a) Draw the isoquants for level of outputs equal to 2 and 4.

(b) Give the cost function of the firm in terms of wage and rental rates.

(c) The demand function for the firm's output is $p = 60 - \frac{1}{2}q$. Suppose $w = \$11$/day and $r = \$3$/day. What price, output, labor input, and land input maximize profits? What if $w = \$5$/day and $r = \$20$/day?

(d) What if the firm is one of many identical firms in a competitive industry. What is the equilibrium price of output for each of the above sets of factor prices?

2.11 (20) A firm has a cost function of the form

$$c(y_1 w_1, w_2) = y^2 w_1^a w_2^b$$

(a) What is b equal to?

(b) What are the marginal and average cost curves?

(c) What is the short-run supply curve of the firm?

(d) Suppose this firm is a member of an industry consisting of a large number of identical firms. Suppose further that the profit level available in the rest of the economy is $10 per day. What is the long-run supply curve of the industry, *given* that there are n firms in the industry in the long run?

(e) What if the number of firms in the industry is variable? How many firms will operate in the long run? Is the above technology a "reasonable" long-run technology? Discuss.

2.12 (10) Suppose we take the supply of housing in a given area to be fixed in the short run. Then the equilibrium price is determined solely by demand. If taxes on apartment house owners are increased how much of this tax will they be able to "pass along" to consumers?

2.13 (10) Consider a simple model of a credit market. Let x be the amount of money borrowed or lent, let $r_B(x)$ be the interest rate borrowers will pay for $\$x$, and let $r_L(x)$ be the rate lenders will charge. The equilibrium interest rate in the loan market is determined by $r_B(x^*) = r_L(x^*)$. Suppose that lenders must pay a tax on their interest income, but the borrowers can *deduct* their interest payments from their taxable income. Suppose further that borrowers and lenders both face the same marginal tax rate t, with $0<t<1$. Is the total amount of loans with the tax larger or smaller than without it? What happens to the equilibrium interest rate?

2.14 (10) (Salop) "In the monopolistic competition model, each firm behaves as a Nash competitor vis-à-vis other firms, but as a Stackelberg competitor vis-à-vis the consumers." Discuss.

2.15 (10) Suppose we have a duopoly industry where $c_i(y_i) = 0$ for $i = 1, 2$ and the market (inverse) demand curve is linear: $p = a - b(y_1 + y_2)$. Solve for the Cournot equilibrium.

2.16 (15) We have an industry composed of a large number of firms each with a cost function $c(y) = y^2 + 1$.

(a) What is the supply curve of an individual firm?

(b) Suppose the demand curve facing the industry is $D(p) = 52 - p$. What are the equilibrium price and profits of each firm?

(c) Suppose the demand curve shifts to $D(p) = 52.5 - p$. What happens to the number of firms and the profits of each firm?

(d) Suppose the demand curve shifts to $D(p) = 53 - p$. What happens?

2.17 (10) A monopolist with cost function $c(y) = y^2 + 1$ faces an inverse demand curve $p_D(y) = 20 - y$.

(a) What levels of price and output will result?

(b) What will the monopolist's profits be?

(c) If the monopolist for some reason behaved as a competitor what would the equilibrium price, quantity, and profits be?

2.18 (15) The demand function for output is $D = 12 - p$. The cost function of the firm is $c(y) = y^2/2$.

(a) What would the equilibrium price and quantity be if the firm behaved as a competitor?

(b) What would the equilibrium price and quantity be if the firm behaved as a monopolist?

(c) How much money would the firm require to forgo the monopoly profits and behave competitively instead?
(d) How much would consumers be willing to pay to the firm if it would agree to behave as a competitor rather than a monopolist? (You may assume zero income effects.)

2.19 (15) Farmers produce corn from land and labor. The labor costs in dollars to produce y bushels of corn is $c(y) = y^2$. There are 100 identical farms which all behave competitively.
(a) What is an individual farmer's supply curve of corn?
(b) What is the market supply curve of corn?
(c) Suppose the demand curve for corn is $D(p) = 200 - 50p$. What is the equilibrium price and quantity sold?
(d) What is the equilibrium rent on the land?

2.20 (20) Suppose we have the same setup as in 2.15 but now firm 1 acts as a follower and firm 2 acts as a leader. Solve for the Stackleberg solution.

2.21 (20) Consider two duopolists producing a homogeneous product facing demand curve $p(y_1 + y_2)$. Suppose that when each duopolist sets his output, he believes the other will respond by adjusting *his* output so as to keep a constant market share. Show that the resulting conjectural variations equilibrium will be the collusive solution (assume costs are zero).

2.22 (15) A monopolist has a cost function $c(y) = cy + F$. Draw the average cost function. Suppose the demand curve facing the monopolist is $x(p) = ap^{-\epsilon}$ where $\epsilon > 1$. Calculate the profit-maximizing levels of price and output. What happens if $\epsilon = 1$?

Notes

Most of the material in this section forms the core of economic theory; it was developed by a number of authors and probably took its present form first under Marshall (1920). The Cournot equilibrium concept is due to Cournot (1897); it was later generalized by Nash (1954).

The concept of monopolistic competition is due to Chamberlin (1956). The location example is due to Salop (1979)). Some other recent work on monopolistic competition can be found in Spence (1976) and Dixit and Stiglitz (1977). A comprehensive survey of market structure and applications to the study of industrial organization can be found in Scherer (1970).

References

CHAMBERLIN, E. 1956. *The Theory of Monopolistic Competition.* Cambridge, Mass.: Harvard University Press.

COURNOT, A. 1897. *Researches into the Mathematical Principles of the Theory of Wealth.* New York: Macmillan.

DIXIT, A., and STIGLITZ, J. 1977. "Monopolistic Competition and Optimum Product Diversity." *American Economic Review* 67:297–308.

MARSHALL, A. 1920. *Principles of Economics.* London: Macmillan.

NASH, J. 1954. "Equilibrium States in N-Person Games." *Proceedings of the National Academy of Sciences* 36:48–49.

SALOP, S. 1979. "Monopolistic Competition with Outside Goods." *The Bell Journal of Economics* 10:141–156.

SCHERER, F. 1970. *Industrial Market Structure and Economic Performance.* Chicago: Rand McNally.

SPENCE, M. 1976. "Product Selection, Fixed Costs, and Monopolistic Competition." *Review of Economic Studies* 43:217–235.

Chapter 3

Theory of the Consumer

In Chapter 2 considerable use was made of the market demand function. In this chapter we will investigate the derivation of such demand functions. In the theory of a competitive firm, the supply function was derived from a model of profit-maximizing behavior and a specification of the underlying technological constants. In the theory of the consumer we will derive demand functions by considering a model of preference-maximizing behavior coupled with a description of underlying economic constraints.

The basic outline of the chapter is as follows. We will first consider the primitive concept of preferences and describe some standard regularity assumptions concerning preferences. Next we investigate the concept of a utility function and its relationship to the idea of a preference ordering. Once this has been done we can investigate the problem of utility maximization subject to a budget constraint and begin to analyze the behavior of demand functions. This study culminates in a description of the properties of demand functions. At the end of the chapter we turn to an analysis of consumer behavior under uncertainty.

3.1 THE CONSUMER'S PREFERENCES

We imagine a consumer faced with possible consumption bundles in some set X, his consumption set. We usually assume that X is the nonnegative orthant in R^k, but more specific consumption sets may be used. For example, we might only include bundles that would give the consumer at least a subsistence existence. We will always assume X is a closed and convex set.

The consumer is assumed to have preferences on the consumption bundles in X. When we write $\mathbf{x} \succsim \mathbf{y}$, we mean "the consumer thinks that the bundle $\mathbf{x}$ is at least as good as the bundle $\mathbf{y}$." We want the preferences to *order* the set of bundles; thus, we assumed:

(COMPLETENESS) For all $\mathbf{x}$, $\mathbf{y}$ in X either $\mathbf{x} \succsim \mathbf{y}$ or $\mathbf{y} \succsim \mathbf{x}$ or both.

(REFLEXIVITY) For all $\mathbf{x}$ in X, $\mathbf{x} \succsim \mathbf{x}$.

(TRANSITIVITY) For all $\mathbf{x}$, $\mathbf{y}$, and $\mathbf{z}$ in X, if $\mathbf{x} \succsim \mathbf{y}$, $\mathbf{y} \succsim \mathbf{z}$, then $\mathbf{x} \succsim \mathbf{z}$.

The first assumption just says that any two bundles can be compared, the second is trivial, and the third is necessary for any discussion of preference *maximization;* for if preferences were not transitive, there might be sets of bundles which had no best elements.

Of course given an ordering $\succsim$ of "weak preference" we can define an ordering $\succ$ of strong preference simply by defining $\mathbf{x} \succ \mathbf{y}$ to mean not $(\mathbf{y} \succsim \mathbf{x})$. We read $\mathbf{x} \succ \mathbf{y}$ as "$\mathbf{x}$ is (strictly) preferred to $\mathbf{y}$." Similarly, we define a notion of "indifference" by $\mathbf{x} \sim \mathbf{y}$ if and only if $\mathbf{x} \succsim \mathbf{y}$ and $\mathbf{y} \succsim \mathbf{x}$.

We often wish to make other assumptions on consumers' preferences; for example,

(CONTINUITY) For all $\mathbf{y}$ in X $\{\mathbf{x}: \mathbf{x} \succsim \mathbf{y}\}$ and $\{\mathbf{x}: \mathbf{x} \precsim \mathbf{y}\}$ are closed sets. It follows that $\{\mathbf{x}: \mathbf{x} \succ \mathbf{y}\}$ and $\{\mathbf{x}: \mathbf{x} \prec \mathbf{y}\}$ are open sets.

This assumption is necessary to rule out certain discontinuous behavior; it says that, if $(\mathbf{x}^i)$ is a sequence of consumption bundles that are all at least as good as a bundle $\mathbf{y}$ and if this sequence converges to some bundle $\mathbf{x}^*$, then $\mathbf{x}^*$ is at least as good as $\mathbf{y}$. The most important consequence of continuity is this: if $\mathbf{y}$ is strictly preferred to $\mathbf{z}$ and if $\mathbf{x}$ is a bundle that is close enough to $\mathbf{y}$, then $\mathbf{x}$ must be strictly preferred to $\mathbf{z}$. This is just a restatement of the assumption that the set of strictly preferred bundles is an open set.

In classical economic theory one often summarizes a consumer's behavior by means of a utility function, that is, a continuous function $u: X \to R$ such that $\mathbf{x} \succ \mathbf{y}$ if and only if $u(\mathbf{x}) > u(\mathbf{y})$. It can be shown that, if the preference ordering is complete, reflexive, transitive, and continuous, then it can be represented by some utility function. We will prove a weaker version of this assertion below. A utility function is often a very convenient way to describe preferences, but it should not be given any psychological interpretation. The only relevant feature of a utility function is its ordinal character. Thus if $u(\mathbf{x})$ represents some preferences $\succsim$ and $f: R \to R$ is a monotonic function, then $f(u(\mathbf{x}))$ will represent exactly the same preferences since $f(u(\mathbf{x})) > f(u(\mathbf{y}))$ if and only if $u(\mathbf{x}) > u(\mathbf{y})$.

There are other assumptions on preferences that are often useful; for example:

(STRONG MONOTONICITY) If $\mathbf{x} \geqq \mathbf{y}$ and $\mathbf{x} \neq \mathbf{y}$, then $\mathbf{x} \succ \mathbf{y}$.

This just says that more is better. This is usually a much stronger assumption than we need; a weaker replacement is:

(LOCAL NONSATIATION) Given any $\mathbf{x}$ in X and any $e > 0$, then there is some bundle $\mathbf{y}$ in X with $|\mathbf{x} - \mathbf{y}| < e$ such that $\mathbf{y} > \mathbf{x}$.

Local nonsatiation says that one can always do a little bit better, even if one is restricted to only small changes in the consumption bundle. You should verify that strong monotonicity implies local nonsatiation but not vice versa. Finally, an assumption which is often used to guarantee nice behavior of the demand curves is:

(STRICT CONVEXITY) Given $\mathbf{x} \neq \mathbf{y}$ and $\mathbf{z}$ in X, if $\mathbf{x} \succsim \mathbf{z}$ and $\mathbf{y} \succsim \mathbf{z}$, then $t\mathbf{x} + (1-t)\mathbf{y} > \mathbf{z}$ for all $0 < t < 1$.

Strict convexity implies that an agent prefers averages to extremes, but, other than that, it has little economic content. Luckily, there are often ways to avoid its use. Strict convexity is a generalization of the neoclassical assumption of "diminishing marginal rates of substitution."

Given a preference ordering, we can often display it graphically. The set of all consumption bundles that are indifferent to each other is called an *indifference curve*. One can think of indifference curves as being level sets of the utility function; they are analogous to the isoquants used in production theory. The set of all bundles on or above an indifference curve, $\{\mathbf{x}$ in X: $\mathbf{x} \succsim \mathbf{x}_0\}$, is called an *upper contour set*. This is analogous to the input requirement set used in production theory.

Example 3.1 The Existence of a Utility Function

PROPOSITION *Suppose preferences are complete, reflexive, transitive, continuous, and strongly monotonic. Then there exists a continuous utility function* u: $R^k_+ \to R$ *which represents those preferences.*

PROOF Let $\mathbf{e}$ be the vector in R^k_+ consisting of all ones. Then given any vector $\mathbf{x}$ let $u(\mathbf{x})$ be that number such that $\mathbf{x} \sim u(\mathbf{x})\,\mathbf{e}$. We have to show that such a number exists and is unique. Let $B = \{t$ in R: $t\mathbf{e} \succsim \mathbf{x}\}$ and $W = \{t$ in R: $\mathbf{x} \succsim t\mathbf{e}\}$. Then strong monotonicity implies B is nonempty; W is certainly nonempty since it contains 0. Continuity implies both sets are closed. Since R is connected, there is some t such that $t\mathbf{e} \sim \mathbf{x}$. Strong monotonicity shows t is unique. It is clear from this construction that the range of u is the entire nonnegative line, since $u(t\mathbf{e}) = t$.

To show that u is continuous, it therefore suffices to show that all inverse images of sets of the form $[u_0; \infty]$ and $[0; u_0]$ are closed sets. But by the above remarks on the range of u,

$$u^{-1}[u_0; \infty] = \{\mathbf{x}: u(\mathbf{x}) \geqq u(\mathbf{x}_0)\} = \{\mathbf{x}: \mathbf{x} \succsim \mathbf{x}_0\}$$

and

$$u^{-1}[0; u_0] = \{\mathbf{x}: u(\mathbf{x}) \leqq u(\mathbf{x}_0)\} = \{\mathbf{x}: \mathbf{x} \precsim \mathbf{x}_0\}$$

which are closed by hypothesis.

Finally we have to show that this utility function actually represents the underlying preferences. Let

$$u(\mathbf{x}) = t_x \quad \text{where } t_x\mathbf{e} \sim \mathbf{x}$$

$$u(\mathbf{y}) = t_y \quad \text{where } t_y\mathbf{e} \sim \mathbf{y}$$

Then if $t_x < t_y$, monotonicity shows that $t_x\mathbf{e} < t_y\mathbf{e}$, and transitivity shows that

$$\mathbf{x} \sim t_x\mathbf{e} < t_y\mathbf{e} \sim \mathbf{y}$$

Similarly, if $\mathbf{x} > \mathbf{y}$, then $t_x\mathbf{e} > t_y\mathbf{e}$ so that t_x must be greater than t_y □.

(M) *Example 3.2 The Nonexistence of a Utility Function*

The lexicographic ordering on R^2_+ is defined by:

$$\mathbf{x} >_l \mathbf{y} \text{ if either } \quad (1)\ x_1 > y_1$$
$$\text{or} \quad (2)\ x_1 = y_1 \quad \text{and} \quad x_2 > y_2$$

In Figure 3.1 we have drawn the set $\{\mathbf{x}: \mathbf{x} >_l \mathbf{y}\}$. Notice that this is *not* an open set of points.

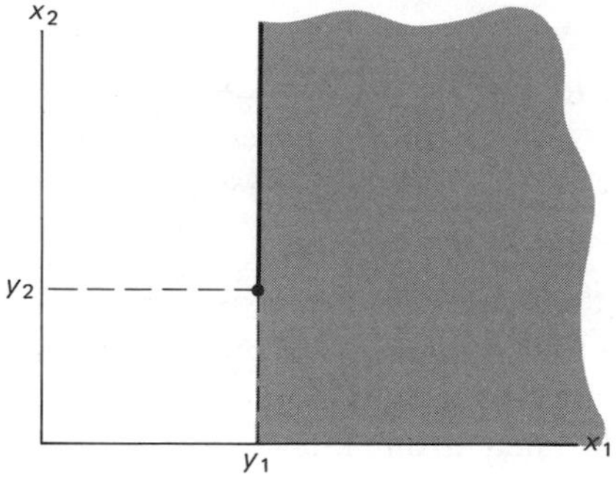

Fig. 3.1 *Lexicographic Preferences*

one directional preference, only willing to make the trade-off in one way.

Since the lexicographic ordering violates the continuity assumption, we might suspect that it cannot be represented by a continuous utility function. This is indeed the case. Suppose that there did exist such a continuous utility function. Then note that the set of numbers

$$\{u(\mathbf{x}): x_1 = a\}$$

must be a nondegenerate interval disjoint from

$$\{u(\mathbf{x}): x_1 = b\} \quad \text{for} \quad b \neq a$$

Hence, with each real number a, we can associate a distinct nondegenerate interval on the real line. But there can only be a countable number of such intervals—since each one contains a distinct rational number—while there are an uncountable number of real numbers.

3.2 CONSUMER BEHAVIOR

Now that we have a convenient way to represent preferences we can begin to investigate consumer behavior. Our basic hypothesis is that a rational consumer will always choose a most preferred bundle from the set of feasible alternatives.

In the basic problem of preference maximization, the set of feasible alternatives is just the set of all bundles that the consumer can afford. Let y be the fixed amount of money available to a consumer, and let $\mathbf{p} = (p_1, \ldots, p_k)$ be the vector of prices of goods $1, \ldots, k$. The set of affordable bundles, the budget set of the consumer, is given by:

$$B = \{\mathbf{x} \text{ in } X: \mathbf{p}\cdot\mathbf{x} \leq y\}$$

The problem of preference maximization can then be written as:

$$\begin{aligned} \max \quad & u(\mathbf{x}) \\ \text{s.t.} \quad & \mathbf{p}\cdot\mathbf{x} \leqq y \\ & \mathbf{x} \text{ is in } X \end{aligned}$$

We note a few basic features of this problem. First, there will generally be a utility-maximizing bundle at least as long as $\mathbf{p} \gg 0$ and $y > 0$. For under this assumption of positive prices the budget set will be a nice compact set. (If some price is zero, the consumer might want an infinite amount of the corresponding good. We will generally ignore such boundary problems.)

Second, the maximizing choice $\mathbf{x}^*$ will be independent of the choice of utility function used to represent the preferences. This is because $\mathbf{x}^*$ must have the property that $\mathbf{x}^* \succsim \mathbf{x}$ for any $\mathbf{x}$ in B, so any utility function that represents the preferences $\succsim$ must pick out $\mathbf{x}^*$ as a constrained maximum.

Third, if we multiply all prices and income by some positive constant we will not change the budget set, and thus we cannot change the optimal choice. Roughly speaking, the optimal choice is "homogeneous of degree zero" in prices and income.

By making a few regularity assumptions on preferences, we can say even more about the consumer's maximizing behavior. For example, suppose that preferences satisfy local nonsatiation; can we ever get an $\mathbf{x}^*$ where $\mathbf{p}\cdot\mathbf{x}^* < y$? Suppose that we could; then, since $\mathbf{x}^*$ costs strictly less than y, every bundle in X close enough to $\mathbf{x}^*$ also costs less than y and is therefore feasible. But, according to the local nonsatiation hypothesis, there must be some bundle $\mathbf{x}$ which is close to $\mathbf{x}^*$ and which is preferred to $\mathbf{x}^*$. But this means that $\mathbf{x}^*$ could not maximize preferences on the budget set B.

Therefore, under the local nonsatiation assumption, a utility-maximizing bundle $\mathbf{x}^*$ must meet the budget constraint with equality. We can thus restate the consumer's problem as

$$\begin{aligned} v(\mathbf{p}, y) = \max \quad & u(\mathbf{x}) \\ \text{s.t.} \quad & \mathbf{p}\cdot\mathbf{x} = y \end{aligned}$$

The function $v(\mathbf{p}, y)$ that gives us the answer to the consumer's problem—that is, the maximum utility achievable at given prices and income—is called the *indirect utility function*. The value of $\mathbf{x}$ that solves this problem is the consumer's *demanded bundle:* it expresses how much of each good the consumer desires at a given level of prices and income. The function that relates $\mathbf{p}$ and y to the demanded bundle is called the consumer's *demand function*. We denote the demand function by $\mathbf{x}(\mathbf{p}, y)$.

Just as in the case of the firm, the consumer's demand function is homogeneous of degree 0 in $(\mathbf{p}, y)$, for multiplying all prices and income by some positive number does not change the budget set at all and thus cannot change the answer to the utility maximization problem.

As in the case of production we can characterize optimizing behavior by calculus. The first-order conditions to the above problem for $\mathbf{x}^* \gg \mathbf{0}$ are:

$$\mathbf{D}u(\mathbf{x}^*) = \lambda\mathbf{p} \qquad \text{where } \lambda \text{ is the Lagrange multiplier described in Section A.10 of the Mathematical Appendix}$$

or $\partial u(\mathbf{x}^*)/\partial x_i = \lambda p_i$ for $i = 1, \ldots, k$. These conditions can be rearranged to give:

$$\frac{\dfrac{\partial u(\mathbf{x}^*)}{\partial x_i}}{\dfrac{\partial u(\mathbf{x}^*)}{\partial x_j}} = \frac{p_i}{p_j} \qquad \text{for } i, j = 1, \cdots, k$$

The fraction on the left is the marginal rate of substitution between good i and j, and the fraction on the right is the economic rate of substitution between i and j. Maximization implies that these two rates of substitution be equal. Suppose they were not; for specificity, suppose

$$\frac{\frac{\partial u(\mathbf{x}^*)}{\partial x_i}}{\frac{\partial u(\mathbf{x}^*)}{\partial x_j}} = \frac{1}{1} \neq \frac{2}{1} = \frac{p_i}{p_j}$$

Then, if the consumer gives up one unit of good i and purchases one unit of good j, he or she will remain on the same indifference curve and have an extra dollar to spend. Hence, total utility can be increased, contradicting maximization.

Figure 3.2 makes the condition even more intuitive. The budget line of the consumer is given by $\{\mathbf{x}: p_1x_1 + p_2x_2 = y\}$. This can also be written as

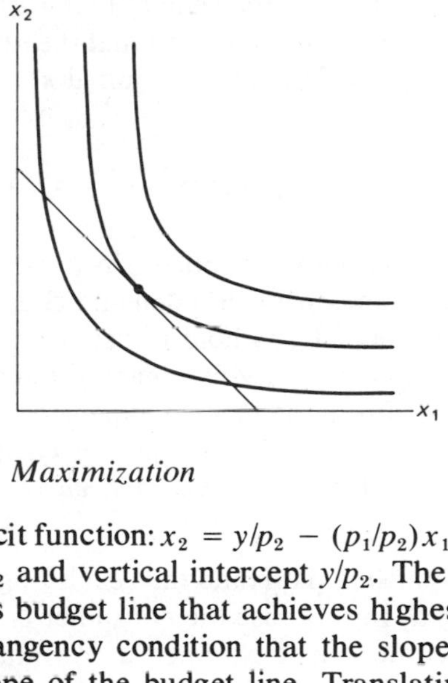

Fig. 3.2 *Preference Maximization*

the graph of an implicit function: $x_2 = y/p_2 - (p_1/p_2)x_1$. Hence, the budget line has slope $-p_1/p_2$ and vertical intercept y/p_2. The consumer wants to find the point on this budget line that achieves highest utility. This must clearly satisfy the tangency condition that the slope of the indifference curve equals the slope of the budget line. Translating this into algebra gives the above condition.

Finally, we can state the condition using vector terminology. Let $\mathbf{x}^*$ be an optimal choice, and let $\mathbf{dx}$ be a perturbation of $\mathbf{x}^*$ that satisfies the budget constraint. Hence, we must have:

$$\mathbf{p}(\mathbf{x}^* \pm \mathbf{dx}) = y, \text{ which implies } \mathbf{pdx} = 0$$

In other words, $\mathbf{dx}$ must be orthogonal to $\mathbf{p}$. For any such perturbation $\mathbf{dx}$ utility cannot change, or else $\mathbf{x}^*$ would not be optimal. Hence, we also have:

$$\mathbf{D}u(\mathbf{x}^*)\mathbf{dx} = 0$$

which says that $\mathbf{D}u(\mathbf{x}^*)$ is also orthogonal to $\mathbf{dx}$. Since this is true for all perturbations for which $\mathbf{pdx} = 0$, we must have $\mathbf{D}u(\mathbf{x}^*)$ proportional to $\mathbf{p}$.

The second-order conditions for utility maximization can be found by applying the results of Section A.10 of the Mathematical Appendix. The Lagrangean expression is:

$$L(\mathbf{x}, \lambda) = u(\mathbf{x}) - \lambda(\mathbf{p}\cdot\mathbf{x} - y)$$

so the second-order conditions can be written as:

$$\mathbf{h}\mathbf{D}^2u(\mathbf{x}^*)\mathbf{h} \leqq 0 \text{ for all } \mathbf{h} \text{ such that } \mathbf{p}\cdot\mathbf{h} = 0$$

Algebraically this means that the Hessian matrix of the utility function is negative semidefinite for all vectors $\mathbf{h}$ orthogonal to the price vector. This is essentially equivalent to the requirement that $u(\mathbf{x})$ be locally quasiconcave. Geometrically, the condition means that the upper contour set must lie above the budget hyperplane at the optimal $\mathbf{x}^*$.

3.3 COMPARATIVE STATICS

Let us examine the two-good problem in a bit more detail. It is of interest to look at how the consumer's demand changes as we change the parameters of the problem. Let's hold prices fixed and allow income to vary; the resulting locus of utility-maximizing bundles is known as the *income expansion path.* From the income expansion path, we can derive a function that relates income to the demand for each commodity (at constant prices). These functions are called *Engle curves.* Several possibilities arise:

(1) The income expansion path (and thus each Engle curve) is a straight line through the origin. In this case the consumer is said to have demand curves with unit income elasticity. Such a consumer will consume the same proportion of each commodity at each level of income as long as prices are held fixed, and just scale this fixed consumption bundle up and down as income changes.

(2) The income expansion path bends towards one good or the other—i.e., as the consumer gets more income he wishes to consume more of both goods but proportionally more of one good (the *luxury good*) than of the other (the *necessary good*).

(3) The income expansion path could bend backwards—in this case an increase in income means the consumer actually wants to consume less of one of the goods. For example, one might argue that as income increases I would want to consume fewer potatoes. Such goods are called *inferior* goods; goods for which more income means more demand are called *normal goods*. (See Figure 3.3.)

We can also hold income fixed and allow prices to vary. If we just let p_1 vary and hold p_2 and y fixed, our budget line will tilt, and the locus of tangencies will sweep out a curve known as the *offer curve*. In the first case in Figure 3.4 we have the standard situation where a lower price for good 1 implies more demand; in the second case we have a situation where a decrease in the price of good 1 brings about a *decreased* demand for good 1. Such a good is called a *Giffen good*. An example might again be

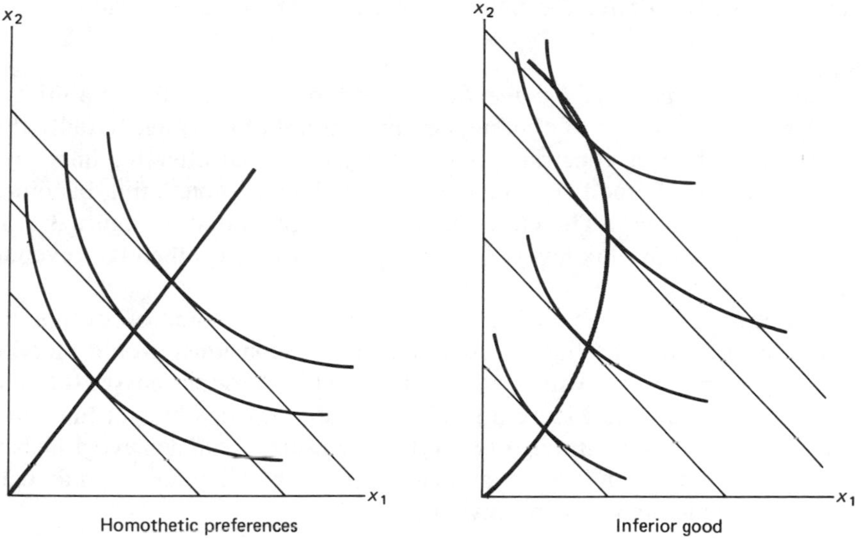

Fig. 3.3 *Income Expansion Paths*

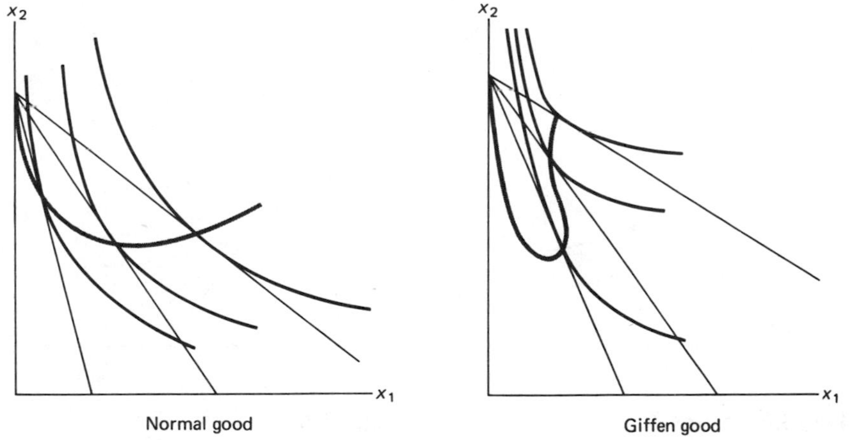

Fig. 3.4 *Offer Curves*

potatoes; if the price of potatoes goes down I can buy just as many of them as I could before and still have some money left over. I could use this leftover money to buy more French bread. But now that I am consuming more French bread I don't even want to consume as many potatoes as I did before.

In the above example we see that a fall in the price of a good may have two sorts of effects—one commodity will become less expensive than another, and total "purchasing power" may change. A fundamental result of the theory of the consumer, the Slutsky equation, relates these two effects. We will derive the Slutsky equation later in several ways.

Example 3.3 Excise and Income Taxes Suppose we wish to tax a utility-maximizing consumer to obtain a certain amount of revenue. Initially the consumer's budget constraint is $p_1x_1 + p_2x_2 = y$, but after we impose a tax on sales of good 1, the consumer's budget constraint becomes $(p_1 + t)x_1 + p_2x_2 = y$. The effect of this tax is illustrated in Figure 3.5. If we denote the after-tax level of consumption by (x_1^*, x_2^*) then the revenue collected by the tax is tx_1^*.

Suppose now that we decide to collect this same amount of revenue by a tax on income. The budget constraint of the consumer would then be $p_1x_1 + p_2x_2 = y - tx_1^*$. This is a line with slope $-p_1/p_2$ that passes through (x_1^*, x_2^*), as shown in Figure 3.6. Notice that since this budget line cuts the indifference curve through (x_1^*, x_2^*), the consumer can achieve a higher level of utility from an income tax than from a commodity tax, even though they both generate the same revenue.

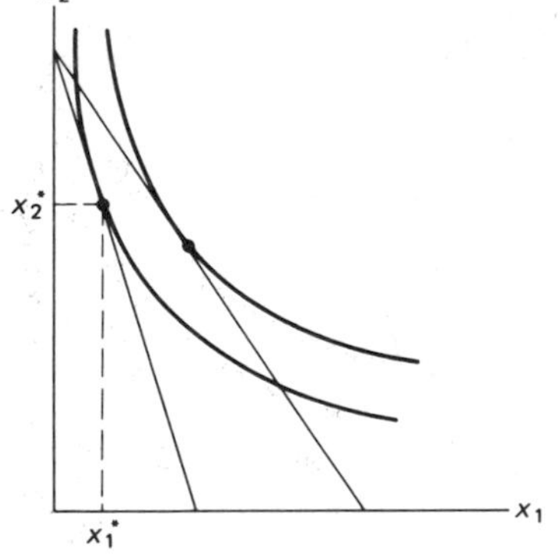

Fig. 3.5 *Sales Tax*

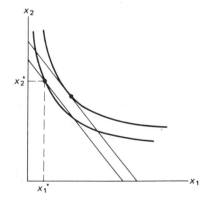

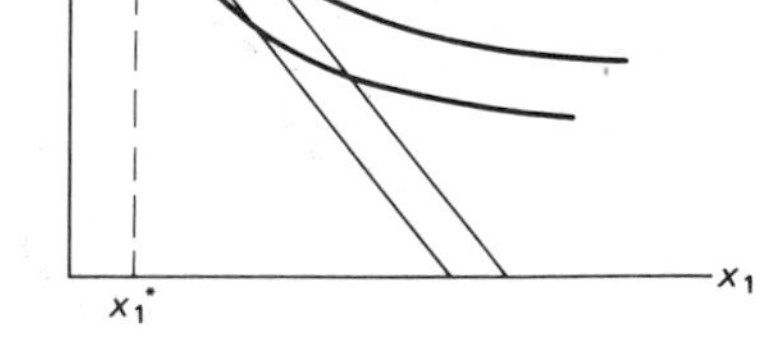

Fig. 3.6 *Income Tax with Revenue* tx*

3.4 *THE EXPENDITURE FUNCTION AND THE INDIRECT UTILITY FUNCTION*

Recall the indirect utility function defined earlier. This function, $v(\mathbf{p}, y)$, gives maximum utility as a function of $\mathbf{p}$ and y. The indirect utility function can be shown to have the following properties:

PROPERTIES OF THE INDIRECT UTILITY FUNCTION

(1) $v(\mathbf{p}, y)$ *is continuous at all* $\mathbf{p} \gg 0$, $y > 0$.

(2) $v(\mathbf{p}, y)$ *is nonincreasing in* $\mathbf{p}$; *that is, if* $\mathbf{p}' \geqq \mathbf{p}$, $v(\mathbf{p}', y) \leqq v(\mathbf{p}, y)$. *Similarly,* $v(\mathbf{p}, y)$ *is nondecreasing in* y.

(3) $v(\mathbf{p}, y)$ *is quasi-convex in* $\mathbf{p}$; *that is,* $\{\mathbf{p}\colon v(\mathbf{p}, y) \leqq k\}$ *is a convex set for all real numbers* k.

(4) $v(\mathbf{p}, y)$ *is homogeneous of degree* 0 *in* $(\mathbf{p}, y)$.

PROOF

(1) This follows from the theorem of the maximum in Section A.12 of the Mathematical Appendix.

(2) Let $B = \{\mathbf{x}\colon \mathbf{p}\cdot\mathbf{x} \leqq y\}$ and $B' = \{\mathbf{x}\colon \mathbf{p}'\cdot\mathbf{x} \leqq y\}$ for $\mathbf{p}' \geqq \mathbf{p}$. Then B' is contained in B. Hence, the maximum of $u(\mathbf{x})$ over B is at least as big as the maximum of $u(\mathbf{x})$ over B'. The argument for y is similar.

(3) Suppose $\mathbf{p}$ and $\mathbf{p}'$ are such that $v(\mathbf{p}, y) \leqq k$, $v(\mathbf{p}', y) \leqq k$. Let $\mathbf{p}'' = t\mathbf{p} + (1-t)\mathbf{p}'$. We want to show that $v(\mathbf{p}'', y) \leqq k$. Define the budget sets

$$B = \{\mathbf{x}\colon \mathbf{p}\cdot\mathbf{x} \leqq y\}$$

$$B' = \{\mathbf{x}\colon \mathbf{p}'\cdot\mathbf{x} \leqq y\}$$

$$B'' = \{\mathbf{x}\colon \mathbf{p}''\cdot\mathbf{x} \leqq y\}$$

We will show that any $\mathbf{x}$ in B'' must be in either B or B'. Assume not; then $\mathbf{x}$ is such that $t\mathbf{p}\cdot\mathbf{x} + (1-t)\mathbf{p}'\cdot\mathbf{x} \leqq y$ but $\mathbf{p}\cdot\mathbf{x} > y$ and $\mathbf{p}'\cdot\mathbf{x} > y$. These can be transformed to:

$$t\mathbf{p}\cdot\mathbf{x} > ty$$

$$(1-t)\mathbf{p}'\cdot\mathbf{x} > (1-t)y$$

Summing, we get: $$t\mathbf{p}\cdot\mathbf{x} + (1-t)\mathbf{p}'\cdot\mathbf{x} > y$$

which contradicts our original assumption.

Now note that

$$v(\mathbf{p}'', y) = \max u(\mathbf{x}) \quad \text{s.t.} \quad \mathbf{x} \text{ is in } B''$$

$$\leqq \max u(\mathbf{x}) \quad \text{s.t.} \quad \mathbf{x} \text{ is in } B, \text{ or } \mathbf{x} \text{ is in } B' \text{ since } B'' \text{ is contained in the union of } B \text{ and } B'.$$

$$\leqq k \quad \text{since} \quad v(\mathbf{p}, y) \leqq k \quad \text{and} \quad v(\mathbf{p}', y) \leqq k$$

(4) If prices and income are both multiplied by a positive number the budget set doesn't change at all. Thus, $v(t\mathbf{p}, ty) = v(\mathbf{p}, y)$ for $t > 0$. □

In Figure 3.7 we have drawn a typical set of "price indifference curves." These are just the level sets of the indirect utility function. By property (2) utility is increasing as we move towards the origin, and by property (3) the lower contour sets are convex. Note that the lower contour sets lie to the northeast of the price indifference curves since indirect utility declines with higher prices.

We note that, if preferences satisfy the local nonsatiation assumption, then $v(\mathbf{p}, y)$ will be *strictly* increasing in y. In Figure 3.8 we have drawn the relationship between $v(\mathbf{p}, y)$ and y for constant prices. Since $v(\mathbf{p}, y)$ is strictly increasing in y, we can invert the function and solve for y as a function of the level of utility; that is, given any level of utility, u, we can read off the above graph the minimal amount of income necessary to achieve u at the prices $\mathbf{p}$. The function that relates income and utility in this way—the inverse of the indirect utility function—is known as the *expenditure function* and is denoted by $e(\mathbf{p}, u)$.

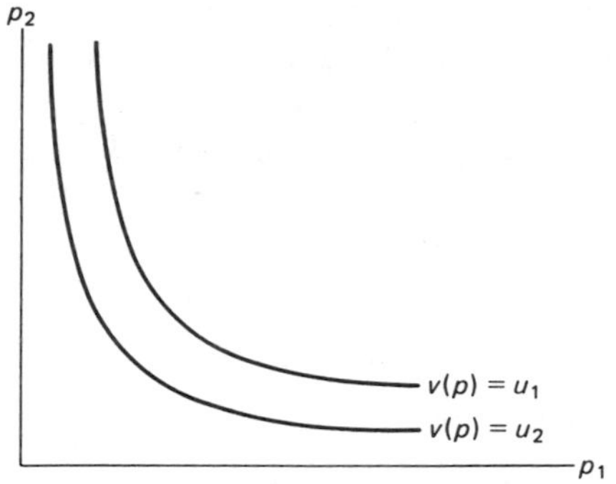

Fig. 3.7 *Price Indifference Curves*

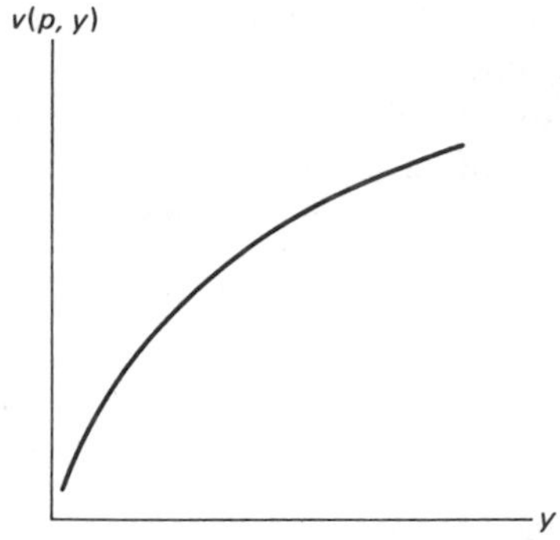

Fig. 3.8 *Utility as a Function of Income*

An equivalent definition is given by the following problem:

$$e(\mathbf{p}, u) = \min \quad \mathbf{p} \cdot \mathbf{x}$$
$$\text{s.t.} \quad u(\mathbf{x}) \geqq u$$

Hence, the expenditure function gives the minimum cost of achieving a fixed level of utility.

The expenditure function is completely analogous to the cost function we considered in Chapter 1. It therefore has all the same properties. These are repeated here for convenience.

PROPERTIES OF THE EXPENDITURE FUNCTION

(1) *Nondecreasing in* **p**.
(2) *Homogeneous of degree* 1 *in* **p**.
(3) *Concave in* **p**.
(4) *Continuous in* **p**, *for* $\mathbf{p} \gg 0$.
(5) *If* $\mathbf{h}(\mathbf{p}, u)$ *is the expenditure-minimizing bundle necessary to achieve utility level* u *at prices* **p**, *then* $h_i(\mathbf{p}, u) = \frac{\partial e(\mathbf{p}, u)}{\partial p_i}$ *for* $i = 1, \cdots, n$ *assuming the derivative is defined and* $\mathbf{p} \gg 0$.

PROOF These are exactly the same properties that the cost function exhibits. □

The function $\mathbf{h}(\mathbf{p}, u)$ is called the *Hicksian* or *compensated demand function*. The last term comes from viewing the demand function as being constructed by varying prices *and income* so as to keep the consumer at a fixed level of utility. Thus, the income changes are arranged to "compensate" for the price changes.

Hicksian demand functions are not directly observable since they depend on utility, which is not directly observable. Demand functions expressed as a function of prices and income are observable; when we want to emphasize the difference between the Hicksian demand function and the usual demand function, we will refer to the latter as the *Marshallian* demand function. The Marshallian demand functions are just the ordinary market demand functions we have been discussing all along.

3.5 *THE COMPENSATION FUNCTIONS*

There is a nice construction involving the expenditure function that comes up in a variety of places in welfare economics known as the *compensation function*. Let us consider some prices **p** and some given bundle of goods **x**. We can ask the following question: How much money would a given consumer need at the prices **p** to be as well off as he could be by consuming the bundle of goods **x**?

Figure 3.9 tells us how to construct the answer to this question if we know the consumer's preferences. We just see how much money the consumer would need to reach the indifference curve passing through x. Mathematically speaking, we simply solve the following problem:

$$\begin{aligned} \min \quad & \mathbf{p}\,\mathbf{z} \\ \text{s.t.} \quad & u(\mathbf{z}) \geq u(\mathbf{x}) \end{aligned}$$

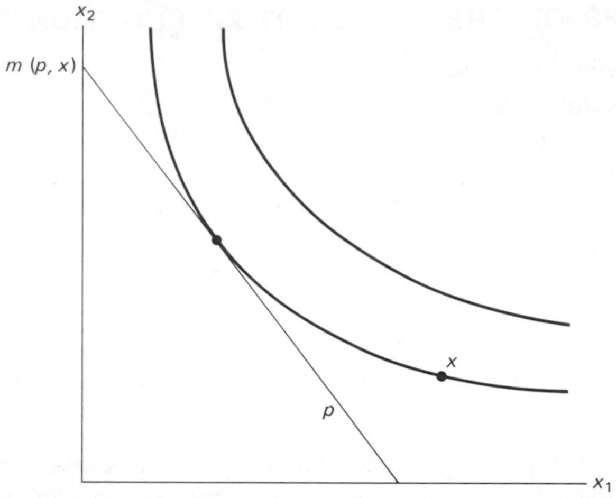

Fig. 3.9 *Direct Compensation Function*

Or, even more simply, we just use the expenditure function and compute $e(\mathbf{p}, u(\mathbf{x}))$.

This type of function occurs so often that it is worthwhile giving it a special name; we will call it the *(direct) compensation function*. (It is also known as the "minimum income function," the "money metric utility function," and by a variety of other names.) It is given by:

$$m(\mathbf{p}, \mathbf{x}) \equiv e(\mathbf{p}, u(\mathbf{x}))$$

It is easy to see that for fixed $\mathbf{x}$, $u(\mathbf{x})$ is fixed so $m(\mathbf{p}, \mathbf{x})$ behaves exactly like an expenditure function: it is monotonic, homogeneous, concave in $\mathbf{p}$, and so on. What is not as obvious is that when $\mathbf{p}$ is fixed, $m(\mathbf{p}, \mathbf{x})$ is in fact a utility function. The proof is simple: for fixed prices the expenditure function is increasing in the level of utility: if you want to get a higher utility level, you have to spend more money. In fact, the expenditure function is strictly increasing in u for preferences that exhibit local nonsatiation. Hence, for fixed $\mathbf{p}$, $m(\mathbf{p}, \mathbf{x})$ is simply a monotonic transform of the utility function and is, therefore, itself a utility function!

This is easily seen in Figure 3.9. All points on the indifference curve passing through $\mathbf{x}$ will be assigned the same level of $m(\mathbf{p}, \mathbf{x})$, and all points on higher indifference curves will be assigned a higher level. This is all it takes to be a utility function.

There is a similar construct for indirect utility known as the *indirect compensation function*. It is given by:

$$\mu(\mathbf{p}; \mathbf{q}, y) \equiv e(\mathbf{p}, v(\mathbf{q}, y))$$

That is, $\mu(\mathbf{p}; \mathbf{q}, y)$ measures how much money one would need at prices $\mathbf{p}$ to be as well off as one would be facing prices $\mathbf{q}$ and having income y. Just as in the direct case, $\mu(\mathbf{p}; \mathbf{q}, y)$ behaves like an expenditure function with respect to $\mathbf{p}$, but now it behaves like an indirect utility function with respect to $\mathbf{q}$ and y. See Figure 3.10 for a graphical example.

A nice feature of the direct and indirect compensation functions is that they contain only *observable* arguments. They are *specific* direct and indirect utility functions that measure something of interest, and there is no ambiguity regarding monotonic transformations. We will find this feature to be useful in our discussion of integrability theory.

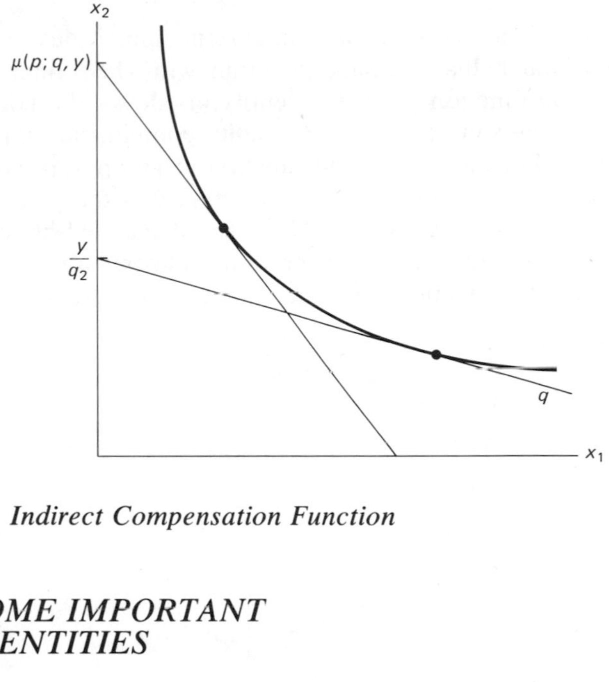

Fig. 3.10 *Indirect Compensation Function*

3.6 *SOME IMPORTANT IDENTITIES*

There are some important identities that tie together the expenditure function, the indirect utility function, the Marshallian demand function, and the Hicksian demand function.

Let us consider the utility maximization problem

$$v(\mathbf{p}, y^*) = \max \; u(\mathbf{x}) \quad \text{s.t.} \quad \mathbf{p}\cdot\mathbf{x} \leqq y^*$$

Let $\mathbf{x}^*$ be the solution to this problem and let $u^* = u(\mathbf{x}^*)$. Consider the expenditure minimization problem:

$$e(\mathbf{p}, u^*) = \min \; \mathbf{p}\cdot\mathbf{x} \quad \text{s.t.} \quad u(\mathbf{x}) \geqq u^*$$

Some inspection of Figure 3.11 should convince you that in nonperverse cases the answers to these two problems should be the same $\mathbf{x}^*$. (A more rigorous argument is given in Appendix 1 to this chapter.) This simple observation leads to four important identities:

(1) $e(\mathbf{p}, v(\mathbf{p}, y)) \equiv y$ The minimal expenditure to reach utility $v(\mathbf{p}, y)$ is y.
(2) $v(\mathbf{p}, e(\mathbf{p}, u)) \equiv u$ The maximal utility from income $e(\mathbf{p}, u)$ is u.
(3) $x_i(\mathbf{p}, y) \equiv h_i(\mathbf{p}, v(\mathbf{p}, y))$ The Marshallian demand at income y is the same as the Hicksian demand at utility $v(\mathbf{p}, y)$.
(4) $h_i(\mathbf{p}, u) \equiv x_i(\mathbf{p}, e(\mathbf{p}, u))$ The Hicksian demand at utility u is the same as the Marshallian demand at income $e(\mathbf{p}, u)$.

This last identity is perhaps the most important since it ties together the "observable" Marshallian demand function with the "unobservable" Hicksian demand function. That is, identity (4) shows the Hicksian demand function—the solution to the expenditure minimization problem—is equal to the Marshallian demand function at an appropriate level of income—namely, the minimum income necessary at the given prices to achieve the desired level of utility. Thus, any demanded bundle can be expressed *either* as the solution to the utility maximization problem or the expenditure minimization problem. This fact will prove to be useful later on.

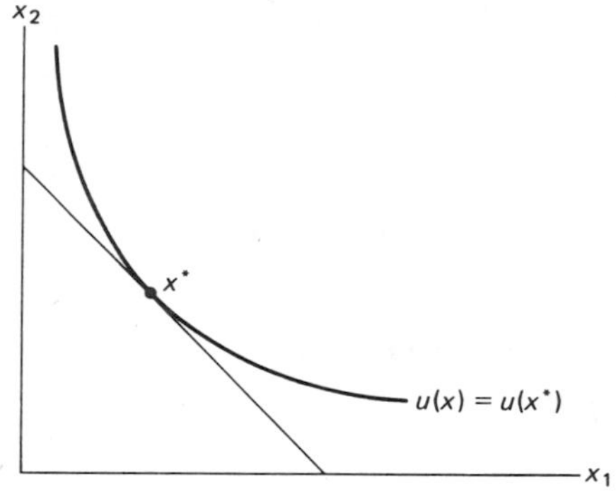

Fig. 3.11 *Utility Maximization and Expenditure Minimization*

A nice application of one of these identities is given in the next proposition:

PROPOSITION (*Roy's identity*) *If* $\mathbf{x}(\mathbf{p}, y)$ *is the Marshallian demand function, then*

$$x_i(\mathbf{p}, y) = \frac{-\dfrac{\partial v(\mathbf{p}, y)}{\partial p_i}}{\dfrac{\partial v(\mathbf{p}, y)}{\partial y}} \quad \textit{for} \quad i = 1, \cdots, n$$

provided, of course, that the right hand side is well defined and that $\mathbf{p} \gg 0$, $y > 0$.

PROOF Suppose that $\mathbf{x}^*$ maximizes utility at $(\mathbf{p}^*, y^*)$; that is, $\mathbf{x}^* = \mathbf{x}(\mathbf{p}^*, y^*)$. Let $u^* = u(\mathbf{x}^*) = u(\mathbf{x}(\mathbf{p}^*, y^*)) = v(\mathbf{p}^*, y^*)$. Then it is identically true that

$$u^* \equiv v(\mathbf{p}, e(\mathbf{p}, u^*))$$

that is, no matter what prices are, if you give the consumer the minimal income to get utility u^* at those prices, then the maximal utility he can get is u^*.

Since this is an identity we can differentiate it to get:

$$0 = \frac{\partial v(\mathbf{p}^*, y^*)}{\partial p_i} + \frac{\partial v(\mathbf{p}^*, y^*)}{\partial y} \frac{\partial e(\mathbf{p}, u^*)}{\partial p_i}$$

or

$$\mathbf{x}_i^* = \frac{\partial e(\mathbf{p}, u^*)}{\partial p_i} = \frac{-\partial v(\mathbf{p}^*, y^*)/\partial p_i}{\partial v(\mathbf{p}^*, y^*)/\partial y}$$

Since this is true for all $\mathbf{p}^*$, y^* and since $\mathbf{x}^* = \mathbf{x}(\mathbf{p}^*, y^*)$, the theorem is proved. □

Here is an alternative direct proof of Roy's identity. The indirect utility function is given by:

$$v(\mathbf{p}, y) \equiv u(\mathbf{x}(\mathbf{p}, y))$$

If we differentiate this with respect to p_j, we find:

$$\frac{\partial v(\mathbf{p}, y)}{\partial p_j} = \sum_{i=1}^{k} \frac{\partial u(\mathbf{x})}{\partial x_i} \frac{\partial x_i}{\partial p_j}$$

Since $\mathbf{x}(\mathbf{p}, y)$ is the demand function, it satisfies the first-order condition for utility maximization. Substituting these into the above:

$$\frac{\partial v(\mathbf{p}, y)}{\partial p_j} = \lambda \sum_{i=1}^{k} p_i \frac{\partial x_i}{\partial p_j}$$

The demand functions also satisfy the budget constraint $\mathbf{p}\mathbf{x}(\mathbf{p}, y) \equiv y$. Differentiating this with respect to p_j, we have:

$$x_j(\mathbf{p}, y) + \sum_{i=1}^{k} p_i \frac{\partial x_i}{\partial p_j} = 0$$

Substitute this into the above expression to find:

$$\frac{\partial v(\mathbf{p}, y)}{\partial p_j} = -\lambda x_j(\mathbf{p}, y)$$

Now we differentiate the definition of the indirect utility function with respect to y to find:

$$\frac{\partial v(\mathbf{p}, y)}{\partial y} = \lambda \sum_{i=1}^{n} p_i \frac{\partial x_i}{\partial y}$$

Similarly differentiating the budget constraint with respect to y we have:

$$\sum_{i=1}^{n} p_i \frac{\partial x_i}{\partial y} = 1$$

Substituting:

$$\frac{\partial v(\mathbf{p}, y)}{\partial y} = \lambda$$

Thus, the Lagrange multiplier in the first-order condition is the marginal utility of income. Combining these two expressions gives us Roy's identity.

Finally, for one last proof of Roy's law, we note that it is an immediate consequence of the envelope theorem. The argument given above is just going through the steps of the proof of this theorem.

Example 3.4 The Cobb-Douglas Utility Function The Cobb-Douglas utility function is given by: $u(x_1, x_2) = x_1^a x_2^{1-a}$. Since any monotonic transform of this function represents the same preferences, we can also define the Cobb-Douglas utility function by $u(x_1, x_2) = a \ln x_1 + (1 - a) \ln x_2$.

The expenditure function and Hicksian demand functions were derived in Chapter 1. They correspond to the cost function and the conditional factor demand functions. The Marshallian demand functions and the indirect utility function can be derived by solving the following problem:

$$\begin{aligned} \max \quad & a \ln x_1 + (1 - a) \ln x_2 \\ \text{s.t.} \quad & p_1 x_1 + p_2 x_2 = y \end{aligned}$$

The first-order conditions are:

$$\frac{a}{x_1} - \lambda p_1 = \frac{(1 - a)}{x_2} - \lambda p_2 = 0$$

or

$$\frac{a}{p_1 x_1} = \frac{(1 - a)}{p_2 x_2}$$

Cross multiply and use the budget constraint to get

$$ap_2x_2 = p_1x_1 - ap_1x_1$$

$$ay = p_1x_1$$

$$x_1(p_1, p_2, y) = \frac{ay}{p_1}$$

Substitute to get the second Marshallian demand:

$$x_2(p_1, p_2, y) = \frac{(1-a)y}{p_2}$$

Substitute into the objective function and eliminate constants to get the indirect utility function:

$$v(p_1, p_2, y) = ln\ y - a\ ln\ p_1 - (1-a)\ ln\ p_2$$

A quicker way to derive the indirect utility function is to invert the Cobb-Douglas expenditure function we derived in Chapter 1. This is

$$e(p_1, p_2, u) = Kp_1^a p_2^{1-a} u$$

where K is some constant depending on a. Inverting the expression by replacing $e(p_1, p_2, u)$ by y, and u by $v(p_1, p_2, y)$, we get:

$$v(p_1, p_2, y) = \frac{y}{Kp_1^a p_2^{1-a}}$$

This is just a monotonic transform of the other expression as can be seen by taking the logarithm of both sides.

The compensation functions can be derived by substitution. We have:

$$\begin{aligned} m(\mathbf{p}, \mathbf{x}) &= Kp_1{}^a p_2{}^{1-a} u(x_1, x_2) \\ &= Kp_1{}^a p_2{}^{1-a} x_1{}^a x_2{}^{1-a} \end{aligned}$$

and

$$\begin{aligned} \mu(\mathbf{p}; \mathbf{q}, y) &= Kp_1{}^a p_2{}^{1-a} v(q_1, q_2, y) \\ &= p_1{}^a p_2{}^{1-a} q_1{}^{-a} q_2{}^{a-1} y \end{aligned}$$

Example 3.5 The CES Utility Function The CES utility function is given by $u(x_1, x_2) = (x_1^\rho + x_2^\rho)^{1/\rho}$. Since preferences are invariant with respect to monotonic transforms of utility, we could just as well choose $u(x_1, x_2) = x_1^\rho + x_2^\rho$.

We have seen in Example 1.13 that the cost function for the CES technology has the form $c(w, y) = (w_1^r + w_2^r)^{1/r}y$ where $r = \rho/(1 - \rho)$. Thus the expenditure function for the CES utility function must have the form:

$$e(\mathbf{p}, u) = (p_1^r + p_2^r)^{1/r}u$$

We can find the indirect utility function by inverting the above equation:

$$v(\mathbf{p}, y) = (p_1^r + p_2^r)^{-1/r}y$$

The demand functions can be found by simple differentiation:

$$x_1(\mathbf{p}, y) = \frac{-\partial v(\mathbf{p}, y)/\partial p_1}{\partial v(\mathbf{p}, y)/\partial y} = \frac{\frac{1}{r}(p_1^r + p_2^r)^{\left(\frac{-1}{r} - 1\right)} yrp_1^{r-1}}{(p_1^r + p_2^r)^{-1/r}}$$

$$= \frac{p_1^{r-1}y}{(p_1^r + p_2^r)}$$

3.7 THE SLUTSKY EQUATION

The expenditure function was introduced in order to simplify the derivation of the Slutsky equation, which concerns the effect of price changes on demand. Here is the promised formula:

PROPOSITION (*The Slutsky equation*)

$$\frac{\partial x_j(\mathbf{p}, y)}{\partial p_i} = \frac{\partial h_j(\mathbf{p}, v(\mathbf{p}, y))}{\partial p_i} - \frac{\partial x_j(\mathbf{p}, y)}{\partial y} \cdot x_i$$

PROOF Let $\mathbf{x}^*$ maximize utility at $(\mathbf{p}^*, y^*)$ and let $u^* = u(\mathbf{x}^*)$. It is identically true that

$$h_j(\mathbf{p}, u^*) \equiv x_j(\mathbf{p}, e(\mathbf{p}, u^*))$$

We can differentiate this with respect to p_i and evaluate the derivative at $\mathbf{p}^*$ to get:

$$\frac{\partial h_j(\mathbf{p}^*, u^*)}{\partial p_i} = \frac{\partial x_j(\mathbf{p}^*, y^*)}{\partial p_i} + \frac{\partial x_j(\mathbf{p}^*, y^*)}{\partial y}\frac{\partial e(\mathbf{p}^*, u^*)}{\partial p_i}$$

Note the meaning of this expression. The lefthand side is how the compensated demand changes when p_j changes. The righthand side says that this change is equal to the change in demand holding expenditure fixed at y^* *plus* the change in demand when income changes *times* how much income has to change to keep utility constant. But this last term, $\partial e(\mathbf{p}^*, u^*)/\partial p_i$, is just x_i^*; rearranging gives us:

$$\frac{\partial x_j(\mathbf{p}^*, y^*)}{\partial p_i} = \frac{\partial h_j(\mathbf{p}^*, u^*)}{\partial p_i} - \frac{\partial x_j(\mathbf{p}^*, y^*)}{\partial y} x_i^*$$

which is the Slutsky equation. □

The Slutsky equation decomposes the demand change induced by a price change Δp_i into two separate effects: the substitution effect and the income effect:

$$\Delta x_j \approx \underbrace{\frac{\partial x_j(\mathbf{p}, y)}{\partial p_1} \cdot \Delta p_i}_{\substack{\text{change in}\\ \text{demand}}} = \underbrace{\frac{\partial h_j(\mathbf{p}, u)}{\partial p_i} \cdot \Delta p_i}_{\substack{\text{substitution}\\ \text{effect}}} - \underbrace{\frac{\partial x_j(\mathbf{p}, y)}{\partial y} \cdot \overbrace{x_i \Delta p_1}^{\substack{\text{change in}\\ \text{income}\\ \text{to keep utility constant}}}}_{\text{income effect}}$$

We can also consider the effects from all prices' changing at once; in this case we just interpret the derivatives as generalized n-dimensional derivatives rather than partial derivatives. In the two-good case the Slutsky equation looks like:

$$\mathbf{D}_p\mathbf{x}(\mathbf{p}, y) = \mathbf{D}_p\mathbf{h}(\mathbf{p}, v(\mathbf{p}, y)) - \mathbf{D}_y\mathbf{x}(\mathbf{p}, y) \cdot \mathbf{x}$$

$$\begin{bmatrix} \frac{\partial x_1(\mathbf{p}, y)}{\partial p_1} & \frac{\partial x_1(\mathbf{p}, y)}{\partial p_2} \\ \frac{\partial x_2(\mathbf{p}, y)}{\partial p_1} & \frac{\partial x_2(\mathbf{p}, y)}{\partial p_2} \end{bmatrix} = \begin{bmatrix} \frac{\partial h_1(\mathbf{p}, u)}{\partial p_1} & \frac{\partial h_1(\mathbf{p}, u)}{\partial p_2} \\ \frac{\partial h_2(\mathbf{p}, u)}{\partial p_1} & \frac{\partial h_2(\mathbf{p}, u)}{\partial p_2} \end{bmatrix} - \begin{bmatrix} \frac{\partial x_1(\mathbf{p}, y)}{\partial y} \\ \frac{\partial x_2(\mathbf{p}, y)}{\partial y} \end{bmatrix} [x_1, x_2]$$

where $u = v(\mathbf{p}, y)$.

Expanding the last term gives

$$\begin{bmatrix} \frac{\partial x_1(\mathbf{p}, y)}{\partial y} \\ \frac{\partial x_2(\mathbf{p}, y)}{\partial y} \end{bmatrix} [x_1, x_2] = \begin{bmatrix} \frac{\partial x_1(\mathbf{p}, y)}{\partial y} x_1 & \frac{\partial x_1(\mathbf{p}, y)}{\partial y} x_2 \\ \frac{\partial x_2(\mathbf{p}, y)}{\partial y} x_1 & \frac{\partial x_2(\mathbf{p}, y)}{\partial y} x_2 \end{bmatrix}$$

Suppose we consider a price change $\Delta\mathbf{p} = (\Delta p_1, \Delta p_2)$ and we are interested in the approximate change in demand $\Delta\mathbf{x} = (\Delta x_1, \Delta x_2)$. According to the Slutsky equation we can calculate this by:

$$(\Delta x_1, \Delta x_2) \approx \begin{bmatrix} \frac{\partial h_1}{\partial p_1} & \frac{\partial h_1}{\partial p_2} \\ \\ \frac{\partial h_2}{\partial p_1} & \frac{\partial h_2}{\partial p_2} \end{bmatrix} \begin{bmatrix} \Delta p_1 \\ \\ \Delta p_2 \end{bmatrix} - \begin{bmatrix} \frac{\partial x_1}{\partial y} x_1 & \frac{\partial x_1}{\partial y} x_2 \\ \\ \frac{\partial x_z}{\partial y} x_1 & \frac{\partial x_1}{\partial y} x_2 \end{bmatrix} \begin{bmatrix} \Delta p_1 \\ \\ \Delta p_2 \end{bmatrix}$$

$$= (\Delta x_1^s, \Delta x_2^s) \qquad + (\Delta x_1^y, \Delta x_2^y)$$

The first vector is the substitution effect. It indicates how the Hicksian demands change. Since changes in Hicksian demands keep utility constant,$(\Delta x_1^s, \Delta x_2^s)$ will lie along an indifference surface. The second vector is the income effect. Income has "changed" by $x_1\Delta p_1 + x_2\Delta p_2$ and the vector $(\Delta x_1^y, \Delta x_2^y)$ measures the impact of this change on demand, with prices held constant at the initial level. This vector therefore lies along the income expansion path.

We can do a similar decomposition for finite changes in demand. This is illustrated in Figure 3.12. Here prices change from $\mathbf{p}^\circ$ to $\mathbf{p}'$. To find the change in the Hicksian demands we shift the new budget line back to the original indifference curve. This gives us $(\Delta x_1^s, \Delta x_2^s)$. To find the income effect, we shift the old budget line out to the new demand. This gives us $(\Delta x_1^y, \Delta x_2^y)$. The total change, $(\Delta x_1, \Delta x_2)$, is (approximately) equal to the sum of these two changes. As $(\Delta p_1, \Delta p_2)$ gets small this approximate relationship becomes exact.

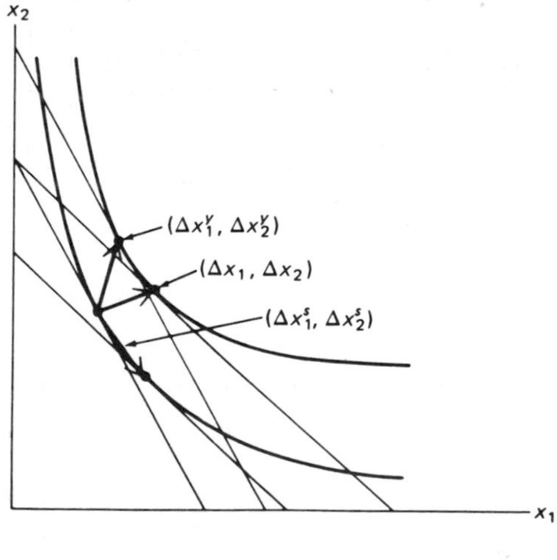

Fig. 3.12 *The Slutsky Decomposition of a Demand Change*

Example 3.6 The Cobb-Douglas Slutsky Equation Let us check Slutsky's equation in the Cobb-Douglas case. As we've seen, in this case we have:

$$v(p_1, p_2, y) = y p_1^{-a} p_2^{a-1}$$
$$e(p_1, p_2, u) = u p_1^{a} p_2^{1-a}$$
$$x_1(p_1, p_2, y) = \frac{ay}{p_1}$$
$$h_1(p_1, p_2, u) = a p_1^{a-1} p_2^{1-a} u$$

Thus

$$\frac{\partial x_1(p, y)}{\partial p_1} = -\frac{ay}{p_1^2} \quad \frac{\partial x_1(p, y)}{\partial y} = \frac{a}{p_1}$$
$$\frac{\partial h_1(p, u)}{\partial p_1} = a(a-1) p_1^{a-2} p_2^{1-a} u$$
$$\frac{\partial h_1(p, v(p, y))}{\partial p_1} = a(a-1) p_1^{a-2} p_2^{1-a} y p_1^{-a} p_2^{a-1}$$
$$= a(a-1) p_1^{-2} y$$

Now plug into the Slutsky equation:

$$\frac{\partial h_1}{\partial p_1} - \frac{\partial x_1}{\partial y} x_1 = \frac{a(a-1)y}{p_1^2} - \frac{a}{p_1}\frac{ay}{p_1}$$
$$= \frac{[a(a-1) - a^2]y}{p_1^2} = \frac{-ay}{p_1^2} = \frac{\partial x_1}{\partial p_1}$$

It checks!

3.8 *PROPERTIES OF DEMAND FUNCTIONS*

The properties of the expenditure function give us an easy way to develop the main propositions of the neoclassical theory of consumer behavior:

(1) *The matrix of substitution terms* $(\partial h_j(\mathbf{p}, u)/\partial p_i)$ *is negative semi-definite.* This follows because $(\partial h_j(\mathbf{p}, u)/\partial p_i) = (\partial^2 e(\mathbf{p}, u)/\partial p_i \partial p_j)$, which is negative semidefinite because the expenditure function is concave. (See Section A.4 of the Mathematical Appendix.)

(2) *The matrix of substitution terms is symmetric*—since

$$\frac{\partial h_j(\mathbf{p}, u)}{\partial p_i} = \frac{\partial^2 e(\mathbf{p}, u)}{\partial p_i \partial p_j} = \frac{\partial^2 e(\mathbf{p}, u)}{\partial p_j \partial p_i} = \frac{\partial h_i(\mathbf{p}, u)}{\partial p_j}$$

(3) *In particular, "the compensated own price effect is nonpositive"*; that is, the Hicksian demand curves slope downward:

$$\frac{\partial h_i(\mathbf{p}, u)}{\partial p_i} = \frac{\partial^2 e(\mathbf{p}, u)}{\partial p_i^2} \leqq 0$$

since the substitution matrix is negative semidefinite and thus has nonpositive diagonal terms.

These restrictions all concern the Hicksian demand functions, which are not directly observable. However, the Slutsky equation allows to express the derivatives of **h** with respect to **p** as derivatives of **x** with respect to **p** and y, and these are observable. For example, Slutsky's equation and the above remarks yield:

(4) *The matrix* $\left(\frac{\partial x_j(\mathbf{p}, y)}{\partial p_i} + \frac{\partial x_j(\mathbf{p}, y)}{\partial y} x_i\right)$ *is a symmetric, negative semidefinite matrix.*

3.9 DIFFERENTIATING THE FIRST-ORDER CONDITIONS

The Slutsky equation can also be derived by differentiating the first-order condition as in Section 1.14. Since the calculations are a bit tedious, we will only sketch the broad outlines and limit ourselves to the case of two goods.

In this case the first-order conditions take the form:

$$\begin{aligned}
\partial u(x_1(p_1, p_2, y)), x_2(p_1, p_2, y))/\partial x_1 - \lambda p_1 &\equiv 0 \\
\partial u(x_1(p_1, p_2, y)), x_2(p_1, p_2, y))/\partial x_2 - \lambda p_2 &\equiv 0 \\
p_1 x_1(p_1, p_2, y) + p_2 x_2(p_1, p_2, y) - y &\equiv 0
\end{aligned}$$

Differentiating with respect to p_1, and arranging in matrix form, we have:

$$\begin{bmatrix} u_{11} & u_{12} & -p_1 \\ u_{21} & u_{22} & -p_2 \\ -p_1 & -p_2 & 0 \end{bmatrix} \begin{bmatrix} \dfrac{\partial x_1}{\partial p_1} \\ \dfrac{\partial x_2}{\partial p_1} \\ \dfrac{\partial \lambda}{\partial p_1} \end{bmatrix} \equiv \begin{bmatrix} \lambda \\ 0 \\ x_1 \end{bmatrix}$$

Solving for $\partial x_1/\partial p_1$ via Cramer's rule:

$$\frac{\partial x_1}{\partial p_1} = \frac{\begin{vmatrix} \lambda & u_{12} & -p_1 \\ 0 & u_{22} & -p_2 \\ x_1 & -p_2 & 0 \end{vmatrix}}{H} =$$

$$= \lambda \frac{\begin{vmatrix} u_{22} & -p_2 \\ -p_2 & 0 \end{vmatrix}}{H} + x_1 \frac{\begin{vmatrix} u_{12} & -p_1 \\ u_{22} & -p_2 \end{vmatrix}}{H}$$

where H is the determinant of the bordered Hessian.

This is beginning to look a bit like Slutsky's equation already. Note that the first term—which turns out to be the substitution effect—is negative as required. Now go back to the first-order conditions and differentiate them with respect to y. We have:

$$\begin{bmatrix} u_{11} & u_{12} & -p_1 \\ u_{21} & u_{22} & -p_2 \\ -p_1 & -p_2 & 0 \end{bmatrix} \begin{bmatrix} \frac{\partial x_1}{\partial y} \\ \frac{\partial x_2}{\partial y} \\ \frac{\partial \lambda}{\partial y} \end{bmatrix} = \begin{bmatrix} 0 \\ 0 \\ -1 \end{bmatrix}$$

So:

$$\frac{\partial x_1}{\partial y} = -\frac{\begin{vmatrix} u_{12} & -p_1 \\ u_{22} & -p_2 \end{vmatrix}}{H}$$

Substituting into the equation for $\partial x_1/\partial p_1$ derived above we have thc income-effect part of Slutsky's equation. In order to derive the substitution effect we need to set up the expenditure minimization problem and calculate $\partial h_1/\partial p_1$. This calculation is analogous to the calculation of the conditional factor demand functions in Section 1.14. The resulting expression can be shown to be equal to the substitution term in the above equation, which establishes Slutsky's equation.

3.10 THE INTEGRABILITY PROBLEM

We have seen that the utility maximization hypothesis imposes certain observable restrictions on consumer behavior. In particular, we know that the matrix of substitution terms,

$$\left(\frac{\partial h_i(\mathbf{p}, u)}{\partial p_j}\right) = \left(\frac{\partial x_i(\mathbf{p}, y)}{\partial p_j} + \frac{\partial x_i(\mathbf{p}, y)}{\partial y} x_j\right)$$

must be a symmetric, negative semidefinite matrix.

Suppose that we were given a system of demand functions which had a symmetric, negative semidefinite substitution matrix. Is there necessarily a utility function from which these demand functions can be derived? This question is known as "the integrability problem."

Subject to certain technical restrictions, the answer is yes. The basic idea of the argument is as follows.

Let us pick some point $\mathbf{x}^0 = \mathbf{x}(\mathbf{q}, y)$ and arbitrarily assign it utility u^0. How can we construct the expenditure function $e(\mathbf{p}, u^0)$?

If such an expenditure function does exist it certainly must satisfy the system of partial differential equations given by:

$$\frac{\partial e(\mathbf{p}, u^0)}{\partial p_i} = x_i(\mathbf{p}, e(\mathbf{p}, u^0)) \qquad i = 1, \ldots, k$$

and initial condition:

$$e(\mathbf{p}^0, u^0) = \mathbf{p}^0 \cdot \mathbf{x}(\mathbf{p}^0, y^0) = \mathbf{p}^0 \cdot \mathbf{x}^0$$

These equations are just the conditions that the Hicksian demands at utility u are the Marshallian demands at income $e(\mathbf{p}, u)$. Now a fundamental mathematical result, the material in Section A.16 of the Mathematical Appendix, says that a system of partial differential equations of the form

$$\frac{\partial f(\mathbf{p})}{\partial p_i} = g_i(\mathbf{p}) \qquad i = 1, \ldots, k$$

has a solution if and only if

$$\frac{\partial g_i(\mathbf{p})}{\partial p_j} = \frac{\partial g_j(\mathbf{p})}{\partial p_i} \qquad \text{all } i \text{ and } j = 1, \ldots, k$$

Applying this condition to the above problem, we see that it reduces to requiring that the matrix

$$\left(\frac{\partial x_i(\mathbf{p}, y)}{\partial p_j} + \frac{\partial x_i(\mathbf{p}, y)}{\partial y} \frac{\partial e(\mathbf{p}, u)}{\partial p_j}\right)$$

is symmetric. But this is just the Slutsky restriction! Thus the Slutsky restrictions imply that the demand functions can be "integrated" to find an expenditure function which can in turn be used to construct a consistent utility function.

Another necessary condition for the system of partial-differential equations to define a bona-fide expenditure function is that $e(\mathbf{p}, u)$ must be concave in prices. That is, the second derivative matrix of $e(\mathbf{p}, u)$ must be negative semidefinite. But, from above, the second derivative matrix $e(\mathbf{p}, u)$ is simply the Slutsky substitution matrix. If this is negative semidefinite, then the solution to the above partial-differential equations must be concave.

There is a nice trick that will allow us to recover the indirect utility function from demand functions, as well as the expenditure function. Let us refer again to the base point $\mathbf{x}^0 = \mathbf{x}(\mathbf{q}, y)$. Now recalling the definition of the compensation function, we know that:

$$e(\mathbf{p}, u(\mathbf{x}^0)) = e(\mathbf{p}, v(\mathbf{q}, y)) = \mu(\mathbf{p}; \mathbf{q}, y)$$

Substituting this definition into the system of partial-differential equations given above, we have the *integrability equations:*

$$\frac{\partial \mu(\mathbf{p}; \mathbf{q}, y)}{\partial p_i} = x_i(\mathbf{p}, \mu(\mathbf{p}; \mathbf{q}, y)) \qquad i = 1, \cdots, k$$

$$\mu(\mathbf{q}; \mathbf{q}, y) = y$$

A solution to these partial-differential equations is simply a compensation function—a particular indirect utility function—that rationalizes the observed demand behavior $\mathbf{x}(\mathbf{p}, y)$. That is, the solution $\mu(\mathbf{p}; \mathbf{q}, y)$ will be an indirect utility function that will generate $\mathbf{x}(\mathbf{p}, y)$ by Roy's law. We consider several examples below.

Example 3.7 Integrability with Only Two Goods If there are only two goods being consumed, the integrability equations take a very simple form since there is only *one* independent variable, the relative price of the two goods. Similarly, there is only one independent equation since if we know the demand for one good, we can find the demand for the other through the budget constraint.

Let us normalize the price of good 2 to be 1, and write p for the price of the first good and $x(p, y)$ for its demand function. Then the integrability equations become the single equation:

$$\frac{d\mu(p;\, q,\, y)}{dp} = x(p,\, \mu(p;\, q,\, y))$$

$$\mu(p;\, q,\, y) = y$$

This is just an ordinary differential equation with boundary condition which can be solved using standard techniques.

For example, suppose that we have a log-linear demand function:

$$ln\ x = a\ ln\ p + b\ ln\ y + c$$

$$x = p^a y^b e^c$$

The integrability equations become:

$$\frac{d\mu(p;\, q,\, y)}{dp} = p^a e^c \mu^b$$

Or,

$$\mu^{-b} \frac{d\mu(p;\, q,\, y)}{dp} = p^a e^c$$

Integrating we have:

$$\int_p^q \mu^{-b} \frac{\partial \mu}{\partial t}\, dt = e^c \int_p^q t^a dt$$

$$\left.\frac{\mu^{1-b}}{1-b}\right]_p^q = e^c \left[\frac{q^{a+1} - p^{a+1}}{a+1}\right]$$

for $b \neq 1$. Solving this equation gives:

$$\frac{y^{1-b} - \mu(p;\, q,\, y)^{1-b}}{1-b} = e^c \left[\frac{q^{a+1} - p^{a+1}}{a+1}\right]$$

or:

$$\mu(p;\, q,\, y) = \left[y^{1-b} + \frac{(b-1)}{(1+a)} e^c [q^{a+1} - p^{a+1}]\right]^{\frac{1}{1-b}}$$

Example 3.8 Integrability with Several Goods We now consider a case where there are three goods and thus two independent demand equations. For definiteness consider the Cobb-Douglas system:

$$x_1 = a_1 y / p_1 \qquad x_2 = a_2 y / p_2$$

We verified earlier that this system satisfies Slutsky symmetry so that we know that the integrability equations will have a solution. We simply have to solve the following system of partial-differential equations:

$$\frac{\partial \mu}{\partial p_1} = \frac{a_1 \mu}{p_1}$$

$$\frac{\partial \mu}{\partial p_2} = \frac{a_2 \mu}{p_2}$$

$$\mu(q_1, q_2; q_1, q_2, y) = y$$

The first equation implies that:

$$\ln \mu = a_1 \ln p_1 + C_1$$

for some constant of integration C_1, and the second equation implies that:

$$\ln \mu = a_2 \ln p_2 + C_2$$

So it is natural to look for a solution of the form:

$$\ln \mu = a_1 \ln p_1 + a_2 \ln p_2 + C_3$$

where C_3 is independent of p_1 and p_2.

Substituting into the boundary condition we have:

$$\ln \mu(\mathbf{q}; \mathbf{q}, y) = \ln y = a_1 \ln q_1 + a_2 \ln q_2 + C_3$$

Solving this equation for C_3 and substituting into the proposed solution, we have:

$$\ln \mu(\mathbf{p}; \mathbf{q}, y) = a_1 \ln p_1 + a_2 \ln p_2 - a_1 \ln q_1 - a_2 \ln q_2 + \ln y$$

which is indeed the compensation function for the Cobb-Douglas utility function.

3.11 DUALITY IN CONSUMPTION

We have seen how one can recover an indirect utility function from observed demand functions by solving the integrability equations. The question arises as to how we can then solve for the direct utility function.

The answer exhibits quite nicely the duality between direct and indirect utility functions. It is most convenient to describe the calculations in terms of the normalized indirect utility function, where we have prices divided by income so that expenditure is identically one. Thus the normalized indirect utility function is given by:

$$v(\mathbf{p}) = \max_{\mathbf{x}} \quad u(\mathbf{x})$$
$$\text{s.t.} \quad \mathbf{px} = 1$$

If we are given the indirect utility function $v(\mathbf{p})$, we can find the direct utility function by solving the following problem:

$$u(\mathbf{x}) = \min_{\mathbf{p}} \quad v(\mathbf{p})$$
$$\text{s.t.} \quad \mathbf{px} = 1$$

The proof is straightforward. Let $\mathbf{x}(\mathbf{p})$ be the demanded bundle at the prices $\mathbf{p}$. Then by definition $v(\mathbf{p}) = u(\mathbf{x}(\mathbf{p}))$. Let $\mathbf{p}'$ be any other price vector that satisfies the budget constraint so that $\mathbf{p}'\mathbf{x} = 1$. Then since $\mathbf{x}(\mathbf{p})$ is always a *feasible* choice at the prices $\mathbf{p}'$, the utility-maximizing choice must yield utility at least as great as the utility yielded by $\mathbf{x}(\mathbf{p})$; that is, $v(\mathbf{p}') \geqslant u(\mathbf{x}(\mathbf{p})) = v(\mathbf{p})$. Hence, the minimum of the indirect utility function over all $\mathbf{p}$'s that satisfies the budget constraint gives us the utility function.

The argument is depicted in Figure 3.13 below. Any price vector $\mathbf{p}$ that satisfies the budget constraint $\mathbf{px} = \mathbf{px}^\circ$ must yield a higher utility than $u(\mathbf{x}^\circ)$, which is simply to say that $u(\mathbf{x}^\circ)$ solves the minimization problem posed above.

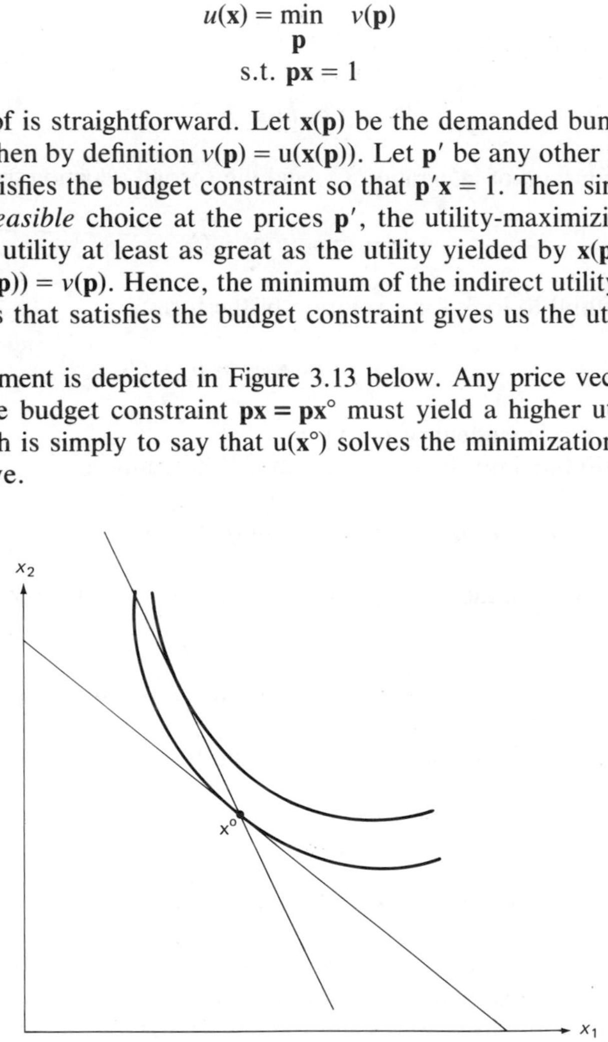

Fig. 3.13 *Solving for the Direct Utility Function*

Example 3.9 Solving for the Direct Utility Function Suppose that we have a normalized indirect utility function given by $v(p_1, p_2) = -a \ln p_1 - b \ln p_2$. What is its associated direct utility function? We set up the minimization problem:

$$\min_{p_1, p_2} \quad -a \ln p_1 - b \ln p_2$$
$$\text{s.t. } p_1 x_1 + p_2 x_2 = 1$$

The first-order conditions are:

$$-a/p_1 = \lambda\, x_1$$
$$-b/p_2 = \lambda\, x_2$$

Or:

$$-a = \lambda\, p_1 x_1$$
$$-b = \lambda\, p_2 x_2$$

Adding together and using the budget constraint:

$$\lambda = -a - b$$

Substitute back into the first-order conditions to find:

$$p_1 = \frac{a}{(a+b)x_1}$$
$$p_2 = \frac{b}{(a+b)x_1}$$

These are the choices of (p_1, p_2) that minimize indirect utility. Now substitute these choices into the indirect utility function:

$$u(x_1, x_2) = -a \ln \frac{a}{(a+b)x_1} - b \ln \frac{b}{(a+b)x_2}$$
$$= a \ln x_1 + b \ln x_2 + \text{constant}$$

This is the familiar Cobb-Douglas utility function.

3.12 REVEALED PREFERENCE

In our study of consumer behavior we have taken preferences as the primitive concept and derived the restrictions that the utility maximization model imposes on the observed demand functions. These restrictions are basically the Slutsky restrictions that the matrix of substitution terms be symmetric and negative semidefinite.

These restrictions are in principle observable, but in practice they leave something to be desired. After all, who has really seen a demand function? The best that we may hope for in practice is a list of the choices made under different circumstances. For example, we may have some observations on consumer behavior that take the form of a list of prices, $\mathbf{p}^i$, and the associated chosen consumption bundles, $\mathbf{x}^i$. How can we tell whether these data could have been generated by a utility-maximizing consumer?

We will say that a utility function *rationalizes* the observed behavior $(\mathbf{p}^i, \mathbf{x}^i)$ $i = 1, \cdots, n$ if $u(\mathbf{x}^i) \geq u(\mathbf{x})$ for all $\mathbf{x}$ such that $\mathbf{p}^i\mathbf{x}^i \geq \mathbf{p}^i\mathbf{x}$. That is, $u(\mathbf{x})$ rationalizes the observed behavior if it achieves its maximum value on the budget set at the chosen bundles. Suppose, first, that the data were generated by such a maximization process. What can we infer about the relationship among the various observations?

First, we note that if $\mathbf{p}^i\mathbf{x}^i \geq \mathbf{p}^i\mathbf{x}$, then it must be the case that $u(\mathbf{x}^i) \geq u(\mathbf{x})$. Since $\mathbf{x}^i$ was chosen when $\mathbf{x}$ could have been chosen, the utility of $\mathbf{x}^i$ must be at least as large as the utility of $\mathbf{x}$. In this case we will say that $\mathbf{x}^i$ is *directly revealed preferred* to x, and write $\mathbf{x}^i \; R^0 \; \mathbf{x}$.

Note that as a consequence of this definition and the assumption that the data were generated by utility maximization, we can conclude that "$\mathbf{x}^i \; R^0 \; \mathbf{x}$ implies $u(\mathbf{x}^i) \geq u(\mathbf{x})$."

Now suppose that we have a sequence of such revealed preference comparisons such that $\mathbf{x}^i \; R^o \; \mathbf{x}^j$, $\mathbf{x}^j \; R^0 \; \mathbf{x}^k$, $\cdots$, $\mathbf{x}^n \; R^0 \; \mathbf{x}$. In this case we will say that $\mathbf{x}^i$ is *revealed preferred* to $\mathbf{x}$ and write $\mathbf{x}^i \; R \; \mathbf{x}$. The relation R is sometimes called the "transitive closure" of the relation R^0.

Just as above, if we assume that the data were generated by utility maximization, we can conclude that "$\mathbf{x}^i \; R \; \mathbf{x}$ implies $u(\mathbf{x}^i) \geq \mathrm{u}(\mathbf{x})$."

Up until now we have imposed no restrictions at all on the utility function $u(\mathbf{x})$ or the underlying preferences that it represents. Let us now assume that $u(\mathbf{x})$ is locally nonsatiated. It is not hard to show that this implies that $\mathbf{p}^i\mathbf{x}^i > \mathbf{p}^i\mathbf{x}$ implies that $u(\mathbf{x}^i) > u(\mathbf{x})$. For we know from the above argument that $u(\mathbf{x}^i) \geq u(\mathbf{x})$; if $u(\mathbf{x}^i) = u(\mathbf{x})$, then there would exist some other $\mathbf{x}'$ close enough to $\mathbf{x}$ so that $\mathbf{p}^i\mathbf{x}^i > \mathbf{p}^i\mathbf{x}'$ and $u(\mathbf{x}') > u(\mathbf{x}) = u(\mathbf{x}^i)$. This contradicts that hypothesis of utility maximization.

If $\mathbf{p}^i\mathbf{x}^i > \mathbf{p}^i\mathbf{x}$, we will say that $\mathbf{x}^i$ is *strictly directly revealed preferred* to $\mathbf{x}$ and write $\mathbf{x}^i \; P^0 \; \mathbf{x}$. We are now in a position to state the fundamental result of this section:

GENERALIZED AXIOM OF REVEALED PREFERENCE (GARP) *If* $\mathbf{x}^i$ *is revealed preferred to* $\mathbf{x}^j$*, then* $\mathbf{x}^j$ *cannot be strictly directly revealed preferred to* $\mathbf{x}^i$*.*

Using the symbols defined above, we have:

$$\text{GARP: } \mathbf{x}^i \; R \; \mathbf{x}^j \textit{ implies not } \mathbf{x}^j \; P^0 \; \mathbf{x}^i$$

GARP is an observable consequence of utility maximization. But does it contain all the implications of that model? If some data satisfy this axiom, is it necessarily true that it must come from utility maximization, or at least be thought of in that way? Is GARP a *sufficient* condition for utility maximization?

It turns out that it is. If a finite set of data is consistent with GARP, then there exists a utility function that rationalizes the observed behavior—i.e., there exists a utility function that could have generated that behavior. Hence, GARP exhausts the list of restrictions imposed by the maximization model.

There are a number of alternative formulations of revealed preference axioms that are related to GARP. Two worthy of special note are:

(1) *Weak Axiom of Revealed Preference (WARP).* If $\mathbf{x}^i \; R^0 \; \mathbf{x}^j$ and $\mathbf{x}^i$ is not equal to $\mathbf{x}^j$, then it is not the case that $\mathbf{x}^j \; R^0 \; \mathbf{x}^i$.

(2) *Strong Axiom of Revealed Preference (SARP).* If $\mathbf{x}^i \; R \; \mathbf{x}^j$ and $\mathbf{x}^i$ is not equal to $\mathbf{x}^j$, then it is not the case that $\mathbf{x}^j \; R \; \mathbf{x}^i$.

Each of these axioms implies that there is a *unique* demanded bundle at each budget, while GARP allows for multiple demanded bundles. Thus, GARP allows for flat spots in the indifference curves that might have generated the observed behavior. Both WARP and SARP are necessary conditions for utility maximization in the case of single-valued demands, but only SARP is sufficient in this case. However, it is worth nothing that if demands are single-valued and there are only *two* goods, then WARP is a necessary and sufficient condition for utility maximization. (This last result is not so easy to prove.)

3.13 COMPARATIVE STATICS FROM REVEALED PREFERENCE

Since GARP is a necessary and sufficient condition for utility maximization, it should imply the comparative statics results derived earlier. These include the Slutsky decomposition of a price change into the income and the substitution effects and the fact that the own substitution effect is negative.

Let us begin with the latter. When we consider finite changes in a price rather than just infinitesimal changes, there are two possible definitions of the compensated demand. The first definition is the natural extension of our earlier definition—namely, the demand for the good in question if we change the level of income so as to restore the prechange level of utility. That is, the value of the compensated demand for good i when prices change from $\mathbf{p}$ to $\mathbf{p} + \Delta\mathbf{p}$ is just $x_i(\mathbf{p} + \Delta\mathbf{p}, y + \Delta y) \equiv x_i(\mathbf{p} + \Delta\mathbf{p}, e(\mathbf{p} + \Delta\mathbf{p}, u))$, where u is the original level of utility achieved at $(\mathbf{p}\ y)$. This notion of compensation is known as the *Hicksian compensation.* The second notion of compensated demand when prices change from $\mathbf{p}$ to $\mathbf{p} + \Delta\mathbf{p}$ is known as the *Slutsky compensation.* It is the level of demand that arises when income is changed so as to make the prechange level of *consumption* possible. This is easily described by the following equations. We want the change in income, Δy, necessary to allow for the old level of consumption, $\mathbf{x}(\mathbf{p}, y)$, to be feasible at the new prices, $\mathbf{p} + \Delta\mathbf{p}$. That is:

$$(\mathbf{p} + \Delta\mathbf{p})\mathbf{x}(\mathbf{p}, y) = y + \Delta y$$

Since $\mathbf{p}\ \mathbf{x}(\mathbf{p}, y) = y$, this reduces to $\Delta\mathbf{p}\ \mathbf{x}(\mathbf{p}, y) = \Delta y$.

The difference between the two notions of compensation is illustrated in Figure 3.14. Here x^h measures the Hicksian compensated level of demand, and x^s measures the Slutsky compensated level of demand. The Slutsky notion is directly measurable without knowledge of the preferences, but the Hicksian notion is more convenient for analytic work.

For infinitesimal changes in price there is no need to distinguish between the two concepts since they coincide. We can prove this simply

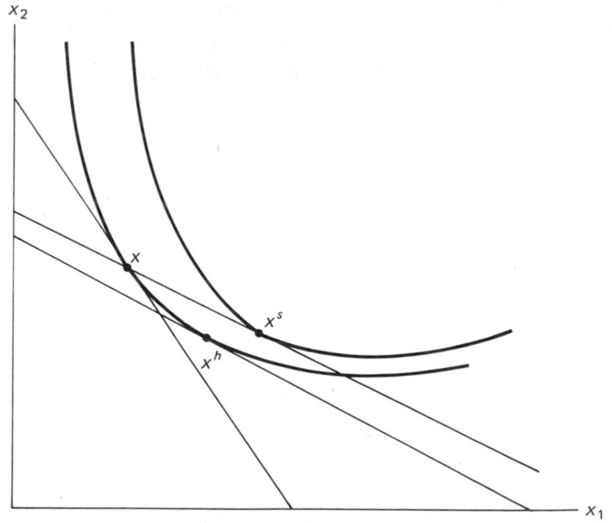

Fig. 3.14 *Hicks and Slutsky Compensation*

by examining the expenditure function. If the price of good j changes by dp_j, we need to change expenditure by $(\partial e(\mathbf{p}, u)/\partial p_j)\, dp_j$ to keep utility constant. If we want to keep the old level of consumption feasible, we need to change income by $x_j\, dp_j$. By the derivative property of the expenditure function, these two magnitudes are the same.

Whichever definition you prefer, we can still use revealed preference to prove that "the compensated own price effect is negative." Suppose we consider the Hicksian definition. We start with a price vector $\mathbf{p}$ and let $\mathbf{x} = \mathbf{x}(\mathbf{p}, y)$ be the demanded bundle. The price vector changes to $\mathbf{p} + \Delta\mathbf{p}$, and the compensated demand, therefore, changes to $\mathbf{x}(\mathbf{p} + \Delta\mathbf{p}, y + \Delta y)$, where Δy is the amount necessary to make $\mathbf{x}(\mathbf{p} + \Delta\mathbf{p}, y + \Delta y)$ indifferent to $\mathbf{x}(\mathbf{p}, y)$.

Since $\mathbf{x}(\mathbf{p}, y)$ and $\mathbf{x}(\mathbf{p} + \Delta\mathbf{p}, y + \Delta y)$ are indifferent to each other, neither can be strictly directly revealed preferred to the other. That is, we must have:

$$\mathbf{p}\,\mathbf{x}(\mathbf{p},y) \leq \mathbf{p}\,\mathbf{x}\,(\mathbf{p}+\Delta\mathbf{p}, y+\Delta y)$$

$$(\mathbf{p} + \Delta\mathbf{p})\mathbf{x}(\mathbf{p} + \Delta\mathbf{p}, y + \Delta y) \leq (\mathbf{p} + \Delta\mathbf{p})\mathbf{x}(\mathbf{p}, y)$$

Adding these inequalities together we have:

$$\Delta\mathbf{p}[\mathbf{x}(\mathbf{p} + \Delta\mathbf{p}, y + \Delta y) - \mathbf{x}(\mathbf{p},y)] \leq 0$$

Or, letting $\Delta\mathbf{x} = \mathbf{x}(\mathbf{p} + \Delta\mathbf{p}, y + \Delta y) - \mathbf{x}(\mathbf{p}, y)$:

$$\Delta\mathbf{p}\;\Delta\mathbf{x} \leq 0$$

Suppose that only one price has changed so that $\Delta\mathbf{p} = (0, \cdots, \Delta p_i, \cdots, 0)$. Then this inequality implies that x_i must change in the opposite direction.

We now turn to the Hicksian definition. We keep the same notation as before, but now interpret Δy as the change in income necessary to make the old consumption bundle feasible. Since $\mathbf{x}(\mathbf{p}, y)$ is thus by hypothesis a feasible level of consumption at $\mathbf{p} + \Delta\mathbf{p}$, the bundle actually chosen at $\mathbf{p} + \Delta\mathbf{p}$ cannot be revealed worse than $\mathbf{x}(\mathbf{p}, y)$. That is,

$$\mathbf{p}\,\mathbf{x}(\mathbf{p}, y) \leq \mathbf{p}\,\mathbf{x}(\mathbf{p} + \Delta\mathbf{p}, y + \Delta y)$$

Since $(\mathbf{p} + \Delta\mathbf{p})\mathbf{x}(\mathbf{p} + \Delta\mathbf{p}, y + \Delta y) = (\mathbf{p} + \Delta\mathbf{p})\mathbf{x}(\mathbf{p}, y)$ by construction of Δy, we can subtract this equality from the above inequality to find:

$$\Delta\mathbf{p}\;\Delta\mathbf{x} \leq 0$$

just as before.

Let us now consider the Slutsky equation. We derived this equation earlier by differentiating an identity involving Hicksian and Marshallian demands. We start here by writing the following arithmetic identity:

$$x_i(\mathbf{p} + \mathbf{\Delta p}, y) - x_i(\mathbf{p}, y) = x_i(\mathbf{p} + \mathbf{\Delta p}, y + \Delta y) - x_i(\mathbf{p}, y) - [x_i(\mathbf{p} + \mathbf{\Delta p}, y + \Delta y) - x_i(\mathbf{p} + \mathbf{\Delta p}, y)]$$

Suppose that $\mathbf{\Delta p} = (0, \cdot\ \cdot, \Delta p_j, \cdot\ \cdot, 0)$. Then the compensating change in income—in the Slutsky sense—is $\Delta y = \Delta p_j x_j$. If we divide each side of the above identity by Δp_j and use the fact that $\Delta p_j = \Delta y / x_j$, we have

$$\frac{x_i(\mathbf{p} + \mathbf{\Delta p}, y) - x_i(\mathbf{p}, y)}{\Delta p_j} = \frac{x_i(\mathbf{p} + \mathbf{\Delta p}, y + \Delta y) - x_i(\mathbf{p}, y)}{\Delta p_j} - x_j \frac{[x_i(\mathbf{p} + \mathbf{\Delta p}, y + \Delta y) - x_i(\mathbf{p} + \mathbf{\Delta p}, y)]}{\Delta y}$$

Or,

$$\frac{\Delta x_i}{\Delta p_j} = \left.\frac{\Delta x_i}{\Delta p_j}\right|_{\text{comp}} - x_j \frac{\Delta x_i}{\Delta y}$$

Note that this last equation is simply a discrete analog of the Slutsky equation. The term on the lefthand side is how the demand for good i changes as price j changes. This is decomposed into the substitution effect—how the demand for i changes when price j changes and income is also changed so as to keep the original level of consumption possible—and the income effect—how the demand for good i changes when prices are held constant but income changes times the demand for good j.

3.14 SEPARABLE UTILITY FUNCTIONS

In many circumstances it is reasonable to model consumer choice by certain "partial" or "conditional" maximization problems. For example, we may want to model the consumer's choice of various types of meat while taking the consumption of other sorts of goods as given. Thus, we can focus our inquiry on the types of consumption of most immediate interest rather than attempting to model the entire consumption decision involved.

In order to describe some useful results concerning this kind of separability, we will have to introduce some new notation. Let us think of partitioning the consumption bundle into two "subbundles" so that the consumption bundle takes the form $(\mathbf{x}, \mathbf{z})$. We partition the price vector analogously into $(\mathbf{p}, \mathbf{q})$.

There are two situations under which the demand behavior of the consumer can be decomposed into smaller problems. The first condition is known as *Hicksian separability*. Suppose that the price vector $\mathbf{q}$ is always proportional to some fixed vector $\mathbf{q}^0$ so that $\mathbf{q} = t\mathbf{q}^0$ for some scalar t. Then the utility maximization problem of the consumer can be written as:

$$v(\mathbf{p}, t, y) = \max \quad u(\mathbf{x}, \mathbf{z})$$
$$\text{s.t.} \quad \mathbf{px} + t\mathbf{q}^0\mathbf{z} = y$$

Since the prices of the z goods move proportionally to $\mathbf{q}^0$, we have written the indirect utility function as depending only on the scalar t. It is straightforward to check that this indirect utility function has all the usual properties. A simple application of the envelope theorem shows that the derivative of $v(\mathbf{p}, t, y)$ with respect to t divided by the marginal utility of income gives us the optimal choice of $\mathbf{q}^0\mathbf{z}$. That is, a version of Roy's law holds.

It is natural to think of the quantity $\mathbf{q}^0\mathbf{z}$ as a kind of a "composite commodity." The price of this composite commodity is, of course, t. The demands for the other goods—the x goods—will depend on only $\mathbf{p}$, y and t.

We can solve for the direct utility function that is dual to $v(\mathbf{p}, t, y)$ by the usual calculation:

$$u(\mathbf{x}, Z) = \min \quad v(\mathbf{p}, t, y)$$
$$\text{s.t.} \quad \mathbf{p}x + tZ = y$$

where $Z = \mathbf{q}^0\mathbf{z}$.

Or, if more convenient, we can define $u(\mathbf{x}, Z)$ by the following maximization problem:

$$u(\mathbf{x}, Z) = \max \quad u(\mathbf{x}, \mathbf{z})$$
$$\text{s.t.} \quad \mathbf{q}^0\mathbf{z} = Z$$

We can think of the demands for the x goods as being generated by maximizing $u(\mathbf{x}, Z)$ and interpret the Z good as a Hicksian composite commodity.

In practice, we usually think of the composite commodity as being "all other goods"—other than the ones we are interested in at the time—and think of its price as being some version of a consumer price index. Hence, the demand function for the $\mathbf{x}$ goods can be thought of as depending on only $\mathbf{p}$, y and t; since demand is homogeneous of degree zero, we can write this as $\mathbf{x}(\mathbf{p}/t, y/t)$. This gives the standard specification that for some category of goods demand depends on "real price" and "real income."

The second case in which we can decompose the consumer's consumption decision is known as the case of *functional separability*.

Let us suppose that the underlying preference ordering has the property that:

$$(\mathbf{x}, \mathbf{z}) \succ (\mathbf{x}', \mathbf{z}) \text{ if and only if } (\mathbf{x}, \mathbf{z}'') \succ (\mathbf{x}', \mathbf{z}'')$$

for all $\mathbf{x}$, $\mathbf{x}'$, $\mathbf{z}$ and $\mathbf{z}''$. That is, if $\mathbf{x}$ is preferred to $\mathbf{x}'$ for some choice of the other goods, then $\mathbf{x}$ is preferred to $\mathbf{x}'$ for all choices of the other goods. Or, even more succinctly, the preferences over the $\mathbf{x}$ goods are independent of the $\mathbf{z}$ goods.

If this "independence" property is satisfied and the preferences are locally nonsatiated, then it can be shown that the utility function for $\mathbf{x}$ and $\mathbf{z}$ can be written in the form $u(v(\mathbf{x}), \mathbf{z})$, where $u(v, \mathbf{z})$ is an increasing function of v. That is, the overall utility from $\mathbf{x}$ and $\mathbf{z}$ can be written as a function of the *subutility* of $\mathbf{x}$ and the level of consumption of $\mathbf{z}$.

We will say that in this case the utility function is (*weakly*) *separable*. What does separability imply about the structure of the utility maximization problem? As usual, we will write the demand function for the goods as $\mathbf{x}(\mathbf{p},\mathbf{q}, y)$ and $\mathbf{z}(\mathbf{p}, \mathbf{q}, y)$. Then, if the overall utility function is weakly separable, the optimal choice of $\mathbf{x}$ can be found by solving the following problem:

$$\begin{aligned} \max \quad & v(\mathbf{x}) \\ \text{s.t.} \quad & \mathbf{px} = \mathbf{px}(\mathbf{p}, \mathbf{q}, \mathbf{y}) \end{aligned}$$

Thus, if we know the *expenditure* on the $\mathbf{x}$ goods, $y^x = \mathbf{px}(\mathbf{p}, \mathbf{q}, y)$, we can solve the subutility maximization problem to determine the optimal choice of the $\mathbf{x}$ goods. In other words, the demand function for the $\mathbf{x}$ goods can be written as a function of the prices $\mathbf{p}$ and the expenditure y^x: $\mathbf{x}(\mathbf{p}, \mathbf{q}, y) = \mathbf{x}(\mathbf{p}, y^x)$.

The proof of this is straightforward. Assume that $\mathbf{x}(\mathbf{p}, \mathbf{q}, y)$ does not solve the above problem. Instead, let $\mathbf{x}'$ be another value of $\mathbf{x}$ that satisfies the budget constraint and yields strictly greater subutility. Then the bundle $(\mathbf{x}', \mathbf{z})$ would give higher overall utility than $(\mathbf{x}(\mathbf{p}, \mathbf{q}, y), \mathbf{z}(\mathbf{p}, \mathbf{q}, y))$, which contradicts the definition of the demand function.

The demand functions $\mathbf{x}(\mathbf{p}, y^x)$ are sometimes known as *conditional demand functions* since they give demand for the $\mathbf{x}$ goods conditional on the level of expenditure on these goods. Thus, for example, we may consider the demand for beef as a function of the prices of beef, pork, and lamb and the total expenditure on meat.

How is this level of expenditure itself determined? In general it will depend on all prices and total income. But in certain cases it might depend on these variables in special and convenient ways.

Suppose, for example, that the subutility function $v(\mathbf{x})$ was homothetic. In this case we know that we can write the indirect utility from the submaximization problem as $\nu(\mathbf{p})y^x$. Then the overall maximization problem takes the form:

$$\begin{array}{ll} \max & u(\nu(\mathbf{p})y^x, \mathbf{z}) \\ \text{s.t.} & y^x + \mathbf{qz} = y \end{array}$$

Let us define a new scalar variable $X = \nu(\mathbf{p})y^x$. Then we can substitute this definition into the above problem to find:

$$\begin{array}{ll} \max & u(X, \mathbf{z}) \\ \text{s.t.} & (1/\nu(\mathbf{p}))X + \mathbf{qz} = y \end{array}$$

We can interpret the new variable X to be a kind of composite commodity whose price is given by the "price index" $1/\nu(\mathbf{p})$. Thus, we can think of the consumption decision as taking place in two stages: first the consumer considers how much of the composite commodity (meat) to consume as a function of a price index of meat; then the consumer considers how much beef to consume given the prices of the various sorts of meat and the total expenditure on meat. Such a two-stage budgeting process is very convenient in applied demand analysis.

3.15 CONTINUITY OF DEMAND FUNCTION

Up until now we have blithely been assuming that the demand functions we have been analyzing are nicely behaved; that is, that they are continuous and even differentiable functions. Are these assumptions justifiable?

Referring to the theorem of the maximum in Section A.10 of the Mathematical Appendix we see that, as long as the demand functions are well defined, they will be continuous, at least when $\mathbf{p} \gg 0$ and $y > 0$; that is, as long as $\mathbf{x}(\mathbf{p}, y)$ is the *unique* maximizing bundle at prices $\mathbf{p}$ and income y, then demand will vary continuously with $\mathbf{p}$ and y.

If we want to ensure that demand is continuous for all $\mathbf{p} \gg 0$ and $y > 0$, then we need to ensure that demand is always unique. The condition we need is that of strict convexity.

PROPOSITION *If preferences are strictly convex, then for each* $\mathbf{p} \gg 0$ *there is a unique bundle* $\mathbf{x}$ *that maximizes* u *on the consumer's budget set,* B($\mathbf{p}$, y).

PROOF Suppose $\mathbf{x}'$ and $\mathbf{x}''$ both maximize u on $B(\mathbf{p}, y)$. Then $\frac{1}{2}\mathbf{x}' + \frac{1}{2}\mathbf{x}''$ is also in $B(\mathbf{p}, y)$ and is strictly preferred to $\mathbf{x}'$ and $\mathbf{x}''$, which is a contradiction. □

Loosely speaking, if demand functions are well defined and everywhere continuous and are derived from preference maximization, then the underlying preferences must be strictly convex. If not, there would be some point of discontinuity, as illustrated in Figure 3.15.

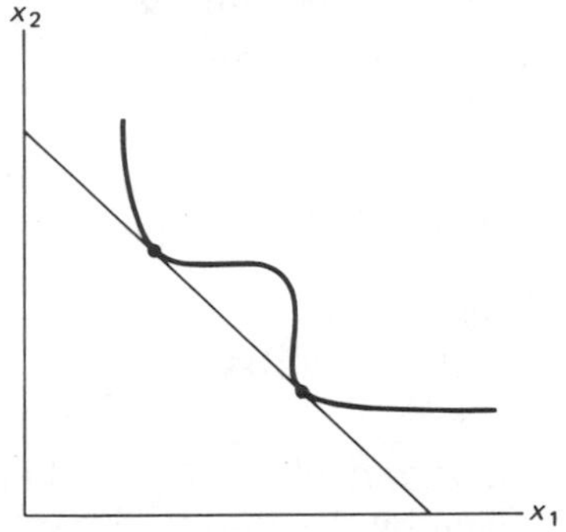

Fig. 3.15 *Discontinuous Demand due to Nonconvex Preferences*

Note that, in the case depicted in Figure 3.13, a small change in the price brings about a large change in the demanded bundles: the demand "function" is discontinuous. (For completeness, we have also provided a self-contained proof that convexity implies continuity in Appendix 2 at the end of this chapter.)

3.16 AGGREGATE CONSUMER DEMAND

We have studied the properties of a neoclassical consumer's demand function, $\mathbf{x}(\mathbf{p}, y)$. Now let us consider some collection of n consumers, each of whom has a demand function for some k commodities, $\mathbf{x}_i(\mathbf{p}, y_1) = (x_i^1(\mathbf{p}, y_i), \cdots, x_i^k(\mathbf{p}, y_i))$ for $i = 1, \cdots, n$. (Note that we have changed our notation slightly: goods are now indicated by superscripts while consumers are indicated by subscripts.) The aggregate demand function is defined to be $\mathbf{X}(\mathbf{p}, y_1, \cdots, y_n) = \sum_{i=1}^{n} \mathbf{x}_i(\mathbf{p}, y_i)$. Thus, the aggregate demand for good j would just be denoted by $X^j(\mathbf{p}, \mathbf{y})$ where $\mathbf{y}$ denotes the vector of incomes $(y_1, \cdots, y_n)$.

The aggregate demand function inherits certain properties of the individual demand functions. For example, if the individual demand functions are continuous, the aggregate demand function will certainly be continuous.

Continuity of the individual demand functions is a sufficient but not necessary condition for continuity of the aggregate demand functions. For example, consider the demand for washing machines. It seems reasonable to suppose that most consumers want one and only one washing machine. Hence, the demand function for an individual consumer i would look like the function depicted in Figure 3.16.

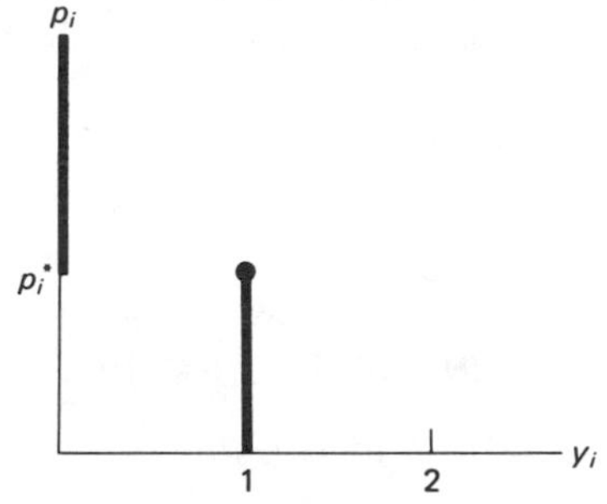

Fig. 3.16 *Demand for a Discrete Commodity*

The price p_i^* is called the ith consumer's *reservation price*. If consumers' incomes and tastes vary, we would expect to see several different reservation prices. The aggregate demand for washing machines would be given by

$$X(p) = \text{number of consumers whose reservation price is greater than or equal to } p$$

If there are a lot of consumers with dispersed reservation prices it would make sense to think of this as a continuous function: if the price goes up by a small amount, only a few of the consumers—the "marginal" consumers—will decide to stop buying the good. Even though their demand changes discontinuously, the *aggregate* demand will change only by a small amount.

What other properties does the aggregate demand function inherit from the individual demands? Is there an aggregate version of Slutsky's equation or of the Strong Axiom of Revealed Preference? Unfortunately, the answer to these questions is no. In fact the aggregate demand function will in general possess no interesting properties other than homogeneity and continuity. Hence, the neoclassical theory of the consumer places no restrictions on aggregate behavior in general.

However, in certain cases it may happen that the aggregate behavior may look as though it were generated by a single "representative" consumer. Below, we consider a circumstance where this may happen.

Suppose that all individual consumers' indirect utility functions take the *Gorman form:*

$$v_i(\mathbf{p}, y_i) = a_i(\mathbf{p}) + b(\mathbf{p})y_i$$

Note that the $a_i(\mathbf{p})$ term can differ from consumer to consumer, but the $b(\mathbf{p})$ term is assumed to be identical for all consumers. By Roy's law the demand function for good j of consumer i will then take the form:

$$x_i^j(\mathbf{p}, y^i) = A_i^j(\mathbf{p}) + B^j(\mathbf{p})y_i$$

where:

$$A_i^j(\mathbf{p}) = [\partial a_i(\mathbf{p})/\partial p_j]/b(\mathbf{p})$$

$$B^j(\mathbf{p}) = [\partial b(\mathbf{p})/\partial p_j]/b(\mathbf{p})$$

Note that the marginal propensity to consume good j—$\partial x_i^j(\mathbf{p}, y_i)/\partial y_i$—is independent of the level of income of any consumer and also constant across consumers since $b(\mathbf{p})$ is constant across consumers. The aggregate demand for good j will then take the form:

$$X^j(\mathbf{p}, y^1, \cdots, y^n) = \sum_{i=1}^{n} [\partial a_i/\partial p_j]/b(\mathbf{p}) + [\partial b(p)/\partial p_j]/b(\mathbf{p})] \sum_{i=1}^{n} y_i$$

This demand function can in fact be rationalized by a representative consumer. His representative indirect utility function is given by:

$$V(\mathbf{p}, Y) = \sum_{i=1}^{n} a_i(\mathbf{p}) + b(\mathbf{p})Y$$

where $Y = \sum_{i=1}^{n} y_i$.

The proof is simply to apply Roy's identity to this indirect utility function and to note that it yields the demand function given above. In fact it can be shown that the Gorman form is the most general form of the indirect utility function that will allow for aggregation in the sense of the representative consumer model. Hence, the Gorman form is not only *sufficient* for the representative consumer model to hold, but it is also *necessary*.

Although a complete proof of this fact is detailed, the following argument is reasonably convincing. Suppose, for the sake of simplicity, that there are only two consumers. Then by hypothesis the aggregate demand for good j can be written as:

$$X^j(\mathbf{p}, y_1 + y_2) \equiv x_1^j(\mathbf{p}, y_1) + x_2^j(\mathbf{p}, y_2)$$

If we first differentiate with respect to y_1 and then with respect to y_2, we find:

$$\partial X^j(\mathbf{p}, Y)/\partial Y \equiv \partial x_1^j(\mathbf{p}, y_1)/\partial y_1 \equiv \partial x_2^j(\mathbf{p}, y_2)/\partial y_2$$

Hence, the marginal propensity to consume good j must be the same for all consumers. If we differentiate this expression once more with respect to y_1, we find that:

$$\partial^2 X^j(\mathbf{p}, Y)/\partial Y^2 \equiv \partial^2 x_1^j(\mathbf{p}, y_1)/\partial y_1^2 \equiv 0$$

Thus, consumer 1's demand for good j—and, therefore, consumer 2's demand—is affine in income. Hence, the demand functions for good j take the form $x_i^j(\mathbf{p}, y_i) = A_i^j(\mathbf{p}) + B^j(\mathbf{p})y_i$. If this is true for all goods, the indirect utility function for each consumer must have the Gorman form.

3.17 INVERSE DEMAND FUNCTIONS

In many applications it is of interest to express demand behavior by describing prices as a function of quantities. That is, given some vector of goods $\mathbf{x}$, we would like to find a vector of prices $\mathbf{p}$ and an income y at which $\mathbf{x}$ would be the demanded bundle.

First, we note that we can simplify this problem by *fixing* the level of income at some predetermined value since all that matters for demand behavior are the values of prices relative to income. The most convenient choice is $y = 1$.

Now the first-order conditions for the utility maximization problem are simply:

$$\frac{\partial u(\mathbf{x})}{\partial x_i} - \lambda p_i = 0$$

$$\sum_{i=1}^{k} p_i x_i = 1$$

Multiply each of the first set of equalities by x_i and sum them over the number of goods to get:

$$\sum_{i=1}^{k} \frac{\partial u(\mathbf{x})}{\partial x_i} x_i - \lambda \sum_{i=1}^{k} p_i x_i = 0$$

Substitute the value of λ back into the first expression to find **p** as function of *x:*

$$p_i = \frac{\dfrac{\partial u(\mathbf{x})}{\partial x_i}}{\displaystyle\sum_{j=1}^{k} \frac{\partial u(\mathbf{x})}{\partial x_j} x_j}$$

Given any vector of demands **x,** we can use this expression to find the price vector **p**(**x**) which will satisfy the necessary conditions for maximization. If the utility function is quasi-concave so that these necessary conditions are indeed sufficient for maximization, then this will give us the inverse demand relationship.

What happens if the utility function is not everywhere quasi-concave? Then there may be some bundles of goods that will not be demanded at any price; any bundle on a nonconvex part of an indifference curve will be such a bundle.

There is a dual version of the above formula for inverse demands that can be obtained from the expression given in Section 3.11. The argument given there shows that the demanded bundle **x** must *minimize* indirect utility over all prices that satisfy the budget constraint. Thus **x** must satisfy the first-order conditions:

$$\frac{\partial v(\mathbf{p})}{\partial p_i} - \mu x_i = 0 \qquad \text{for } i = 1, \cdot \cdot \cdot , k$$

$$\sum_{i=1}^{n} p_i x_i = 1$$

Now multiply each of the first inequalities by p_i and sum them to find that $\mu = \sum_{i=1}^{k} \frac{\partial v(\mathbf{p})}{\partial p_i} p_i$. Hence, we have an expression for the demanded bundle as a function of the normalized indirect utility function:

$$x_i(\mathbf{p}) = \frac{\dfrac{\partial v(\mathbf{p})}{\partial p_i}}{\displaystyle\sum_{j=1}^{k} \frac{\partial v(\mathbf{p})}{\partial p_j} \mathbf{p}_j}$$

Note the nice duality: the equation for the direct demand and that for the indirect demand have the same form. Of course, this expression can also be derived from the definition of the normalized indirect utility function and Roy's law.

3.18 EXPECTED UTILITY

Until now, we have been concerned with the behavior of a consumer under conditions of certainty. However, many choices made by consumers take place under partial or even total ignorance. In this section we explore how the theory can be modified to describe such behavior.

The first task is to describe the space of choices facing the consumer. We shall imagine that the choices facing the consumer take the form of *lotteries*. A lottery is denoted by $p \circ x + (1-p) \circ y$ and is interpreted in the following way: "the consumer receives prize x with probability p and prize y with probability $(1-p)$." The prizes may be money, bundles of goods, or even further lotteries. Nearly all situations involving behavior under risk can be put into this lottery framework.

We will make several assumptions about the consumer's perception of the lotteries open to him.

(L1) $1 \circ x + (1-1) \circ y = x$. Getting a prize with probability one is the same as getting the prize for certain.

(L2) $p \circ x + (1-p) \circ y = (1-p) \circ y + p \circ x$

(L3) $q \circ (p \circ x + (1-p) \circ y) + (1-q) \circ y = (qp) \circ x + (1-qp) \circ y$. A consumer's perception of a lottery depends only on the net probabilities of receiving the various prizes.

Under these assumptions, we can define $\mathcal{L}$, the space of lotteries open to the consumers. The consumer is assumed to have preferences on this lottery space: given any two lotteries, he can choose between them. As before we will assume the preferences are complete, reflexive, and transitive.

The fact that lotteries have only two outcomes is not restrictive since we have allowed the outcomes to be further lotteries. For example, suppose we want to represent a situation with three prizes x, y, and z where the probability of getting each prize is one third. This can be represented by the lottery:

$$(2/3) \circ [(1/2) \circ x + (1/2) \circ y] + (1/3) \circ z$$

According to assumption L3 above, the consumer only cares about the net probabilities involved, so this is indeed equivalent to the original lottery.

Under minor additional assumptions, the theorem concerning the existence of a utility function mentioned earlier may be applied to show that there exists a continuous utility function u which describes the consumer's preferences; that is, $p \circ x + (1-p) \circ y > q \circ w + (1-q) \circ z$ if and only if:

$$u\,(p \circ x + (1-p) \circ y) > u\,(q \circ w + (1-q) \circ z)$$

Of course, this utility function is not unique; any monotonic transform would do as well. Under some additional hypotheses, we can find a particular utility function that has a very convenient property, namely, the *expected utility property:*

$$u\,(p \circ x + (1-p) \circ y) = pu\,(x) + (1-p)\,u\,(y)$$

Thus, the utility of a lottery is just the expected utility of its prizes. It should be emphasized that the *existence* of a utility function is not at issue; any well-behaved preferences can be represented by a utility function. What is of interest here is the existence of a utility function with the above convenient property. For that we need these additional axioms:

(C1) $\{p \text{ in } [0;\ 1]: p \circ x + (1-p) \circ y \succsim z\}$ and $\{p \text{ in } [0;\ 1]: z \succsim p \circ x + (1-p) \circ y\}$ are closed sets for all x, y and z in $\mathcal{L}$.
(C2) If $x \sim y$ then $p \circ x + (1-p) \circ z \sim p \circ y + (1-p) \circ z$.

The first assumption is an assumption of continuity; the second says that lotteries with indifferent prizes are indifferent.

In order to avoid some technical details we will make two further assumptions.

(C3) There is some best lottery b and some worst lottery w. For any x in $\mathcal{L}$, $b \succsim x \succsim w$.
(C4) A lottery $p \circ b + (1-p) \circ w$ is preferred to $q \circ b + (1-q) \circ w$ if and only if $p > q$.

Assumption (C3) is purely for convenience. Assumption (C4) can be derived from the other axioms. It just says that if one lottery on $(b,\ w)$ is better than another it must be because it gives higher probability of getting the best prize.

Under these assumptions we can state the main theorem.

Theorem *If $(\mathcal{L}, \succsim)$ satisfy the above axioms, there is a utility function* u *defined on $\mathcal{L}$ such that:*

$$u\,(p \circ x + (1-p) \circ y) = pu\,(x) + (1-p)\,u\,(y)$$

PROOF Define $u(b) = 1$, $u(w) = 0$. To find the utility of an intermediate element z, set $u(z) = p_z$ where p_z is defined by $p_z \circ b + (1 - p_z) \circ w \sim z$. To ensure that this is well defined we have to check two things:

(1) Does such a p_z exist? The two sets $\{p \text{ in } [0;\ 1]: p \circ b + (1 - p) \circ w \succsim z\}$ and $\{p \text{ in } [0;\ 1]: z \succsim p \circ b + (1 - p) \circ w\}$ are closed and nonempty, and every point in [0; 1] is in one or the other of the two sets. Since the unit interval is connected, there must be some p in both—but this will just be the desired p_z.

(2) Is p_z unique? Suppose p_z and p_z' both satisfy the above definition. Then one must be larger than the other. By assumption (C4), the lottery that gives a bigger probability of getting the best prize cannot be indifferent to one that gives a smaller probability. Hence, p_z is unique and u is well defined.

We next check that u has the expected utility property. This follows by some elementary substitutions:

$$\begin{aligned} p \circ x + (1 - p) \circ y &\sim p \circ [p_x \circ b + (1 - p_x) \circ w] + (1 - p) \circ [p_y \circ b + (1 - p_y) \circ w] \sim [pp_x + (1 - p)p_y] \circ b \\ &+ [1 - pp_x - (1 - p)p_y] \circ w \sim [pu(x) + (1 - p)u(y)] \circ b + [1 - pu(x) - (1 - p)u(y)] \circ w \end{aligned}$$

Hence,

$$u(p \circ x + (1 - p) \circ y) = pu(x) + (1 - p)u(y).$$

Finally we verify that u is a utility function. Suppose that $x \succ y$. Then

$$u(x) = p_x \text{ such that } x \sim p_x \circ b + (1 - p_x) \circ w$$

$$u(y) = p_y \text{ such that } y \sim p_y \circ b + (1 - p_y) \circ w$$

By axiom (C4), we must have $u(x) > u(y)$. □

3.19 THE UNIQUENESS OF THE EXPECTED UTILITY FUNCTION

We have now shown that there exists an expected utility function $u: \mathcal{L} \to R$. Of course, any monotonic transform of u will also be a utility function which describes the consumer's choice behavior. But will such a monotonic transform preserve the expected utility property? Does the construction described above *characterize* expected utility functions in any way?

Now it is easy to see that, if $u(\ )$ is an expected utility function describing some consumer, then so is $v(\ ) = au(\ ) + b$ where $a > 0$; that is, any affine transformation of an expected utility function is also an expected utility function. This is clear since:

$$v(p \circ x + (1-p) \circ y) = au(p \circ x + (1-p) \circ y) + b = a(pu(x) + (1-p)u(y)) + b$$
$$= pv(x) + (1-p)v(y)$$

It is not much harder to see the converse: that any monotonic transform of u that has the expected utility property must be an affine transform. Stated another way:

PROPOSITION *An expected utility function is unique up to an affine transformation.*

PROOF According to the above remarks we only have to show that, if a monotonic transformation preserves the expected utility property, it must be an affine transformation. Let $f: R \to R$ be a monotonic transform of u that has the expected utility property. Then

$$f(u\ (p \circ x + (1-p) \circ y)) = pf(u\ (x)) + (1-p)f(u\ (y))$$

or

$$f(pu\,(x) + (1-p)\,u\,(y)) = pf(u\,(x)) + (1-p)\,f(u\,(y))$$

But this is equivalent to the definition of an affine transformation. (See Section A.6 of the Mathematical Appendix.) □

3.20 RISK AVERSION

Let us consider the simple case where the lottery space consists solely of gambles with money prizes. Then the expected utility theorem says we can represent the consumer's behavior over all money gambles if we only know his expected utility function for money. For example, to compute the consumer's expected utility of a gamble $p \circ x + (1-p) \circ y$, we just look at $pu\,(x) + (1-p)\,u\,(y)$. This construction is illustrated in Figure 3.17 for $p = \frac{1}{2}$.

Notice that in this example the consumer prefers to get the expected value of the gamble, $px + (1-p)\,y$, rather than the gamble. Such behavior is called *risk aversion.* A consumer may also be *risk loving;* in such a case, the consumer prefers a gamble to its expected value.

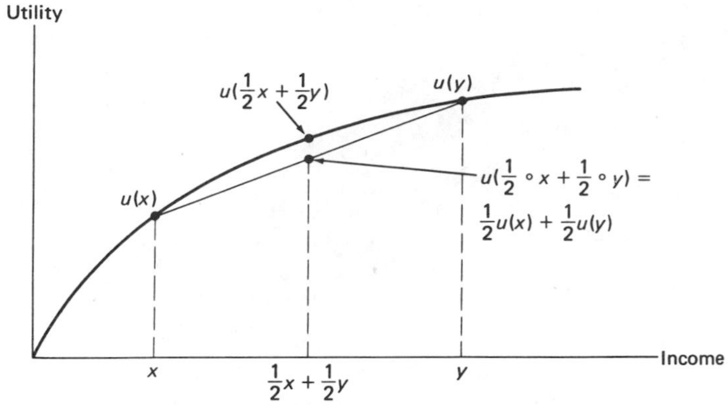

Fig. 3.17 *Expected Utility of a Monetary Gamble*

If a consumer is risk averse over some region, the chord drawn between any two points of the graph of his utility function in this region must lie below the function. This is equivalent to the mathematical definition of concavity. Hence concavity of the expected utility function is equivalent to risk aversion.

It is often convenient to have a measure of risk aversion. Intuitively the more concave the expected utility function, the more risk averse the consumer. Thus, we might think we could measure risk aversion by the second derivative of the expected utility function. However, this definition is not invariant to changes in the expected utility function: if we multiply the expected utility function by 2, the consumer's behavior doesn't change, but our proposed measure of risk aversion does. However, if we normalize the second derivative by dividing by the first, we get a reasonable measure, known as the Arrow-Pratt measure of (absolute) risk aversion: $r(y) = -u''(y)/u'(y)$.

The following "state-preference" analysis gives further rationale for this measure. Let us represent a gamble now by a pair of numbers (x_1, x_2) where the consumer gets x_1 if some event E occurs and x_2 if not-E occurs. Then we define the consumer's acceptance set $A(w)$ to be the set of all gambles the consumer would accept at an initial wealth level w. If the consumer is risk averse, $A(w)$ will be a convex set. The boundary of this set—the set of indifferent gambles—can be given by an implicit function $x_2(x_1)$, as depicted in Figure 3.18.

Suppose that the consumer's behavior can be described by the maximization of expected utility given a subjective probability p that the event E occurs. Then $x_2(x_1)$ must satisfy the identity:

$$pu(w + x_1) + (1 - p)\,u(w + x_2(x_1)) \equiv u(w)$$

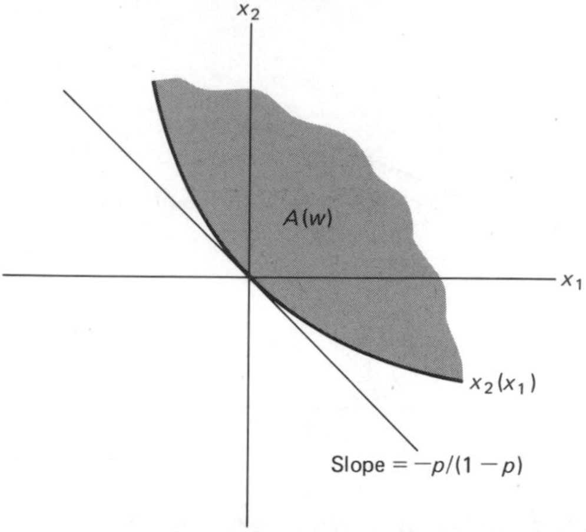

Fig. 3.18 *The Acceptance Set*

The slope of the acceptance set boundary at (0, 0) can be found by differentiating this identity and evaluating it at $x_1 = 0$:

$$pu'(w) + (1-p)u'(w)x_2'(x_1) = 0$$

$$x_2'(0) = -p/(1-p)$$

that is, the slope of the acceptance set at (0, 0) gives us the subjective odds. This gives us a nice way for eliciting subjective probabilities—find the odds at which a consumer is just willing to accept a small bet on the event in question.

Now suppose that we have two consumers who have identical subjective probabilities on the event E. It is natural to say that consumer i is more risk averse than consumer j if consumer i's acceptance set is contained in consumer j's acceptance set. This is clearly a global statement about risk aversion for it says that j will accept *any* gamble that i will accept. If we limit ourselves to small gambles we get a more useful measure:

DEFINITION Consumer i is *locally more risk averse* than consumer j if there is some neighborhood N of (0, 0) such that $(A_i(w_i) \cap N)$ is contained in $(A_j(w_j) \cap N)$.

This measure of risk aversion is clearly given by the second derivative of the acceptance set frontier. Again assuming expected utility maximization and differentiating the identity given above, we get:

$$pu''(w) + (1-p)\,u''(w)\,x_2'(x_1)\,x_2'(x_1) + (1-p)\,u'(w)\,x_2''(x_1) = 0$$

Using the fact that $x_2'(x_1) = -p/(1-p)$ we get:

$$x_2''(x_1) = \frac{p}{(1-p)^2}\left[\frac{-u''(w)}{u'(w)}\right]$$

This is just proportional to the Arrow-Pratt measure defined above. We can conclude that an agent j will take more small gambles than agent i if and only if agent i has a larger Arrow-Pratt measure of local risk aversion.

Example 3.10 The Demand for Insurance Suppose a consumer initially has monetary wealth W. There is some probability p that he will loose an amount L—for example, there is some probability his house will burn down. The consumer can however purchase insurance that will pay him q dollars in the event that he incurs this loss. The premium he has to pay for q dollars of coverage will be denoted by πq.

How much coverage will the consumer purchase? We look at the utility maximization problem:

$$\max pu(W - L - \pi q + q) + (1-p)u(W - \pi q)$$

Taking the derivative with respect to q and setting it equal to zero we find:

$$pu'(W - L + q^*(1-\pi))(1-\pi) - (1-p)u'(W - \pi q^*)\pi = 0$$
$$\frac{u'(W - L + (1-\pi)q^*)}{u'(W - \pi q^*)} = \frac{(1-p)}{p}\frac{\pi}{1-\pi}$$

If the event occurs, the insurance company receives $\pi q - q$ dollars. If the event doesn't occur, the insurance company receives πq dollars. Hence the expected profit of the company is:

$$-p(1-\pi)q + (1-p)\pi q$$

Let us suppose that competition in the insurance industry forces these profits to zero:

$$-p(1-\pi)q + (1-p)\pi q = 0$$
$$(1-p)\pi = p(1-\pi)$$

Under this assumption the insurance firm charges an *actuarially fair premium:* the cost of a policy is precisely its expected value. Inserting the above equations into the first-order conditions for utility maximization, we find:

$$u'(W - L + (1 - \pi)q^*) = u'(W - \pi q^*)$$

If the consumer is strictly risk averse so that $u''(W) < 0$, then the above equation implies:

$$W - L + (1 - \pi)q^* = W - \pi q^*$$
$$L = q^*$$

Thus the consumer will completely insure himself against the loss L.

(M) *APPENDIX 1: EXPENDITURE MINIMIZATION AND UTILITY MAXIMIZATION*

In this appendix, we give a precise statement of when utility maximization and expenditure minimization are compatible. We consider the two problems:

$$\text{MAX:} \quad \max \ u(\mathbf{x}) \quad \text{s.t.} \ \mathbf{p}\cdot\mathbf{x} \leqq y \qquad\qquad \text{MIN:} \quad \min \ \mathbf{p}\cdot\mathbf{x} \quad \text{s.t.} \ u(\mathbf{x}) \geqq u$$

We will suppose:

(1) the utility function is continuous,
(2) preferences satisfy local nonsatiation,
(3) answers to both problems exist.

PROPOSITION *Suppose that the above assumptions are met and that* $\mathbf{x}^*$ *solves* MAX. *Let* $u = u(\mathbf{x}^*)$. *Then* $\mathbf{x}^*$ *solves* MIN.

PROOF Suppose not, and let $\mathbf{x}'$ solve MIN, so that $\mathbf{p}\cdot\mathbf{x}' < \mathbf{p}\cdot\mathbf{x}^*$ and $u(\mathbf{x}') \geqq u(\mathbf{x}^*)$. By local nonsatiation, there is a bundle $\mathbf{x}''$ close enough to $\mathbf{x}'$ so that $\mathbf{p}\cdot\mathbf{x}'' < \mathbf{p}\cdot\mathbf{x}^* = y$ and $u(\mathbf{x}'') > u(\mathbf{x}^*)$. But then $\mathbf{x}^*$ couldn't solve MAX. □

PROPOSITION *Suppose that the above assumptions are met and that* $\mathbf{x}^*$ *solves* MIN. *Let* $y = \mathbf{p}\cdot\mathbf{x}^*$ *and suppose* $y > 0$. *Then* $\mathbf{x}^*$ *solves* MAX.

PROOF Suppose not, and let $\mathbf{x}'$ solve MAX so that $u(\mathbf{x}') > u(\mathbf{x}^*)$ and $\mathbf{p}\cdot\mathbf{x}' = \mathbf{p}\cdot\mathbf{x}^*$. Since $\mathbf{p}\cdot\mathbf{x}^* > 0$ and preferences are continuous we can find $0 < t < 1$ so that $\mathbf{p}\cdot t\mathbf{x}' < \mathbf{p}\cdot\mathbf{x}^*$ and $u(t\mathbf{x}') > u(\mathbf{x}^*)$. Thus, $\mathbf{x}^*$ cannot solve MIN. □

(M) *APPENDIX 2: CONTINUITY OF DEMAND*

In this appendix, we present a direct proof of the continuity of the consumer's demand function when preferences are convex.

PROPOSITION *Suppose preferences are strictly convex, locally non-satiated, and continuous. The consumer's demand function* $\mathbf{x}(\mathbf{p}, y)$ *is continuous for all* $\mathbf{p} \gg 0$, *and* $y > 0$.

PROOF Let $(\mathbf{p}^i)$ be a sequence of prices converging to $\mathbf{p}^* \gg 0$. For i large each component of $\mathbf{p}^i$ is bounded away from zero; let $\mathbf{p}_{\min}$ be the vector of these bounds. Again for i large, the sequence of demands $\mathbf{x}(\mathbf{p}^i, y)$ lies in the compact set $\{\mathbf{x} \text{ in } R^n\colon \mathbf{p}_{\min} \cdot \mathbf{x} \leqq y\}$ so it has a convergent subsequence that converges to some point $\mathbf{x}^*$. We need to show that $\mathbf{x}(\mathbf{p}^*, y) = \mathbf{x}^*$. Assume not.

First, we note that $\mathbf{x}^*$ is in the consumer's budget set at $\mathbf{p}^*$, for if not there would be some i such that $\mathbf{p}^i \cdot \mathbf{x}(\mathbf{p}^i, y) > y$.

Now $\mathbf{x}(\mathbf{p}^*, y)$ is either worse than or at least as good as $\mathbf{x}^*$. Consider each of these cases:

(1) $\mathbf{x}^* \succsim \mathbf{x}(\mathbf{p}^*, y)$ and $\mathbf{x}^* \neq \mathbf{x}(\mathbf{p}^*, y)$—then $\frac{1}{2}\mathbf{x}^* + \frac{1}{2}\mathbf{x}(\mathbf{p}^*, y)$ is in the consumer's budget set and is preferred to $\mathbf{x}(\mathbf{p}^*, y)$, a contradiction.

(2) $\mathbf{x}^* < \mathbf{x}(\mathbf{p}^*, y)$—by continuity we choose $s < 1$ such that $s\mathbf{x}(\mathbf{p}^*, y) > \mathbf{x}^*$. For all i larger than some number n, $s\mathbf{x}(\mathbf{p}^*, y) \succ \mathbf{x}(\mathbf{p}^i, y)$ and therefore $s\mathbf{p}^i \cdot \mathbf{x}(\mathbf{p}^*, y) > \mathbf{p}^i \cdot \mathbf{x}(\mathbf{p}^i, y) = y$.

On the other hand, $s\mathbf{p}^* \cdot \mathbf{x}(\mathbf{p}^*, y) < y$ since $s < 1$, so, for large enough i, $s\mathbf{p}^n \cdot \mathbf{x}(\mathbf{p}^*, y) < y$ which gives us the contradiction.

To show continuity of $\mathbf{x}(\mathbf{p}, y)$ in y, we let (y^i) be a sequence of incomes converging to y^*. We have to show that $\mathbf{x}(\mathbf{p}, y^i)$ converges to $\mathbf{x}(\mathbf{p}, y^*)$. We can assume that since $y^* > 0$ we have all $y^i > 0$. Then consider the sequence of demands $\mathbf{x}(\mathbf{p}/y^i, 1)$. By homogeneity of $\mathbf{x}(\mathbf{p}, y)$ in $(\mathbf{p}, y)$ we see that $\mathbf{x}(\mathbf{p}/y^i, 1) \equiv \mathbf{x}(\mathbf{p}, y^i))$. But the sequence $(\mathbf{x}(\mathbf{p}/y^i, 1))$ clearly converges to $\mathbf{x}(\mathbf{p}, y^*)$ by the first part of the proof. □

Exercises

3.1 (10) Let $x^i(\mathbf{p}, y)$ be the consumer's demand for good i. The income elasticity of demand for good i is defined as: $e_i = \dfrac{y}{x_i} \dfrac{dx^i(\mathbf{p}, y)}{dy}$. Show that, if all income elasticities are constant and equal, they must be equal to one.

3.2 (15) Suppose that b is an upper bound on the income elasticity of demand for good 1 over some region of the price-income space, R. That is:

$$\frac{\partial x_1(\mathbf{p}, y)}{\partial y} \frac{y}{x_1(\mathbf{p}, y)} \leqq b \qquad \text{for all } (p, y) \text{ in } R$$

Then show that:

$$\frac{x_1(\mathbf{p}, y)}{x_1(\mathbf{p}, y_o)} \leqq \left[\frac{y}{y_o}\right]^b \qquad \begin{array}{l}\text{for all} \\ (p, y) \text{ in } R \\ (p, y_o) \text{ in } R\end{array}$$

3.3 (30) One can show that the "compensated own price effect is negative" by an argument similar to that in Exercise 1.4. Supply the details.

3.4 (10) State marginal conditions for utility maximization that are valid even on the boundary of the consumption set.

3.5 (20) In general equilibrium analysis, a consumer's income y depends on the value of his endowment which in turn depends on prices: $y(\mathbf{p}) = \mathbf{p} \cdot \mathbf{W}$. Derive the Slutsky equation in this circumstance.

3.6 (15) Suppose that two goods i and j have the same income elasticity at $(\mathbf{p}, y)$. Show that $\partial x_i(\mathbf{p}, y)/\partial p_j = \partial x_j(\mathbf{p}, y)/\partial p_i$.

3.7 (10) Show that, if one allows "thick" indifference curves, then expenditure minimization and preference maximization do not coincide.

3.8 (20) A consumer has a utility function of the form $u(x_1, x_2) = -1/x_1 - 1/x_2$.
(a) Compute the Marshallian demand functions.
(b) Show the indirect utility function is $-(\sqrt{p_1} + \sqrt{p_2})^2/y$.
(c) Compute the expenditure function.
(d) Compute the Hicksian demand curves.

3.9 (20) Let $v(p_1, p_2, y) = \dfrac{y}{p_1} + \dfrac{y}{p_2}$
(a) Verify that this satisfies all of the properties of an indirect utility function.
(b) What is its associated expenditure function?
(c) What are the associated demands for the two goods?

3.10 (15) Given the following expenditure function (Diewert),

$$e(\mathbf{p}, u) = \left(\frac{1}{3} p_1 + p_1^{1/2} p_2^{1/2} + \frac{2}{3} p_2\right) u$$

(a) Derive the Marshallian demands for x_1 and x_2.
(b) Derive the Hicksian demands for x_1 and x_2.

3.11 (20) Suppose at prices $(p_1, p_2) = (5, 10)$ and income $y = \$100$ a rational consumer demands the bundle (6, 7). Assume we have measured the following derivatives,

$$\frac{\partial h_1(p_1, p_2, u)}{\partial p_1} = -2$$

$$\frac{\partial h_1(p_1, p_2, u)}{\partial p_2} = +1$$

$$\frac{\partial x_1(p_1, p_2, y)}{\partial y} = 2/7$$

Find an estimate of the consumption bundle of the consumer at $(p_1, p_2) = (5, 11)$.

3.12 (15) Suppose that $u(\mathbf{x})$ is homothetic. Show that the normalized indirect utility function $v(\mathbf{q}) = v(\mathbf{p}/y, 1)$ is homogeneous of degree -1 in $\mathbf{q}$.

3.13 (20) Suppose there are two goods. Let good 0 be the numéraire, p the price of good 1 relative to the numéraire, and y income relative to the numéraire. Suppose the demand function for good 1 takes the form $x(p, y) = ap + by + c$. What is the form of the indirect income compensation function?

3.14 (30) Ms. Smith has a utility function of the form $u(x_1, x_2) = \min(x_1, x_2)$. How much money does Ms. Smith need at prices (q_1, q_2) to have the same level of utility she had at (p_1, p_2, y)—that is, what is Ms. Smith's indirect income compensation function $\mu(q_1, q_2; p_1, p_2, y)$?

3.15 (15) Suppose a consumer has an expenditure function of the form:

$$e(p^1, p^2, u) = (p^1 + p^2)u$$

Calculate the compensated demand functions, and illustrate a typical indifference curve.

3.16 (20) Suppose a consumer has an expenditure function of the form $e(\mathbf{p}, u) = ug(\mathbf{p})$. Show that his utility function is homogeneous of degree 1. Suppose $e(\mathbf{p}, u)$ is of the form $e(\mathbf{p}, u) = h(u)g(\mathbf{p})$ with h positive monotonic. How does the consumer's behavior differ?

3.17 (20) Consumer A has expenditure function $e_A(\mathbf{p}, u) = g(\mathbf{p})u$, and consumer B has expenditure function $e_B(\mathbf{p})u^3$. (Note that $g(\mathbf{p})$ and u are the same for each consumer, but consumer B has *u cubed*.) How does the observed market behavior of A and B differ?

3.18 (5) A consumer has expenditure function $e(p_1, p_2, u) = p_1^{1/4}p_2^b u$. What is the value of b?

3.19 (15) A consumer has indirect utility function $v(\mathbf{p}, y) = -(1/r)\log(p_1^r + p_2^r) + \log y$. (The logarithms are natural logarithms —to the base e.) Calculate:
(a) The expenditure function.
(b) The market demand functions.

3.20 (20) Suppose a consumer consumes only two goods. We suppose the demand functions are given by:

$$x_1(\mathbf{p}, y) = (p_2/p_1)$$

$$x_2(\mathbf{p}, y) = \frac{y}{p_2} - 1$$

What is the consumer's indirect utility function? (Hint: set $p_2 = 1$.)

3.21 (20) Suppose a consumer has a differentiable expected utility function for money with $du(y)/dy$ strictly positive. The consumer is offered a bet with probability $\frac{2}{3}$ of winning \$$t$ and probability $\frac{1}{3}$ of losing \$$t$. Show that if t is small enough the consumer will always take the bet.

3.22 (20) A consumer has a utility function of the form:

$$u(x_1, x_2, x_3) = u_1(x_1) + u_2(x_2) + u_3(x_3)$$

$$u_i'(x_i) > 0$$

$$u_i''(x_i) < 0$$

$$i = 1, \cdots, 3$$

(a) How many of the three goods can be inferior goods?
(b) When p_1 rises, what are the possible kinds of behavior for x_1?
(c) When p_1 rises, what are the possible kinds of behavior for x_2?
(d) What sign patterns are possible in the substitution matrix?

3.23 (15) At a given wage rate an individual would choose to work six hours per day, but institutional constraints force that person to work eight hours or not at all. Show that the unemployment benefit necessary to induce the person to quit is less than if he/she were allowed to work six hours.

3.24 (15) Suppose that a union has a fixed supply of labor to sell and that unemployed workers are paid unemployment insurance at a rate u per worker. Show that if the union wishes to maximize the wage bill it should set a lower wage than if it wished to maximize the sum of the wage bill plus the unemployment compensation.

3.25 (10) A college student's budget is entirely spent on milk and pizza. Here are his consumption patterns for two months.

	September	*October*
milk price	3	8
pizza price	4	6
milk consumption	4	3
pizza consumption	3	4

Is the consumer's behavior consistent with the utility maximization model?

3.26 (10) The Laspeyres quantity index is defined by $Q_L = \Sigma p_i^0 q_i^1 / \Sigma p_i^0 q_i^0$. Show that if $Q_L < 1$ the consumer is surely worse off at $\mathbf{p}^1$ than at $\mathbf{p}^0$.

3.27 (10) The Paasche quantity index is defined by $Q_p = \Sigma p_i^1 q_i^1 / \Sigma p_i^1 q_i^0$. Show that if $Q_p > 1$ the consumer is surely better off at $\mathbf{p}^1$ than at $\mathbf{p}^0$.

3.28 (10) The following price index numbers can be defined:

$$P_L = \Sigma p_i^1 q_i^0 / \Sigma p_i^0 q_i^0 \qquad \text{Laspeyres}$$

$$P_p = \Sigma p_i^1 q_i^1 / \Sigma p_i^0 q_i^1 \qquad \text{Paasche}$$

$$Y = \Sigma p_i^1 q_i^1 / \Sigma p_i^0 q_i^0 \qquad \text{money-income}$$

(a) If $Y > P_L$ the consumer is surely better off.
(b) If $Y < P_p$ the consumer is surely worse off.

3.29 (10) The true cost of living index is defined by $i = e(\mathbf{p}^1, u^0)/\mathbf{p}^0 \cdot x^0$. Show that $i \leqq P_L$.

3.30 (20) Consider the substitution matrix $(\partial h_i(\mathbf{p}, u)/\partial p_j)$ of a utility-maximizing consumer.

(a) Show that $\sum_{i=1}^{k} \dfrac{\partial u(\mathbf{x})}{\partial x_i} \dfrac{\partial h_i(\mathbf{p}, u)}{\partial p_j} = 0$

(b) Conclude that the substitution matrix is singular and that the price vector $\mathbf{p}$ lies in its null space.
(c) Show that this implies that there is some entry in each row and column of the substitution matrix that is nonnegative.

3.31 (30) Suppose preferences are convex and monotonic. Show that the utility function can be chosen to be homogeneous of degree 1 if and only if the indirect utility function is separable in the sense that $v(\mathbf{p}, y) = y\, h(\mathbf{p})$.

3.32 (10) Show that a good can be a Giffen good only if it is an inferior good.

3.33 (15) Suppose the consumer's demand function for good i has constant income elasticity η. Show that the demand function can be written as $x_i(\mathbf{p}, y) = x_i(\mathbf{p}, y_0)\,[y/y_0]^{\eta}$.

3.34 (20) Suppose the consumer's utility function is homogeneous of degree 1 so that $u(t\mathbf{x}) = tu(\mathbf{x})$ for $t > 0$. Show that the consumer's demand functions have constant income elasticity equal to 1.

3.35 (15) Use the envelope theorem to show that the Lagrange multiplier associated with the budget constraint gives the marginal utility of income; that is, $\lambda = \partial v(\mathbf{p}, y)/\partial y$.

3.36 (15) Use the envelope theorem to show that $x_i(\mathbf{p}, y) = -(\partial v(\mathbf{p}, y)/\partial p_i)/(\partial v(\mathbf{p}, y)/\partial y)$.

3.37 (10) Suppose the expected utility function can be written as a quadratic function $u(y) = a_0 + a_1 y - a_2 y^2$. Show that expected utility of a random payoff X is a function only of the mean and variance of X.

3.38 (20) A sports fan has an expected utility function of the form $u(w) = \ln w$. He has subjective probability p that the Lions will win their next football game and probability $1 - p$ that they will not win. He chooses to bet \$$x$ on the Lions so that if the Lions win, he wins \$$x$ and if the Lions lose he loses \$$x$.

You know the fan's initial wealth W_O. How can you determine his subjective odds $p/(1 - p)$ by observing the size of his bet x?

3.39 (30) Suppose that the utility function is additively separable and homothetic so that $U(x_1, x_2) = u_1(x_1) + u_2(x_2)$. Show that the utility function must be CES.

3.40 Suppose $U(\mathbf{x})$ is additively separable. Show that

$$\frac{\dfrac{\partial h_i}{\partial p_j}}{\dfrac{\partial h_i}{\partial p_k}} = \frac{\dfrac{\partial x_j}{\partial y}}{\dfrac{\partial x_k}{\partial y}}$$

3.41 (30) Let $x_i(p_i, y)$ $i = 1, \cdots, k$ be the demands of a neoclassical consumer for goods $1, \cdots, k$. Suppose that the demand for each good depends only on its own price and money income. Show that in this case the demand functions must be of the Cobb-Douglas form—i.e.,

$$x_i(p_i, y) = \frac{a_i y}{p_i} \qquad \sum_{i=1}^{k} a_i = 1 \qquad \text{for } i = 1, \cdots, k$$

3.42 (20) (Hausman) Consider a utility-maximizing consumer who chooses bundles of 2 goods at prices (p_1, p_2). We write the substitution matrix as:

$$\begin{bmatrix} \dfrac{\partial h_1(\mathbf{p}, u)}{\partial p_1} & \dfrac{\partial h_1(\mathbf{p}, u)}{\partial p_2} \\ \\ \dfrac{\partial h_2(\mathbf{p}, u)}{\partial p_1} & \dfrac{\partial h_2(\mathbf{p}, u)}{\partial p_2} \end{bmatrix} = \begin{bmatrix} a & b \\ c & d \end{bmatrix}$$

(a) Suppose you are given a. How can you determine b, c, and d?
(b) Suppose you are given b. How can you determine a, c, and d?

3.43 (20) Suppose that the utility function can be written as a function of a vector of goods x and money m: $u(x) + m$. (This is known as a *quasilinear* utility function.) The budget constraint is $\mathbf{p} \cdot \mathbf{x} + m = y$.
(a) Show that the demand for goods is independent of the level of income.
(b) Show that the indirect utility function has the form $v(\mathbf{p}, y) = \phi(\mathbf{p}) + y$.
(c) Show that the expenditure function has the form $e(\mathbf{p}, u) = \psi(\mathbf{p}) + u$.
(d) Show that $\mathbf{Dx}(\mathbf{p}, y) = [\mathbf{D}^2 u(\mathbf{x})]^{-1}$.

3.44 (20) Suppose an expected utility function has the property that its Arrow-Pratt measure of risk aversion is constant $-u''(x)/u'(x) = \mathrm{r}$. What must the form of the utility function be?

3.45 (30) The Arrow-Pratt measure of relative risk aversion is defined as $-u''(x)x/u'(x)$.
(i) Show that this measure follows from the analysis in the text if we interpret gambles as *relative* gambles; i.e. the gamble (x, y) means that we have an absolute gamble of the form (xW, yW) where W is the initial wealth level.
(ii) Suppose relative risk aversion is constant. What is the form of the utility function?

3.46 (30) Let individual a have an expected utility function $A(x)$, and let b have an expected utility function $B(x)$ where x is income.

Let $G: \mathbf{R} \to \mathbf{R}$ be a monotonic increasing, strictly concave function, and suppose that:

$$A(x) = G(B(x))$$

That is, A is a concave monotonic transformation of B.
(a) Show that individual a is more risk-averse than individual b in the sense of the Arrow-Pratt measure of (absolute) risk aversion.
(b) Let ϵ be a random variable with $E\epsilon = 0$. (E is the expected value operation.) Define "risk premiums" π_A, π_B by:

$$A(W - \pi_A) = E[A(W + \epsilon)]$$
$$B(W - \pi_B) = E[B(W + \epsilon)]$$

Here W is initial wealth. If $A(x) = G(B(x))$, show that $\pi_A \geqq \pi_B$.
(c) Interpret the risk premium in words.

Notes

The lexicographic preference example is due to Debreu (1959). The existence of a utility function example is due to Wold (1943). A general theorem on the existence of a utility function may be found in Debreu (1964).

The concept of the indirect utility function was developed by Roy (1942), (1947). The expenditure function seems to be due to Hicks (1946). The derivative property of the indirect utility function was first proved by Roy (1942). The dual approach to consumer theory described here follows that of McFadden and Winter (1968). The proof of the Slutsky equation given here is due to McKenzie (1957) and Cook (1972). The conditions for continuity of a demand function were derived from Berge (1963).

Expected utility theory is due to von Neumann and Morgenstern (1944). The treatment here follows Herstein and Milnor (1953). The measures of risk aversion are due to Arrow (1970) and Pratt (1964). The treatment here follows Yaari (1969). Essays on consumer behavior under uncertainty with historical notes may be found in Arrow (1970). Some recent work on the foundations of expected utility theory may be found in Machina (1982).

The problem of integrability has its origin in the work of Samuelson (1966). The approach here follows that of Hurwicz and Uzawa (1971).

Revealed preference theory was discovered by Samuelson (1948). The approach taken here follows Afriat (1967), Diewert (1973), and Varian (1982).

The finite approach to Slutsky's equation is based on Yokoyama (1953).

For more on separability, consult Blackorby, Primont, and Russell (1979). Shaefer and Sonnenschein (1982) contains a nice review of positive and negative aggregation results.

References

AFRIAT, S. 1967. "The Construction of a Utility Function from Expenditure Data." *International Economic Review* 8:67–77.

ARROW, K. 1970. *Essays in the Theory of Risk Bearing*. Chicago: Markham.

BERGE, C. 1963. *Topological Spaces*. New York: Macmillan.

BLACKORBY, C., PRIMONT, D., and RUSSELL, R. 1979. *Duality, Separability and Functional Structure: Theory and Economic Applications*. Amsterdam: North-Holland.

COOK, P. 1972. "A One Line Proof of the Slutsky Equation." *American Economic Review* 42:139.

DEBREU, G. 1959. *Theory of Value*. New York: Wiley.

———. 1964. "Continuity Properties of Paretian Utility." *International Economic Review* 5:285–293.

DIEWERT, E. 1973. "Afriat and Revealed Preference Theory." *Review of Economic Studies* 40:419–426.

HERSTEIN, I., and MILNOR, J. 1953. "An Axiomatic Approach to Measurable Utility." *Econometrica* 21:291–297.

HICKS, J. 1946. *Value and Capital*. Oxford, Eng.: Clarendon Press.

HURWICZ, L., and UZAWA, H. 1971. "On the Integrability of Demand Functions." In *Preferences, Utility, and Demand*, ed. J. Chipman et al. New York: Harcourt, Brace, Jovanovich.

MCFADDEN, D., and WINTER, S. 1968. "Lecture Notes on Consumer Theory." University of California at Berkeley, unpublished

MCKENZIE, L. 1957. "Demand Theory without a Utility Index." *Review of Economic Studies* 24:185–189.

MACHINA, M. 1982. " 'Expected Utility' Analysis without the Independence Axiom." *Econometrica* 50:277–323.

NEUMANN, J. VON, and MORGENSTERN, O. 1944. *Theory of Games and Economic Behavior*. Princeton, N.J.: Princeton University Press.

PRATT, J. 1964. "Risk Aversion in the Small and in the Large." *Econometrica* 32:1–2.

ROY, R. 1942. *De l'utilité*. Paris: Hermann.

———. 1947. "La Distribution de Revenu entre les Divers Biens." *Econometrica* 15:205–225.

SAMUELSON, P. 1966. *Collected Scientific Papers of Paul A. Samuelson,* vol. 1, ed. J. Stiglitz. Cambridge, Mass.: MIT Press.

SCHAEFER, W., and SONNENSCHEIN, H. 1982. "Market Demand and Excess Demand Functions." In *Handbook of Mathematical Economics,* K. Arrow and M. Intriligator, vol. 1. Amsterdam: North/Holland.

VARIAN, H. 1982. "The Nonparametric Approach to Demand Analysis." *Econometrica* 50:945–973.

WOLD, H. 1943. "A Synthesis of Pure Demand Analysis" I–III. *Skandinavisk Aktuarietidskrift* 26, 27.

YAARI, M. 1969. "Some Remarks on Measures of Risk Aversion and Their Uses.' *Journal of Economic Theory* 1:315–329.

YOKOYAMA, T. 1953. "A Logical Foundation of the Theory of Consumer's Demand." *Osaka Economic Papers* 2:71–79. Reprinted in P. Newman, *Readings in Mathematical Economics,* vol. 1. Baltimore: Johns Hopkins Press, 1968.

Chapter 4

Econometrics and Economic Theory

The previous three chapters have described consistent models of consumer, producer, and market behavior. We have investigated in some detail the empirical restrictions imposed by these models and some examples of applications of the models to economic problems. In most concrete applications of economic analysis to policy questions, it is necessary to know specific parameters describing the agents' behavior. What is the elasticity of demand for gasoline? Does the oil industry exhibit constant, decreasing, or increasing returns to scale? What is the degree of substitution of capital and labor in agricultural production?

The answers to questions such as these may have serious implications for policy analysis; and answers can be found only by examining the data describing agents' behavior. Such an examination will generally involve the use of statistical tools such as regression analysis. The study of how to use such statistical tools in economic research is known as *econometrics*.

In this chapter we will describe some of the contributions of economic theory to the field of econometrics. In particular we will see how the models of producer and consumer behavior described in the last three chapters aid us in determining appropriate methods to estimate economic behavioral relationships. This discussion will be rather cursory due to limitations on space. Nevertheless, it is hoped that this chapter will give some flavor of the kinds of problems that arise.

Throughout this chapter, some familiarity with elementary regression theory will be assumed; consult the notes at the end of the chapter for suitable references.

4.1 ESTIMATING PRODUCTION FUNCTIONS

Let us imagine that we are interested in estimating a production function for some industry. We have cross-sectional data giving measures of output and inputs of a large number of plants. How would one go about estimating a production relationship from this data?

The first problem we are faced with is that of specifying a functional form for the production process. How are the outputs of the plants related to the inputs? We desire a simple, flexible functional form which meets the economically reasonable restrictions described in Chapter 1 and which does not present unreasonable estimation problems. Unfortunately, as will be seen later, these requirements are difficult to fulfill.

Let us beg the question of functional form for a while and just postulate a production function of the generalized Cobb-Douglas form, so that the output of firm i is related to the inputs X_1, X_2, and X_3 by the function:

$$Y = AX_1^bX_2^cX_3^d$$

where A, b, c, and d are parameters to be estimated.

What exactly are the inputs to the production function anyway? The classical economic "factors of production" are labor (L), capital (K), and land (T). (Raw materials are generally interpreted as coming under the category of land, or products of the earth.) Thus our functional form claims that the output of product in firm i (Y_i) is a function of the capital (K_i), labor (L_i), and land (T_i) used in that firm; this function is more conveniently given by:

$$ln\ Y_i = a + b\ ln\ K_i + c\ ln\ L_i + d\ ln\ T_i$$

Such a linear-in-logarithms form is amenable to estimation by the use of ordinary least squares techniques. If we could only get accurate measurements of the inputs, we would be ready to estimate.

Here some serious problems arise. Each of the three factors of production are not simple quantities but are, rather, aggregate quantities. "Capital" is presumably some weighted average of the number of machines used. "Labor" is likewise some measure of the aggregate amount of labor, counting blue collar, white collar, managerial, and production personnel. Although each of the factors suffers from this problem of measurement, the measurement of capital is often felt to be the most serious problem.

The ideal measure would be of *capital services;* since output is measured as units of the good per unit time, capital should be measured as machine hours. This has the additional advantage of recognizing the fact that the same number of machines may be used more or less intensively (capital utilization) and that different vintages of machines may provide different levels of capital services due to technological differences.

Unfortunately, data on capital services are quite difficult to obtain. The usual procedure is to measure capital value and then deflate by a price index; in some sense, this should measure the level of capital stock. This level is then adjusted by a utilization rate which gives us the final figures.

Let us bypass these important problems by assuming that we do have acceptable measures of the outputs and inputs of the plants in our cross-sectional study. How do we go about estimating the parameters of the production process?

As hinted earlier, the straightforward method would be to regress the natural logarithm of output on a constant and the natural logarithms of the factor inputs. Will this provide us with acceptable estimates of the parameters?

The answer to this question depends in a large part on the intended use of the estimates. For example, if we are primarily interested in *forecasting* the level of output of a firm given a description of its inputs, estimates derived by the above technique may be acceptable.

On the other hand if we are interested in *estimating* the marginal product of the various factors—for example, determining how much extra output will be produced if we add extra workers—the estimates described above may be quite poor.

To see why, we must pose the estimation problem in a more rigorous way. In accordance with the standard regression model, we postulate that the output of the firm i is a *random variable,* with mean given by the appropriate production relationship and some variance which is assumed constant across firms. Let lowercase letters denote logarithms of the uppercase quantities; then our statistical model can be written as:

$$y_i = a + bk_i + cl_i + dt_i + \epsilon_i$$

where ϵ_i is a random variable with mean zero and variance σ^2.

We interpret this stochastic specification in the following way: if we were to choose at random a plant in this industry and observe its inputs, the *expected value* of its level of output would be $a + bk_i + cl_i + dt_i$. We are interested in estimating the parameters (a, b, c, d).

According to the Gauss-Markov theory, good estimates of these parameters can be obtained by the use of ordinary least squares when the right-hand variables are uncorrelated with the error term ϵ_i. Is this likely to be the case in practice?

To answer this question, we have to consider the nature of the error term. What effects are supposed to be represented by this term? The usual interpretation is that the error term represents the cumulative effect of all left-out variables. To answer the question about the acceptability of the estimates of the coefficients, we have to ask ourselves what sort of variables we have left out of the model in question.

In general, there will be two types of left-out variables: the first type will be variables that neither we nor the managers of the firm observe.

Examples of this sort of variable would be errors in the data, unknown variations in the quality of the inputs, unpredicted inputs to production such as weather, and so on. Since the managers of the firms do not observe these variables, their choice of input levels should be uncorrelated with these effects.

The second sort of left-out variable poses much more serious problems: these would be variables that *we* don't observe but the managers of the firm *do* observe. Examples of this sort of variable would be variation in quality of inputs that are known to managers, variations in technology from firm to firm, left-out factors of production that are known to managers, and so on. The problem with these left-out variables is that it is very unlikely that they will be uncorrelated with the observed factor inputs. *If the managers observe these effects, then they will certainly take that information into account when they determine their optimal choice of inputs.* Thus, the right-hand variables will not be statistically independent from (some component of) the error term, and biased estimates may result.

To fix this idea in our minds let us consider an extended example of how we might estimate an agricultural production function.

Suppose that the output of corn in farm *i*, C_i, depends on the amount of corn planted, K_i, and the number of sunny days in the growing season, S_i. Suppose, for now, that these are the *only* two variables that affect the output of corn and that the production relationship is given explicitly by:

$$C_i = K_i^a S_i^{1-a}$$

Taking logs, we can write this production function as:

$$ln\ C_i = a\ ln\ K_i + (1 - a) ln\ S_i$$

Now suppose that we have data only on C_i and K_i; that is, we do not have data about the weather input. Is it reasonable to suppose that applying least squares to the regression

$$ln\ C_i = a\ ln\ K_i + \epsilon_i$$

will give us a good estimate of a? Well, is it reasonable to suppose that ($ln\ K_i$) and ($\epsilon_i = (1 - a) ln\ S_i$) are uncorrelated? If the farmers do not observe S_i before choosing K_i then their choice of K_i cannot be affected by it. Thus, the method of least squares should give a good estimate of a.

Now let us suppose that the production relationship also depends on the quality of the land used at each farm, Q_i. We write the production function as:

$$C_i = Q_i K_i^a S_i^{1-a}$$

or $$\ln C_i = \ln Q_i + a \ln K_i + (1 - a)\ln S_i$$

As before, we assume that neither the farmers nor the econometrician observes S_i. However let us now suppose that the farmers observe Q_i, but the econometrician doesn't.

From the viewpoint of the econometrician, both S_i and Q_i are random variables. Now is it likely that the regression

$$\ln C_i = a \ln K_i + \epsilon_i$$

will give us a good estimate of a? The answer is *no:* since each farmer i observes Q_i, the farmers' choice of K_i will be influenced by this knowledge. Hence, K_i will be correlated with the error term and biased estimates of a will result.

We can actually be quite explicit about how the farmers will use the information about their land quality in their choice of K_i. The profit maximization problem for farmer i is:

$$\max \quad pQ_iK_i^aS_i^{1-a} - qK_i$$

where p is the price of corn and q is the price of seed. For simplicity, we will just assume that the farmer sets S_i equal to its average value. The first-order condition is:

$$paQ_iK_i^{a-1}S_i^{1-a} - q = 0$$

which can be solved to give

$$K_i = [apQ_i/q]^{\frac{1}{1-a}}S_i$$

Then it is clear that the farmer's observation on Q_i directly affects his decision of how much to plant and thus his decision of how much output to produce.

Suppose that our observations on $\ln K_i$ and $\ln C_i$ have the shape depicted in Figure 4.1. The true relationship between $\ln K_i$ and $\ln C_i$ is also plotted, for Q_i fixed at its average level.

If we observe a farm with a very large input of K_i, this is probably a farm with a large Q_i—hence, the output will be larger than the output for a farm with the average quality land. Thus, the data points associated with large K_is will lie *above* the true relationship for average Q farms. Similarly, farms with small inputs of K_i will have smaller than average Q_is as depicted.

The net result is that a line fitted to such data points will give us an estimate for a that is larger than the true value of a. This is exactly the

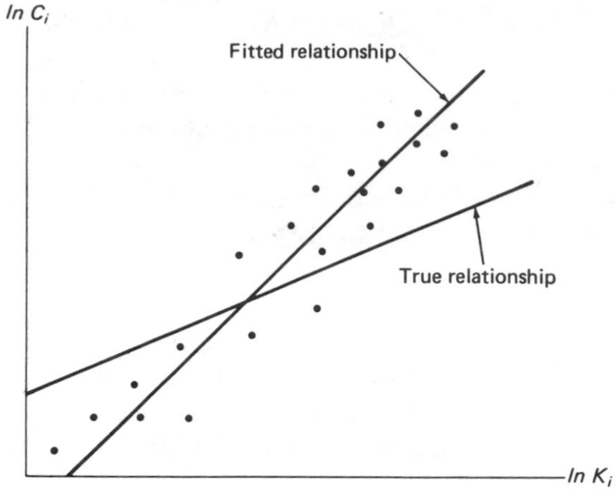

Fig. 4.1 *Example of Biased Estimate*

kind of bias mentioned earlier. The problem is that the large values of output are not due entirely to the large value of corn input. Rather, there is a third omitted variable, land quality, that affects both the level of output and the choice of input.

Bias of this sort is very common in econometric work. The statistical theory of regression was developed to analyze controlled experiments, where errors were present but their effect could be isolated from the effects of the explanatory variable. In economics, the explanatory variables are hardly ever given, but instead are chosen by economic agents. This choice is generally made using all of the information available to the agents which undoubtably includes some components of the error term.

These considerations make it imperative to examine explicitly the decision process of the firm. Only in this way can an empirical model consistent with economic theory and sound econometric analysis be developed.

4.2 *THE DUAL APPROACH*

Let us further consider the problem of the farmer described in the last section. For algebraic simplicity, we will forget about the S_i input and just think of the farmer's using a technology of the form

$$c_i = Q_i K_i^a$$

or

$$\ln C_i = a \ln K_i + \ln Q_i$$

Again, we think of the farmer's observing Q_i when he chooses C_i and K_i.

According to our model of firm behavior, the farmer will choose the output and input levels so as to maximize his profits. As shown in the last section this means we will get a factor demand function of the form:

$$K_i = [aQ_i(p_i/q_i)]^{1/1-a}$$

or

$$lnK_i = (1/1 - a)[lna + lnQ_i + ln(p_i/q_i)]$$

Here p_i and q_i are the prices of corn and seed observed by farmer i. Notice that this factor demand function is of the form:

$$lnK_i = m_0 + m_1 ln(p_i/q_i) + \epsilon_i$$

If we can estimate the parameter m_1 we can construct an estimate of a just by taking $(m_1 - 1)/m_1$.

We then ask the question: is the above equation for lnK_i likely to have the property that the right-hand variables are independent of the error term? The answer is pretty clearly yes; for the right-hand variables are prices, and in a competitive market prices are determined by the market, not by the individual farmers. The prices and the left-out variables—the error term—should be uncorrelated.

Thus to find a good estimate of the technological parameter a, we should not estimate the production function directly; an alternative, and probably better approach is to estimate the factor demand function and infer the underlying technological structure.

4.3 SOME EXTENSIONS

Suppose we now have a more complicated technology where we may have many inputs. Let us write the production function as $f(\mathbf{x}; \mathbf{a})$ where $\mathbf{x}$ is a vector of inputs and $\mathbf{a}$ is a vector of parameters to be estimated. If we want to get good estimates of the parameters $\mathbf{a}$ it would seem reasonable to solve for the factor demand functions $\mathbf{x}(\mathbf{w}; \mathbf{a})$ and use this system of equations to estimate the parameters $\mathbf{a}$.

Suppose for concreteness that we had two factor demands of the form

$$x_1 = a_1 w_1 + a_2 w_2 + \epsilon_1$$

$$x_2 = b_1 w_1 + b_2 w_2 + b_3 w_3 + \epsilon_2$$

(This example is only hypothetical since the functional form of these factor demand functions is rather implausible.) Now we could just estimate these two equations directly and construct estimates of the technological parameters by using the estimates of (a_1, a_2, b_1, b_2). However, to do this would be rather silly. For the parameters (a_1, a_2, b_1, b_2) are not all unrelated. In fact, according to the neoclassical restrictions described in Chapter 1, we know that $\partial x_1/\partial w_2 = \partial x_2/\partial w_1$ so that a_2 must equal b_1. In order to get efficient estimates of the parameters we would like to take account of such restrictions.

A convenient way to do this is to solve for the profit function and then estimate the parameters in terms of that function; that is, given the production function $f(\mathbf{x}; \mathbf{a})$, we solve for the profit function $\pi(p, \mathbf{w}; \mathbf{a})$. We then apply least squares to a regression with observed profits as the dependent variable and prices as the independent variables. We then use the results of this regression to construct estimates of the technological parameters $\mathbf{a}$. Since the profit function contains all the economically relevant information about the technology, this procedure can identify all the parameters.

Now in practice, this is not often done, primarily because it is hard to get data on economic profits and one is not always willing to assume pure competition in the output market. However, it is often feasible to try to estimate cost functions.

If one has data on factor prices and costs, one can try to estimate the parameters of a cost function. Suppose for example we postulate a cost function of the Cobb-Douglas variety. As we saw in Example 1.10, this cost function has the form:

$$c(w_1, w_2, y) = Kw_1^a w_2^{1-a} y$$

or $$\log c(w_1, w_2, y) = \log K + a \log w_1 + (1 - a) \log w_2 + \log y$$

If we have observations on a number of firms we can postulate the statistical relationship:

$$\log c_i = \log K + a \log w_{1i} + (1 - a) \log w_{2i} + \log y_i + \epsilon_i$$

and proceed to estimate the parameters K and a. Just as in the case of the profit function, w_{1i} and w_{2i} can reasonably be assumed to be independent from ϵ_i. However, the relationship between y_i and ϵ_i poses some serious problems. It seems rather implausible that the level of output of a firm should be independent from left-out factors of production that are possibly observed by the individual firms.

Under certain circumstances such an assumption might make sense. For example, suppose that the firms in question generated electric power so that the amount of output supplied was determined exogenously; i.e., the output of the firm was determined solely by demand conditions. In such a circumstance the independence assumption might be plausible, and estimates derived from the cost functions may be acceptable.

We have seen that direct least squares estimates of production relationships are not likely to result in good estimates of the underlying technological parameters. A better procedure seems to be to estimate the factor demand and supply (or the conditional demand and supply functions) and infer the underlying technological parameters. If proper account is taken of the cross equation restrictions, this comes down to estimating the profit function or the conditional cost function.

On the other hand, there are problems with this procedure also. First, the construction of the demand and supply functions involves the maintained hypothesis of competitive markets. Secondly, the independent variables in the demand functions—the factor prices—may vary little from firm to firm. The resulting lack of variation may make accurate estimation difficult. Third, if one is attempting to estimate industry or aggregate production relationship using time series data, the hypothesis of exogenous prices seems unrealistic.

4.4 *FUNCTIONAL FORM AND DUALITY*

Although most of the examples in this book have dealt with two factor production functions, it is clear that most real world applications involve production processes which involve many inputs. When one actually attempts to estimate parameters of a production process, one needs a description of technology that can handle large numbers of inputs.

The Cobb-Douglas technology describes in several previous examples can easily be extended to the case of n inputs. It takes the form:

$$y = A \prod_{i=1}^{n} x_i^{a_i}$$

or

$$\log y = \log A + \sum_{i=1}^{n} a_i \log x_i$$

This form is especially convenient for estimation since it is linear in the parameters A and (a_i).

Unfortunately, the Cobb-Douglas form does impose serious and perhaps unrealistic restrictions on the production process. For example, we have shown in Example 1.23 that the "elasticity of substitution" between each pair of factors must be identically one for a Cobb-Douglas technology. There seems to be no particular reason to impose such a restriction on a priori grounds. Thus, it is desirable to have a functional form for a production function that places fewer restrictions on the nature of the technology.

One such form is the *constant elasticity of substitution* or CES production function given by:

$$y = [a_0 + \sum_{i=1}^{n} a_i x_i^{\rho}]^{1/\rho}$$

As its name implies, the production function allows the elasticity of substitution between pairs of factors to differ from unity, but it can be shown that the CES function does force the elasticities between each pair of factors to be the same. The CES function is a step in the right direction but still seems too restrictive. One might think that it would not be that difficult to find function forms for the production functions that were (1) simple enough to estimate easily and (2) did not impose too many a priori restrictions on economic parameters. Unfortunately, it is rather difficult to find such forms. It is safe to say that most empirical studies that use *production function* specifications of technology use a form of either the CES or the Cobb-Douglas variety.

The situation is not quite as bleak as it appears. Recall that the only econometrically useful feature of a production function is the associated cost or profit function. Thus we might be able to find functional forms for cost functions, for example, that allowed for a lot of flexibility and still were fairly simple to estimate. The search for such flexible forms for cost functions is greatly aided by the duality results described in Chapter 1. Recall that any positive homogeneous, nondecreasing, concave function of factor prices is a cost function for some nice neoclassical technology. Thus, in order to estimate various technological parameters, we only need to choose a nice cost function and estimate its parameters. These considerations have led to the discovery of several convenient forms for cost functions, some of which are described below.

Example 4.1 The Diewert (Generalized Leontief) Cost Function

$$c(\mathbf{w}, y) = y \sum_{i=1}^{n} \sum_{j=1}^{n} b_{ij} w_i^{1/2} w_j^{1/2} \qquad \text{where } b_{ij} = b_{ji}$$

This has conditional factor demands of the form

$$x_i(\mathbf{w}, y) = \sum_{j=1}^{n} b_{ij}(w_j/w_i)^{1/2}\, y$$

The factor demands are linear in the b_{ij} parameters, which is convenient for linear regression estimation. If all the $b_{ij} \geqq 0$ and some $b_{ij} > 0$, it is straightforward to verify that this functional form satisfies the necessary requirements to be a cost function. If $b_{ij} = 0$ for $i \neq j$ then the system collapses to a Leontief system.

The b_{ij} parameters can be related to the elasticities of substitution between the various factors. The equation is a bit messy to give here, but we will content ourselves with the statement that, the greater the b_{ij} term, the larger the elasticity of substitution between factors i and j. Furthermore, all $n/2$ elasticities are unconstrained by the functional form.

Finally, we note one important theoretical justification for the Diewert cost function: it can be viewed as a second-order (local) approximation to an arbitrary cost function.

Example 4.2 The Translog Cost Function

$$ln\ c(\mathbf{w}, y) = \left[a_0 + \sum_{i=1}^{n} a_i\ ln\ w_i + \frac{1}{2} \sum_{i=1}^{n} \sum_{j=1}^{n} b_{ij}\ ln\ w_i\ ln\ w_j\right] + ln\ y$$

where $\sum_{i=1}^{n} a_i = 1, b_{ij} = b_{ji}, \sum_{j=1}^{n} b_{ij} = 0 \quad \text{for} \quad i = 1, \ldots, n$

Under the stated restrictions the translog cost function is homogeneous in prices. If $a_i > 0$ for all i, $\Sigma a_i = 1$, and $b_{ij} = 0$ for all i and j the translog function collapses to a Cobb-Douglas cost function. It can be shown that, like the Diewert cost function, the translog function can serve as a local, second-order approximation to an arbitrary cost function.

The conditional factor demands are not linear in the parameters. However, the factor shares $s_i(\mathbf{w}, y) = w_i x_i(\mathbf{w}, y)/c(\mathbf{w}, y)$ are linear in the unknown parameters:

$$s_i(\mathbf{w}, y) = a_i + \sum_{j=1}^{n} b_{ij}\ ln\ w_j$$

(Of course, we have the restriction that $\sum_{i=1}^{n} s_i(\mathbf{w}, y) = 1$.) Since s_i can be observed, the equation for the factor shares can be used to estimate the parameters of the cost—and hence production—function.

4.5 ESTIMATING CONSUMER DEMAND FUNCTIONS

At an abstract level, the problem of estimating parameters of demand functions can be viewed as analogous to the problem of estimating the parameters of factor demand functions as discussed in the last chapter. The study of demand functions presents three extra problems that make it somewhat more difficult:

(1) In production estimation we observe the level of output of the system—the amount of product produced. In demand estimation, the level of output of the system is the utility level and this is not observed.

(2) In production estimation it seemed reasonable to assume that all firms operated under the same technology. In the estimation of demand systems it is clear that utility functions and income vary from agent to agent.

(3) In production estimation we observe directly the output of each individual firm. In demand estimation we often observe only the aggregate traded amounts. According to our elementary economic theory, observed prices are supposed to be *equilibrium* prices, i.e., prices where aggregate supply equals aggregate demand. This equilibrium nature of the aggregate equations raises several new econometric problems such as *the identification problem* and *simultaneous equation bias*. For the rest of the section we will ignore these problems, supposing that the equilibrium prices are determined exogenously and that the demand behavior we observe is only a small part of some larger system. The reader interested in the estimation problems of simultaneous equation systems should consult one of the references listed at the end of this chapter.

4.6 ESTIMATION OF A SINGLE DEMAND EQUATION

Let us consider first the commonly encountered empirical problem of estimating the demand for a single good given cross-sectional data. Thus we imagine that in each of several locations we have observations on the amount of the good consumed Q_i and the (exogenously determined) price of the good in that location, P_i. The first problem is to choose a functional form for the demand equation.

One form often used is the *linear demand equation:*

$$Q_i = a + bP_i + \epsilon_i$$

A somewhat more convenient form is the *multiplicative demand equation:*

$$Q_i = AP_i^b\epsilon_i$$

Upon taking logarithms of both sides we find:

$$\log Q_i = \log A + b \log P_i + \log \epsilon_i$$

This has the convenient property that b directly measures the price elasticity of demand.

As before, ϵ_i is interpreted as a random error term. We know from the Gauss-Markov theorem that ordinary least squares will give us good estimates of the parameter b when p_i is uncorrelated with ϵ_i. Is this likely to be the case?

To answer this question we have to ask ourselves what kind of left-out effects are subsumed in ϵ_i. Referring to our basic theory of consumer behavior, we recall that demand functions are in general functions of all prices and of income. These effects must certainly be counted as part of the error term.

Now is it reasonable to assume that other prices and income are uncorrelated with p_i? Suppose that we are estimating the demand for coffee as a function of its price. We do not have data on the price of tea, but the consumers do observe such prices. The demand for coffee will presumably depend on the price of tea, so that the price of tea will be a component of the error term. If coffee and tea prices are correlated in the sample, ordinary regression techniques may produce biased estimates of the parameters.

Even with the simplest kind of demand estimation it is often necessary to incorporate variables other than own prices and income. Let us return to our basic methodology of consumer behavior and see how to construct a demand system.

4.7 SYSTEMS OF DEMAND EQUATIONS

We imagine that a *representative consumer* has a utility function of the Cobb-Douglas sort:

$$u(x^1, \cdots, x^k) = \sum_{j=1}^{k} a^j \ln x^j$$

Then maximization of utility subject to a budget constraint gives us demand functions of the form:

$$x^j(p, y) = \frac{a^j y}{p^j}$$

We observe agents $i = 1, \cdots, n$. The above form makes it reasonable to postulate that agent i's demand for good j is of the form:

$$x_i^j(p, y_i) = a^j\left(\frac{y_i}{p^j}\right) + \epsilon_i$$

Thus demand functions are linear in the income price ratio. This system of equations can be estimated using standard techniques.

In this particular case, the demand for good j depends only on the price of good j and income. Hence one can estimate individual demand equations quite easily.

The linear expenditure system described above imposes some serious restrictions on the form of the demand equations. Most serious of these is the *independence* assumption: the cross price elasticities are all zero. For many applications this is implausible. As before, it is convenient to use duality theory to find new functional forms for demand systems.

According to the chapter on consumer behavior, the specification of an indirect utility function is *equivalent* to the specification of a direct utility function. Furthermore we know that *any* continuous, nonincreasing, quasi-convex function of prices is an indirect utility function for some direct utility function. Hence all we need to do is examine such convenient forms.

Example 4.3 Indirect Addilog Demand Model The indirect utility function has the form:

$$v(\mathbf{p}, y) = \sum_{i=1}^{k} a_i \left(\frac{y}{p_i}\right)^{b_i}$$

Demand functions can be found by differentiation:

$$x_i(\mathbf{p}, y) = \frac{a_i b_i y^{b_i} p_i^{-b_i-1}}{\sum_{j=1}^{k} a_j b_j y^{b_j-1} p_j^{-b_j}}$$

This is rather inconvenient for linear estimation techniques. However, the log of the ratio of x_i and x_j gives us a linear form:

$$ln\ (x_i/x_j) = ln\ (a_i b_i/a_j b_j) + (b_i - b_j)\ ln\ y + (b_j - b_i)\ ln\ (p_i/p_j)$$

It should be noted that the a_i terms are only determined up to a scale factor.

Example 4.4 The Diewert Reciprocal Indirect Utility Function Define $q_i = p_i/y$ and let $h(\mathbf{q}) = 1/v(\mathbf{p}, y)$. Consider the following functional form for $h(\mathbf{q})$:

$$h(\mathbf{q}) = \sum_{i=1}^{n} \sum_{j=1}^{n} b_{ij} q_i^{1/2} q_j^{1/2} + 2 \sum_{j=1}^{n} b_{0j} q_j^{1/2} + b_{00}$$

where $b_{ij} = b_{ji}$.

If all $b_{ij} \geqq 0$ and some $b_{ij} > 0$ then this form satisfies the conditions to be the reciprocal of an indirect utility function.

The demand equation for good i is given by:

$$x_i(q_1 \cdots q_n) = \frac{\sum_{j=1}^{n} b_{ij} q_i^{-1/2} q_j^{1/2} + b_{0i} q_i^{-1/2}}{\sum_{k=1}^{n} \sum_{m=1}^{n} b_{km} q_k^{1/2} q_n^{1/2} + \sum_{m=1}^{n} b_{0m} q_m^{1/2}}$$

The demand equations are homogeneous in degree zero in the b_{ij} so we generally impose a convenient normalization. Preferences will be homothetic if $b_{0i} = 0$ for $i = 0, 1, \cdots, n$. In this case the system of demand equations will be given by:

$$x_i(p_1 \cdots p_n, y) = \frac{\left(\sum_{j=1}^{n} b_{ij} p_i^{-1/2} p_j^{1/2} \right) y}{\sum_{k=1}^{n} \sum_{m=1}^{n} b_{km} p_k^{1/2} p_m^{1/2}}$$

Example 4.5 The Translog Reciprocal Indirect Utility Function This function is given by:

$$ln\ h(\mathbf{q}) = a_0 + \sum_{i=1}^{n} a_i\ ln\ q_i + \frac{1}{2} \sum_{i=1}^{n} b_{ij}\ ln\ q_i\ ln\ q_j$$

where $b_{ij} = b_{ji}$ for all i and j. The consumer demand functions are given by:

$$x_i(\mathbf{q}) = \frac{q_i^{-1} \left(a_i + \sum_{j=1}^{n} b_{ij}\ ln\ q_j \right)}{\sum_{k=1}^{n} a_k + \sum_{k=1}^{n} \sum_{m=1}^{n} b_{km}\ ln\ q_m}$$

If the $b_{ij} \neq 0$ for any i and j then the translog function will not satisfy the requirements for an indirect utility function globally but may be regarded as a local approximation to *any* indirect utility function.

The translog function will be homogeneous of degree 1 if $\sum_{i=1}^{n} a_i = 1$, $b_{ij} = b_{ji}$, and $\sum_{j=1}^{n} b_{ij} = 0$ for every i.

Since the demand equations are homogeneous of degree zero in the parameters a_i and b_{ij}, it is necessary to impose a normalization. The most convenient such normalization is: $\sum_{i=1}^{n} \sum_{j=1}^{n} b_{ij} = 0$.

In the previous two examples we have specifically assumed that we observe all consumers' incomes and that all consumers have the same preferences. This is rather implausible.

The identical utility function assumption is not really so bad. A reasonable way to view the problem of distribution of tastes is to imagine that consumers have utility functions "distributed around" a given utility function. Then if we could observe utilities we can imagine choosing an agent i at random and recording his (indirect) utility as:

$$v_i(\mathbf{p}, y_i) = v(\mathbf{p}, y_i) + \epsilon_i$$

Here the error terms have a very direct interpretation: they are due to variations in tastes within the population.

The problem of observing income for each agent is more difficult since this information is rarely known. However, the next example shows that some specifications can be used that greatly reduce this problem:

Example 4.6 Translog Utility and Income Distribution Imagine that the average consumer in the economy has translog preferences and that income is distributed according to some known density function $f(y)$; i.e., the number of people having income between y_0 and y_1 is given by $N \int_{y_0}^{y_1} f(y)\,dy$ where N is the total number of people in the economy.

Then the observed *aggregate* market demand for good i can be given by

$$x_i(\mathbf{p}, f) = N \int_0^{\infty} f(y)\, x_i(\mathbf{p}, y)\, dy$$

If we impose the normalization given above, that $\sum_{i=1}^{n} \sum_{j=1}^{n} b_{ij} = 0$, the average demand for good i can be written as:

$$\frac{p_i x_i(\mathbf{p}, f)}{N} = \frac{a_i y^* + \sum_{j=1}^{n} b_{ij} \ln p_j y^* - \sum_{j=1}^{n} b_{ij} y^{**}}{\sum_{k=1}^{n} a_k + \sum_{k=1}^{n} \sum_{m=1}^{n} b_{km} \ln p_m}$$

where $y^* = \int y f(y)\, dy$ is average income and $y^{**} = \int y \ln y f(y)\, dy$ measures the dispersion of income. The above form, although somewhat messy, can be estimated by nonlinear least squares techniques. It has the remarkable property that the preferences of an "average" consumer can be estimated using only market data plus data on the distribution of income.

We have seen that consumer theory can contribute to the specification and estimation of demand systems. However, its contribution must be taken with a grain of salt. The problem comes again in the fact that preferences may vary significantly from agent to agent.

Recall that we have shown that individual demand behavior must obey certain demand restrictions—the Slutsky equation, symmetry, and so on. These properties are not carried over to aggregate demand functions. In fact, it can be shown that any continuous function that satisfies Walras' law can be generated by some set of preference-maximizing consumers with some distribution of income. For a proof, see Debreu (1974).

Hence it may be a mistake to impose the Slutsky-type restrictions by assuming that aggregate behavior is representable by utility-maximizing demand functions. On the other hand, it seems that, if preferences can be regarded as distributed closely around some average representative utility function, aggregate demand behavior can be represented by neoclassical demand curves plus a random error component. The decision as to which type of specification is most useful must ultimately rest on empirical results.

Exercises

4.1 (10) How would one estimate the parameters of a constant returns Cobb-Douglas production function if one were given information about factor prices (w_i) and factor shares ($w_i x_i$)?

4.2 (10) Assume we have a cross-sectional sample of firms who produce some output y_i using capital and labor via a Cobb-Douglas production function. Assume the price of capital is constant across firms but the price of labor varies from firm to firm. What equation would be appropriate to estimate the parameters of the production function?

4.3 (10) Why do we require that $b_i = b_j$ in the Diewert cost function?

4.4 (10) Suppose that we want to estimate the parameters of a production function, where we can control the production process. We choose K and L at random, plug these into the production process, and observe the output $y + \epsilon$. Suggest a reasonable way to estimate the parameters of the production function.

Notes

An elementary book on statistics and econometrics is Beals (1972). More advanced works include Kmenta (1971), Johnston (1972), Theil (1971), Malinvaud (1966), and Pindyck and Rubinfeld (1976).

A useful survey of the problems involved in estimating production functions is in Walters (1970). A more detailed study with examples and much methodological discussion is Nerlove (1965). A quite useful survey of the dual approach to estimation is Diewert (1974).

An elementary exposition of the problems of estimating consumer demand may be found in Walters (1970). Diewert (1974) gives a very useful survey of duality theory and demand estimation. The examples in this chapter were taken from this latter work. There is an extensive literature on the estimation problems described in this chapter; the above works contain useful bibliographies. A nice collection of reading is Zellner (1968). For problems involved in estimating production functions see in particular Zellner, Kmenta, and Drèze (1966), which is reprinted in Zellner (1968). A wealth of information on estimating production functions and cost functions can be found in Fuss and McFadden (1978). See especially the chapter by Fuss, McFadden, and Mundlak (1978).

References

BEALS, R. 1972. *Statistics for Economists*. Chicago: Rand McNally.

DEBREU, G. 1974. "Excess Demand Functions." *Journal of Mathematical Economics* 1 (no. 1):15–22.

DIEWERT, E. 1974. "Applications of Duality Theory." In *Frontiers of Quantitative Economics*, vol. 2, ed. M. Intriligator and D. Kendrick. Amsterdam: North Holland.

FUSS, M., and MCFADDEN, D. 1978. *Production Economics: A Dual Approach to Theory and Applications*. Amsterdam: North Holland.

FUSS, M.; MCFADDEN, D.; and MUNDLAK, Y. 1978. "A Survey of Functional Forms in the Economic Analysis of Production." In M. Fuss and D. McFadden, 1978.

JOHNSTON, J. 1972. *Econometric Methods*. 2d ed. New York: McGraw-Hill.

KMENTA, J. 1971. *Elements of Econometrics*. New York: Macmillan.

MALINVAUD, E. 1966. *Statistical Methods of Econometrics*. Chicago: Rand McNally.

NERLOVE, M. 1965. *Estimation and Identification of Cobb-Douglas Production Functions*. Chicago: Rand McNally.

PINDYCK, R., and RUBINFELD, D. 1976. *Econometric Models and Economic Forecasts*. New York: McGraw-Hill.

THEIL, H. 1971. *Principles of Econometrics*. New York: Wiley.

WALTERS, A. 1970. *An Introduction to Econometrics*. New York: Norton.

ZELLNER, A. 1968. *Readings in Economic Statistics and Econometrics*. Boston: Little, Brown.

———; KMENTA, J.; and DRÈZE, J. 1966. "Specification and Estimation of Cobb-Douglas Production Function Models." *Econometrica* 34:784–795. Reprinted in Zellner (1968).

Chapter 5

General Equilibrium Theory and Welfare Economics

In Chapter 2 we discussed the economic theory of a single market. We saw that when there were many economic agents each had an incentive to act as a price taker. Given prices each agent could then determine his or her demands and supplies for the good in question. When the price was such that supply equaled demand, the market was in equilibrium in the sense that no agent would desire to change his or her actions.

The single-market story described above is a *partial equilibrium* model in that all prices other than the price of the good being studied are assumed to remain fixed. In the general equilibrium model *all* prices are variable, and equilibrium requires that all markets clear. Thus, general equilibrium theory takes account of all of the interactions between markets, as well as the functioning of the individual markets.

In the interests of exposition, we will examine first the special case of the general equilibrium model where all of the economic agents are consumers. This situation, known as the case of *pure exchange,* contains many of the phenomena present in the more extensive case involving firms. The theory of production in general equilibrium will be discussed in Chapter 6.

The setup of the pure exchange economy is as follows. We imagine that we have n consumers, each of whom holds some initial bundle of k commodities. The initial bundle of agent i is represented by a k vector $\mathbf{W}_i$. The agents then trade among themselves, each attempting to maximize his or her preferences.

What will be the outcome of such a process? What are desirable outcomes of such a process? What allocative mechanisms are appropriate for achieving desirable outcomes? These questions involve a mixture of both positive and normative issues. It is precisely the interplay between the two types of questions that provides much of the interest in the theory of resource allocation.

5.1 AGENTS AND GOODS

The concept of good considered here is very broad. Goods can be distinguished by time, location, and state of world. Services, such as labor services, are taken to be just another kind of good. There is assumed to be a market for each good, in which a price of that good is determined.

In the pure exchange model the only kind of economic agent is the consumer. Each consumer i is described completely by his preference, $>_i$ (or his utility function, u_i), and his endowment of the k commidities, $\mathbf{W}_i$. Each consumer is assumed to behave competitively—that is, to take prices as given, independent of his or her actions. The objective of the consumer is taken to be preference maximization.

The basic concern of the theory of general equilibrium is how goods are allocated among the economic agents. Agent i's *consumption bundle* will be denoted by $\mathbf{x}_i$; it is a k-vector describing how much of each good agent i consumes. The amount of good j that agent i holds will be denoted by x_i^j. An *allocation* $\mathbf{x} = (\mathbf{x}_1, \cdots, \mathbf{x}_n)$ is a collection of n consumption bundles describing what each of the n agents holds. A *feasible allocation* is one that is possible; in the pure exchange case, this is just an allocation that uses up all the goods, i.e., one in which $\sum_{i=1}^{n} \mathbf{x}_i = \sum_{i=1}^{n} \mathbf{W}_i$. (Sometimes the equality is replaced by less than or equal to.)

There is a convenient way of representing allocations, preferences, and endowments in a two-dimensional form, which is depicted in Figure 5.1.

Suppose that there are two goods W^1 and W^2 of each good, and two agents. In the *Edgeworth box* below we can draw how much agent 1 has of

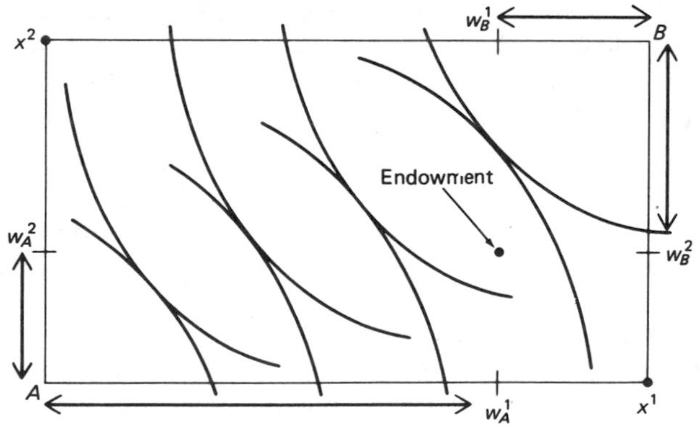

Fig. 5.1 *The Edgeworth Box*

each of the two goods; this automatically determines how much agent 2 has of each good. Thus all feasible allocations can be represented in the box. In particular, the *initial endowment* is a feasible allocation and can be represented by a point in the box.

Similarly, the agents' indifference curves can be drawn in; now of course there are two sets, one set for each of the agents. All of the information contained in a two-person, two-good pure exchange economy can in this way be represented in a convenient graphical form.

5.2 *WALRASIAN EQUILIBRIUM*

We have argued that, when there are many agents, it is reasonable to suppose that each agent takes the market prices as independent of his or her actions. Consider the particular case of pure exchange being described here. We imagine that there is some vector of market prices $\mathbf{p} = (p_1, \cdots, p_k)$, one price for each good. Each consumer takes these prices as given and chooses the most preferred bundle from his or her consumption set; that is, each consumer i acts as if he or she were solving the following problem:

$$\begin{aligned} \max \quad & u_i(\mathbf{x}_i) \\ \text{s.t.} \quad & p \cdot \mathbf{x}_i = y_i = p \cdot \mathbf{W}_i \end{aligned}$$

The answer to this problem, $\mathbf{x}_i(\mathbf{p}, \mathbf{p} \cdot \mathbf{W}_i)$, is just the consumer's demand function, which we have already studied in Chapter 3. The only difference is that the consumer's income is now taken to be the value of his or her initial bundle, so that it will depend on $\mathbf{p}$. We saw in Chapter 3 that, under an assumption of strict convexity of preferences, the demand functions will be nice continuous functions.

Of course, for arbitrary $\mathbf{p}$, it may not be possible actually to make the desired transactions for the simple reason that the total amount of desired demand, $\sum_i \mathbf{x}_i(\mathbf{p}, \mathbf{p} \cdot \mathbf{W}_i)$, may not be equal to the total amount of supply, $\sum_i \mathbf{W}_i$.

The question then arises: is there some price vector $\mathbf{p}^*$ that will equate supply and demand in all markets? It may sometimes be too much to require the *equality* of supply and demand. After all, if some goods are undesirable, they may well be in excess supply in equilibrium. Hence, we often define a *Walrasian equilibrium* to be a pair $(\mathbf{p}^*, \mathbf{x}^*)$ such that

$$\sum_i \mathbf{x}_i^* = \sum_i \mathbf{x}_i(\mathbf{p}^*, \mathbf{p}^* \cdot \mathbf{W}_i) \leqq \sum_i \mathbf{W}_i$$

that is, $\mathbf{p}^*$ is a Walrasian equilibrium if there is no good for which there is positive excess demand. It will be shown later that if all goods are desirable—in a sense to be made precise—then no good can be in excess supply in equilibrium. In such economies, equilibrium means that all markets must clear and that we have equality of demand and supply in all markets. We will usually be concerned with this case.

5.3 GRAPHICAL ANALYSIS OF WALRASIAN EQUILIBRIA

Walras equilibria can be examined geometrically by use of the Edgeworth box. Given any price vector, we can determine the budget line of each agent and use the tangency condition to find the demanded bundles of each agent. We then search for a price vector such that the demanded points of the two agents are compatible.

In Figure 5.2 we have drawn such an equilibrium allocation. Each agent is maximizing his preferences on his budget line and these demands are compatible with the total supplies available.

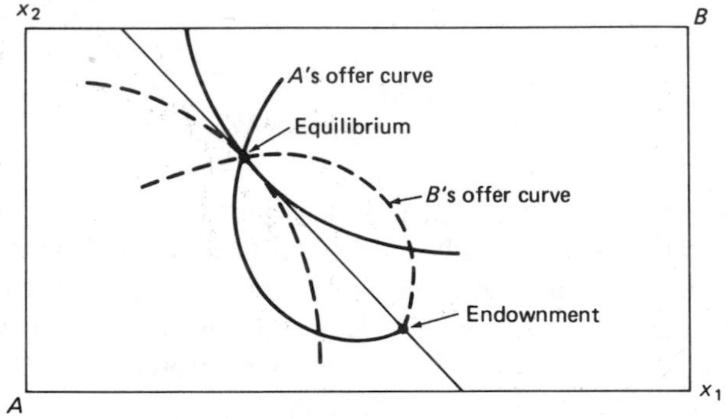

Fig. 5.2 *Walrasian Equilibrium in the Edgeworth Box*

Note that the Walras equilibrium occurs at a point where the two indifference curves are tangent. This is clear, since preference maximization requires that each agent's marginal rates of substitution be equal to the common price ratio.

Another way to describe equilibrium is through the use of the offer curves introduced in Chapter 3. Recall that a consumer's offer curve describes the locus of tangencies—i.e., the set of demanded bundles. Thus, equilibrium in the Edgeworth box is precisely the point where the offer curves of the agents intersect. At such an intersection the demanded bundles of each agent are compatible with the available supplies.

5.4 EXISTENCE OF WALRASIAN EQUILIBRIA

Will there always exist a price vector where all markets clear? We will analyze this question of the existence of a Walras equilibrium in this section.

Let us notice a few facts about this existence problem. First of all, the budget set B_i remains unchanged if we multiply all prices by any positive constant; thus, each consumer's demand function has the property that $\mathbf{x}_i(\mathbf{p}, \mathbf{p}\cdot\mathbf{W}_i) = \mathbf{x}_i(k\mathbf{p}, k\mathbf{p}\cdot\mathbf{W}_i)$; i.e., the demand function is homogeneous of degree zero in prices. As the sum of homogeneous functions is homogeneous, the aggregate excess demand function

$$z(\mathbf{p}) = \sum_i \mathbf{x}_i(\mathbf{p}, \mathbf{p}\cdot\mathbf{W}_i) - \sum_i \mathbf{W}_i$$

is also homogeneous of degree zero in prices. (Notice that we have dropped the dependence of $\mathbf{z}$ on $\mathbf{W}_i$ since the initial endowments remain constant.) If all of the individual demand functions are continuous, then $\mathbf{z}$ will be a continuous function.

Since the aggregate excess demand function is homogeneous, we can normalize prices and express demands in terms of relative prices. A convenient normalization is to replace each absolute price p_i' by a normalized price $p_i = \dfrac{p_i'}{\sum_{j=1}^{k} p_j'}$. This has the consequence that the relative prices p_i must always sum up to 1. Hence, we can restrict our attention to price vectors belonging to the $k - 1$ dimensional unit simplex:

$$S^{k-1} = \{\mathbf{p} \text{ in } R^k_+ \colon \sum_{i=1}^{k} p_i = 1\}.$$

For a picture of S^1 and S^2 see Figure 5.3.

We can already establish an important result about the excess demand function.

PROPOSITION (*Walras' law*) *For any* $\mathbf{p}$ *in* S^{k-1}, *we have* $\mathbf{p}\cdot\mathbf{z}(\mathbf{p}) = 0$; *i.e., the value of the excess demand is identically zero.*

PROOF $\mathbf{p}\cdot\mathbf{z}(\mathbf{p}) = \mathbf{p}\cdot(\Sigma\mathbf{x}_i(\mathbf{p}, \mathbf{p}\cdot\mathbf{W}_i) - \Sigma\mathbf{W}_i) = \Sigma(\mathbf{p}\cdot\mathbf{x}_i(\mathbf{p}, \mathbf{p}\cdot\mathbf{W}_i) - \mathbf{p}\cdot\mathbf{W}_i) = 0$ since $\mathbf{x}_i(\mathbf{p}, \mathbf{p}\cdot\mathbf{W}_i)$ must lie in the ith agent's budget set $B_i = \{\mathbf{x} \text{ in } R^k\colon \mathbf{p}\cdot\mathbf{x} = \mathbf{p}\cdot\mathbf{W}_i\}$. □

Walras' law actually says something quite obvious: if each individual satisfies his budget constraint, so that the value of his excess demand is

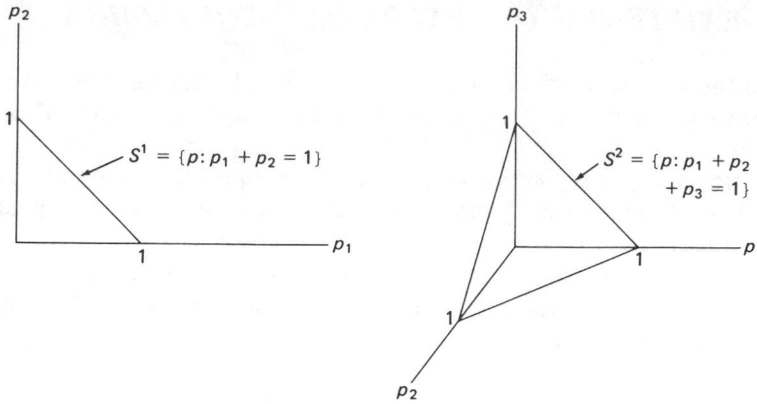

Fig. 5.3 *Price Simplices*

zero, then of course the value of the *sum* of the excess demands must be zero.

One implication of Walras' law is this: if, at some $\mathbf{p} \gg 0$, $k - 1$ of the markets all clear, then the kth market must also clear. Another important consequence of Walras' law is the following:

PROPOSITION (*Free goods*) *If* $\mathbf{p}^*$ *is a Walrasian equilibrium and* $z_j(\mathbf{p}^*) < 0$, *then* $p_j^* = 0$; i.e., *if some good is in excess supply at a Walras equilibrium it must be a free good.*

PROOF Since $\mathbf{p}^*$ is a Walras equilibrium, $\mathbf{z}(\mathbf{p}^*) \leqq \mathbf{0}$ and thus $\mathbf{p}^* \cdot \mathbf{z}(\mathbf{p}^*) = \Sigma p_i^* z_i(\mathbf{p}^*) \leqq 0$. If $z_j(\mathbf{p}^*) < 0$ and $p_j^* > 0$, we would have $\mathbf{p}^* \cdot \mathbf{z}(\mathbf{p}^*) < 0$, contradicting Walras' law. □

Suppose that all goods are desirable in the following sense:

(DESIRABILITY) If $p_i = 0$, then $z_i(\mathbf{p}) > 0$ for $i = 1, \cdots, k$

that is, if some price is zero, the aggregate excess demand for that good is strictly positive. Then:

PROPOSITION (*Equality of demand and supply*) *If all goods are desirable and* $\mathbf{p}^*$ *is a Walrasian equilibrium, then* $\mathbf{z}(\mathbf{p}^*) = \mathbf{0}$.

PROOF Assume $z_i(\mathbf{p}^*) < 0$. Then by the free goods proposition, $p_i^* = 0$. But then by the desirability assumption, $z_i(\mathbf{p}^*) > 0$, a contradiction. □

To summarize: in general all we require for equilibrium is that there is no excess demand for any good. But the above propositions indicate that if some good is actually in excess supply in equilibrium then its price must be zero. Thus, if each good is desirable in the sense that a zero price implies it will be in excess demand, then equilibrium will in fact be characterized by the equality of demand and supply in every market.

We return now to the question of the existence of a Walras equilibrium: is there a $\mathbf{p}^*$ that clears all markets? Our basic proof of existence will make use of the Brouwer fixed-point theorem:

Theorem *If* $\mathbf{f}: S^{k-1} \rightarrow S^{k-1}$ *is a continuous function from the unit simplex to itself, there is some* $\mathbf{x}$ *in* S^{k-1} *such that* $\mathbf{x} = \mathbf{f}(\mathbf{x})$.

"PROOF" The proof for the general case is beyond the scope of this book; a good proof is in Scarf (1973). However, we will prove the theorem for $k = 2$.

In this case, we can identify the unit 1-dimensional simplex S^1 with the unit interval. So we have a continuous function f: $[0; 1] \rightarrow [0; 1]$ and we want to establish that there is some x in $[0; 1]$ such that $x = f(x)$.

Consider the function g: $[0; 1] \rightarrow [-1; 1]$ defined by $g(x) = f(x) - x$. Geometrically, g just measures the difference between $f(x)$ and the diagonal in the box depicted in Figure 5.4. A fixed point of the mapping f is just an x^* where $g(x^*) = 0$.

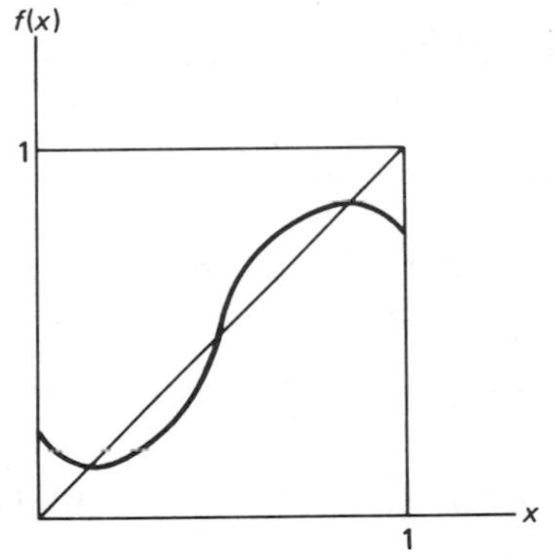

Fig. 5.4 *Proof of Brouwer's Theorem for* S^1

Now $g(0) = f(0) - 0 \geqq 0$ since $f(0)$ is in $[0; 1]$, and $g(1) = f(1) - 1 \leqq 0$ for the same reason. Since f is continuous, we can apply the intermediate value theorem and conclude that there is some x in $[0; 1]$ such that $g(x) = 0 = f(x) - x$, which proves the theorem. □

We are now in a position to prove the main existence theorem.

Theorem *If* $\mathbf{z}: S^{k-1} \rightarrow R^k$ *is continuous and satisfies* $\mathbf{p} \cdot \mathbf{z}(\mathbf{p}) \equiv 0$, *then there is a* $\mathbf{p}^*$ *in* S^{k-1} *such that* $\mathbf{z}(\mathbf{p}^*) \leqq \mathbf{0}$.

PROOF Define a map $\mathbf{g}: S^{k-1} \to S^{k-1}$ by

$$g_i(\mathbf{p}) = \frac{p_i + \max(0, z_i(\mathbf{p}))}{1 + \sum_{j=1}^{k} \max(0, z_j(\mathbf{p}))} \qquad \text{for } i = 1, \cdots, k$$

Notice that this map is continuous since z and $\max(\cdot, \cdot)$ are continuous functions and that $\mathbf{g}(\mathbf{p})$ does lie in S^{k-1} since $\Sigma\, g_i(\mathbf{p}) = 1$.

This map also has a reasonable economic interpretation: if there is excess demand in some market, so that $z_i(\mathbf{p}) > 0$, then the price of that good tends to increase.

By Brouwer's fixed-point theorem there is a $\mathbf{p}^*$ such that $\mathbf{p}^* = \mathbf{g}(\mathbf{p}^*)$; i.e.,

$$p_i^* = \frac{p_i^* + \max(0, z_i(\mathbf{p}^*))}{1 + \sum_j \max(0, z_j(\mathbf{p}^*))} \qquad \text{for } i = 1, \cdots, k$$

We will show that this $\mathbf{p}^*$ is indeed a Walras equilibrium. Cross multiply the above equation to get

$$p_i^* \sum_j \max(0, z_j(\mathbf{p}^*)) = \max(0, z_i(\mathbf{p}^*)) \qquad i = 1, \cdots, k$$

and multiply each equation by $z_i(\mathbf{p}^*)$:

$$z_i(\mathbf{p}^*)\, p_i^* \left[\sum_j \max(0, z_j(\mathbf{p}^*))\right] = z_i(\mathbf{p}^*) \max(0, z_i(\mathbf{p}^*)) \qquad i = 1, \cdots, k$$

Sum these k equations to get:

$$\left[\sum_j \max(0, z_j(\mathbf{p}^*))\right] \sum_i p_i^* z_i(\mathbf{p}^*) = \sum_i z_i(\mathbf{p}^*) \max(0, z_i(\mathbf{p}^*))$$

Now $\sum_i p_i^* z_i(\mathbf{p}^*) = 0$ by Walras' law so we have:

$$\sum_i z_i(\mathbf{p}^*) \max(0, z_i(\mathbf{p}^*)) = 0$$

Each term of this sum is greater than or equal to zero since each term is either 0 or $(z_i(\mathbf{p}^*))^2$. But if any term were *strictly* greater than zero, the equality wouldn't hold. Thus, every term must be equal to zero, which says

$$z_i(\mathbf{p}^*) \leqq 0 \qquad \text{for } i = 1, \cdots, k. \ \square$$

It is worth emphasizing the very general nature of the above theorem. All that is needed is that excess demand be continuous and satisfy Walras' law. Walras' law arises directly from the hypotheses that the consumer has to meet some kind of budget constraint; such behavior would seem to be necessary in any type of economic model. The hypothesis of continuity is more restrictive but not unreasonably so. We have seen in Chapter 3 that if consumers all have strictly convex preferences then their demand functions will be well defined and continuous. The aggregate demand function will therefore be continuous. But even if the individual demand functions display discontinuities it may still turn out the aggregate demand function is continuous if there are a large number of consumers. Thus, continuity of aggregate demand seems like a relatively weak requirement.

(To be honest, there is one slight problem with the above argument for existence. It is true that aggregate demand is likely to be continuous for *positive* prices, but it is rather unreasonable to assume it is continuous even when some price goes to zero. If, for example, preferences were monotonic and the price of some good is zero, we would expect that the demand for such a good might be infinite. Thus, the excess demand function might not even be well defined on the boundary of the price simplex—i.e., on that set of price vectors where some prices are zero. However, this sort of "discontinuity" can be handled by using a slightly more complicated mathematical argument.)

Example 5.1 The Cobb-Douglas Economy Let agent 1 have utility function $u_1(x_1, x_2) = x_1^a x_2^{1-a}$ and endowment $\mathbf{W}_1 = (1, 0)$. Let agent 2 have utility function $u_2(x_1, x_2) = x_1^b x_2^{1-b}$ and endowment $\mathbf{W}_2 = (0, 1)$. Then agent 1's demand function for good 1 is $x_1^1(p_1, p_2, y_1(\mathbf{p})) = \frac{ay_1}{p_1} = \frac{ap_1}{p_1} = a$, and agent 2's demand function for good 1 is $x_2^1(p_1, p_2, y_2(\mathbf{p})) = \frac{by_2}{p_1} = \frac{bp_2}{p_1}$. The equilibrium price is where total demand for each good equals total supply.

By Walras' law, this occurs where total demand for good 1 equals total supply of good 1:

$$x_1^1(p_1, p_2, y_1(\mathbf{p})) + x_2^1(p_1, p_2, y_2(\mathbf{p})) = 1$$

$$a + \frac{bp_2}{p_1} = 1$$

$$\frac{p_2^*}{p_1^*} = \frac{1-a}{b}$$

Note that, as always, only relative prices are determined by the equilibrium condition.

5.5 WELFARE PROPERTIES OF WALRASIAN EQUILIBRIA

The existence of a Walrasian equilibrium is interesting as a positive result insofar as we believe the behavioral assumptions—primarily that agents take prices as given—which underly the above model. However, even if this does not seem to be an especially plausible assumption in many circumstances, we may still be interested in Walrasian equilibria for their normative content. Let us consider the following definition.

DEFINITION A feasible allocation $\mathbf{x}$ is a *Pareto efficient* allocation if there is no feasible allocation $\mathbf{x}'$ such that all agents prefer $\mathbf{x}'$ to $\mathbf{x}$.

An alternative definition of Pareto efficiency is: "There is no feasible allocation where everyone is at least as well off and at least one agent is strictly better off." The two definitions are equivalent under the weak hypotheses of monotonicity and continuity of preferences. To see this, we consider the following argument. It is clear that, if everyone can be made better off, then one person can be made better off. What we need to show is that, if we can make one person better off and everyone else no worse off, then there is a way to make everyone better off. The argument is quite simple. If we can make one person better off, then by continuity we can take a little bit of all the goods he has away from him and he will still be better off. But then if we redistribute the extra goods to all the other agents, monotonicity of preferences implies they will all be made better off too. Thus, the two definitions of Pareto efficiency are equivalent. Since the first definition is slightly more convenient, we will generally use it. However, we will henceforth always assume preferences are continuous and monotonic so that either definition is applicable.

Notice that the concept of Pareto efficiency is quite weak as a normative concept; an allocation where one agent gets everything there is in the economy and all other agents get nothing will be Pareto efficient, assuming the agent who has everything is not satiated.

Pareto efficient allocations can easily be depicted in the Edgeworth box diagram introduced earlier. We only need note that, in the two-person case, Pareto efficient allocations can be found by fixing one agent's utility function at a given level and maximizing the other agent's utility function subject to this constraint. Formally, we only need solve the following maximization problem:

$$\begin{aligned} \max \quad & u_1(\mathbf{x}_1) \\ \text{s.t.} \quad & u_2(\mathbf{x}_2) \geqq u \\ & \mathbf{x}_1 + \mathbf{x}_2 = \mathbf{W}_1 + \mathbf{W}_2 \end{aligned}$$

This can be solved by inspection in the Edgeworth box case. Simply find the point on one agent's indifference curve where the other agent reaches the highest utility. By now it should be clear that the resulting Pareto efficient point will be characterized by a tangency condition: the marginal rates of substitution between the two goods will be equal between the two agents.

For each fixed value of agent 2's utility, we will find an allocation where agent 1's utility is maximized and thus the tangency condition will be satisfied. The set of Pareto efficient points—the Pareto set—will thus be the locus of tangencies drawn in the Edgeworth box depicted in Figure 5.5.

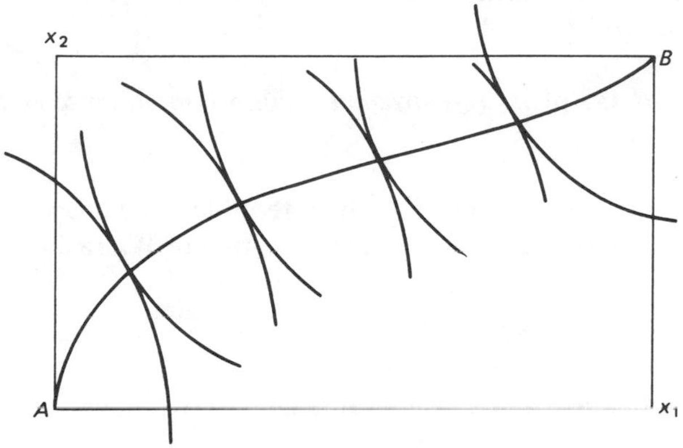

Fig. 5.5 *Pareto Efficiency in the Edgeworth Box*

The comparison of Figure 5.5 with Figure 5.2 reveals a striking fact: there seems to be a one-to-one correspondence between the set of Walrasian equilibria and the set of Pareto efficient allocations. Each Walrasian equilibrium satisfies the first-order condition for preference maximization that the marginal rate of substitution between the two goods for each agent be equal to the price ratio between the two goods. Since all agents face the same price ratio at a Walras equilibrium, all agents must have the same marginal rates of substitution.

Furthermore, if we pick an arbitrary Pareto efficient allocation, we know that the marginal rates of substitution must be equal across the two agents, and we can thus pick a price ratio equal to this common value. Graphically, given a Pareto efficient point we simply draw the common tangency line separating the two indifference curves. We then pick any point on this tangent line to serve as a initial endowment. If the agents try to maximize preferences on their budget sets, they will end up precisely at the Pareto efficient allocation.

The next two theorems give this correspondence precisely. First, we restate the definition of a Walras equilibrium in a more convenient form:

DEFINITION An allocation-price pair $(\mathbf{x}, \mathbf{p})$ is a *Walrasian equilibrium*

(1) if $\Sigma \mathbf{x}_i = \Sigma \mathbf{W}_i$ (total supply = total demand) i.e., the allocation is feasible; and

(2) if $\mathbf{x}_i'$ is preferred by i to $\mathbf{x}_i$, then $\mathbf{p} \cdot \mathbf{x}_i' > \mathbf{p} \cdot \mathbf{W}_i$ (each agent is maximized in his budget set).

This definition is equivalent to the original definition of Walrasian equilibrium, as long as the desirability assumption is satisfied.

The following theorem is generally known as the *First Theorem of Welfare Economics.*

Theorem *If* $(\mathbf{x}, \mathbf{p})$ *is a Walrasian equilibrium, then* $\mathbf{x}$ *is Pareto efficient.*

PROOF Suppose not, and let $\mathbf{x}'$ be a feasible allocation that all agents prefer to $\mathbf{x}$. Then by property 2 of the definition of Walrasian equilibrium, we have

$$\mathbf{p} \cdot \mathbf{x}_i' > \mathbf{p} \cdot \mathbf{W}_i \text{ for } i = 1, \cdots, n$$

Summing and using the definition of feasibility we have

$$\mathbf{p} \cdot \Sigma \mathbf{W}_i = \mathbf{p} \cdot \Sigma \mathbf{x}_i' > \mathbf{p} \cdot \Sigma \mathbf{W}_i$$

which is a contradiction. □

The content of the theorem is that if the behavioral assumptions of our model are satisfied then the market equilibrium is efficient. It is by no means optimal in any other ethical sense, since the market equilibrium may be very "unfair." The outcome depends entirely on the original distribution of endowments. What is needed is some further ethical criterion to choose among the efficient allocations. Such a concept, the concept of a welfare function, will be discussed in the next section.

Here we continue to investigate the relationship between efficient allocations and Walras equilibria. For example, we may want to consider the possibility of using the market mechanism to support an arbitrary efficient allocation. The next theorem shows that, under some reasonable hypotheses, essentially all Pareto efficient allocations are Walrasian equilibria for appropriate distribution of endowments. This theorem is generally known as the *Second Theorem of Welfare Economics.*

Theorem *Suppose* $\mathbf{x}^*$ *is a Pareto efficient allocation with* $\mathbf{x}_i^* \gg 0$ *for* $i=1, \cdots, n$ *and preferences are convex, continuous, and monotonic.*

Then $\mathbf{x}^*$ *is a Walrasian equilibrium for initial endowment* $\mathbf{W}_i = \mathbf{x}_i^*$ *for* $i = 1, \cdots, n$.

PROOF Let $P_i = \{\mathbf{x} \text{ in } R^k\text{: } \mathbf{x} \succ_i \mathbf{x}_i^*\}$. Then define $P = \sum_{i=1}^{n} P_i = \{\mathbf{z}\text{: } \mathbf{z} = \Sigma \mathbf{x}_i \text{ with } \mathbf{x}_i \text{ in } P_i\}$. P is the set of all aggregate bundles that can be distributed among the n agents so as to make them all better off. Since each P_i is a convex set by hypothesis and the sum of convex sets is convex, we can conclude that P is a convex set.

Let $\mathbf{W} = \Sigma \mathbf{x}_i^*$ be the current *aggregate* bundle. Since $\mathbf{x}^*$ is Pareto efficient, there is no redistribution of $\mathbf{x}^*$ that makes everyone better off; i.e., $\mathbf{W}$ is not an element of P.

Hence, by the separating hyperplane theorem (Section A.5 of the Mathematical Appendix) there is a $\mathbf{p}$ such that

$$\mathbf{p}\cdot\mathbf{z} \geqq \mathbf{p}\cdot\Sigma\mathbf{x}_i^* = \mathbf{p}\cdot\mathbf{W} \qquad \text{for all } \mathbf{z} \text{ in } P$$

Rearranging this gives us:

$$\mathbf{p}\cdot(\mathbf{z} - \Sigma\mathbf{x}_i^*) \geqq 0 \qquad \text{for all } \mathbf{z} \text{ in } P$$

We want to show that $\mathbf{p}$ is in fact an equilibrium price vector. The proof proceeds in three steps:

(1) $\mathbf{p}$ is nonnegative; that is, $\mathbf{p} \geqq 0$.

To see this, let $\mathbf{e}_i = (0, \cdots, 1, 0 \cdots 0)$ with 1 in the ith place. Since preferences are monotonic, $\mathbf{W} + \mathbf{e}_i$ must lie in P, since if we have one more unit of any good it is possible to redistribute it to make everyone better off. The above inequality shows us that

$$\mathbf{p}\cdot(\mathbf{W} + \mathbf{e}_i - \mathbf{W}) \geqq 0 \qquad \text{for } i = 1, \cdots, k$$

so

$$\mathbf{p}\cdot\mathbf{e}_i \geqq 0 \qquad \text{for } i = 1, \cdots, k.$$

which implies $p_i \geqq 0$ for $i = 1, \cdots, k$.

(2) if $\mathbf{y}_j \succ_j \mathbf{x}_j^*$, then $\mathbf{p}\cdot\mathbf{y}_j \geqq \mathbf{p}\cdot\mathbf{x}_j^*$, for each agent $j = 1, \cdots, n$. We already know that, if every agent i prefers $\mathbf{y}_i$ to $\mathbf{x}_i^*$, then

$$\mathbf{p}\cdot\Sigma\mathbf{y}_i \geqq \mathbf{p}\cdot\Sigma\mathbf{x}_i^*$$

Now suppose only that some particular agent j prefers some bundle $\mathbf{y}_j$ to $\mathbf{x}_j$. Then construct an allocation $\mathbf{z}$ by taking some of each good away from j and distributing it to the other agents:

$$\mathbf{z}_j = \mathbf{y}_j\,(1 - \theta)$$

$$\mathbf{z}_i = \mathbf{x}_i^* + \frac{\mathbf{y}_j\,\theta}{n-1} \qquad i = 1, \cdots, n \quad i \neq j$$

For small enough θ, strong monotonicity implies $\mathbf{z}$ is Pareto preferred to $\mathbf{x}^*$, and thus $\Sigma\mathbf{z}_i$ lies in P. The above inequality implies:

$$\mathbf{p}\cdot\Sigma\mathbf{z}_i \geqq \mathbf{p}\cdot\Sigma\mathbf{x}_i^*$$

$$\mathbf{p}\cdot(\mathbf{y}_j\,(1-\theta) + \sum_{i\neq j}\mathbf{x}_i^* + \mathbf{y}_j\,\theta) \geqq \mathbf{p}\cdot(\mathbf{x}_j^* + \sum_{i\neq j}\mathbf{x}_i^*)$$

$$\mathbf{p}\cdot\mathbf{y}_j \geqq \mathbf{p}\cdot\mathbf{x}_j^*$$

This says that if agent j prefers $\mathbf{y}_j$ to $\mathbf{x}_j^*$ it can cost no less than $\mathbf{x}_j^*$. It remains to show that we can make this inequality strict; that is,

(3) if $\mathbf{y}_j \succ_j \mathbf{x}_j^*$ we must have $\mathbf{p}\cdot\mathbf{y}_j > \mathbf{p}\cdot\mathbf{x}_j^*$.

We already know that $\mathbf{p}\cdot\mathbf{y}_j \geqq \mathbf{p}\cdot\mathbf{x}_j^*$, and from the assumption that $\mathbf{x}_j^* \gg 0$ we know that $\mathbf{p}\cdot\mathbf{x}_j^* > 0$. Assume that $\mathbf{p}\cdot\mathbf{y}_j = \mathbf{p}\cdot\mathbf{x}_j^*$. We will derive a contradiction.

From the assumption of continuity of preferences, we can find some $0 < \theta < 1$ such $\theta\mathbf{y}_j$ is strictly preferred to $\mathbf{x}_j^*$. By the argument of part (2), then $\theta\mathbf{y}_j$ must cost at least as much as $\mathbf{x}_j^*$:

$$\theta\mathbf{p}\cdot\mathbf{y}_j \geqq \mathbf{p}\cdot\mathbf{x}_j^*$$

However, if $\mathbf{p}\cdot\mathbf{y}_j = \mathbf{p}\cdot\mathbf{x}_j^* > 0$, it follows that

$$\theta\mathbf{p}\cdot\mathbf{y}_j < \mathbf{p}\cdot\mathbf{x}_j^*$$

This contradiction establishes the theorem. □

It is worth considering the hypotheses of this proposition. Convexity and continuity of preferences are crucial, of course, but strong monotonicity can be relaxed considerably. One can also relax the assumption that $\mathbf{x}_i^* \gg 0$.

There is a very simple but somewhat indirect proof of the second welfare theorem that is based on a revealed preference argument and the existence theorem described earlier in this chapter.

Theorem *Suppose that* $\mathbf{x}^*$ *is a Pareto efficient allocation and that preferences are nonsatiated. Suppose further that a competitive equilibrium exists from the initial endowments* $\mathbf{W}_i = \mathbf{x}_i^*$ *and let it be given by* $(\mathbf{p}', \mathbf{x}')$. *Then, in fact,* $(\mathbf{p}', \mathbf{x}^*)$ *is a competitive equilibrium.*

PROOF Since $\mathbf{x}_i^*$ is feasible for each consumer by construction, we must have $\mathbf{x}_i' \succsim_i \mathbf{x}_i^*$. Since $\mathbf{x}^*$ is Pareto efficient this implies that $\mathbf{x}_i' \sim_i \mathbf{x}_i^*$. Thus if $\mathbf{x}_i'$ provides maximum utility on the budget set, so does x_i^*. Hence, $(\mathbf{p}', \mathbf{x}^*)$ is a Walrasian equilibrium. □

This argument shows that if a competitive equilibrium *exists* from a Pareto efficient allocation, then that Pareto efficient allocation is *itself* a competitive equilibrium. The remarks following the existence theorem in this chapter indicate that the only real requirement for existence is continuity of the aggregate demand function, which is in turned implied either by convexity of individual preferences or follows automatically if we have a "large" economy. Thus, the second welfare theorem holds under the same circumstances.

5.6 *PARETO EFFICIENCY AND CALCULUS*

We have seen in the last section that every competitive equilibrium is Pareto efficient and essentially every Pareto efficient allocation is a competitive equilibrium for some distribution of endowments. In this section we will investigate this relationship more closely through the use of differential calculus. Essentially, we will derive first-order conditions that characterize market equilibria and Pareto efficiency and then compare these two sets of conditions.

The conditions characterizing the market equilibrium are very simple.

PROPOSITION *If* $(\mathbf{x}^*, \mathbf{p}^*)$ *is a market equilibrium with* $\mathbf{x}^* \gg 0$ *then there exists a set of numbers* $(\lambda_1, \cdots, \lambda_n)$ *such that:*

$$\mathbf{D}u_i(\mathbf{x}^*) = \lambda_i \mathbf{p}^* \qquad i = 1, \cdots, n$$

PROOF If we have a market equilibrium, then each agent is maximized on his budget set, and these are just the first-order conditions for such utility maximization, where λ_i has the standard interpretation of being i's marginal utility of income. □

The first-order conditions for Pareto efficiency are a bit harder to formulate. However, the following trick is very useful:

PROPOSITION *A feasible allocation* $\mathbf{x}^*$ *is Pareto efficient if and only if* $\mathbf{x}^*$ *solves the following problems for* $i = 1, \cdots, n$.

$$\begin{aligned} \max \quad & u_i(\mathbf{x}_i) \\ \text{s.t.} \quad & \Sigma \mathbf{x}_i^l \leqq W^l \qquad l = 1, \cdots, k \\ & u_j(\mathbf{x}_j^*) \leqq u_j(\mathbf{x}_j) \qquad j = 1, \cdots, n \\ & \qquad\qquad\qquad\qquad j \neq i \end{aligned}$$

PROOF Suppose $\mathbf{x}^*$ solves all the problems but $\mathbf{x}^*$ is not Pareto efficient. Then there is some allocation $\mathbf{x}'$ where everyone is better off. But then $\mathbf{x}^*$ couldn't solve all—or any—of the problems.

Conversely, suppose $\mathbf{x}^*$ is Pareto efficient, but it doesn't solve one of the problems. Then there is a way to make one of the agents better off without hurting anyone else, which contradicts the assumption that $\mathbf{x}^*$ is Pareto efficient. □

Now we can use the Kuhn-Tucker theorem described in Section A.9 of the Mathematical Appendix to get first-order conditions for maximizing the above problems. By the above proposition, such first-order conditions will characterize all Pareto efficient allocations.

We write the Lagrangian for such a problem:

$$L = u_i(\mathbf{x}_i) - \sum_{l=1}^{k} q^l \left[\sum_{i=1}^{n} x_i^l - W^l\right] - \sum_{j \neq i} t_j[u_j(\mathbf{x}_j^*) - u_j(\mathbf{x}_j)]$$

Here $(q_1, \cdots, q_k)$ are the Kuhn-Tucker multipliers on the resource constraints and $(t_1, \cdots, t_n)$ are the Kuhn-Tucker multipliers on the utility constraints.

We differentiate L with respect to x_j^l where $l = 1, \cdots, k$ and $j = 1, \cdots, n$. We get:

$$\frac{\partial u_i(\mathbf{x}_i^*)}{\partial x_i^l} - q_l = 0 \qquad l = 1, \cdots, k$$

$$t_j \frac{\partial u_j(\mathbf{x}_j^*)}{\partial x_j^l} - q_l = 0 \qquad j = 1, \cdots, n;\ j \neq i \quad l = 1, \cdots, k$$

In vector notation, these conditions are:

$$\mathbf{D}u_i(\mathbf{x}_i^*) = \mathbf{q}$$

$$t_j\mathbf{D}u_j(\mathbf{x}_j^*) = \mathbf{q}$$

(Of course, we are assuming an interior solution so that $\mathbf{x}_i^* \gg 0$.)

Now at first these conditions seem rather paradoxical since they seem to be asymmetric. For each choice of i, we get different values for (q_l) and (t_j). However, the paradox is resolved when we note that the *relative* values of the qs are independent of the choice of agent. This is clear since from the above conditions:

$$\frac{\dfrac{\partial u_i(\mathbf{x}_i^*)}{\partial x_i^l}}{\dfrac{\partial u_i(\mathbf{x}_i^*)}{\partial x_i^h}} = \frac{q_l}{q_h} \qquad \text{all } i = 1, \cdots, n \quad l, h = 1, \cdots, k$$

Since $\mathbf{x}^*$ is given, q^l/q^h must be independent of which maximization problem we solve. The same reasoning shows that t_i/t_j is independent of which maximization problem we solve. The solution to the asymmetry problem now becomes clear: if we maximize agent i's utility and use the other agent's utilities as constraints, then it is just as if we are arbitrarily setting agent i's weight to be $t_i = 1$.

Now using the first welfare theorem we can derive nice interpretations of the weights (t_i) and (q_h): if $\mathbf{x}^*$ is a market equilibrium then

$$\mathbf{D}u_i(\mathbf{x}_i^*) = \lambda_i\mathbf{p} \qquad i = 1, \cdots, n$$

but all market equilibria are Pareto efficient and thus must satisfy:

$$t_i\mathbf{D}u_i(\mathbf{x}_i^*) = \mathbf{q} \qquad i = 1, \cdots, n$$

From this it is clear that we can choose $\mathbf{p} = \mathbf{q}$ and $t_i = 1/\lambda_i$. In words, the Kuhn-Tucker multipliers on the resource constraints are just the competitive prices, and the Kuhn-Tucker multipliers on the agent's utilities are just the reciprocals of their marginal utilities of income.

If we eliminate the Kuhn-Tucker multipliers in the first-order conditions we get the following conditions:

$$\frac{\dfrac{\partial u_i(\mathbf{x}_i^*)}{\partial x_i^l}}{\dfrac{\partial u_i(\mathbf{x}_i^*)}{\partial x_i^h}} = \frac{p_l}{p_h} = \frac{q_l}{q_h} \qquad \begin{matrix} i = 1, \cdots, n \\ h, l = 1, \cdots, k \end{matrix}$$

The interpretation of these conditions is as follows: every Pareto efficient allocation must satisfy the condition that the marginal rate of substitution between each pair of goods is the same for every agent. This marginal rate of substitution is precisely the ratio of the competitive prices.

The intuition behind this condition is fairly clear: if two agents had different marginal rates of substitution between some pair of goods, they could arrange a small trade that would make them both better off, contradicting the assumption of Pareto efficiency.

It is often useful to note that the first-order conditions for a Pareto efficient allocation are the same as the first-order conditions for maximizing a weighted sum of utilities; that is, consider the problem:

$$\begin{aligned} &\max \quad \Sigma a_i u_i(\mathbf{x}_i) \\ &\text{s.t.} \quad \Sigma \mathbf{x}_i^l \leqq W^l \qquad l = 1, \cdots, k \end{aligned}$$

The first-order conditions for a solution to this problem are just:

$$a_i \mathbf{D}u_i(\mathbf{x}_i^*) = \mathbf{q}$$

which are precisely the same as the necessary conditions for Pareto efficiency. We will explore this relationship a bit further in the next section.

For now we note that this calculus characterization of Pareto efficiency gives us a simple proof of the second welfare theorem. Let us assume that all consumers have concave utility functions, although this is not really required. Then if $\mathbf{x}^*$ is a Pareto efficient allocation, we know from the first-order conditions that:

$$\mathbf{D}u_i(\mathbf{x}^*) = \mathbf{q}/t_i \text{ for } i = 1, \cdots, n$$

Thus, the gradient of each consumer's utility function is proportional to some fixed vector $\mathbf{q}$. Let us choose $\mathbf{q}$ to be the vector of competitive prices. We need to check that each consumer is maximized on his budget set $\{\mathbf{x}_i : \mathbf{q}\mathbf{x}_i \leqq \mathbf{q}\mathbf{x}_i^*\}$. But this follows quickly from concavity; according to the mathematical properties of concave functions:

$$u(\mathbf{x}_i) \leq u(\mathbf{x}_i^*) + Du(\mathbf{x}_i^*)(\mathbf{x}_i - \mathbf{x}_i^*)$$

so:

$$u(\mathbf{x}) \leq u(\mathbf{x}_i^*) + (\mathbf{q}/\mathrm{t}_i)(\mathbf{x}_i - \mathbf{x}_i^*)$$

Thus, if $\mathbf{x}_i$ is in the consumer's budget set, $u(\mathbf{x}) \leq u(\mathbf{x}_i^*)$.

(Yet another proof of the second fundamental welfare theorem is given in Section 6.1.)

5.7 WELFARE MAXIMIZATION

One problem with the concept of Pareto efficiency as a normative criterion is that it is not very specific. Pareto efficiency is only concerned with efficiency and has nothing to say about distribution of welfare. Even if we agree that we should be at a Pareto efficient allocation, we still don't know which one we should be at.

One way to resolve these problems is to hypothesize the existence of some *social welfare function*. This is supposed to be some sort of function that aggregates the individual utility functions to come up with some sort of social utility. We will refrain from making philosophical comments here and just postulate that some such function exists; that is, we will suppose that we have

$$W: R^h \to R$$

so that $W(u_1, \cdots, u_n)$ gives us the "social utility" resulting from any distribution $(u_1, \cdots, u_n)$ of private utilities. We will suppose that W is increasing in each of its arguments—if you increase any agent's utility without decreasing anybody else's utility then society is made better off.

Now according to the social welfare approach, society should operate at a point that maximizes social welfare; that is, we should choose an allocation $\mathbf{x}^*$ such that $\mathbf{x}^*$ solves:

$$\begin{aligned} \max \quad & W(u_1(\mathbf{x}_1), \cdots, u_n(\mathbf{x}_n)) \\ \text{s.t.} \quad & \sum_i x_i^l \leqq W^l \qquad l = 1, \cdots, k \end{aligned}$$

The following is a trivial consequence of the monotonicity hypothesis:

PROPOSITION *If* $\mathbf{x}^*$ *maximizes a social welfare function then* $\mathbf{x}^*$ *is Pareto efficient.*

PROOF If $\mathbf{x}^*$ were not Pareto efficient, then there would be some feasible allocation $\mathbf{x}'$ such that $u_i(\mathbf{x}_i') > u_i(\mathbf{x}_i^*)$, $i = 1, \cdots, n$. But then $\mathbf{x}^*$ couldn't maximize welfare either. □

Since welfare maxima are Pareto efficient they must satisfy the same first-order conditions as Pareto efficient allocations; furthermore, under convexity assumptions, every Pareto efficient allocation is a competitive equilibrium, so that same goes for welfare maxima: every welfare maximum is a competitive equilibrium for some distribution of endowments.

This last observation gives us one further interpretation of the competitive prices: they are exactly the Kuhn-Tucker multipliers for the welfare maximization problem. Thus, the competitive prices really measure the (marginal) social value of a good: how much welfare would increase if we had one more unit of the good.

We have seen above that every welfare maximum is Pareto efficient, but is the converse necessarily true? We saw in the last section that every Pareto efficient allocation satisfied the same first-order conditions as the problem of maximizing a weighted sum of utilities, so it might seem plausible that under convexity and concavity assumptions things might work out nicely. Indeed they do:

PROPOSITION *Let* $\mathbf{x}^*$ *be a Pareto efficient allocation with* $\mathbf{x}_i^* \gg \mathbf{0}$, $i = 1, \cdots, n$. *Let the utility functions* u_i *be concave, continuous, and monotonic functions. Then there is some choice of weights* a_i^* *such that*

$\mathbf{x}^*$ *maximizes* $\Sigma a_i^* u_i(\mathbf{x}_i)$ *subject to the resource constraints. Furthermore, the weights are such that* $a_i^* = 1/\lambda_i^*$ *where* λ_i^* *is the ith agent's marginal utility of income; that is,* $\lambda_i^* = \dfrac{\partial v_i(\mathbf{p}, \mathbf{p}\cdot\mathbf{x}_i^*)}{\partial y}$.

PROOF Since $\mathbf{x}^*$ is Pareto efficient, it is a Walrasian equilibrium. There therefore exist prices $\mathbf{p}$ such that each agent is maximized on his or her budget set; this in turn implies:

$$\mathbf{D}u_i(\mathbf{x}_i^*) = \lambda_i \mathbf{p} \qquad \text{for } i = 1, \cdots, n$$

Consider now the welfare maximization problem:

$$\begin{aligned} \max \quad & \Sigma a_i u_i(\mathbf{x}_i) \\ \text{s.t.} \quad & \Sigma x_i^1 \leqq \Sigma x_i^{*1} \\ & \quad \vdots \\ & \Sigma x_i^k \leqq \Sigma x_i^{*k} \end{aligned}$$

According to the sufficiency theorem for concave constrained maximization problems (Section A.8 of the Mathematical Appendix), $\mathbf{x}^*$ solves this problem if there exist nonnegative numbers $(q_1 \cdots q_k) = \mathbf{q}$ such that:

$$a_i \mathbf{D}u_i(\mathbf{x}_i^*) = \mathbf{q}$$

If $a_i = 1/\lambda_i$ then the prices $\mathbf{p}$ serve as the appropriate nonnegative numbers and the proof is done. □

The interpretation of the weights as reciprocals of the marginal utilities of income makes good economic sense. If some agent has a large income at some Pareto efficient allocation then his marginal utility of income will be small and his weight in the implicit social welfare function will be large.

The above two propositions complete the set of relationships between market equilibria, Pareto efficient allocations, and welfare maxima. To recapitulate briefly:

(1) competitive equilibria are always Pareto efficient;
(2) Pareto efficient allocations are competitive equilibria under convexity assumptions and endowment redistribution;
(3) welfare maxima are always Pareto efficient;
(4) Pareto efficient allocations are welfare maxima under concavity assumptions for some choice of welfare weights.

Inspecting the above relationships we can see the basic moral: a competitive market system will give efficient allocations but it says nothing about distribution. The choice of distribution of income is the same as the choice of a reallocation of endowments, and this in turn is equivalent to choosing a particular welfare function.

Exercises

5.1 (10) Draw an Edgeworth box example of an economy with multiple price equilibria, each being locally isolated. Then draw an Edgeworth box example with a continuum of price equilibria.

5.2 (20) Show that, in the diagram depicted below, $\mathbf{x}^*$ is a Pareto efficient allocation, but $\mathbf{x}^*$ cannot be supported by competitive prices. Which assumption is violated?

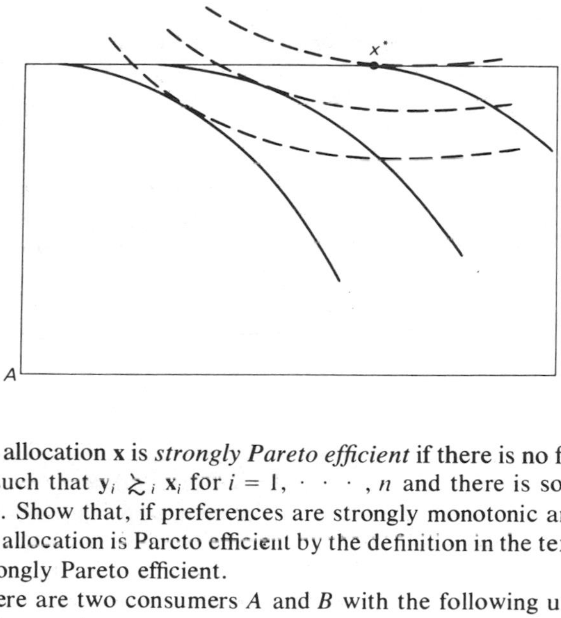

5.3 (20) An allocation $\mathbf{x}$ is *strongly Pareto efficient* if there is no feasible allocation $\mathbf{y}$ such that $\mathbf{y}_i \succsim_i \mathbf{x}_i$ for $i = 1, \cdots, n$ and there is some j such that $\mathbf{y}_j \succ_j \mathbf{x}_j$. Show that, if preferences are strongly monotonic and continuous, then an allocation is Pareto efficient by the definition in the text if and only if it is strongly Pareto efficient.

5.4 (20) There are two consumers A and B with the following utility functions and endowments:

$$u_A(x_A^1, x_A^2) = a \ln x_A^1 + (1-a) \ln x_A^2 \qquad \mathbf{W}_A = (0, 1)$$

$$u_B(x_B^1, x_B^2) = \min(x_B^1, x_B^2) \qquad \mathbf{W}_B = (1, 0)$$

Calculate the market clearing prices and the equilibrium allocation.

5.5 (20) We have n agents with identical strictly concave utility functions. There is some initial bundle of goods $\mathbf{W}$. Show that equal division is a Pareto efficient allocation.

5.6 (20) We have two agents with *indirect* utility functions

$$v_1(p_1, p_2, y) = \ln y - a \ln p_1 - (1 - a) \ln p_2$$

$$v_2(p_1, p_2, y) = \ln y - b \ln p_1 - (1 - b) \ln p_2$$

and initial endowments

$$\mathbf{W}_1 = (1, 1) \qquad \mathbf{W}_2 = (1, 1)$$

Calculate the market clearing prices.

5.7 (30) Suppose we have a general equilibrium price vector $\mathbf{p}^*$ so that $\Sigma x_i(\mathbf{p}^*, \mathbf{p}^* \cdot \mathbf{W}_i) = \Sigma \mathbf{W}_i$. Show that if all agents have identical marginal propensities to consume each good $\left(\frac{\partial \mathbf{x}_i}{\partial y} = \frac{\partial \mathbf{x}_j}{\partial y} \text{ for all } i \text{ and } j\right)$ then all aggregate demand curves must be downward sloping at p^*. More generally show that $\mathbf{D}_p(\Sigma \mathbf{x}_i(\mathbf{p}^*, \mathbf{p}^* \cdot \mathbf{W}_i))$ is negative definite and conclude that $\mathbf{p}^*$ are the unique equilibrium prices.

5.8 (20) Suppose we have two consumers A and B with identical utility functions $u_A(x_1, x_2) = u_B(x_1, x_2) = \max(x_1, x_2)$. Suppose the total amount of goods 1 and 2 available is $\mathbf{W} = (1, 2)$. Draw an Edgeworth box that illustrates the strongly Pareto efficient and the (weakly) Pareto efficient sets. (Compare to Exercise 5.3.)

5.9 (15) Consider an economy with 15 consumers, 2 goods, and 7 firms. Consumer 3 has a Cobb-Douglas utility function $u_3(x_3^1, x_3^2) = \ln x_3^1 + \ln x_3^2$. At a certain Pareto efficient allocation x^*, consumer 3 holds (10, 5). What are the competitive prices that support x^*?

5.10 (15) Consider a two-consumer, two-good economy. Both consumers have the same Cobb-Douglas utility function:

$$u_i(x_i^1, x_i^2) = \ln x_i^1 + \ln x_i^2 \qquad i = 1, 2$$

There is one unit of each good available. Calculate the set of Pareto efficient allocations and illustrate it in an Edgeworth box.

5.11 If we allow for the possibility of satiation, the consumer's budget constraint takes the form $\mathbf{px}_i \leqq \mathbf{pW}_i$. Walras' law then becomes $\mathbf{pz(p)} \leqq 0$ for all $\mathbf{p} \leqq 0$. Show that the proof of existence of a Walrasian equilibrium given in the text still applies for this generalized form of Walras' law.

Notes

The general equilibrium model was first formulated by Walras (1954). The first proof of existence was due to Wald (1951); more general treatments of existence were provided by McKenzie (1954) and Arrow and Debreu (1954). The definitive modern treatments are Debreu (1959) and (1962) and Arrow and Hahn (1971). The treatment of existence given here follows Arrow and Hahn (1971).

The basic welfare results have a long history. The proof of the first welfare theorem used here follows Koopmans (1957). The importance of convexity in the second theorem was recognized by Arrow (1951) and Debreu (1953). The differentiable treatment of efficiency was first developed rigorously by Samuelson (1947). The relationship between welfare maxima and Pareto efficiency follows Negishi (1960).

The approach of this chapter follows that of McFadden and Winter (1969). The most up-to-date treatment of general equilibrium theory is Arrow and Hahn (1971). This work also contains extensive historical notes.

The revealed preference proof of the second welfare theorem is due to Maskin and Roberts (1980).

References

ARROW, K. 1951. "An Extension of the Basic Theorems of Classical Welfare Economics." In *Readings in Mathematical Economics,* P. Newman. Baltimore: Johns Hopkins Press.

———, and DEBREU, G. 1954. "Existence of Equilibrium for a Competitive Economy." *Econometrica* 22:265–290.

ARROW, K., and HAHN, F. 1971. *General Competitive Analysis*. San Francisco: Holden-Day.

DEBREU, G. 1953. "Valuation Equilibrium and Pareto Optimum." In *Readings in Welfare Economics,* K. Arrow and T. Scitovsky. Homewood, Ill.: Irwin.

———. 1959. *Theory of Value*. New York: Wiley.

———. 1962. "New Concepts and Techniques for Equilibrium Analysis." *International Economic Review* 3:257–273.

EDGEWORTH, F. 1881. *Mathematical Psychics,* London: Kegan Paul.

KOOPMANS, T. 1957. *Three Essays on the State of Economic Science*. Cowles Foundation Monograph. New Haven: Yale University Press.

MCFADDEN, D., and WINTER, S. 1969. "Lecture Notes on Price and Resource Allocation Theory." University of California at Berkeley, mimeo.

MCKENZIE, L. 1954. "On Equilibrium in Graham's Model of World Trade and Other Competitive Systems." *Econometrica* 22:147–161.

MASKIN, E., and ROBERTS, K. 1980. "On the Fundamental Theorems of General Equilibrium." Economic Theory Discussion Paper 43, Cambridge University.

NEGISHI, T. 1960. "Welfare Economics and the Existence of an Equilibrium for a Competitive Economy." *Metroeconomica* 12:92–97.

SAMUELSON, P. 1947. *Foundations of Economic Analysis*. Cambridge, Mass.: Harvard University Press.

SCARF, H. 1973. *The Computation of Economic Equilibrium*. New Haven: Yale University Press.

WALD, A. 1951. "On Some Systems of Equations in Mathematical Economics." *Econometrica* 19:368–403.

WALRAS, L. 1954. *Elements of Pure Economics*. London: Allen and Unwin.

Chapter 6

Topics in General Equilibrium Theory

6.1 EQUILIBRIUM AND PRODUCTION

The previous chapter dealt only with a pure exchange economy. In this section we will describe how one extends such a general equilibrium model to a productive economy. First we will discuss how one describes firm behavior, then how consumer behavior differs when firms are present, and finally how the basic existence and efficiency theorems should be modified.

FIRM BEHAVIOR We shall represent firm actions in a very general way. Let Y_j be the *production possibilities* set of the jth firm. This is the set of all feasible production plans for firm j; each production plan is summarized by a netput vector $\mathbf{y}_j$ with negative entries indicating net inputs and positive signs indicating net outputs. Examples of production possibilities sets are given in Chapter 1.

We will deal exclusively with competitive, price-taking firms in this section. Thus if $\mathbf{p}$ is a vector of prices of the various goods, $\mathbf{p} \cdot \mathbf{y}_j$ is the amount of profits associated with the production plan $\mathbf{y}_j$. Firm j is assumed to choose a feasible production plan $\mathbf{y}_j^*$ that maximizes profits.

In Chapter 1 we dealt with the consequences of this model of behavior. There we described the idea of the net supply function $\mathbf{y}_j(\mathbf{p})$ of a competitive firm. This is simply the function that associates to each vector $\mathbf{p}$ the profit-maximizing netput vector at those prices. At this point we encounter a problem with the model. Will a profit-maximizing netput bundle always exist? Recall that, in a constant-returns-to-scale technology, at some prices there are netput bundles that make arbitrarily large profits. Evidently no profit-maximizing netput bundle exists in this case.

To ensure the existence of profit-maximizing netput bundles we need to make some kind of boundedness assumption. In practice this is done by showing that the availability of inputs to production bounds the set of feasible production plans; that is, we assume that there is only a finite amount of "primary" resources and that it is impossible to produce something out of nothing. Given such resource constraints we can bound the set of feasible netput vectors and only consider a bounded part of the original production sets.

For purposes of exposition, we shall simply assume that production possibilities are bounded, presumably by some sort of resource constraint as indicated above:

(A1) Y_j is closed and bounded for $j = 1, \cdots, m$

For demand *functions* to be well defined, we need it to be the case that there is only one profit-maximizing bundle associated with a given price vector. Again the constant-returns-to-scale technology poses a problem in that at some prices—where the firm makes zero profits—the firm is willing to produce at any scale. In such a circumstance there are many profit-maximizing bundles associated with one price.

In general treatments of existence of equilibria, this problem is solved through the use of *correspondences*, or *multivalued functions*. An appropriate notion of continuity is applied to such functions, and a generalization of Brouwer's Fixed Point Theorem is used to prove existence.

For our purposes, it seems better to avoid these technicalities and restrict ourselves to the more straightforward case. Hence we will assume:

(A2) Y_j is strictly convex; $j = 1, \cdots, m$

Combining this with the boundedness assumption we have:

PROPOSITION *If* Y_j *is closed, bounded, and strictly convex, the demand function of the* j^{th} *firm is well defined.*

PROOF The function $\mathbf{p} \cdot \mathbf{y}$ is certainly continuous, so it achieves a maximum on the closed and bounded set Y_j.

Suppose $\mathbf{y}$ and $\mathbf{y}'$ both maximized profits on Y_j, so that $\mathbf{p} \cdot \mathbf{y} = \mathbf{p} \cdot \mathbf{y}'$. Then due to strict convexity $t\mathbf{y} + (1 - t)\mathbf{y}'$ is in the interior of Y_j for $0 < t < 1$. Therefore there is some $s > 1$ such that $st\mathbf{y} + s(1 - t)\mathbf{y}'$ is in Y_j. But the profit associated with this netput bundle is greater than $\mathbf{p} \cdot \mathbf{y}$ since:

$$s[t\mathbf{p} \cdot \mathbf{y} + (1 - t)\mathbf{p} \cdot \mathbf{y}'] = s\mathbf{p} \cdot \mathbf{y} > \mathbf{p} \cdot \mathbf{y}. \ \square$$

Actually, the assumptions of this proposition are not too bad since it seems reasonable that one could approximate a bounded convex set by a strictly convex set without too much trouble.

Finally, there is the problem of continuity of the firm's demand and supply functions. This is the most important of the problems we are considering here. Suppose we first consider the simple case of a firm which produces output from some input good. In Figure 6.1 we have drawn three possible technologies and the associated demand functions for the input.

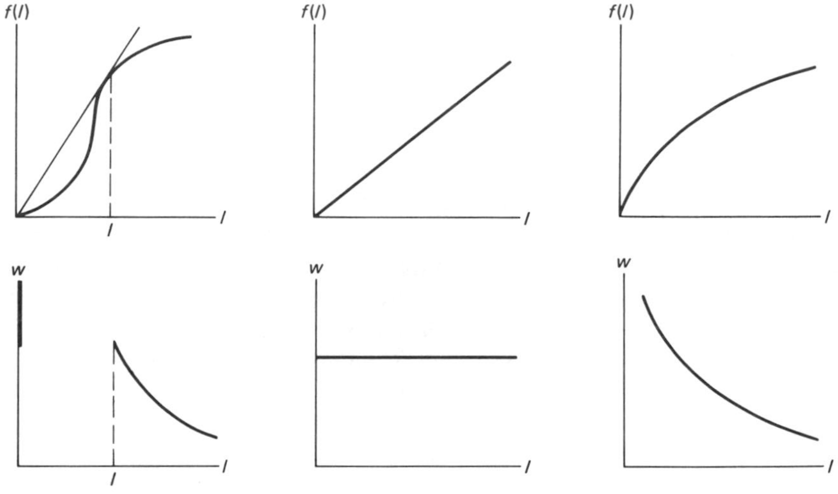

Fig. 6.1 *Continuity of the Firm's Demand Function*

In the first example, we have a technology that exhibits a region of increasing returns to scale. The associated demand function is discontinuous. The second example exhibits constant returns to scale. The demand "function" is multivalued at a certain wage but it seems to be "continuous" in an appropriate sense. The third case is the most well behaved. Here we have diminishing returns to scale and a nice continuous demand function.

If the technology exhibited increasing returns to scale, it is clear that the supply function of the input could happen to be at a position where no equilibrium price would exist. On the other hand the constant-returns-to-scale and diminishing-returns-to-scale technologies seem compatible with the existence of an equilibrium price.

In fact, it is not hard to show that the assumptions we have already made have excluded the first two cases and are sufficient to prove the continuity of the firm's demand function:

(M) PROPOSITION *Suppose the production set* Y *is closed and bounded and strictly convex. Then the net supply function* **y(p)** *is well defined and continuous.*

PROOF As we have shown above, the maximizing choice is well defined since Y is strictly convex. Let $(\mathbf{p}^i)$ be a sequence converging to $\mathbf{p}^0$, and consider the corresponding sequence $(\mathbf{y}(\mathbf{p}^i))$. This sequence has a subsequence that converges to some point $\mathbf{y}^*$ since Y is compact. We need to show that $\mathbf{y}^* = \mathbf{y}(\mathbf{p}^0)$.

Suppose

$$\mathbf{p}^0 \cdot \mathbf{y}^* > \mathbf{p}^0 \cdot \mathbf{y}(\mathbf{p}^0)$$

This contradicts the fact that $\mathbf{y}(\mathbf{p}^0)$ maximizes profits at $\mathbf{p}^0$.

Suppose

$$\mathbf{p}^0 \cdot \mathbf{y}^* < \mathbf{p}^0 \cdot \mathbf{y}(\mathbf{p}^0)$$

Then for $\mathbf{p}^i$ close enough to $\mathbf{p}^0$ and $\mathbf{y}(\mathbf{p}^i)$ close enough to $\mathbf{y}^*$,

$$\mathbf{p}^i \cdot \mathbf{y}(\mathbf{p}^i) < \mathbf{p}^i \cdot \mathbf{y}(\mathbf{p}^0)$$

which contradicts the fact that $\mathbf{y}(\mathbf{p}^i)$ maximizes profits at $\mathbf{p}^i$. Hence, $\mathbf{p}^0 \cdot \mathbf{y}^* = \mathbf{p}^0 \cdot \mathbf{y}(\mathbf{p}^0)$. But since Y is strictly convex, there is only one $\mathbf{y}$ that maximizes $\mathbf{p}^0 \cdot \mathbf{y}$, so $\mathbf{y}^* = \mathbf{y}(\mathbf{p}^0)$. □

Under the above assumptions the supply and demand behavior of an individual firm will be well defined and nicely behaved. Given any firm j with production set $\mathbf{Y}_j$, we will denote its net supply function by $\mathbf{y}_j(p)$. If we have m firms, the *aggregate* net supply function will be $\mathbf{y}(p) = \sum_{j=1}^{m} \mathbf{y}_j(p)$.

We can also consider the *aggregate production possibilities set,* **Y**. This set indicates all feasible net output vectors for the economy as a whole. This aggregate production possibilities set will typically be the sum of the individual production possibility sets so that we can write:

$$\mathbf{Y} = \sum_{i=1}^{m} \mathbf{Y}_i$$

What does this mean? It simply means that each production plan $\mathbf{y}$ in **Y** is expressible as the sum of n production plans $\mathbf{y}_j$, $j = 1, \cdots, n$ with each production plan $\mathbf{y}_j$ an element of $\mathbf{Y}_j$.

This has the following interesting consequence.

PROPOSITION *An aggregate production play* $\mathbf{y} = \Sigma \mathbf{y}_j$ *maximizes aggregate profits* $\mathbf{p}\ \mathbf{y}$ *for* $\mathbf{y}$ *in* **Y** *if and only if each firm's production plan* $\mathbf{y}_j$ *maximizes its profits* $\mathbf{p}\ \mathbf{y}_j$ *over all the plans* $\mathbf{y}_j$ *available in* $\mathbf{Y}_j$.

PROOF Suppose that $\mathbf{y} = \sum_{j=1}^{m} \mathbf{y}_j$ maximizes aggregate profits but some firm k could have higher profits by choosing $\mathbf{y}'_k$. Then aggregate profits could be higher by choosing the same plan $\mathbf{y}'_k$ for firm k and do exactly what was done before for the other firms.

Conversely, let $(\mathbf{y}_j)$ for $j = 1, \cdots, n$ be a set of profit-maximizing production plans for the individual firms. Suppose that $\mathbf{y} = \sum_{j=1}^{m} \mathbf{y}_j$ is not profit-maximizing at prices $\mathbf{p}$. This means that there is some other production plan $\mathbf{y}' = \Sigma \mathbf{y}'_j$ with $\mathbf{y}'_j$ in Y_j that has higher profits:

$$\Sigma \mathbf{p}\mathbf{y}'_j = \mathbf{p}\Sigma\mathbf{y}'_j > \mathbf{p}\Sigma\mathbf{y}_j = \Sigma\mathbf{p}\,\mathbf{y}_j$$

But by inspecting the sums on each side of this inequality we see that some individual firms must have higher profits at $\mathbf{y}'_j$ than at $\mathbf{y}_j$. □

CONSUMER BEHAVIOR Production introduces two new complications into our model of consumer behavior: labor supply and profit distribution.

In the pure exchange model the consumer was supposed to own some vector $\mathbf{W}$ of commodities. If the consumer sold this vector of commodities he would receive an income of $\mathbf{p} \cdot \mathbf{W}$. It is immaterial whether the consumer sells his entire bundle and buys some goods back or whether he sells only part of his bundle. The observed amount of income may differ, but the economic income is the same.

If we introduce labor into the model we introduce a new possibility: consumers now will presumably supply different amounts of labor depending on the wage rates.

We first consider a very simple model of an individual consumer who has a total amount L of "time" available which he has to divide between labor, l, and leisure, $L - l$. We assume the consumer cares about leisure, $L - l$, and a consumption good, c. The price of labor—the wage rate—will be denoted by w and the price of the consumption good will be denoted by p. The consumer may already own an endowment of the consumption good $\bar{c}$ which contributes to his nonlabor income.

We can write the consumer's maximization problem as:

$$\begin{aligned} \max \quad & u(c, L - l) \\ \text{s.t.} \quad & pc = p\bar{c} + wl \end{aligned}$$

It is often more convenient to write the budget constraint as:

$$pc + w(L - l) = p\bar{c} + wL$$

$$(p, w)\cdot(c, L - l) = (p, w)\cdot(\bar{c}, L)$$

The second way of writing the budget constraint treats leisure as just another good: one has an endowment of it, L, and one "sells" the endowment to a firm at a price w, then "buys back" some of the leisure at the same price.

The same strategy can be used in the more complex case where the consumer has many different types of labor. We regard these as types of leisure and postulate some vector of endowments of these various types. For any vector of prices of goods and labor, the consumer can consider selling off his or her endowment and then buying back the desired bundle of goods and leisure. When we view the labor supply problem in this way, we see that it fits exactly into the previous model of consumer behavior. Given an endowment vector $\mathbf{W}$ and a price vector $\mathbf{p}$, the consumer solves the problem:

$$\begin{aligned} &\max \quad u(\mathbf{x}) \\ &\text{s.t.} \quad \mathbf{p}\cdot\mathbf{x} = \mathbf{p}\cdot\mathbf{W} \end{aligned}$$

(The only complication is that there are now more constraints on the problem—for example, the total amount of leisure consumed has to be less than 24 hours a day. Formally such constraints can be incorporated into the definition of the consumption set described in Chapter 2.)

We now turn to a discussion of profit distribution. In a capitalist economy, consumers own firms and are entitled to a share of the profits. We will summarize this ownership relation by a set of numbers (T_{ij}), where T_{ij} represents consumer i's share of the profits of firm j. For any firm we will require that $\sum_i T_{ij} = 1$, so that it is completely owned by individual consumers. We will take the ownership relations as being historically given, although more complicated models can incorporate the existence of a "stock market" for such shares. At a price vector $\mathbf{p}$ each firm j will choose a production plan that will yield (potential) profits $\mathbf{p}\cdot\mathbf{y}_j(\mathbf{p})$. The total profit income derived by consumer i will then be $\sum_j T_{ij}\mathbf{p}\cdot\mathbf{y}_j(\mathbf{p})$. The budget constraint of the consumer is then:

$$\mathbf{p}\cdot\mathbf{x}_i = \mathbf{p}\cdot\mathbf{W}_i + \sum_j T_{ij}\mathbf{p}\cdot\mathbf{y}_j(\mathbf{p})$$

We assume that the consumer will choose a preference-maximizing bundle that satisfies this budget constraint. Hence consumer i's demand function can be written as a function of the price vector $\mathbf{p}$. Again it is necessary to make an assumption of strict convexity of preferences to ensure $\mathbf{x}_i(\mathbf{p})$ is a (single valued) function. However, we have seen in Chapter 3 that under such an assumption $\mathbf{x}_i(\mathbf{p})$ will be continuous, at least at strictly positive prices and income.

Adding together all of the consumers' demand functions gives the aggregate consumer demand function $\mathbf{X}(\mathbf{p}) = \sum_i \mathbf{x}_i(\mathbf{p})$. The aggregate supply vector comes from adding together the aggregate supply from consumers, which we denote by $\mathbf{W} = \sum_{i=1}^{n} \mathbf{W}_i$, and the aggregate net supply of firms, $\mathbf{Y}(\mathbf{p})$. Finally we define the aggregate excess demand function by:

$$\mathbf{z}(\mathbf{p}) = \mathbf{X}(\mathbf{p}) - \mathbf{Y}(\mathbf{p}) - \mathbf{W}$$

Notice that the sign conventions for supplied commodities works out nicely: a component of $\mathbf{z}(\mathbf{p})$ is negative if the relevant commodity is in net excess supply and positive if the commodity is in net excess demand.

WALRAS' LAW An important part of the existence argument in a pure exchange economy was the application of Walras' law. Does such a relationship hold in a productive economy? The answer is yes.

PROPOSITION *If* $\mathbf{z}(\mathbf{p})$ *is as defined above,* $\mathbf{p}\cdot\mathbf{z}(\mathbf{p}) = 0$ *for all* $\mathbf{p}$.

PROOF We expand $\mathbf{z}(\mathbf{p})$ according to its definition.

$$\begin{aligned}\mathbf{p}\cdot\mathbf{z}(\mathbf{p}) &= \mathbf{p}\cdot[-\mathbf{Y}(\mathbf{p}) + \mathbf{X}(\mathbf{p}) - \mathbf{W}]\\ &= \mathbf{p}\cdot\left[-\sum_j \mathbf{y}_j(\mathbf{p}) + \sum_i \mathbf{x}_i(\mathbf{p}) - \sum_i \mathbf{W}_i\right]\\ &= -\sum_j \mathbf{p}\cdot\mathbf{y}_j(\mathbf{p}) + \sum_i \mathbf{p}\cdot\mathbf{x}_i(\mathbf{p}) - \sum_i \mathbf{p}\cdot\mathbf{W}_i\end{aligned}$$

Using the budget constraint of the consumer i:

$$\begin{aligned}\mathbf{p}\cdot\mathbf{z}(\mathbf{p}) &= -\sum_j \mathbf{p}\cdot\mathbf{y}_j(\mathbf{p}) + \sum_i \mathbf{p}\cdot\mathbf{W}_i + \sum_i\sum_j T_{ij}\mathbf{p}\cdot\mathbf{y}_j(\mathbf{p}) - \sum_i \mathbf{p}\cdot\mathbf{W}_i\\ &= -\sum_j \mathbf{p}\cdot\mathbf{y}_j(\mathbf{p}) + \sum_i T_{ij}\sum_j \mathbf{p}\cdot\mathbf{y}_j(\mathbf{p})\\ &= -\sum_j \mathbf{p}\cdot\mathbf{y}_j(\mathbf{p}) + \sum_j \mathbf{p}\cdot\mathbf{y}_j(\mathbf{p}) = 0\end{aligned}$$

since $\sum_i T_{ij} = 1$ for each j. □

EXISTENCE OF AN EQUILIBRIUM If $\mathbf{z}(\mathbf{p})$ is a continuous function defined on the price simplex that satisfies Walras' law, the argument of Chapter 5 can be applied to show that there exists a $\mathbf{p}^*$ such that $\mathbf{z}(\mathbf{p}^*) \leqq 0$. We have seen that continuity follows if the production possibilities set for each firm is strictly convex. It is not too hard to see that we only need to have the *aggregate* production possibilities set convex. Even if the individual firms have technologies that exhibit slight nonconvexities, such as a small region of increasing returns to scale, the induced discontinuities may be smoothed out in the aggregate.

Recall that the argument for existence we have sketched here is valid only when we are dealing with demand *functions*. The only serious restriction that this imposes is that it rules out constant-returns-to-scale technologies, which we have argued is a rather important case. Therefore we will state an existence theorem for the general case and discuss the economic meanings of the assumptions.

Theorem *An equilibrium exists for an economy if the following assumptions are satisfied:*

(1) *Each consumer's consumption set is closed, convex, and bounded below;*
(2) *There is no satiation consumption bundle for any consumer;*
(3) *For each consumer* i, *the sets* $\{\mathbf{x}_i: \mathbf{x}_i \succsim \mathbf{x}_i'\}$ *and* $\{\mathbf{x}_i: \mathbf{x}_i \precsim \mathbf{x}_i'\}$ *are closed;*
(4) *Each consumer holds an initial endowment vector in the interior of his consumption set;*
(5) *For each consumer* i, *if* $\mathbf{x}_i$, $\mathbf{x}_i'$ *are two consumption bundles, then* $\mathbf{x}_i \succ_i \mathbf{x}_i'$ *implies* $t\mathbf{x}_i + (1-t)\mathbf{x}_i' \succ_i \mathbf{x}_i'$ *for any* $0 < t < 1$;
(6) *For each firm* j, 0 *is an element of* Y_j;
(7) Y_j *is closed and convex for* $j = 1, \cdots, n$;
(8) $Y_j \cap (-Y_j) = \{0\} \qquad j = 1, \cdots, n$;
(9) $Y_j \supset (-R_+)$.

PROOF See Debreu (1959). □

Let us make sure we understand what each assumption is used for. Assumptions (1), (2), (3), (4), and (5) are used to prove a form of continuity of the consumers' (multivalued) demand functions; we are already familiar with their economic meaning. Assumption (6) is an assumption that a firm can always go out of business: this ensures that equilibrium profits will be nonnegative. Assumption (7) is to guarantee continuity of each firm's (multivalued) demand function. Assumption (8) ensures that production is irreversible in the sense that you can't produce a netput vector $\mathbf{y}$ and then turn around and use the outputs as inputs and produce all the inputs as outputs. It is used to guarantee the feasible set of allocations will be bounded. Finally, assumption (9) says that any production plan that uses all goods as inputs is feasible; this is essentially an assumption of free disposal.

WELFARE PROPERTIES OF AN EQUILIBRIUM An allocation $(\mathbf{x}, \mathbf{y})$ is *feasible* if aggregate holdings are compatible with the aggregate supply: $\mathbf{X} - \mathbf{Y} - \mathbf{W} = \mathbf{0}$. In expanded form this becomes:

$$\sum_i \mathbf{x}_i - \sum_j \mathbf{y}_j - \sum_i \mathbf{W}_i = \mathbf{0}$$

As before, a feasible allocation $(\mathbf{x}, \mathbf{y})$ is Pareto efficient if there is no other feasible allocation $(\mathbf{x}', \mathbf{y}')$ such that $\mathbf{x}_i' >_i \mathbf{x}_i$ for all $i = 1, \cdots, n$.

Theorem *If* $(\mathbf{x}, \mathbf{y}, \mathbf{p})$ *is a Walras equilibrium, then* $(\mathbf{x}, \mathbf{y}, \mathbf{p})$ *is Pareto efficient.*

PROOF Suppose not, and let $(\mathbf{x}', \mathbf{y}')$ be a dominating allocation. Then since consumers are utility maximizing we must have:

$$\mathbf{p}\cdot\mathbf{x}_i' > \mathbf{p}\cdot\mathbf{W}_i + \sum_j T_{ij}\mathbf{p}\cdot\mathbf{y}_j \qquad \text{for all } i = 1, \cdots, n$$

Summing we get:

$$\mathbf{p}\cdot\sum_i \mathbf{x}_i' > \sum_i \mathbf{p}\cdot\mathbf{W}_i + \sum_i \mathbf{p}\cdot\mathbf{y}_j$$

where we have used the fact that $\sum_i T_{ij} = 1$. Now we use the definition of feasibility of $\mathbf{x}'$ and replace $\sum_i \mathbf{x}_i'$ by $\sum_j \mathbf{y}_j' + \sum_i \mathbf{W}_i$:

$$\mathbf{p}\cdot\left[\sum_j \mathbf{y}_j' + \sum_i \mathbf{W}_i\right] > \sum_i \mathbf{p}\cdot\mathbf{W}_i + \sum \mathbf{p}\cdot\mathbf{y}_j$$

$$\sum_j \mathbf{p}\cdot\mathbf{y}_j' > \sum_j \mathbf{p}\cdot\mathbf{y}_j$$

But this says that aggregate profits for the production plan $(\mathbf{y}_j')$ are greater than aggregate profits for the production plan $(\mathbf{y}_j)$. This contradicts individual profit maximization by firms. □

The other basic welfare theorem is just about as easy. We will content ourselves with a sketch of the proof.

Theorem *Suppose* $(\mathbf{x}^*, \mathbf{y}^*)$ *is a Pareto efficient allocation with* $\mathbf{x}_i^* \gg 0$. *Suppose preferences are convex, continuous, and strongly monotonic. Suppose firms' production possibility sets,* Y_j, *are each convex. Then there exists a set of prices* $\mathbf{p} \geqq \mathbf{0}$ *such that:*

(1) *if* $\mathbf{x}_i' >_i \mathbf{x}_i^*$, $\mathbf{p}\cdot\mathbf{x}_i' > \mathbf{p}\cdot\mathbf{x}_i^*$ $\quad i = 1, \cdots, n$
(2) *if* $\mathbf{y}_j'$ *is in* Y_j, *then* $\mathbf{p}\cdot\mathbf{y}_j \geqq \mathbf{p}\cdot\mathbf{y}_j'$ *for* $j = 1, \cdots, m$.

"PROOF" (Sketch) As before, let P be the set of all aggregate preferred bundles. Let F be the set of all *feasible* aggregate bundles; that is:

$$F = \left\{W + \sum_j \mathbf{y}_j \colon \mathbf{y}_j \text{ is in } Y_j\right\}$$

Then F and P are both convex sets, and, since $(\mathbf{x}^*, \mathbf{y}^*)$ is Pareto efficient, F and P are disjoint. We can therefore apply the separating hyperplane theorem and find a price vector $\mathbf{p}$ such that

$$\mathbf{p}\cdot\mathbf{z}_P \geqq \mathbf{p}\cdot\mathbf{z}_F \quad \text{for all} \quad \begin{array}{l}\mathbf{z}_P \text{ in } P\\ \mathbf{z}_F \text{ in } F\end{array}$$

Monotonicity of preferences implies that $\mathbf{p} \geqq 0$. We can use the construction given in the pure exchange case to show that at these prices each consumer is maximizing preferences and each firm is maximizing profits. □

The above proposition shows that every Pareto efficient allocation can be achieved by a suitable reallocation of "income." We determine the allocation $(\mathbf{x}^*, \mathbf{y}^*)$ that we want, then determine the relevant prices $\mathbf{p}$. If we give consumer i income $\mathbf{p}\cdot\mathbf{x}_i^*$, he or she will not want to change his or her consumption bundle.

We can interpret this result in several ways: first, we can think of the state as confiscating the consumers' original endowments of goods and leisure and redistributing the endowments in some way compatible with the desired income redistribution. Notice that this redistribution may involve a redistribution of goods, profit shares, and leisure. In a sense, redistributing endowments of labor may involve slavery, i.e., giving some of one consumer's labor to another consumer.

On the other hand, we can think of consumers as keeping their original endowments but being subject to a lump sum tax. This tax is unlike usual taxes in that it is levied on "potential" income rather than "realized" income; that is, the tax is levied on endowments of labor rather than on labor sold. The consumer has to pay the tax regardless of his actions. In a pure economic sense, taxing an agent by a lump sum tax and giving the proceeds to another agent is the same as giving some of the first agent's labor to the other agent and letting him sell it at the going wage rate.

Of course, agents may differ in ability, or—equivalently—in their endowments of various kinds of potential labor. In practice it may be very difficult to observe such differences in ability so as to know how to levy the appropriate lump sum taxes. There are substantial problems involved in efficient redistribution of income when abilities vary across individuals.

Here is a simple but somewhat indirect proof of the second welfare theorem based on a revealed preference argument that generalizes the similar theorem given in Chapter 5.

Theorem *Suppose that* $(\mathbf{x}^*, \mathbf{y}^*)$ *is a Pareto efficient allocation and that preferences are nonsatiated. Suppose further that a competitive equilibrium exists from the initial endowments* $\mathbf{W}_i = \mathbf{x}_i^*$ *and profit shares* $T_{ij} = 0$ *for all* i *and* j, *and let it be given by* $(\mathbf{p}', \mathbf{x}', \mathbf{y}')$. *Then in fact,* $(\mathbf{p}', \mathbf{x}^*, \mathbf{y}^*)$ *is a competitive equilibrium.*

PROOF Since $\mathbf{x}_i^*$ is feasible for each consumer by construction, we must have $\mathbf{x}_i' \succsim_i \mathbf{x}_i^*$. Since $\mathbf{x}^*$ is Pareto efficient, this implies that $\mathbf{x}_i' \sim_i \mathbf{x}_i^*$. Thus, if $\mathbf{x}_i'$ provides maximum utility on the budget set, so does $\mathbf{x}_i^*$.

Each agent will satisfy his budget constraint with equality so that:

$$\mathbf{p}'\mathbf{x}'_i = \mathbf{p}'\mathbf{x}^*_i \qquad i = 1, \cdots, n$$

Summing and using feasibility:

$$\mathbf{p}'\left(\sum_{j=1}^{m} \mathbf{y}_j' + \sum_{i=1}^{n} \mathbf{W}_i\right) = \mathbf{p}'\left(\sum_{j=1}^{m} \mathbf{y}_j^* + \sum_{i=1}^{n} \mathbf{W}_i\right)$$

or

$$\mathbf{p}' \sum_{j=1}^{m} \mathbf{y}_j' = \mathbf{p}' \sum_{j=1}^{m} \mathbf{y}_j^*$$

Hence, if $\mathbf{y}^*$ maximizes aggregate profits, then $\mathbf{y}'$ maximizes aggregate profits. By the usual argument, each individual firm must be maximizing profits. □

This proposition states that if an equilibrium exists from the Pareto efficient allocation $(\mathbf{x}^*, \mathbf{y}^*)$, then $(\mathbf{x}^*, \mathbf{y}^*)$ is *itself* a competitive equilibrium. We may well ask what is necessary for an equilibrium to exist. According to the earlier discussion concerning existence, two things alone are necessary: (1) that all demand functions be continuous; and (2) that Walras' law be satisfied. The continuity of demand will follow from the convexity of preferences and production sets. The Walras law requirement can be checked as follows:

$$\begin{aligned}\mathbf{p}\cdot\mathbf{z}(\mathbf{p}) &= \mathbf{p}\ \mathbf{X}(\mathbf{p}) - \mathbf{p}\ \mathbf{W} - \mathbf{p}\mathbf{Y}(\mathbf{p}) \\ &= \mathbf{p}\mathbf{X}(\mathbf{p}) - \mathbf{p}\ \mathbf{X}^* - \mathbf{p}\ \mathbf{Y}(\mathbf{p}) \\ &= 0 - \mathbf{p}\ \mathbf{Y}(\mathbf{p}) \leq 0.\end{aligned}$$

We see in this model that the value of excess demand is always nonpositive. This occurs because we did not give the consumers a share of the firms' profits. Since these profits are being "thrown away," the value of excess demand may well be negative. However, by Exercise 5.11 there will still exist a competitive equilibrium as long as the demand functions are continuous.

This result indicates that the crucial conditions for the second welfare theorem are simply the conditions that a competitive equilibrium exists—i.e., the convexity conditions.

WELFARE ANALYSIS IN A PRODUCTIVE ECONOMY It should come as no surprise that the analysis of welfare maximization in a productive economy proceeds in much the same way as in the pure exchange case. The only real issue is how to describe the feasible set of allocations in the case of production.

The easiest way is to use the transformation function mentioned in Example 1.5. Recall that this is a function that picks out efficient production plans in the sense that $\mathbf{y}$ is an efficient production plan if and only if $T(\mathbf{y}) = 0$. It turns out that nearly any reasonable technology can be described by means of a transformation function.

The welfare maximization problem can then be written as:

$$\begin{aligned} \max \quad & W(u_1(\mathbf{x}_1), \cdots, u_n(\mathbf{x}_n)) \\ \text{s.t.} \quad & T(X^1, \cdots, X^k) = 0 \end{aligned}$$

where $X^j = \sum_{i=1}^{n} x_i^j \qquad \text{for } j = 1, \cdots, k$

The Lagrangean is:

$$L = W(u_1(\mathbf{x}_1), \cdots, u_n(\mathbf{x}_n)) - tT(\mathbf{X}) = 0$$

and the first-order conditions are:

$$\frac{\partial W(\mathbf{u}^*)}{\partial u_i} \frac{\partial u_i(\mathbf{x}_i^*)}{\partial x_i^l} - t \frac{\partial T(\mathbf{X}^*)}{\partial X^l} = 0 \qquad \begin{array}{l} i = 1, \cdots, n \\ l = 1, \cdots, k \end{array}$$

These can be rearranged to give:

$$\frac{\dfrac{\partial u_i(\mathbf{x}_i^*)}{\partial x_i^l}}{\dfrac{\partial u_i(\mathbf{x}_i^*)}{\partial x_i^h}} = \frac{\dfrac{\partial T(\mathbf{X}^*)}{\partial X^l}}{\dfrac{\partial T(\mathbf{X}^*)}{\partial X^h}} \qquad \begin{array}{l} i = 1, \cdots, n \\ l = 1, \cdots, k \\ h = 1, \cdots, k \end{array}$$

Now the conditions characterizing welfare maximization are expressed by saying that the marginal rate of substitution between each pair of commodities must be equal to the marginal rate of transformation between those commodities.

Just as in the case of pure exchange the same conditions characterize Pareto efficient allocations and market equilibrium allocations as well. For example, suppose a producer considers the problem of maximizing profits subject to the technological restrictions represented by the transformation function. This problem can be written as:

$$\begin{aligned} \max \quad & \mathbf{p} \cdot \mathbf{X} \\ \text{s.t.} \quad & T(\mathbf{X}) = 0 \end{aligned}$$

The first-order conditions are:

$$\frac{p_l}{p_h} = \frac{\dfrac{\partial T(\mathbf{X}^*)}{\partial X^l}}{\dfrac{\partial T(\mathbf{X}^*)}{\partial X^h}} \qquad \begin{array}{l} l = 1, \cdots, k \\ h = 1, \cdots, k \end{array}$$

All the results described in the pure exchange case carry over in a natural way to the production case.

GRAPHICAL TREATMENT There is a generalization of the Edgeworth box that is very helpful in understanding production and general equilibrium. Suppose that we consider a one-consumer economy. The consumer leads a rather schizophrenic life: on the one hand he is a profit-maximizing producer who produces a consumption good from labor inputs while on the other hand he is a utility-maximizing consumer who owns the profit-maximizing firm. This is sometimes called a Robinson Crusoe economy.

In Figure 6.2 we have drawn the production set of the firm. Notice that labor is measured as a negative number since it is an input to the production process. Notice also that the technology exhibits constant returns to scale.

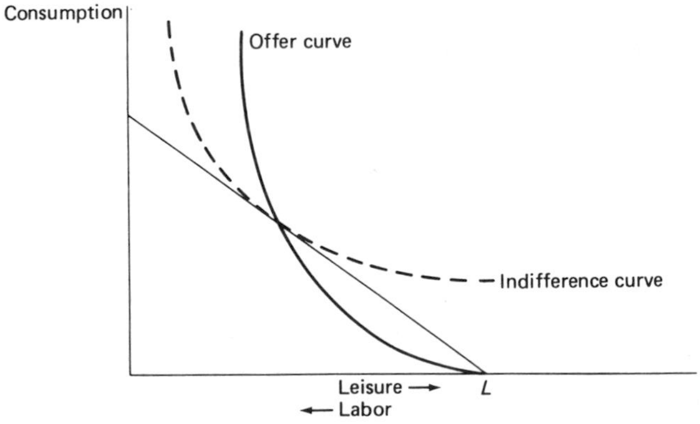

Fig. 6.2 *Robinson Crusoe Economy—Constant Returns*

There is some maximum amount of labor that can be supplied, L. The consumer has preferences over consumption-leisure bundles which are given by the indifference curves in the diagram. What will the equilibrium wage be?

If the real wage is given by the slope of the production set, the consumer's budget set will coincide with the production set. He will demand the bundle that gives him maximal utility. The producer is willing to supply the bundle since he gets zero profits. Hence, both the consumption and the labor markets clear.

Notice the following interesting point: the real wage is determined entirely by the technology while the level of operation is determined by consumer demand. This observation can be generalized to the "nonsubstitution theorem," which states that, if there is only one nonproduced input to production and the technology exhibits constant returns to scale, then the equilibrium prices are independent of tastes—they are determined entirely by technology. We will prove this theorem in the next section.

The decreasing-returns-to-scale case is depicted in Figure 6.3. Notice that we can find the equilibrium allocation directly by looking for the points where the marginal rate of substitution equals the marginal rate of transformation. This slope gives us the equilibrium real wage.

Of course, at this real wage the budget line of the consumer does not pass through the endowment point $(0, L)$. The reason is that the consumer is receiving some profits from the firm. The amount of profits the firm is making, measured in units of the consumption good, is given by the vertical intercept. Since the consumer owns the firm, he receives all of these profits as "nonlabor" income. Thus, his budget set is as indicated, and both markets do indeed clear.

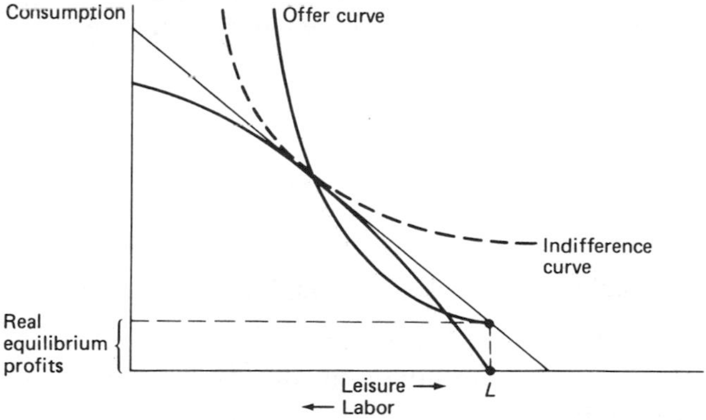

Fig. 6.3 *Robinson Crusoe Economy—Decreasing Returns*

This brings up an interesting point about profits in a general equilibrium model. In the treatment above, we have assumed that the technology exhibits decreasing returns to labor without any particular explanation of why this might be so. A possible reason for such decreasing returns to labor might be the presence of some fixed factor—land, for example. In this interpretation Robinson's production function for consumption depends on the (fixed) land input, T, and the labor input, l. The production function may well exhibit constant returns to scale if we increase both factors of production, but, if we fix the land input and look at output as a function of labor alone, we would presumably see decreasing returns to labor.

From this point of view the "profits"—or nonlabor income—can be interpreted as *rent* to the fixed factor land. If we do use this interpretation then profits broadly speaking are zero—the value of the output must be equal to the value of the factors, almost by definition. Whatever is left over is automatically counted as a factor payment, or rent, to the fixed factor.

Example 6.1 The Cobb-Douglas Constant Returns Economy Suppose we have one consumer with a Cobb-Douglas utility function for consumption (x) and leisure $(1 - l)$: $u(x, 1 - l) = a \ln x + (1 - a) \ln (1 - l)$. We have one firm with a constant-returns-to-scale technology; $x = al$.

By inspection we see that the equilibrium real wage should be the marginal product of labor; hence, $w^*/p^* = a$. The maximization problem of the consumer is:

$$\begin{aligned} \max \quad & a \ln x + (1 - a) \ln (1 - l) \\ \text{s.t.} \quad & px + w(1 - l) = w \end{aligned}$$

We have used the fact that equilibrium profits are zero. Using the by now familiar result that the demand functions for a Cobb-Douglas utility function have the form $x(p) = ay/p$ where y is income, we find:

$$x(p, w) = \frac{aw}{p}$$

$$1 - l(p, w) = \frac{(1 - a)w}{w} = 1 - a$$

Hence, equilibrium supply of labor is a, and the equilibrium output is a^2.

Example 6.2 A Decreasing-Returns-to-Scale Economy Suppose the consumer has a Cobb-Douglas utility function as in the last example, but the producer has a production function $x = l^{1/2}$.

We arbitrarily normalize the price of output to be 1. The profit maximization problem is:

$$\max l^{1/2} - wl$$

This has first-order conditions

$$\tfrac{1}{2}l^{-1/2} - w = 0$$

which implies

$$l = (2w)^{-2} \qquad x = (2w)^{-1}$$

The profit function is found by substitution:

$$\begin{aligned}\pi(w) &= (2w)^{-1} - w(2w)^{-2}\\ &= (4w)^{-1}\end{aligned}$$

The income of the consumer now includes profit income so that the demand for leisure is:

$$1 - l(w) = \frac{(1-a)}{w}\left(w + \frac{1}{4w}\right) = (1-a)\left(1 + \frac{1}{4w^2}\right)$$

By Walras' law we only need find a real wage that clears the labor market:

$$\frac{1}{4w^2} = 1 - (1-a)\left(1 + \frac{1}{4w^2}\right)$$

Solving this equation we find:

$$w^* = \left(\frac{2-a}{4a}\right)^{1/2}$$

The equilibrium level of profits is therefore

$$\pi^* = \frac{1}{4}\left(\frac{2-a}{4a}\right)^{-1/2}$$

An alternative approach to this problem is suggested by the discussion in section on "Graphical Treatment." Presumably the decreasing-returns-to-scale feature of this technology is due to the presence of a fixed factor. Let us call this factor *land* and measure it in units so that the total amount of land is $L = 1$. The price of land will be denoted by q.

The profit maximization problem of the firm is:

$$\max l^{1/2}L^{1/2} - wl - qL$$

which has first-order conditions:

$$\tfrac{1}{2}l^{-1/2}L^{1/2} - w = 0$$

$$\tfrac{1}{2}l^{1/2}L^{-1/2} - q = 0$$

In equilibrium the land market will clear so that $L = 1$. Inserting this into the above equations gives:

$$l = (2w)^{-2}$$

$$l = (2q)^2$$

$$q = \frac{1}{4w}$$

The consumer's income now consists of his income from his endowment of labor, $w \cdot 1$, plus his income from his endowment of land, $q \cdot 1$. His demand for leisure is therefore given by

$$1 - l = \frac{(1-a)y}{w} = \frac{(1-a)(w+q)}{w}$$

or

$$l = 1 - (1-a)(1 + q/w)$$

The condition that the labor market clear is given by the statement that labor demand equals labor supply:

$$\frac{1}{4w^2} = 1 - (1-a)(1 + q/w) = 1 - (1-a)\left(1 + \frac{1}{4w^2}\right)$$

which can be solved to give:

$$w^* = \left(\frac{2-a}{4a}\right)^{1/2}$$

The equilibrium rent to land is:

$$q^* = \frac{1}{4}\left(\frac{2-a}{4a}\right)^{-1/2}$$

Note that this is the same as the earlier solution.

THE NONSUBSTITUTION THEOREM Here we will present an argument for the nonsubstitution theorem in the n-good case. We will assume that there are n industries producing outputs y_i, $i = 1, \cdots, n$. Each industry produces only one output—no joint production is allowed. There is only one nonproduced input to production, usually thought of as labor, denoted by y_0. The prices of each of the $n + 1$ goods will be denoted by $w_0, w_1, \cdots w_n$.

As usual, the equilibrium prices will only be determined as relative prices. We will assume that labor is a necessary input to each industry. Thus, in equilibrium $w_0 > 0$, and we can choose it as numéraire; that is, we can arbitrarily set $w_o = 1$.

We will assume that the technology exhibits constant returns to scale. We have seen in Chapter 1, Example 1.9, that this implies that each industry's cost function can be written as $c_i(\mathbf{w}, y_i) = c_i(\mathbf{w})y_i \; i = 1, \cdots, n$. The functions $c_i(\mathbf{w})$ are interpreted as unit cost functions—how much it costs to produce one unit of output at the prices $\mathbf{w}$, measured in terms of the numéraire price w_0.

We also assume that labor is indispensable to production so that $0 < x_{i0}(\mathbf{w}, y_i) = \partial c_i(\mathbf{w}, y_i)/\partial w_0$; i.e., the conditional factor demand for labor is strictly positive for y_i positive. Note that this had the implication that the cost functions are *strictly* increasing in w_0, so that in particular $c_i(t\mathbf{w}) > c_i(\mathbf{w})$ for $t > 1$.

NONSUBSTITUTION THEOREM *Suppose there is only one nonproduced input to production, this input is indispensable to production, there is no joint production, and the technology is constant returns to scale. Let* $(\mathbf{x}, \mathbf{y}, \mathbf{w})$ *be a Walrasian equilibrium with* $y_i > 0$ *for* $i = 0, \cdots, n$. *Then* $\mathbf{w}$ *is the unique solution to* $w_i = c_i(\mathbf{w})$, $i = 1, \cdots, n$.

PROOF If $\mathbf{w}$ is an equilibrium price vector in a constant-returns-to-scale economy, then profits must be zero in each industry; that is:

$$w_i y_i - c_i(\mathbf{w})y_i = 0 \qquad i = 1, \cdot \cdot \cdot, n$$

Since $y_i > 0$ for $i = 1, \cdot \cdot \cdot, n$ this reduces to:

$$w_i - c_i(\mathbf{w}) = 0 \qquad i = 1, \cdot \cdot \cdot, n$$

Hence any equilibrium price vector must satisfy the condition that price equals average cost. Note that since $w_0 > 0$ and labor is an indispensable factor of production $c_i(\mathbf{w}) > 0$ so $w_i > 0, i = 1, \cdot \cdot \cdot, n$; hence, all equilibrium price vectors are strictly positive.

Furthermore, there is only one such equilibrium price vector. For suppose $\mathbf{w}'$ and $\mathbf{w}$ were two distinct solutions to the above system of equations. Define

$$t = w'_k/w_k = \max_i w'_i/w_i$$

Suppose that $t > 1$. Then we would have:

$$w'_k \overset{1}{=} tw_k \overset{2}{=} tc_k(\mathbf{w}) \overset{3}{=} c_k(t\mathbf{w}) \overset{4}{>} c_k(\mathbf{w}') \overset{5}{=} w'_k$$

The justifications for these equalities and inequalities are as follows:

(1) definition of t,
(2) assumption that $\mathbf{w}$ is a solution,
(3) linear homogeneity of cost function,
(4) definition of t, assumption $t > 1$, and strict monotonicity of cost function,
(5) assumption that $\mathbf{w}'$ is a solution.

The result of assuming $t > 1$ is a contradiction, so $t \leqq 1$, and thus $\mathbf{w} \geqq \mathbf{w}'$. The role of $\mathbf{w}$ and $\mathbf{w}'$ is symmetric in the above argument so we also have $\mathbf{w}' \geqq \mathbf{w}$. Putting these together we have $\mathbf{w}' = \mathbf{w}$, as required. □

This theorem says that, if there is an equilibrium price vector for the economy, it must be the solution to $w_i = c_i(\mathbf{w})$ for $i = 1, \cdots, n$. The surprising thing is that $\mathbf{w}$ does not depend on demand conditions at all; i.e., $\mathbf{w}$ is completely independent of preferences and endowments.

Let $\mathbf{w}^*$ be the vector of prices that solves the zero-profit conditions. Then we can determine the equilibrium net supply vector of each firm by differentiating the cost function:

$$\mathbf{x}_i(\mathbf{w}^*, y_i) = \mathbf{D}c_i(\mathbf{w}^*)y_i$$

Since the equilibrium prices are independent of demand conditions, the equilibrium factor demands will be independent of demand conditions. The level of output of the different goods may change, but the *method* of production will remain constant.

INDUSTRY STRUCTURE IN GENERAL EQUILIBRIUM Recall that the number of firms is a given in the Walrasian model. In Chapter 2 we argued that the number of firms in an industry was a variable. How can we reconcile these two models?

Let us consider first the constant-returns case. Then we know that the only profit-maximizing level of profits compatible with equilibrium is that of zero profits. Furthermore, at the prices compatible with zero profits, the firms are willing to operate at any level. Hence, the industry structure of the economy is indeterminate—firms are indifferent as to what market share they hold. If the number of firms is a variable, it is also indeterminate.

Consider now the decreasing-returns case. If all technology is decreasing returns, we know that there will be some equilibrium profits. In the general equilibrium model as we have described it up until now, there is no reason to have constant profits across firms. The usual argument for constant profits is that firms will enter the industry with the highest profits; but if the number of firms is fixed this cannot occur.

What would in fact happen if the number of firms were variable? Presumably we would see entry occur. If the technology really exhibits decreasing returns to scale, the optimum size of the firm is infinitesimal, simply because it is always better to have two small firms than one large one. Hence, we would expect continual entry to occur, pushing down the profit level. In long-run equilibrium we would expect to see an infinite number of firms, each operating at an infinitesimal level.

This seems rather implausible. One way out is to return to the argument we mentioned in Chapter 2: if we can always replicate, the only sensible long-run technology is a constant-returns-to-scale technology. Hence, the decreasing-returns-to-scale technology really must be due to the presence of some fixed factor. In this interpretation the equilibrium "profits" should really be regarded as returns to the fixed factor.

6.2 GENERAL EQUILIBRIUM OVER TIME

As mentioned earlier, the concept of goods used in general equilibrium theory is very broad. In particular, goods which are to be available at different times may be—and should be—regarded as different goods. One way to think about this is to think of *contracts* being traded rather than goods.

Thus, agents offer contracts of the form: "At date t I will deliver to the holder of this contract one unit of commodity X." Given a list of potential prices for the various contracts, agents can consult their intertemporal preferences and their intertemporal technologies to determine their demands and supplies of the various contracts. Note that contracts are traded and payed for at time 0 but are carried out at the appropriate time stated in the contract. An equilibrium price vector is one where the demand for each contract equals the supply of each contract. From the point of view of the abstract theory, the contracts are just goods, so the standard existence and welfare results apply.

Certain markets for future delivery exist in the real life economies. An example might be the Chicago futures markets for commodities. In such markets one can buy or sell contracts for future delivery of some commodity. Another example is the market for money. Here we can sell or buy contracts of the form "I will pay you \$$x$ at time t." In real life selling such contracts is known as borrowing money, and buying such contracts is known as loaning money.

There is an interesting interpretation to the sequence of intertemporal prices for a single good. Suppose p_i^t and p_i^{t+1} are the prices at time 0 of a certain commodity delivered at time t and time $t + 1$. Then we can define

$$r_{t,t+1} = p_i^t/p_i^{t+1} - 1$$

The number r is interpreted as an "own rate of interest" over the period t to $t + 1$. This is because it measures the value of the good at time $t + 1$ relative to the value at time t.

Consider for example a particular case of a monetary contract described above. Suppose it is now t_0 = January 1, 1980. The current price of \$100 is clearly p^{t_0} = \$100. Suppose that the current price for \$100 delivered one year from now is \$50; that is, a contract of the form "I will pay you \$100 on January 1, 1981" now sells for \$50 so that p^{t_0+1} = \$50. Then the implied rate of interest is 100/50-1, or 100 per cent.

6.3 *TEMPORARY EQUILIBRIUM*

If only some subset of markets exist, we can only require that the existing markets clear in equilibrium. In the real world futures markets are quite rare, and hence observed equilibria are only equilibria for current markets. Such equilibria are called *temporary equilibria*.

To be more precise, let us consider a model with k goods, n agents, and t time periods. At time 0, agents face current prices $\mathbf{p}$ (a k-vector) and expect futures prices to be $\mathbf{q}$ ($\mathbf{q}$ will be an nkt vector representing the expectations of each of the n agents about each of the k prices for each of the t time periods). There exist only spot markets for each of the first $k - 1$ goods, but the kth good can be traded on a futures market. We think of the kth good as being some kind of money. The ratio between its future price and current price gives the rate of return on holding money.

Given these prices and expectations, agents determine their current demands and supplies. These current demands and supplies can be thought of as coming from some kind of utility maximization planning. The important feature is that each agent j must meet a one-period budget constraint of the form:

$$\sum_{i=1}^{k-1} p^i x_j^i(\mathbf{p}, \mathbf{q}) = p^k x_j^k(\mathbf{p}, \mathbf{q}) + \sum_{i=1}^{k} p^i W_j^i$$

Here x_j^i is the jth agent's demand function for the ith good and W_j^i is his endowment of the ith good. The budget constraint says that the value of the agent's demand for goods equals the value of his endowment plus the value of the money he desires to "purchase." Presumably he must "sell" some money at a future date if he wants to purchase some now. In more prosaic language, if the consumer borrows money now, he must presumably pay it back later.

Let us define $\mathbf{z}(\mathbf{p}, \mathbf{q})$ to be the aggregate "excess demand" vector for current goods:

$$\mathbf{z}(\mathbf{p}, \mathbf{q}) = \sum_{j=1}^{n} \{[x_j^1(\mathbf{p}, \mathbf{q}), \cdots, x_j^{k-1}(\mathbf{p}, \mathbf{q}), -x_j^k(\mathbf{p}, \mathbf{q})] - \mathbf{W}_j\}$$

There are several natural assumptions we can make about the function $\mathbf{z}$.

(CONTINUITY) We assume $\mathbf{z}$ is continuous in $\mathbf{p}$. We may allow the agents' expectations $\mathbf{q}$ to be a function of $\mathbf{p}$, in which case we assume the function $\mathbf{z}(\mathbf{p}, \mathbf{q}(\mathbf{p}))$ to be continuous.

(HOMOGENEITY) We assume $\mathbf{z}(\mathbf{p}, \mathbf{q}) = \mathbf{z}(k\mathbf{p}, k\mathbf{q})$ for all positive k.

(WALRAS' LAW) $\mathbf{p} \cdot \mathbf{z}(\mathbf{p}, \mathbf{q}) \equiv 0$ for all current prices $\mathbf{p}$. This means that the value of excess demand *including* the excess demand for money is identically zero. As before, this follows from adding the individual budget constraints.

Under these assumptions it is quite easy to show the existence of a temporary Walrasian equilibrium, simply by mimicking the earlier proof.

Theorem *There exists a price vector* $\mathbf{p}^*$ *such that* $\mathbf{z}(\mathbf{p}^*, \mathbf{q}(\mathbf{p}^*)) \leq 0$.

PROOF Normalize the prices $(\mathbf{p}, \mathbf{q}(\mathbf{p}))$ to lie on the unit simplex, S. Then define a continuous map from the simplex to itself by:

$$f_i(\mathbf{p}, \mathbf{q}) = \frac{p_i + \max\,[0, z_i(\mathbf{p}, \mathbf{q})]}{1 + \sum_j \max\,[0, z_j(\mathbf{p}, \mathbf{q})]} \qquad i = 1, \cdots, k$$

$$f_i(\mathbf{p}, \mathbf{q}) = \frac{q_i(\mathbf{p})}{1 + \sum_j \max\,[0, z_j(\mathbf{p}, \mathbf{q})]} \qquad i = k + 1, \cdots nkt$$

As before, this mapping has a fixed point; that is, there is some vector $(\mathbf{p}^*, \mathbf{q}^*)$ such that:

$$p_i^* = \frac{p_i^* + \max\,[0, z_j(\mathbf{p}^*, \mathbf{q}^*)]}{1 + \sum_j \max\,[0, z_j(\mathbf{p}^*, \mathbf{q}^*)]} \qquad i = 1, \cdots, k$$

and

$$q_i^* = \frac{q_i(\mathbf{p}^*)}{1 + \sum_j \max\,[0, z_j(\mathbf{p}^*, \mathbf{q}^*)]} \qquad i = k + 1, \cdots, nkt$$

Now apply the same arithmetical operations as before to the first set of equations to conclude that $\mathbf{z}(\mathbf{p}^*, \mathbf{q}^*) \leqq 0$ and substitute this into the second set of equations to conclude that $q_i^* = q_i(\mathbf{p}^*)$. □

It would be nice to be able to complement this existence proof with a proof of efficiency. Unfortunately, there is no reason to believe that temporary equilibria are efficient. The equilibria depend very much on the expectations of the agents and these expectations may be radically different. If agents happen to have "rational" expectations—expectations that are consistent with *all* markets (spot and future) clearing—then the economy will be efficient since $(\mathbf{p}^*, \mathbf{q}(\mathbf{p}^*))$ will be a Walrasian equilibrium for the intertemporal economy. Otherwise, the situation will undoubtedly reveal intertemporal inefficiencies.

6.4 *GENERAL EQUILIBRIUM OVER STATES OF NATURE*

Let us suppose that agents are considering trading at time t, but there is some uncertainty about what will happen at time $t + 1$, when the trades are actually supposed to be carried out. For example, people may be trading contracts for ice cream cones and umbrellas at time t; these contracts will be carried out at date $t + 1$. There may be some uncertainty about the weather on date $t + 1$; if it rains, for example, it seems plausible that umbrellas will be worth a lot more than if it is sunny.

Suppose that agents issue "contingency contracts" of the form: "on date $t + 1$ I will deliver to the holder of this contract one umbrella if and only if it rains." More generally, we can imagine there being a large number of states of the world indexed by s. Contracts to supply goods in the various states can be issued. Given any price vector for the contracts, agents can consult their preferences and their technologies and determine how much they wish to demand and supply of the various contracts. Note that contracts are traded and payed for with certainty at time t but will only be exercised at time $t + 1$ if the appropriate state of the world occurs. An *equilibrium price vector* is one where there is no excess demand for any contract. From the viewpoint of the abstract theory the contracts are just goods like any other goods. The standard existence and efficiency results apply.

It is important to understand the efficiency result correctly. Preferences are defined over the space of lotteries. If the von Neumann-Morgenstern axioms are met, the preferences over random events can be summarized by an expected utility function. To say that there is no other feasible allocation that makes all consumers better off is to say that there is no pattern of contingent contracts that increases each agent's *expected utility*.

6.5 THE CORE OF AN EXCHANGE ECONOMY

We have seen that market equilibria have certain desirable normative properties, and furthermore that for arbitrary initial endowments market equilibria will generally exist. But of course the use of a price system is a very specific way to allocate resources and to facilitate trade. Thus it is worthwhile to question the robustness of the market allocation as the outcome of a trading process.

Let us consider a "market game" where agents come with an initial endowment of $\mathbf{W}_i$ to trade. Instead of postulating a price mechanism, we just imagine agents wandering around and making potential arrangements to trade with each other. (Notice that we have returned to a pure exchange model and are ignoring production possibilities.)

What kind of outcome might we expect from such a process? Suppose we were given a suggested allocation as the outcome of such a process; how could we tell if it was reasonable? One suggestion is formulated as follows:

DEFINITION A group of agents S (a coalition S) is said to *improve upon* a given allocation $\mathbf{x}$ if there is some allocation $\mathbf{x}'$ such that

(1) $\sum_{i \text{ in } S} \mathbf{x}_i' = \sum_{i \text{ in } S} \mathbf{W}_i$ ($\mathbf{x}'$ is feasible for S);

(2) $\mathbf{x}_i'$ is preferred to $\mathbf{x}_i$ for all i in S

A feasible allocation $\mathbf{x}$ is in the *core* of the economy if it cannot be improved upon by any coalition.

If an allocation $\mathbf{x}$ can be improved upon, then there is some group of agents that can do better by not engaging in the market at all; they would do better by only trading among themselves. An example of this in "real life" might be a group of consumers who organize a co-op to counteract high prices at the supermarket.

Notice that, if $\mathbf{x}$ is in the core, $\mathbf{x}$ must be Pareto efficient. For if $\mathbf{x}$ were not Pareto efficient, then the coalition consisting of all the agents (the coalition of the whole) could improve upon $\mathbf{x}$.

Notice further that the idea of the core places great informational requirements on the agents—the people in the dissatisfied coalition have to be able to find each other. Furthermore, it is assumed that there are no costs to forming coalitions so that, even if only very small gains can be made by forming coalitions, they will nevertheless be formed.

A geometrical picture of the core can be obtained from the standard Edgeworth box diagram for the 2-person, 2-good case. (See Figure 6.4.)

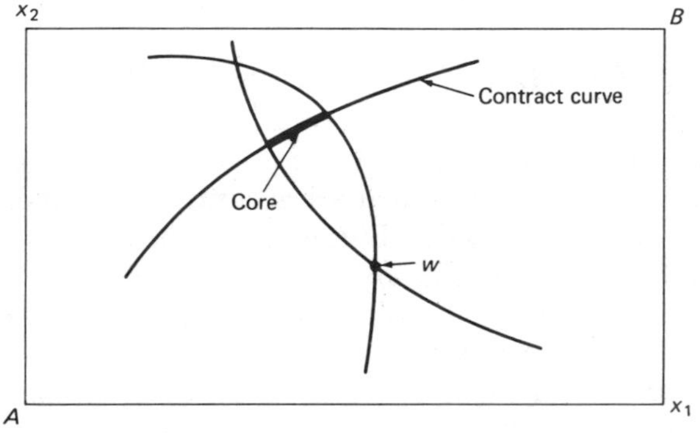

Fig. 6.4 *Core of an Edgeworth Box Economy*

Will the core of an economy generally be nonempty? If we continue to make the assumptions that ensure the existence of a market equilibrium, it will, since the market equilibrium is always contained in the core.

PROPOSITION *If* $(\mathbf{x}^*, \mathbf{p})$ *is a Walrasian equilibrium with initial endowments* $\mathbf{W}_i$, *then* $\mathbf{x}^*$ *is in the core.*

PROOF Assume not; then there is some coalition S and some feasible allocation $\mathbf{x}'$ such that all agents i in S prefer $\mathbf{x}_i'$ to $\mathbf{x}_i^*$ and furthermore

$$\sum_{i \text{ in } S} \mathbf{x}_i' = \sum_{i \text{ in } S} \mathbf{W}_i$$

But the definition of the market equilibrium $\mathbf{x}^*$ implies

$$\mathbf{p}\cdot\mathbf{x}_i' > \mathbf{p}\cdot\mathbf{W}_j \qquad \text{for all } i \text{ in } S$$

so
$$\mathbf{p}\cdot \sum_{i \text{ in } S} \mathbf{x}' > \mathbf{p}\cdot \sum_{i \text{ in } S} \mathbf{W}_i$$

which contradicts the above equality. □

We can see from the Edgeworth box diagram that generally there will be other points in the core than just the market equilibrium. However, if we allow our 2-person economy to grow we will have more possible coalitions and hence more opportunities for improvement. Therefore one might suspect that the core might shrink as the economy grows.

One problem with the above idea is that the core is a subset of the allocation space and thus as the economy grows the core keeps changing dimension. Thus we want to limit ourselves to a particularly simple type of growth.

We will say two agents are of the same *type* if both their preferences and their initial endowments are the same. We will say that one economy is an *r- replica* of another if there are r times as many agents of each type in one economy as in the other. Thus if a large economy replicates a smaller one, it is just a "scaled up" version of the small one. For simplicity we will limit ourselves to only two types of agents, type A and type B. Consider now a fixed 2-person economy; by the r-core of this economy, we mean the core of the rth replication of the given economy.

***Lemma** (Equal Treatment in the Core)* *Suppose agents' preferences are strictly convex, strongly monotonic, and continuous. Then if* $\mathbf{x}$ *is an allocation in the* r-core *of a given economy, then any two agents of the same type must receive the same bundle.*

PROOF Index the $2r$ agents by $A1 \cdots Ar$ and $B1 \cdots Br$. If all agents of the same type do not get the same allocation, there will be one agent of each type who is most poorly treated. We will call these two agents the "type-A underdog" and the "type-B underdog." (If there are ties, select any of the tied agents.)

Let $\bar{\mathbf{x}}_A = \frac{1}{r}\sum_{j=1}^{r} \mathbf{x}_{A_j}$ and $\bar{\mathbf{x}}_B = \frac{1}{r}\sum_{j=1}^{r} \mathbf{x}_{B_j}$ be the "average allocations" of the type-A and type-B agents.

By feasibility,

$$\frac{1}{r}\sum_{j=1}^{r} \mathbf{x}_{A_j} + \frac{1}{r}\sum_{j=1}^{r} \mathbf{x}_{B_j} = \frac{1}{r}\sum_{j=1}^{r} \mathbf{W}_{A_j} + \frac{1}{r}\sum_{j=1}^{r} \mathbf{W}_{B_j}$$

$$= \frac{1}{r} r\mathbf{W}_A + \frac{1}{r} r\mathbf{W}_B$$

$$\bar{\mathbf{x}}_A + \bar{\mathbf{x}}_B = \mathbf{W}_A + \mathbf{W}_B$$

so that $(\bar{\mathbf{x}}_A, \bar{\mathbf{x}}_B)$ is feasible for the coalition consisting of the two underdogs. We are assuming that at least for one type, say type A, two of the type-A agents receive different bundles. Hence the A underdog will strictly prefer $\bar{\mathbf{x}}_A$ to his present allocation by strict convexity of preferences (since it is a weighted average of bundles that are at least as good as $\mathbf{x}_A$), and the B underdog will think $\bar{\mathbf{x}}_B$ is at least as good as his present allocation. Strong monotonicity allows A to remove a little from $\bar{\mathbf{x}}_A$, leaving him $\bar{\mathbf{x}}_A - \epsilon$, and bribe B by offering him $\bar{\mathbf{x}}_B + \epsilon$, thus forming a coalition that can improve upon the allocation.□

Since any allocation in the core must award agents of the same type the same bundle, we can examine the cores of replicated 2-agent economies by use of the Edgeworth box diagram. Instead of a point $\mathbf{x}$ in the core representing how much A gets and how much B gets, we think of $\mathbf{x}$ as telling us how much *each* agent of type A gets and how much *each* agent of type B gets. The above lemma tells us that all points in the r-core can be represented in this manner.

The following proposition shows that any allocation that is not a market equilibrium allocation must eventually not be in the r-core of the economy. Hence core allocations in large economies look just like market equilibria.

PROPOSITION *Suppose that preferences are strictly convex and strongly monotonic and that there is a unique market equilibrium* $\mathbf{x}^*$ *from initial endowment* $\mathbf{W}$. *Then if* $\mathbf{y}$ *is not the market equilibrium, there is some replication* r *such that* $\mathbf{y}$ *is not in the* r *core.*

PROOF Refer to the Edgeworth box in Figure 6.5. We want to show that a point like y can eventually be improved upon. Since $\mathbf{y}$ is not a Walrasian equilibrium, the line through $\mathbf{y}$ and $\mathbf{W}$ must cut at least one

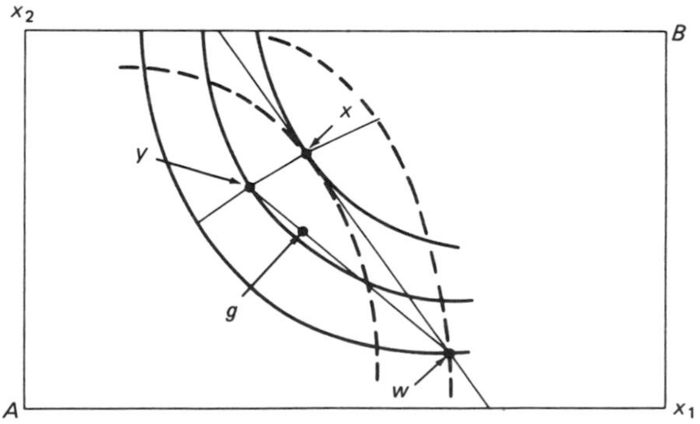

Fig. 6.5 *Proof that the Core Shrinks as the Economy Replicates*

agent's indifference curve through $\mathbf{y}$. Thus it is possible to choose a point such as $\mathbf{g}$ which, for example, agent A prefers to $\mathbf{y}$. (There are several cases to treat, depending on the location of $\mathbf{g}$; however, the arguments are essentially the same, so we treat only the case depicted.)

By continuity of preferences we can imagine $\mathbf{g} = \theta \mathbf{W} + (1 - \theta)\ \mathbf{y}$ where $\theta = T/V$ with T and V integers (i.e., θ is a rational number.) So, $\mathbf{g}_A = (T/V)\ \mathbf{W}_A + (1 - T/V)\ \mathbf{y}_A$.

Suppose the economy has replicated V times. Then form a coalition consisting of V consumers of type A and V-T consumers of type B, and consider the allocation $\mathbf{z}$ where agents of type A in the coalition receive $\mathbf{g}_A$ and agents of type B receive $\mathbf{y}_B$. This allocation is preferred to $\mathbf{y}$ by all members of the coalition (we can remove a little from the A agents and give it to the B agents to get strict preference) and furthermore it is feasible for the members of the coalition: for consider

$$V\mathbf{g}_A + (V - T)\mathbf{y}_B = V \underbrace{\left[\frac{T}{V}\ \mathbf{W}_A + \left(1 - \frac{T}{V}\right)\ \mathbf{y}_A\right]}_{g_A} + (V - T)\mathbf{y}_B$$

$$= T\mathbf{W}_A + (V - T)\mathbf{y}_A + (V - T)\mathbf{y}_B$$

$$= T\mathbf{W}_A + (V - T)[\mathbf{y}_A + \mathbf{y}_B] = T\mathbf{W}_A + (V - T)[\mathbf{W}_A + W_B]$$

$$= T\mathbf{W}_A + V\mathbf{W}_A - T\mathbf{W}_A + (V - T)W_B$$

$$= V\mathbf{W}_A + (V - T)\mathbf{W}_B$$

which is exactly the endowment of our coalition since it has V agents of type A and $(V - T)$ agents of type B. Thus this coalition can improve upon $\mathbf{y}$, proving the proposition. □

Again many of the restrictive assumptions in the above proposition can be relaxed. In particular we can easily get rid of the assumptions of strong monotonicity and the uniqueness of the market equilibrium. Convexity seems to be crucial to the proposition, but, as in the existence theorem, one can get rid of that assumption also for large economies. Of course, we can also allow for there to be more than only 2 types of agents.

In the study of Walrasian economy we found that the price mechanism leads to a well-defined equilibrium position. In the study of Pareto efficient allocations we found that nearly all Pareto efficient allocation can be obtained through a suitable reallocation of endowments and a price mechanism. And here, in the study of a general pure exchange economy, prices appear in a third and different light: the only allocations that are viable in large pure exchange economies are precisely those allocations that are market equilibria with respect to an appropriate price system.

6.6 *CONVEXITY AND SIZE*

Recall the role of convexity in the general equilibrium models we have been discussing: the assumption of convexity has been used only to assure the single valuedness and the continuity of the various demand and supply functions. It is easy to construct examples where nonconvexities cause discontinuities of demand and thus nonexistence of equilibrium prices.

Consider, for example, the Edgeworth box diagram in Figure 6.6. Here agent A has nonconvex preferences while agent B has convex preferences. It is easy to see that no equilibrium prices may exist because of the discontinuity in demand.

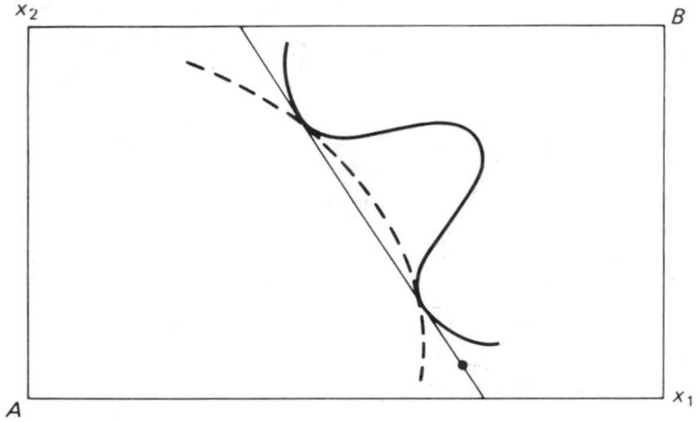

Fig. 6.6 *Nonexistence of an Equilibrium with Nonconvex Preferences*

The demand curves for good 1 that go along with this Edgeworth diagram have the shapes depicted in Figure 6.7.

At the price p^*, we have total demands of $x_A^* + x_B$ or $x_A' + x_B$; one is too big and the other is too small. There is no price where supply will equal demand.

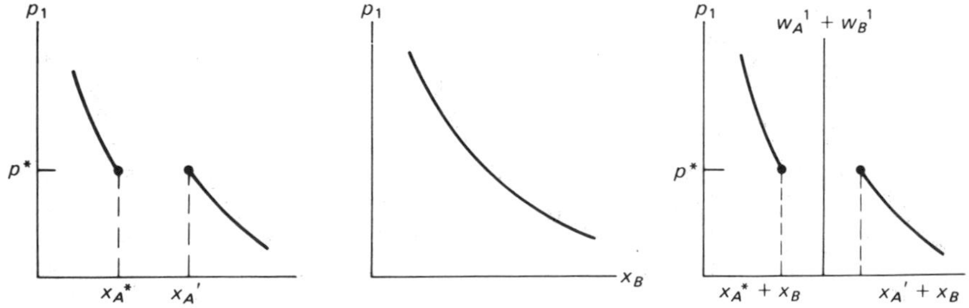

Fig. 6.7 *Nonexistence of an Equilibrium with Discontinuous Demand Function*

Let us consider a specific example. Suppose that the total supply of the good is just halfway between the two demands at p^* as in Figure 6.6.

Now let us think what would happen if the economy would replicate once so that there were two agents of type A and two agents of type B. Then at the price p^*, one type-A agent could demand x_A^* and the other could demand x'_A. In that case, the total demand by the agents would in fact be equal to the total amount of the good supplied. An equilibrium exists for the replicated economy.

It is easy to see that a similar construction will work no matter where the supply curve lies: if it were two-thirds of the way between x_A^* and x'_A, we would just replicate three times, and so on. Thus, we have a rather fundamental principal: *if there are sufficiently many agents, equilibrium prices will always exist, regardless of any nonconvexities of the individual preferences.*

6.7 THE UNIQUENESS OF EQUILIBRIUM

We know from the section on existence of general equilibrium that under appropriate conditions a price vector will exist that clears all markets; i.e., there exists a $\mathbf{p}^*$ such that $\mathbf{z}(\mathbf{p}^*) \leqq 0$. The question we ask in this section is that of uniqueness: when is there only one price vector that clears all markets?

The free goods case is not of great interest here, so we will rule it out by means of the desirability assumption: we will just assume that the excess demand for each good is strictly positive when its relative price is zero. Economically this means that, when the price of a good goes to zero, everyone demands a lot of it, which seems reasonable enough. This has the obvious consequence that, at all equilibrium price vectors $\mathbf{p}^*$, p_i^* must be strictly positive.

As before, we will want to assume $\mathbf{z}$ is continuous, but now we need even more than that—we want to assume continuous differentiability. The reasons for this are fairly clear; if indifference curves have kinks in them, we can find whole ranges of prices that are market equilibria. Not only are the equilibria not unique, they aren't even *locally* unique.

Given these assumptions, we have a purely technical problem: given a smooth mapping $\mathbf{z}$ from the price simplex to R^k, when is there a unique point that maps into zero? It is too much to hope that this will occur in general, since one can construct easy counterexamples, even in the two-dimensional case. Hence, we are interested in finding restrictions on the excess demand functions that ensure uniqueness. We will then be interested in whether these restrictions are strong or weak, what their economic meaning is, and so on.

We will here consider two restrictions on $\mathbf{z}$ that ensure uniqueness. The first case, that of *gross substitutes,* is interesting because it has clear economic meaning and allows a simple, direct proof of uniqueness. The second case, that of *index analysis,* is interesting because it is very general. In fact it contains almost all other uniqueness results as special cases. Unfortunately, the proof utilizes a rather advanced theorem from differential topology. Since the index analysis gives necessary and sufficient conditions for uniqueness, it is about the best one can do and is therefore worthy of study.

GROSS SUBSTITUTES

DEFINITION Two goods, i and j, are gross substitutes at a price vector $\mathbf{p}$ if $\frac{\partial z_j(\mathbf{p})}{\partial p_i} > 0$ for $i \neq j$.

This definition simply says that two goods are gross substitutes if an increase in price i brings about an increase in the excess demand for good j. Thus the Jacobian matrix of $\mathbf{z}$, $\mathbf{Dz}(\mathbf{p})$, has all off diagonal terms positive.

Theorem *If all goods are gross substitutes for all prices, then if* $\mathbf{p}^*$ *is an equilibrium price vector, it is the unique equilibrium price vector.*

PROOF Suppose $\mathbf{p}'$ is some other equilibrium price vector. Since $\mathbf{p}^* \gg 0$ we can define $m = \max p_i'/p_i^* \neq 0$. By homogeneity and the fact that $\mathbf{p}^*$ is an equilibrium, we know that $\mathbf{z}(\mathbf{p}^*) = \mathbf{z}(m\mathbf{p}^*) = \mathbf{0}$. We know that for some price, p_k, we have $mp_k^* = p_k'$ by the definition of m. We now lower each price mp_i^* other than p_k successively to p_i'. Since the price of each good other than k goes down in the movement from $m\mathbf{p}^*$ to $\mathbf{p}'$, we must have the demand for good k going down. Thus $z_k(\mathbf{p}') < 0$ which implies $\mathbf{p}'$ cannot be an equilibrium. □

INDEX ANALYSIS Consider an economy with only two goods. Choose the price of the second good as the numéraire, and draw the excess demand curve for the good one as a function of its own price. Walras' law implies that, when the excess demand for good 1 is zero, we have an equilibrium. The desirability assumption we have made implies that, when p^1 is large, the excess demand for good 1 is negative and when p^1 is small the excess demand for good 1 is positive.

Refer to Figure 6.8, where we have drawn some examples of what can happen. Notice that (1) the equilibria are usually isolated (locally unique); (2) the cases where they are not isolated are not "stable" with respect to minor perturbations; (3) there is usually an odd number of equilibria; (4) if the excess demand curve is downward sloping at all equilibria, there can be only one equilibrium; and (5) if there is only one equilibrium, the excess demand curve must be downward sloping at the equilibrium.

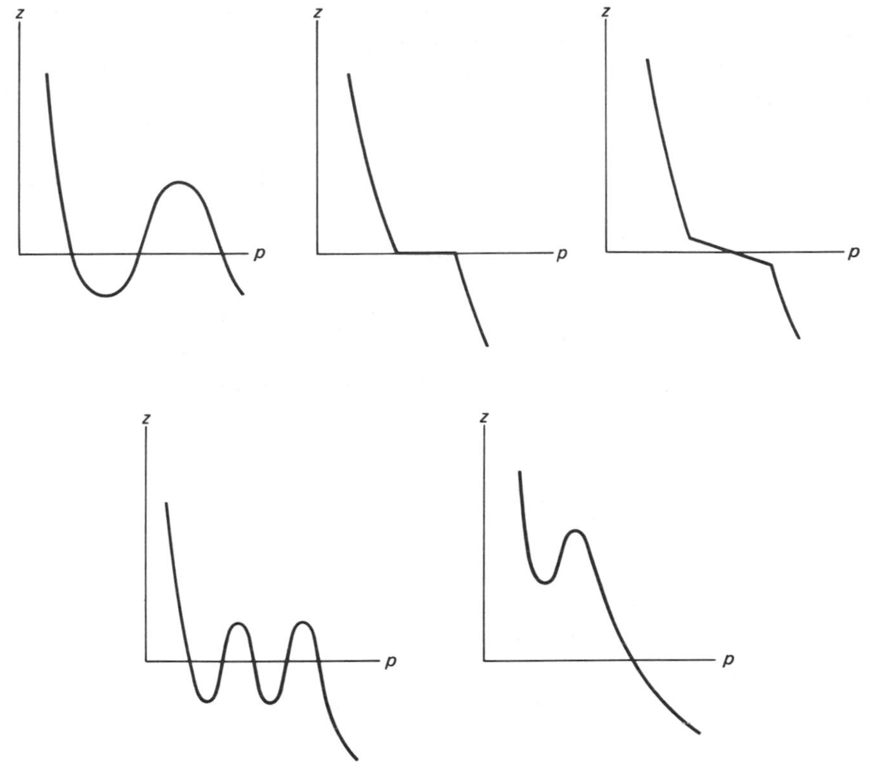

Fig. 6.8 *Uniqueness and Local Uniqueness of Equilibria*

Index analysis is a way of generalizing the above remarks to k dimensions. It gives us a simple necessary and sufficient condition for uniqueness. In the above one-dimensional case we observe that, if $p_i = 0$ implies $z_i(\mathbf{p}) > 0$ and if $\frac{\partial \mathbf{z}(\mathbf{p}^*)}{\partial p_1} < 0$ at all equilibria, then there can be only one equilibrium. The k-dimensional generalization of this goes as follows:

Given an equilibrium $\mathbf{p}^*$, define the *index* of $\mathbf{p}^*$ in the following way: write down the negative of the Jacobian matrix of $\mathbf{z}(\mathbf{p}^*)$, delete the last row and column of this matrix, and take the determinant of the resulting submatrix. If the sign of this determinant is positive, assign $\mathbf{p}^*$ index $+1$, if it is negative, assign $\mathbf{p}^*$ index -1. (Removing the last row and column is equivalent to choosing the last good to be numéraire.)

We also need a boundary condition; there are several general possibilities, but the simplest is to assume $z_i(\mathbf{p}) > 0$ when $p_i = 0$. In this case, a fundamental theorem of differential topology states that, if all equilibria have positive index, there can be only one of them. Hence we have a general uniqueness theorem:

Theorem *Suppose* $\mathbf{z}$ *is a continuously differentiable demand function on the price simplex with* $z_i(\mathbf{p}) > 0$ *when* p_i *equals zero. If the* $(k-1)$ *by* $(k-1)$ *matrix* $(-\mathbf{Dz}(\mathbf{p}^*))$ *has positive determinant at all equilibria then there is only one equilibrium.*

We now have a nice theorem, but what does it mean? We can use Slutsky's equation to get an expression for $\mathbf{Dz}(\mathbf{p}^*)$ that sheds a little light:

$$(-\mathbf{Dz}(\mathbf{p}^*)) = -\left(\sum_{i=1}^{n} \mathbf{D_p h}_i(\mathbf{p}^*, u_i)\right) + \sum_{i=1}^{n} \mathbf{D}_y\mathbf{x}_i(\mathbf{p}, y_i)\cdot[\mathbf{x}_i - \mathbf{W}_i]$$

The first term is the sum of positive definite matrices, which of course all have positive determinants. Hence if the second term—the income effect—is not large enough to "wipe out" the substitution effect, we will have a unique equilibrium.

6.8 GENERAL EQUILIBRIUM DYNAMICS

We have shown that under plausible assumptions on the behavior of economic agents there will always exist a price vector that equates demand and supply. But we have given no guarantee that the economy will actually operate at this "equilibrium" point. What forces exist that might tend to adjust prices to a market-clearing price vector? In this section we will examine some of the problems encountered in trying to model the price adjustment mechanism in a competitive economy.

The biggest problem is one that is the most fundamental, namely the paradoxical relationship between the idea of competition and price adjustment: if all economic agents take market prices as given and outside their control, how can prices move? Who is left to adjust prices?

This puzzle has led to the erection of an elaborate mythology which postulates the existence of a "Walrasian auctioneer" whose sole function is to search for the market clearing prices. According to this construction, a competitive market functions as follows:

> At time zero the Walrasian auctioneer calls out some vector of prices which includes both spot and futures prices. All agents present their demands and supplies of current and futures goods at those prices. The auctioneer examines the vector of aggregate excess demands and adjusts prices according to some rule, presumably raising the price of goods for which there is excess demand and lowering the price of goods for which there is excess supply. The process continues until an equilibrium price vector is found. At this point, all trades are made including the exchanges of contracts for future trades. The economy then proceeds through time, each agent carrying out the agreed upon contracts.

This is, of course, a very unrealistic model. However, the basic idea that prices move in the direction of excess demand seems plausible. The question arises, under what conditions will this sort of adjustment process lead one to an equilibrium?

6.9 TATONNEMENT PROCESSES

Let's consider an economy that takes place over time. Each day the market opens and people present their desired, Walrasian, demands and supplies to the market. Of course at an arbitrary price vector **p**, there will in general be excess demands and supplies in some markets. We will assume that prices adjust according to the following rule, the so-called law of supply and demand.

ADJUSTMENT RULE $\dot{p}_i = G_i(z_i(\mathbf{p}))$ for $i = 1, \cdots, k$ where G_i is some smooth sign-preserving function of excess demand.

It is convenient to make some sort of desirability assumption to rule out the possibility of equilibria at a zero price, so we will generally assume that $z_i(\mathbf{p}) > 0$ when $p_i = 0$.

It is useful to have a picture of the orbit structure of the dynamical system defined by the above system. Let's consider a special case where $G_i(z_i)$ equals the identity function for each i. Then, along with the boundary assumption, we have a system in R^k defined by:

$$\dot{\mathbf{p}} = \mathbf{z}(\mathbf{p})$$

From the usual considerations we know that this system obeys Walras' law, $\mathbf{p} \cdot \mathbf{z}(\mathbf{p}) \equiv 0$.

This system has a very convenient property. Let's look at how the norm of the price vector changes over time; i.e., let's calculate $\frac{d}{dt}\left(\sum_{i=1}^{k} p_i^2(t)\right)$.

$$\frac{d}{dt}\left(\sum_{i=1}^{k} p_i^2(t)\right) = \sum_{i=1}^{k} 2p_i(t)\dot{p}_i(t) = 2\sum_{i=1}^{k} p_i(t)z_i(p(t)) = 0$$

by Walras' law. Hence $\sum_{i=1}^{k} p_i^2(t)$ remains constant along paths of prices. This means that the paths of prices are restricted by Walras' law to lie on the surface of a k-dimensional sphere. Furthermore, since $z_i(\mathbf{p}) > 0$ where $p_i = 0$, we know that the paths of price movements always point inwards near the points where $p_i = 0$. In Figure 6.9 we have some pictures for $k = 2$ and $k = 3$.

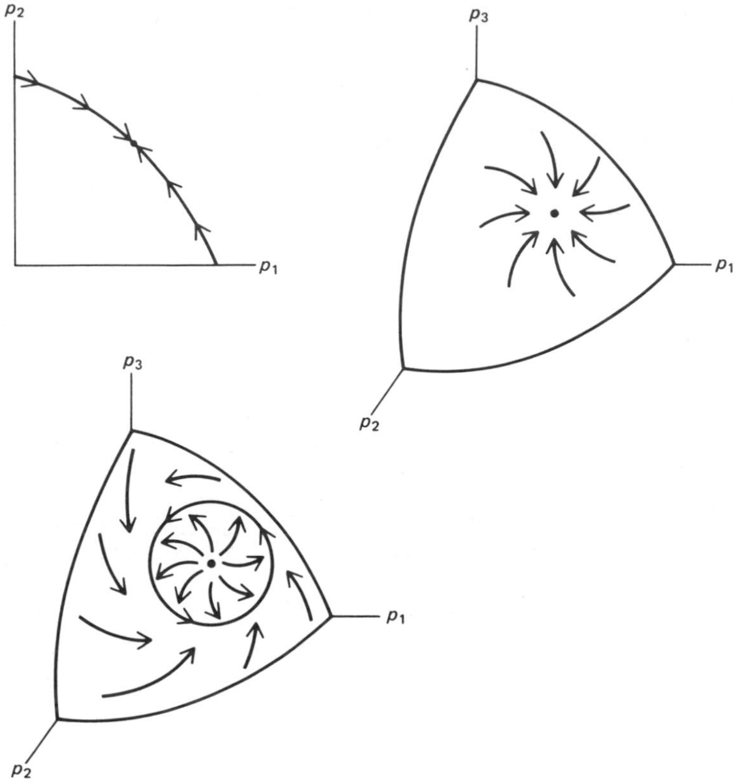

Fig. 6.9 *Example of Price Dynamics*

The third picture is especially unpleasant. It depicts a situation where we have a unique equilibrium, but it is completely unstable. The adjustment process we have described will almost never converge to an equilibrium. This seems like a perverse case, but it can easily happen.

It can be shown that *any* continuous function that satisfies Walras' law is an excess demand function for some economy; i.e., the utility maximization hypothesis places no restrictions on *aggregate* demand behavior. (See reference in Section 3.15) Thus, any dynamical system on the price sphere can arise from our model of economic behavior.

Clearly to get global stability results one has to assume special conditions on demand functions. The value of the results will then depend on the economic naturalness of the conditions assumed.

We will sketch an argument of global stability for one such special assumption under a special adjustment process, to get some idea of what is involved.

PROPOSITION *Suppose the adjustment rule is given by* $\dot{p}_i = k_i z_i(\mathbf{p})$ $i = 1, \cdots, k$ *and the excess demand function obeys the weak axiom of revealed preference; i.e., if* $\mathbf{p}^*$ *is an equilibrium of the economy, then* $\mathbf{p}^*\mathbf{z}(\mathbf{p}) > 0$ *for all* $\mathbf{p} \neq \mathbf{p}^*$. *Then all paths of prices following the above rule converge to* $\mathbf{p}^*$.

PROOF (Sketch) We will construct a Liapunov function for the economy. (See Section A.15 of the Mathematical Appendix.) Let $V(\mathbf{p}) = \sum_i [(p_i - p_i^*)^2/k_i.]$ Then

$$\frac{dV(\mathbf{p})}{dt} = \sum_i \left[\frac{2(p_i - p_i^*)\dot{p}_i(t)}{k_i}\right] = 2\sum_i \left[\frac{(p_i - p^*)k_i z_i(\mathbf{p})}{k_i}\right]$$

$$= 2\sum_i (p_i z_i(\mathbf{p}) - p_i^* z_i(\mathbf{p})) = 0 - 2\mathbf{p}^*\cdot\mathbf{z}(\mathbf{p}) < 0$$

This implies that $V(\mathbf{p})$ is monotonically declining along solution paths for $\mathbf{p} \neq \mathbf{p}^*$. We need only to show boundedness of $\mathbf{p}$ to conclude that $V(\mathbf{p})$ is a Liapunov function and that the economy is globally stable. □

The weak axiom of revealed preference essentially requires that the aggregate excess demand function behave as if it were an excess demand function for a single individual. To see this, let us recall the usual statement of the weak axiom of revealed preference from Chapter 3. "If $\mathbf{p}\cdot\mathbf{x}(\mathbf{p}) \geqq \mathbf{p}\cdot\mathbf{x}(\mathbf{p}^*)$ then $\mathbf{p}^*\cdot\mathbf{x}(\mathbf{p}) > \mathbf{p}^*\cdot\mathbf{x}(\mathbf{p}^*)$." Subtracting $\mathbf{p}\cdot\mathbf{W}$ and $\mathbf{p}^*\cdot\mathbf{W}$ from all these inequalities, we get: "If $\mathbf{p}\cdot\mathbf{z}(\mathbf{p}) \geqq \mathbf{p}\cdot\mathbf{z}(\mathbf{p}^*)$ then $\mathbf{p}^*\cdot\mathbf{z}(\mathbf{p}) > \mathbf{p}^*\cdot\mathbf{z}(\mathbf{p}^*)$." But it is always the case that $\mathbf{p}\cdot\mathbf{z}(\mathbf{p}) \geqq \mathbf{p}\cdot\mathbf{z}(\mathbf{p}^*)$ since both sides are zero, and thus we must have $\mathbf{p}^*\cdot\mathbf{z}(\mathbf{p}) > 0$ for all $\mathbf{p} \neq \mathbf{p}^*$.

6.10 NONTATONNEMENT PROCESSES

The tatonnement story makes sense in two sorts of situations, one being the situation where no trade takes place until equilibrium is reached, so that the adjustment process is really just an "auctioneer's rule." The other situation is where all goods are unstorable so that each day the market reopens with new goods and all agents start their attempts to trade all over again.

The first story makes sense if goods are stocks or flows, but the second makes sense only if the goods are flow goods. For if stock goods are available, unsold goods will accumulate and endowments will change from day to day. This change in endowments will presumably affect agents' demands and supplies.

Models that take account of such changes in endowment are known as *nontatonnement models*. In this section we will try to give the flavor of some analysis connected with the stability of such models.

Since endowments will change over time, we now characterize the *state* of the economy by the reigning price vector, $\mathbf{p}(t)$, and the current allocation of endowments, $\mathbf{W}(t)$. At any state $(\mathbf{p}, \mathbf{W})$, we assume the economy evolves according to some rules of the following sort.

$$\dot{p}_j = G_j[z_j(\mathbf{p}, \mathbf{W})] \qquad j = 1, \cdots, k$$

$$\dot{W}_i^j = H_{ij}[\mathbf{p}, \mathbf{W}] \qquad i = 1, \cdots, n \quad j = 1, \cdots, k$$

The price adjustment mechanism is assumed to have exactly the same properties as before. The H_{ij} functions are functions that express the actual trading process that occurs. At an arbitrary state $(\mathbf{p}, \mathbf{W})$, not all desired trades can be carried out. But some kind of transfer of goods presumably takes place. This transfer process is summarized by the H_{ij} functions. What properties are reasonable for such functions? What properties should the trading rules possess? We will consider two types of assumptions concerning the trading process that result in convergence to an equilibrium.

Notice that the equilibrium of a nontatonnement process may be rather different from the equilibrium of a tatonnment process, even if the initial endowments and tastes of the agents are the same. For the tatonnement equilibrium requires the value of the demanded bundle to be consistent with the *initial* endowments of the consumers while a nontatonnement equilibrium requires the demanded bundle to be consistent with the level of the *current* endowments. In fact, it is reasonably clear that any Pareto efficient allocation should be an equilibrium for nontatonnement process—for the second welfare theorem says that, if we are at a Pareto efficient allocation and prices are right, no agents will want to trade.

We return now to the discussion of the trading process. What might we require for a reasonable process?

It seems plausible that agents will engage in trades only if it increases their utility. Hence, H_{ij}, which specifies the trading rules of the agents, will be such that $\frac{d\,u_i(\mathbf{W}_i(t))}{dt} > 0$ for $i = 1, \cdots, n$. This kind of trading process, called the *Edgeworth process,* leads us very quickly to a stability theorem: for we simply define a Liapunov function by $V(\mathbf{p}, \mathbf{W}) = -\Sigma u_i(\mathbf{W}_i(t))$. By the above assumption V is continually declining and a simple boundedness argument will give us the required convergence proof.

An alternative process, the Hahn process, is described by different assumptions concerning the trading process. We will assume that the trading process defined by the H functions is of sufficient flexibility to ensure that no good is in excess demand by some agents at the same time it is in excess supply by other agents. Hence, at any point in time, if some agent has excess demand for some good, then the *aggregate* excess demand for that good is positive. But the price adjustment rule will raise the price of goods in excess demand. This will tend to lower the *indirect* utility of the agents who desire that good. The agents who have committed themselves to supply that good at current prices do not find their utility affected; hence, aggregate indirect utility declines along the adjustment paths of the economy.

We can make this argument rigorous after clarifying one further point concerning the endowment adjustment process.

We are assuming that at each point in time all agents know the value of all goods. Thus the change in the value of endowments due to trade, $\mathbf{p} \cdot \dot{\mathbf{W}}_j$, should presumably be zero for all agents. This is just saying that agents trade a dollar's worth of goods for a dollar's worth of goods at each instant. The value of the consumers endowments may change over time, but that is because the prices change, not because agents manage to make advantageous trades at constant prices.

Now it is quite simple to show that the sum of the indirect utility function decreases along trajectories of the system. The time derivative of v_i is:

$$\frac{dv_i(\mathbf{p}, \mathbf{p} \cdot \mathbf{W}_i)}{dt} = \mathbf{D}_p v_i(\mathbf{p}, \mathbf{p} \cdot \mathbf{W}_i) \cdot \dot{\mathbf{p}} + \frac{\partial v_i(\mathbf{p}, \mathbf{p} \cdot \mathbf{W}_i)}{\partial y}(\mathbf{p} \cdot \dot{\mathbf{W}}_i + \dot{\mathbf{p}} \cdot \mathbf{W}_i)$$

Substitute $\mathbf{x}_i = -\mathbf{D}_p v_i \Big/ \frac{\partial v}{\partial y}$ and use the fact that $\mathbf{p} \cdot \dot{\mathbf{W}}_i = 0$ to get

$$\frac{dv_i(\mathbf{p}, \mathbf{p} \cdot \mathbf{W}_i)}{dt} = \frac{-\partial v(\mathbf{p}, \mathbf{p} \cdot \mathbf{W}_i)}{\partial y}(\mathbf{x}_i(\mathbf{p}, \mathbf{p} \cdot \mathbf{W}_i) - \mathbf{W}_i) \cdot \dot{\mathbf{p}}$$

By assumption, when $(\mathbf{x}_i - \mathbf{W}_i)$ has a positive component so does $\dot{\mathbf{p}}$ and when $(\mathbf{x}_i - \mathbf{W}_i)$ has a negative component so does $\dot{\mathbf{p}}$. Since the marginal utility of income, $\frac{\partial v_i(\mathbf{p}, \mathbf{p} \cdot \mathbf{W}_i)}{\partial y}$ is positive, the whole expression will be negative as long as $\mathbf{x}_i(\mathbf{p}, \mathbf{p} \cdot \mathbf{W}_i)$ is not equal to $\mathbf{W}_i$. Thus the sum of the indirect utilities will always decrease as long as the economy is out of equilibrium: we have a Liapunov function.

Exercises

6.1 (10) Suppose we have a price adjustment mechanism defined by $\dot{p}_i = G_i(z_i(\mathbf{p}))$ and $\frac{\partial G_i(z_i)}{\partial z_i} > 0$ for $i = 1, \cdots, k$. Show that it is possible to choose units of measurement for the goods such that $\dot{p}_i = z_i(\mathbf{p})\ i = 1, \cdots, k$ when z_i is measured in those units.

6.2 (10) Draw a picture of the orbit structure of a three-good tatonnement economy that has three equilibria.

6.3 (20) Let $\mathbf{y}(\mathbf{p})$ be the profit-maximizing netput vector of a competitive firm. Suppose the firm faces a constant demand for its outputs and a constant supply of its inputs. Let $\mathbf{k}$ be this vector of constants, appropriately signed. Suppose prices adjust according to the rule $p_i = k_i - x_i(\mathbf{p})\ i = 1, \cdots, n$. Find a Liapunov function for this process.

6.4 (20) (Arrow and Hahn) Suppose that the Walrasian actioneer follows the price adjustment rule $\dot{\mathbf{p}} = [\mathbf{Dz}(\mathbf{p})]^{-1}\ \mathbf{z}(\mathbf{p})$ where we suppose that $\mathbf{Dz}(\mathbf{p})$ is always nonsingular. Show that $V(\mathbf{p}) = -\mathbf{z}(\mathbf{p})\cdot\mathbf{z}(\mathbf{p})$ is a Liapunov function for this process.

6.5 (20) Let $\mathbf{z}(\mathbf{p}, \mathbf{W})$ be a differentiable excess demand function containing as arguments the k prices and n endowments. The prices are normalized by $\Sigma\ p_i = 1$ and the endowments are normalized by $\Sigma\ \mathbf{W}_i = \overline{\mathbf{W}}$, with $\overline{\mathbf{W}}$ some fixed bundle of goods. Show that there always exists *some* distribution of initial endowments $\mathbf{W}^*$ such that there is a *unique* equilibrium price vector $\mathbf{p}^*$ associate with $\mathbf{W}^*$.

6.6 (20) Suppose we have a pure exchange economy where all consumers have nice utility functions linear in good 1, so that $u_i(\mathbf{x}) = x^1 + \phi_i(x^2, \cdots, x^k)$. Show that the equilibrium must necessarily be unique. (Assume the standard boundary conditions and differentiability conditions; use Exercise 3.27.)

6.7 (20) Consider an economy with two firms and two consumers. Firm 1 is owned by consumer 1; it produces guns from oil via a production function

$$g = 2x$$

Firm 2 is owned by consumer 2. It produces butter from oil via a production function:

$$b = 3x$$

Each consumer initially owns 10 units of oil. Consumer 1's preferences are given by:

$$u_1(g, b) = g^{.4}b^{.6}$$

Consumer 2's preferences are given by:

$$u_2(g, b) = 10 + .5\ ln\ g + .5\ ln\ b$$

(a) Find the market clearing prices for oil, guns, and butter.
(b) How many guns and how much butter does each consumer consume?
(c) How much oil does each firm use?

6.8 (20) Consider the two assumptions below:
(i) There is a *unique* cost-minimizing bundle at each set of factor prices;
(ii) The firm always uses some of every input.
Show that either of these assumptions implies that $c(\mathbf{w}, y)$ is strictly increasing in $\mathbf{w}$ in the sense that $\mathbf{w}' \geqq \mathbf{w}$ and $\mathbf{w}' \neq \mathbf{w}$ implies $c(\mathbf{w}', y) > c(\mathbf{w}, y)$.

6.9 (20) We have two agents with identical strictly convex preferences and equal endowments. Describe the core of this market and illustrate in an Edgeworth box.

Notes

The existence theorem for a productive economy stated here is due to Debreu (1959). The nonsubstitution theorem is due to Samuelson (1951). The approach here follows von Weizsäcker (1971). The concept of temporary equilibrium is due to Hicks (1939); a survey of existence of temporary equilibrium is described in Grandmont (1975). The contingency contracts approach to uncertainty is due to Arrow (1970).

The dynamic tatonnement approach was first formulated by Samuelson (1947). Global stability analysis was first studied by Arrow and Hurwicz (1958). The nontatonnement model was first studied by Negishi (1961). The two adjustment processes are due to Uzawa (1962) and Hahn and Negishi (1962). The treatment here follows Arrow and Hahn (1971), which includes much more discussion and historical references. Fisher (1975) has provided a very readable survey.

The concept of the core is due to Edgeworth (1954). The uniqueness question was first posed by Wald (1951). The index approach to uniqueness is due to Dierker (1972). The approach here follows that of Varian (1975).

References

ARROW, K. 1970. *Essays in the Theory of Risk Bearing*. Chicago: Markham.

———, and HAHN, F. 1971. *General Competitive Analysis*. San Francisco: Holden-Day.

———, and HURWICZ, L. 1958. "On the Stability of the Competitive Equilibrium, I." *Econometrica* 26:522–552.

DEBREU, G. 1959. *Theory of Value*. New York: Wiley.

DIERKER, E. 1972. "Two Remarks on the Number of Equilibria of an Economy." *Econometrica* 40:951–953.

EDGEWORTH, F. 1954. *Mathematical Psychics*. New York: Kelley and Milman.

FISHER, F. "The Stability of General Equilibrium: Results and Problems." MIT Working Paper no. 153.

GRANDMONT, J. M. 1975. "Temporary General Equilibrium Theory." *Econometrica* 45:535–572.

HAHN, F., and NEGISHI, T. 1962. "A Theorem on Nontatonnement Stability." *Econometrica* 30:463–469.

HICKS, J. 1946. *Value and Capital*. 2d ed. Oxford, Eng.: Clarendon Press.

NEGISHI, T. 1961. "On the Formation of Prices." *International Economic Review* 2:122–126.

SAMUELSON, P. 1947. *Foundations of Economic Analysis*. Cambridge, Mass.: Harvard University Press.

———. 1951. "Abstract of a Theorem Concerning Substitutability in an Open Leontief Model." In *Collected Scientific Papers of Paul A. Samuelson*, vol. 1, ed. J. Stiglitz. Cambridge, Mass.: MIT Press, 1966.

UZAWA, H. 1962. "On the Stability of Edgeworth's Barter Process." *International Economic Review* 3:218–232.

VARIAN, H. 1975. "A Third Remark on the Number of Equilibria of an Economy." *Econometrica* 43:985–986.

WALD, A. 1951. "On Some Systems of Equations in Mathematical Economics." *Econometrica* 19:368–403.

WEIZSÄCKER, C. VON. 1971. *Steady State Capital Theory*. New York: Springer-Verlag.

Chapter 7

Topics in Welfare Economics

In the last two chapters we have examined some of the welfare properties of a competitive equilibrium. The fundamental welfare theorems show that in this special case of competitive market structure things work out quite nicely as far as efficiency is concerned.

But economics is a policy science, and as such its primary focus is—or should be—on those cases where things don't work out nicely. What happens when we don't meet the assumptions of the basic welfare theorems? If inefficiencies result, how can they be rectified? We will analyze some of these problems in this chapter.

7.1 PUBLIC GOODS

Up until now our discussion of resource allocation has been concerned solely with private goods, that is, goods consumed exclusively by individual economic agents. Consider, for example, bread. You and I can consume different amounts of bread, and, if I consume a particular loaf of bread, you are excluded from consuming the same loaf of bread.

Certain goods do not have these properties. A nice example is street lights. The amount of street lights in a given area is fixed—you and I both have the same potential consumption. Furthermore my consumption of street lights does not preclude your consumption. Goods of this type are called *public goods;* other examples are police and fire protection, highways, national defense, lighthouses, clean air, and so on.

Public goods are goods with a specific kind of externality. If I am to consume x units of defense, then you also must "consume" x units of defense, like it or not. As might be expected, such external effects are not handled by the theory we have developed in the previous chapters.

In this section we will examine the problem of efficient allocation of public goods. Purely for notational simplicity we will restrict our analysis to a two-person, two-good economy. The amount of the public good will be denoted by x, and the amounts of the private good will be denoted by y_1 and y_2. The technological possibilities of the economy will be described by a transformation function $T(x, y_1 + y_2)$.

The welfare maximization problem can be written as:

$$\begin{aligned} \max \quad & W(u_1(x, y_1), u_2(x, y_2)) \\ \text{s.t.} \quad & T(x, y_1 + y_2) = 0 \end{aligned}$$

Notice that the level of consumption of the public good must be the same for each consumer, while the levels of the private good will in general differ.

The first-order conditions for the solution of this problem are:

$$a \frac{\partial u_1(x^*, y_1^*)}{\partial x} + b \frac{\partial u_2(x^*, y_2^*)}{\partial x} - t \frac{\partial T(x^*, y^*)}{\partial x} = 0$$

$$a \frac{\partial u_1(x^*, y_1^*)}{\partial y_1} - t \frac{\partial T(x^*, y^*)}{\partial y} = 0$$

$$b \frac{\partial u_2(x^*, y_2^*)}{\partial y_2} - t \frac{\partial T(x^*, y^*)}{\partial y} = 0$$

where $a = \dfrac{\partial W(\mathbf{u}^*)}{\partial u_1}$, $b = \dfrac{\partial W(\mathbf{u}^*)}{\partial u_2}$, and $y^* = y_1^* + y_2^*$.

Eliminating the Lagrange multiplier gives us:

$$\frac{a\, \partial u_1(x^*, y_1^*)/\partial x + b\, \partial u_2(x^*, y_2^*)/\partial x}{\partial T(x^*, y^*)/\partial x} = \frac{a\, \partial u_1(x^*, y_1^*)/\partial y_1}{\partial T(x^*, y^*)/\partial y} = \frac{b\, \partial u_2(x^*, y_2^*)/\partial y_2}{\partial T(x^*, y^*)/\partial y}$$

The last equality establishes that $a\, \partial u_1(x^*, y_1^*)/\partial y_1 = b\, \partial u_2(x^*, y_2^*)/\partial y_2$.

Cross multiplying the first equality and using this fact gives us:

$$\frac{\partial u_1(x^*, y_1^*)/\partial x}{\partial u_1(x^*, y_1^*)/\partial y_1} + \frac{\partial u_2(x^*, y_2^*)/\partial x}{\partial u_2(x^*, y_2^*)/\partial y_2} = \frac{\partial T(x^*, y^*)/\partial x}{\partial T(x^*, y^*)/\partial y}$$

In terms of marginal rates of substitution and marginal rates of transformation between the public and private good, we have

$$\text{MRS}_1 + \text{MRS}_2 = \text{MRT}$$

Note that the conditions for optimality differ from the conditions characterizing a competitive market solution. Instead of MRS = MRT for each consumer, we instead require $\sum_i \text{MRS}_i = \text{MRT}$. The MRS_i can be interpreted as individualized prices—how much consumer i is willing to sacrifice of the private good to pay for one more unit of the public good. This can be thought of as how much consumer i "should" be taxed. Under this interpretation we see the basic "duality" between public and private goods: in the private-goods case we all consume different amounts of the good but pay the same price; in the public-goods case, we all consume the same amount of good but have different prices.

The determination of the optimal allocation of a public and a private good is illustrated geometrically in Figures 7.1 and 7.2. In Figure 7.1 we

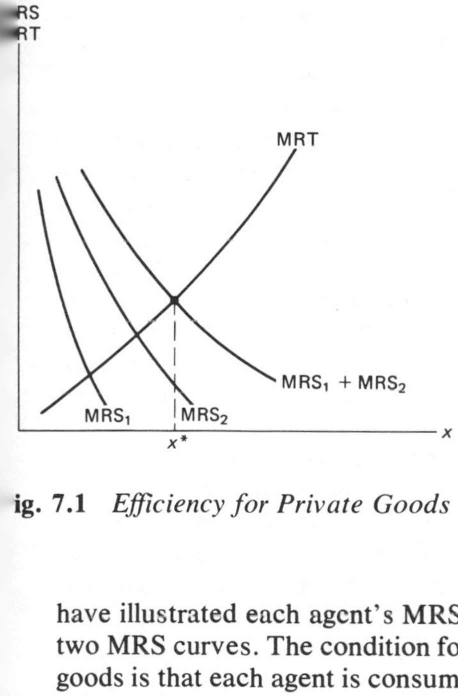

ig. 7.1 *Efficiency for Private Goods*

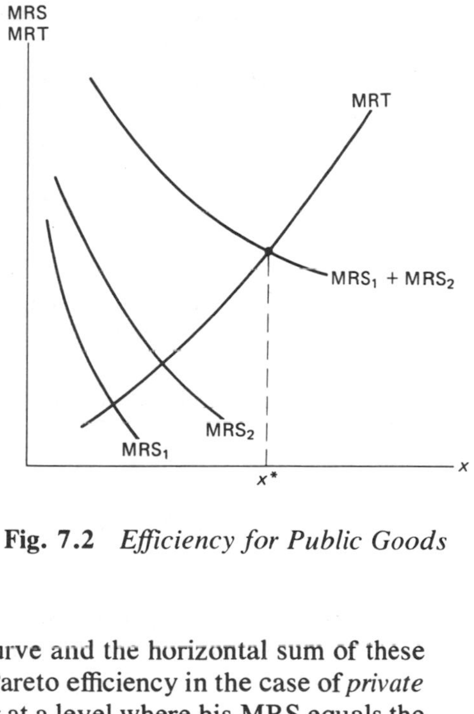

Fig. 7.2 *Efficiency for Public Goods*

have illustrated each agent's MRS curve and the horizontal sum of these two MRS curves. The condition for Pareto efficiency in the case of *private* goods is that each agent is consuming at a level where his MRS equals the price ratio, which in turn is equal to the MRT. To find these levels of consumption we find where the horizontal sum of the MRS curves intersects the MRT curve in order to determine the price, then look at the individual MRS curves to determine the levels of consumption of each agent.

The *public* goods case is illustrated in Figure 7.2. The condition for Pareto efficiency in this case is that the level of consumption of the public good is where the *sum* of the MRSs equals the MRT, i.e., the total willingness to pay equals the social cost. To find this point, we add the MRS curves *vertically* and look for the intersection of this total MRS curve with the MRT curve. The point of intersection gives us the level of output of the public good. We can find each agent's willingness to pay at that level of output by inspecting the individual MRS curves. If we want, we could use this information to tax the individual consumers in order to pay for the public good. Then each agent would be paying exactly his or her true valuation of the public good. This type of taxation scheme—called a Lindahl equilibrium—seems to be an especially "fair" way of paying for the public good. However, notice that it is not the only way of achieving Pareto efficiency—other sorts of taxation schemes may be perfectly compatible with the ΣMRS = MRT condition.

The conditions for efficient allocation of public goods are simple to state, but they may be rather difficult to implement.

To determine the optimal level of a public good we need to know *each* agent's marginal rate of substitution between the public and private goods. For private goods, marginal rates of substitution are revealed in the market: each agent adjusts his consumption bundle so that his marginal rate of substitution between each pair of goods is equal to the price ratio between that pair of goods. But the essence of a public good is that an individual cannot adjust his level of consumption unilaterally, and this inflexibility effectively destroys the possibility of a market for a public good.

How can one elicit the individual agent's marginal rates of substitution between a public and some private good? The simplest solution is just to ask each consumer his willingness to pay for the public good in terms of the private good. (The usual private good used is money, so that one asks, for example, how many dollars you are willing to give up to have an extra streetlight.) Unfortunately, it is not at all clear that people have the correct incentives to reveal their true willingness to pay. If for example you believe that you may be taxed on the basis of your willingness to pay, you have a clear-cut incentive to understate your true value of the public good. If you believe your own taxes will be unaffected by your response, then there is a clear incentive to overstate your willingness to pay—you would thereby increase the level of provision of the public good, which presumably makes you better off, without affecting your own costs at all. This problem of eliciting the true willingness to pay for public goods is known as the *free rider problem*.

7.2 *TRUTHFUL REVELATION OF PREFERENCE*

We have seen in the last section that the presence of public goods leads to definite problems for a decentralized resource allocation mechanism. A necessary condition for Pareto efficiency is that the sum of the marginal rates of substitution between the public and private good must equal the marginal rate of transformation between these two goods. It is difficult to see how such a condition could be satisfied without having some centralized authority which could collect the necessary information, do the necessary computation, and report the results.

But such a centralized agency may have trouble in effectively carrying out such activities if it does not have the cooperation of the individual economic agents. And under many organizational structures, it is hard to see how such cooperation can be elicited.

Let us consider a simple example. Ten people who live in a neighborhood are contemplating erecting a streetlight that will cost \$100. It has been determined that each agent will be taxed \$10 to pay for this public good. Each person can attach some "true value" to the public good—how much (in dollars) he or she is willing to pay for the streetlight. By the "net willingness to pay of agent i" we mean the difference between the true value of the light to agent i and the cost of light to agent i. We denote this net willingness to pay by v_i. Clearly the streetlight is worth building only if $\Sigma v_i \geqq 0$.

Now suppose that the citizen's group appoints an economic consultant to survey the populace in order to determine if the total willingness to pay, Σv_i, is nonnegative. The simplest procedure to follow is simply to ask each agent to report his or her net willingness to pay and to build the streetlight if the sum of these reported values is nonnegative.

The trouble with such a scheme is that it does not provide good incentives for the individual agents to reveal their true willingness to pay. For example, suppose your true net value was \$.10—that is, you would be willing to pay \$10.10 for the services offered by the streetlight. When asked by the survey team for your net value, it would be in your interest to exaggerate this reported value in order to ensure that the light would be built. You might as well report that your net value is \$1,000,000! Similarly, if your net value were −\$.10, you might as well report −\$2,000,000. The naive scheme proposed above does not provide proper incentives for true revelation of preferences and thus may not encourage the correct provision of the public good. Problems of this sort were referred to in the last section as free rider problems.

Are there schemes for eliciting preferences that will result in correct revelation? It turns out that there are. As an example let us consider the following scheme. We denote individual i's reported value by w_i and his true value by v_i. As before, the streetlight (or other public good) will be constructed if $\Sigma w_i \geqq 0$. Now however, we will add some side payments to the structure of the bidding process. If the streetlight is built—i.e., if $\sum_i w_i \geqq 0$—then each agent i will get a side payment in the amount $\sum_{j \neq i} w_j$; that is, each agent will get the sum of what everyone else bid. If the streetlight is not built, the side payment will be zero.

To see that such a system does elicit true revelation of preferences, consider Table 7.1:

Table 7.1

	built	not built
reported values	$w_i + \sum_{j \neq i} w_j \geqq 0$	$w_i + \sum_{j \neq i} w_j < 0$
agent i's payoff	$v_i + \sum_{j \neq i} w_j$	0

Now suppose agent i's payoff if the project is built is nonnegative. Then he or she can ensure that it gets built by reporting his or her true value; that is, if $v_i + \sum_{j \neq i} w_j \geqq 0$, the agent i can ensure that $w_i + \sum_{j \neq i} w_j \geqq 0$ by reporting $w_i = v_i$. Similarly, if $v_i + \sum_{j \neq i} w_j < 0$, agent i can ensure the project is not built by reporting $w_i = v_i$. In each case, reporting the truth is a "dominant" strategy since there is never an incentive to misrepresent preferences, regardless of what the other agents do. In effect, the information-gathering mechanism has been modified so that each agent faces the social decision problem rather than the individual decision problem, and thus each agent has an incentive to reveal his own preferences correctly.

Unfortunately, the preference revelation scheme presented here has a major fault. The total side payments may potentially be very large. Someone presumably must make these side payments, and that cost may be prohibitive: it may be quite expensive to induce people to tell the truth!

Although this problem that the side payments do not sum to zero can not be entirely eliminated, mechanisms do exist that will reduce the amount of the side payments. The basic observation is the following: notice that we can add an extra payment to agent i's side payment that depends only on what the other agents do. Since this payment does not depend on what i does, it cannot affect his or her actions. When such side payments are present, the payoff of agent i takes the form:

$$v_i + \sum_{j \neq i} w_j + h_i(w_{-i}) \qquad \text{if } \Sigma w_i \geqq 0$$

$$h_i(w_{-i}) \qquad \text{if } \Sigma w_i < 0$$

where w_{-i} is notation for the vector of bids, omitting agent i's bid, and $h_i(\ )$ is the side payment mentioned above.

It is clear that such mechanisms give truthful revelation for exactly the reasons mentioned above. If the $h_i(\ )$ functions are cleverly chosen, the size of the side payments can be reduced. One nice choice for the $h_i(\ )$ function is as follows:

$$h_i(w_{-i}) = -\sum_{j \neq i} w_j \quad \text{if } \sum_{j \neq i} w_j \geqq 0$$
$$= 0 \quad \text{if } \sum_{j \neq i} w_j < 0$$

Such a choice gives rise to the *pivotal mechanism*. The payoff to agent i is of the form:

$$\begin{array}{lll} v_i & \text{if } \sum_i w_i \geqq 0 & \text{and } \sum_{j \neq i} w_j \geqq 0 \\ v_i + \sum_{j \neq i} w_j & \text{if } \sum_i w_i \geqq 0 & \text{and } \sum_{j \neq i} w_j < 0 \\ -\sum_{j \neq i} w_j & \text{if } \sum_i w_i < 0 & \text{and } \sum_{j \neq i} w_j \geqq 0 \\ 0 & \text{if } \sum_i w_i < 0 & \text{and } \sum_{j \neq i} w_j < 0 \end{array}$$

Notice several features about this mechanism. First, it only taxes agents and never subsidizes them. Second, it only taxes an agent if his bid would change the social decision. The amount of the tax is precisely the amount by which agent i's bid damages the other agents. Third, every agent finds it advantageous to use this decision process since he is never taxed by more than the decision is worth to him. Finally, it can be shown that, in a certain sense, the average total payments are much less than under the previous mechanism. For details, see the references cited at the end of this chapter.

7.3 EXTERNALITIES

In the basic general equilibrium model economic agents interact only through their effect on prices. When the actions of one agent affect the environment of another agent other than by affecting prices, we will say that there is an *externality*.

An example of a *consumption externality* would be a situation where the utility of one agent is affected directly by the actions of another agent. For example, some consumers may be affected by other agents' consumption of tobacco, alcohol, loud music, and so on. Consumers might also be adversely affected by firms who produce pollution or noise.

A *production externality* is a situation where the production function of a firm is affected directly by the actions of another agent. For example, the production of smoke by a steel mill may directly affect the production of clean clothes by a laundry, or the production of honey by a beekeeper might directly affect the level of output of an apple orchard next door.

Let's try to model such interactions in a simple way. Suppose we have a steel firm producing upstream from a fishery. The steel firm produces steel from labor according to a production function

$$s = f(l_s)$$

If s units of steel are produced, the firm unavoidably produces $h(s)$ units of waste, which is expelled into the river. The fishery produces c units of fish according to the amount of labor it employs and the amount of pollution in the water:

$$c = g(l_c, h)$$

Let the prices of steel, fish, and labor be given by p, q, and w. Then the steel mill will employ labor until:

$$p \frac{df(l_s)}{dl_s} = w$$

The fishery will employ labor until:

$$q \frac{\partial g(l_c, h(s^*))}{\partial l_c} = w$$

It is fairly clear that this situation is not socially efficient. The output of the steel mill adversely affects the output of fish, but this effect is being ignored by the steel producers. As a result they are producing "too much" steel. What would a socially efficient production plan look like?

We know that price-taking profit maximization is efficient in the *absence* of externalities; let us therefore consider what would happen if *one* firm owned both the steel mill and the fishery. It would attempt to maximize aggregate profits:

$$\max \quad pf(l_s) + qg(l_c, h(f(l_s))) - wl_s - wl_c$$

The first-order conditions for this problem are:

$$p \frac{df(l_s^*)}{dl_s} + q \frac{\partial g(l_c^*, h^*)}{\partial h} \frac{\partial h(s^*)}{\partial s} \frac{\partial f(l_s^*)}{\partial l_s} - w = 0$$

and
$$q \frac{\partial g(l_c^*, h^*)}{\partial l_c} - w = 0$$

The first-order conditions are certainly different. Rewriting the first condition, we find:

$$\left[p + q \frac{\partial g(l_c^*, h^*)}{\partial h} \frac{\partial h(s^*)}{\partial s} \right] f'(l_s^*) = w$$

Since the production of steel adversely affects the production of fish, the second term in the bracketed expression above will be negative. Since $f''(l_s)$ is generally negative because of diminishing marginal returns to labor, the optimal choice of labor in steel production will be less when the externality is taken into account than when the two firms operate independently.

If externalities are present, price-taking profit-maximizing behavior will not necessarily lead to an efficient allocation of resources. How can we correct for this deficiency of the market mechanism? There are several ways of viewing externalities, each of which offers a solution to this problem.

(1) Taxes and subsidies. Thc idea here is that the steel mill faces the wrong price. When the steel mill determines the optimal output of steel it just considers the private price of steel. But in our simple model, the production of steel unavoidably affects the production of fish. The *social* price of steel is thus $p + q \frac{\partial g(l_c^*, h(s^*))}{\partial s}$; that is, the social price of steel includes the adverse affect on the value of fish production.

In order to ensure proper resource allocation we only need to ensure that the steel producer faces the social price of steel rather than the private price. In practice this could be done by taxing steel by an amount $q \frac{\partial g(l_c^*, h(s^*))}{\partial s}$.

A dcfinite problem with this proposal is that it may be difficult to determine exactly what the tax should be. In order to compute the optimal tax one needs to know the marginal effect of steel production on fish production at the optimal level of output. Thus one needs to have a pretty good idea of the technological interactions between the two firms.

(2) Missing markets. According to this view the basic problem is that there is no market for pollution. The steel firm produces two outputs, steel and pollution. If there were a price for pollution, the mill would automatically produce the right mix of its two outputs.

What would the equilibrium price of pollution be? Clearly the most that the fishery would be willing to pay for a slight decrease in pollution would be the marginal increase in its profits that such a decrease would bring. From the viewpoint of the fishery, the level of pollution is exogenous. The fishery's demand function for labor will therefore depend on h. Hence, we can write the profits of the fishery as: $\pi(l_c(h), h)$. (Here we have omitted the dependence on w and p for simplicity.) The change in profits resulting from a change in h is:

$$\frac{\partial \pi(l_c, h)}{\partial l_c} \frac{dl_c(h)}{dh} + \frac{\partial \pi(l_c, h)}{\partial h}$$

In this expression, $\frac{\partial \pi(l_c, h)}{\partial l_c} = 0$ by the envelope theorem since l_c is already adjusted to be at a profit-maximizing level. Hence, we only need to evaluate $\partial \pi(l_c, h)/\partial h$. This is clearly given by:

$$r = q \frac{\partial g(l_c, h)}{\partial h}$$

So r is the price of pollution. Then the steel mill's profit maximization problem is:

$$\max \quad pf(l_s) + rh(f(l_s)) - wl_s$$

The first-order conditions for this problem are:

$$p \frac{df(l_s^*)}{dl_s} + r \frac{dh(s^*)}{ds} \frac{df(l_s^*)}{dl_s} - w = 0$$

If we make the substitution for r we see that this is identical to the first-order condition for social efficiency.

Actually, one can see from more general considerations that a market for pollution will produce a Pareto efficient allocation; this follows directly from the basic welfare theorem, once one identifies pollution as just another output of production.

The primary problem with this solution is that setting up markets for pollution may be very costly. Of course, one firm may just *bribe* the other firm to produce the right amount of the externality. If the externality affects only one other firm, such transfer payments may work. On the other hand, if the externality is a *public good*—in the sense described in the last section—a market for the externality will not be effective anyway.

Consider, for example, the apple orchard and the beekeeper mentioned previously. If there is only one beekeeper and one apple orchard, the beekeeper and the orchard owner may be able to arrange for optimal side payments—either through a market or through more informal means. If there are several apple orchards, the bees become a public good, and all the problems about providing the public good at the optimal level will arise.

(3) Property rights. According to the third view, the basic problem is that property rights are not conducive to full efficiency. If one firm owned both the steel mill and the fishery, we have seen that there is no problem. Of course, there is an incentive for property rights to actually sort themselves out in the desired manner.

If the externality of one firm adversely affects the operation of another, it always will pay one firm to buy out the other. It is clear that by coordinating the actions of both firms one can always produce more profits than by acting separately. Therefore, one firm could afford to pay the other firm its current value (in the presence of the externality) since its value when the externality is optimally adjusted would exceed this current value. Hence, the market mechanism itself provides a way to adjust property rights to avoid externalities.

Again, this solution will work well for a private externality, but all the problems mentioned in the last section arise when the externality is public.

For example, suppose we have a simple economy with two consumers and two goods, energy (e) and pollution (b). Energy is a private good while pollution is a public "bad." The welfare maximization problem is:

$$\begin{aligned} \max \quad & W(u_1(e_1, b), u_2(e_2, b)) \\ \text{s.t.} \quad & F(b, e_1 + e_2) = 0 \end{aligned}$$

From the section on public goods, we know that the first-order conditions for efficient allocation are $\text{MRS}_1 + \text{MRS}_2 = \text{MRT}$. But how are we to determine the actual marginal rates of substitution between energy and pollution? How much are people willing to pay to get clean air? The only way to find out is to ask them. However, the accuracy of the responses may depend on how consumers think the clean air will be financed. The free rider problem may well pose a problem for getting true revelation of preferences.

7.4 CONSUMER'S SURPLUS

When prices change, a consumer's welfare changes. When evaluating the impact of various sorts of public policies, such changes in welfare should be taken into account. Consumer's surplus is a way of measuring such welfare changes. In this section we shall investigate measurement of welfare changes for a single consumer and investigate several consumers in the following section.

Let us first consider what an "ideal" measure of welfare change may be. The obvious answer is that we would like to have a measure of the change in utility resulting from some policy. Suppose that we have two budgets $(\mathbf{p}^0, y^0)$ and $(\mathbf{p}', y')$ that measure the prices and incomes that a given consumer would face under two different policy regimes. It is convenient to think of $(\mathbf{p}^0, y^0)$ as being the status quo and $(\mathbf{p}', y')$ as being a proposed change, although this is not the only interpretation.

Then the obvious measure of the welfare change involved in moving from $(\mathbf{p}^0, y^0)$ to $(\mathbf{p}', y')$ is just the difference in indirect utility:

$$v(\mathbf{p}', y') - v(\mathbf{p}^0, y^0)$$

If this utility difference is positive, then the policy change is worth doing, at least as far as this consumer is concerned; and if it is negative, the project is not worth doing.

For the purely ordinal comparison of whether or not a project is preferred by a given consumer, this is about the best that we can do. However, when we want to compare different consumer's welfare, it is convenient to choose a "standard" measure of utility differences. A reasonable measure to adopt is the money metric utility function (i.e., the compensation function) described in Section 3.5.

Recall that $\mu(\mathbf{q}; \mathbf{p}, y)$ measures how much income the consumer would need at prices $\mathbf{q}$ to be as well off as he or she would be facing prices $\mathbf{p}$ and having income y. That is, $\mu(\mathbf{q}; \mathbf{p}, y)$ is defined to be $e(\mathbf{q}, v(\mathbf{p}, y))$. If we adopt this measure of utility, we find that the above utility difference becomes:

$$\mu(\mathbf{q}; \mathbf{p}', y') - \mu(\mathbf{q}; \mathbf{p}^0, y^0)$$

It remains to choose the base prices $\mathbf{q}$. There are two obvious choices: we may set $\mathbf{q}$ equal to $\mathbf{p}^0$ or to $\mathbf{p}'$. This leads to the following two measures for the utility difference:

$$EV = \mu(\mathbf{p}^0; \mathbf{p}', y') - \mu(\mathbf{p}^0; \mathbf{p}^0, y^0) = \mu(\mathbf{p}^0; \mathbf{p}', y') - y^0$$
$$CV = \mu(\mathbf{p}'; \mathbf{p}', y') - \mu(\mathbf{p}'; \mathbf{p}^0, y^0) = y' - \mu(\mathbf{p}'; \mathbf{p}^0, y^0)$$

The first measure is known as the *equivalent variation*. It uses the status-quo prices as the base and asks what income change at the current prices would be *equivalent* to the proposed change. The second measure is known as the *compensating variation*. It uses the new prices as the base and asks what income change would be necessary to *compensate* the consumer for the price change. (Compensation takes place *after* some change, so the compensating variation uses the after-change prices.)

Both of these numbers are reasonable measures of the welfare effect of a price change. Their magnitudes will generally differ because the value of a dollar will depend on what the reigning prices are. However, their *sign* will always be the same since they both measure utility differences. Figure 7.3 depicts an example of the equivalent and compensating variations in a simple two-good case.

Which measure is the most appropriate depends on the circumstances involved and what question you are trying to answer. If you are considering trying to arrange for some compensation scheme at the new prices, then the compensating variation seems reasonable. However, if you are simply trying to get a reasonable measure of "willingness to pay," the equivalent variation is probably better. This is so for two reasons. First, the equivalent variation measures the income change at *current* prices, and it is much easier for decision makers to judge the value of a dollar at current prices than at some hypothetical prices. Second, if we are comparing more than one proposed policy change, the compensating variation keeps changing the base prices while the equivalent variation keeps the base prices fixed at the status quo. Thus, the equivalent variation is more suitable for comparisons among a variety of projects.

Given, then, that we accept the compensating and equivalent variations as reasonable indicators of utility change, how can we measure them in practice? This is equivalent to the question: How we can measure $\mu(\mathbf{q}; \mathbf{p}, y)$ in practice?

We have already answered this question in Sections 3.10 and 4.7. There we investigated how to recover the preferences represented by $\mu(\mathbf{q}; \mathbf{p}, y)$ by observing the demand behavior $x(\mathbf{p}, y)$. Given any observed demand behavior, one could solve the integrability equations, at least in principle, and derive the associated compensation function. In Section

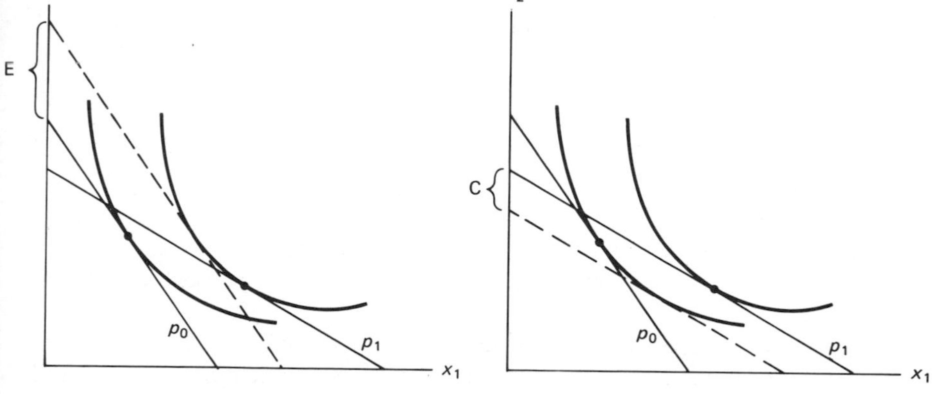

Fig. 7.3 *Equivalent Variation and Compensating Variation*

4.7 we argued that in practice it was usually simpler to specify a functional form for the indirect utility function and then derive the form of the demand functions by Roy's identity. Then estimating the parameters of the demand function immediately gave us the parameters of the underlying utility function.

Thus, the compensating and equivalent variations are in fact observable if the demand functions are observable. The observed demand behavior can be used to construct a measure of welfare change.

The classic case of this measurement is the case of consumer's surplus. Suppose that the observed demand for some single good is independent of income. Then the integrability equations become:

$$d\mu/dq = x(q)$$
$$\mu(p;\, p,\, y) = y$$

These equations imply that $\mu(q;\, p,\, y) = A(q,\, p) + y$, where $A(q,\, p)$ is the definite integral of $x(\,\cdot\,)$ between p and q. (See Section A.16.) For this form of the compensation function the compensating and equivalent variations take the form:

$$CV = \mu(p';\, p',\, y') - \mu(p';\, p^0,\, y^0) = A(p^0,\, p') + y' - y^0$$
$$EV = \mu(p^0;\, p',\, y') - \mu(p^0;\, p^0,\, y^0) = A(p^0,\, p') + y' - y^0$$

Thus, in this special case the compensating and equivalent variations coincide. It is not hard to see the intuition behind this result. Since the compensation function is linear in income with a constant coefficient, the value of an extra dollar—the marginal utility of income—is independent of price. Hence, the value of a compensating or equivalent change in income is independent of the prices at which the value is measured.

Example 7.1 Welfare Analysis of a Tax in General Equilibrium In this example we will analyze the impact of a tax in a simple economy. First we will describe the theoretically ideal procedure and then describe the kind of approximations that are often made in practice.

Let us suppose that we have a set of consumers $i = 1, \ldots, n$, and we are given their preferences, their endowments, and their profit shares of the firms in the economy. We are also given the technologies of the firms in the economy, which we will represent by the profit functions $\pi_j(\mathbf{p})$, $j = 1, \ldots, m$. From this information we can compute the original price vector $\mathbf{p}^0$ facing the consumer and each consumer's wealth $= \mathbf{pW}_i + \Sigma T_{ij}\pi_j(\mathbf{p}^0)$.

We now consider imposing a tax t on one of the goods; we wish to compute the equivalent variation—i.e., how much each consumer would pay to avoid such a tax. In order to do this we must first calculate the resulting general equilibrium—that is, we must calculate what the final price vector $\mathbf{p}'$ will be when the tax is imposed. In general this is a difficult problem. Typically, many prices will change when one imposes a tax on a single good. In theory, we must be able to calculate the entire vector of equilibrium prices that will result.

Let us suppose that this has been accomplished and that we now have the final equilibrium prices facing the consumers and the firms. We denote these prices by $\mathbf{p}'$ and $\mathbf{q}'$.

Consumer i's wealth after the imposition of the tax will be given by $\mathbf{p}'\mathbf{W}_i + \sum_{j=1}^{m} T_{ij}\pi_j(\mathbf{q}')$, which is composed of both his endowment income and his profit income. Finally, we need to consider what happens to the revenues raised by the tax. If we knew what the tax was being spent on, we would use that information to evaluate the consumer's utility from this expenditure. This is the preferred way to analyze a tax, but it is common to simply assume that the tax is paid back to the consumers in the form of a lump-sum grant R_i. Hence, consumer i's wealth after the tax is imposed is given by $y_i' = \mathbf{p}'\mathbf{W}_i + \Sigma T_i\pi_j(\mathbf{q}') + R_i$ for $i = 1, \ldots, n$.

Thus, the equivalent variation for consumer i will be

$$EV_i = \mu_i(\mathbf{p}^0; \mathbf{p}', y_i') - y_i^0$$

This is about as far as we can proceed at this level of generality. The final information about the welfare impact of the tax is a list of the equivalent variations for each consumer in the economy.

It is clear that a rigorous analysis of the impact of a tax is complex to carry out in practice. It is common—but not necessarily desirable—to make several simplifying assumptions concerning the above problem. First, we often assume that the partial equilibrium analysis of the tax described in Example 2.3 is accurate enough for our purposes so that the price changes in other markets can be ignored. Thus p^0 and p' can be calculated by the simple supply and demand diagram given in Figure 2.7.

Second, we often assume that the underlying demand function is independent of income so that the compensation function takes the linear-in-income form described above. This has two effects. First, it will allow us to compute the equivalent variation simply as the change in consumer's surplus plus the change in profits and tax revenues, so that the equivalent variation becomes:

$$EV_i = A_i(p^0, p') + \sum_{j=1}^{m} T_{ij}[\pi_j(q') - \pi_j(p^0)] + R_i(t) \quad i = 1, \cdots, n$$

Second, it will allow us to aggregate the consumers in a convenient way. If we simply sum up the equivalent variations given above, we will find a total equivalent variation of:

$$EV = \Sigma_i A_i(p^0, p') + \Sigma_j[\pi_j(p^0)] + \Sigma_i R_i(t)$$

This equivalent variation can be depicted graphically as in Figure 7.4. The sum of the consumer's surpluses is just the area to the left of the aggregate demand curve, and the sum of the producer surpluses is just the area to the left of the aggregate supply curves. The total tax revenue is the area of the box:

$$\begin{aligned} A(p^0, p') &= A + B \\ \pi(p') - \pi(p^0) &= C + D \\ R(t) &= A + C \\ EV &= B + C \end{aligned}$$

The equivalent variation in this diagram is usually known as the *deadweight loss*. Note that the consumer's surplus case can be treated as a single consumer economy.

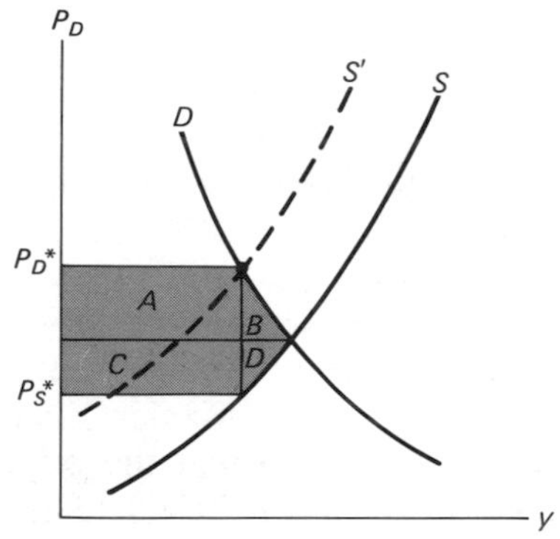

Fig. 7.4 *Deadweight Loss due to Taxation*

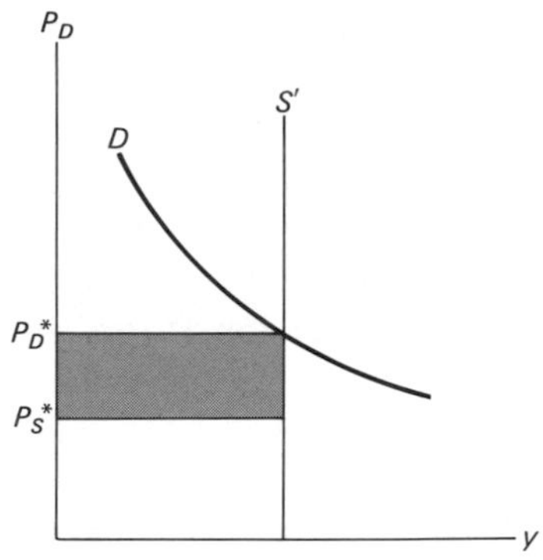

Fig. 7.5 *Deadweight Loss with Vertical Supply Curve*

7.5 MEASUREMENT OF ECONOMIC WELFARE

It is often desirable to know when a government project will improve social welfare. For example, constructing a dam may have economic benefits such as decreasing the price of electric power and water. However, against these benefits we must weigh the costs of possible environmental damage and the cost of constructing the dam. In general, the benefits and cost of a project will affect different people in different ways—the increased water supply from the dam may lower water fees in some areas and raise water fees in other areas. How should these differential benefits and costs be compared?

In Section 7.4 we analyzed the problem of measuring the benefits or costs accruing to one individual due to a change in the price or quantity consumed of some good. In this section we try to extend that sort of analysis to a community of individuals.

There are two distinct approaches to the problem of measuring the welfare impact of public projects. We have already briefly mentioned one approach to social decision making, namely the *welfare function* approach that we analyzed in Chapter 5. The second approach is that of the so-called *compensation criterion.* We will first discuss the ideas behind the compensation criterion and then relate it to the aforementioned welfare function.

The basic idea of the compensation criterion is derived from the concept of the *Pareto criterion.* Consider two allocations, $\mathbf{x}$ and $\mathbf{x}'$. The allocation $\mathbf{x}'$ is said to *Pareto dominate* $\mathbf{x}$ if everyone prefers $\mathbf{x}'$ to $\mathbf{x}$. (As has been mentioned in Section 5.5, we could weaken this definition and require that everyone be at least as well off and someone be strictly better off.) If each individual prefers $\mathbf{x}'$ to $\mathbf{x}$ it seems uncontroversial to assert that $\mathbf{x}'$ is better than $\mathbf{x}$ and any projects that move us from $\mathbf{x}$ to $\mathbf{x}'$ should be undertaken.

However, projects that are unanimously preferred are rather rare. In the usual case, some people prefer $\mathbf{x}'$ to $\mathbf{x}$ and some people may prefer $\mathbf{x}$ to $\mathbf{x}'$. How can these disputes be resolved?

The compensation criterion suggests the following test: $\mathbf{x}'$ is better than $\mathbf{x}$—in the compensation sense—if there is some way to reallocate $\mathbf{x}'$ so that everyone prefers the *reallocation* to the original allocation $\mathbf{x}$. Let us state this definition a bit more formally: $\mathbf{x}'$ is better than $\mathbf{x}$ in the compensation sense, if there is some allocation $\mathbf{x}''$ with $\Sigma \mathbf{x}_i'' = \Sigma \mathbf{x}_i'$ (i.e., $\mathbf{x}''$ is a reallocation of $\mathbf{x}$) such that $\mathbf{x}_i'' \succ_i \mathbf{x}_i$ for all agents i.

Thus the compensation criterion only requires that $\mathbf{x}'$ be a *potential* Pareto improvement on $\mathbf{x}$. The original terminology expresses this very clearly: call a person a *winner* if he prefers $\mathbf{x}'$ to $\mathbf{x}$, and call him a *loser* if he prefers $\mathbf{x}$ to $\mathbf{x}'$. Then $\mathbf{x}'$ is better than $\mathbf{x}$ if the winners can compensate the losers—that is, the winners can give away enough of their gains so as to ensure that everyone is made better off.

Now it is clear that if the winners *do in fact* compensate the losers, the proposed change in the allocation will certainly be acceptable to all. But it is not clear why one should think $\mathbf{x}'$ is better than $\mathbf{x}$ merely because it is *possible* for the winners to compensate the losers.

The usual argument in defense of the compensation principle is that the question of whether the compensation is carried out is really a question about income distribution, and the basic welfare theorems show that the question of income distribution can be separated from the question of allocative efficiency. The compensation criterion is concerned solely with allocative efficiency, and the question of proper income distribution can best be handled by alternative means such as redistributive taxation.

Let us restate this discussion in graphical terms. Suppose that there are only two individuals, and they are considering two allocations $\mathbf{x}$ and $\mathbf{x}'$. We associate with each allocation its *utility possibility set*

$$U = \{u_1(\mathbf{y}_1), u_2(\mathbf{y}_2) : \mathbf{y}_1 + \mathbf{y}_2 = \mathbf{x}_1 + \mathbf{x}_2\} \text{ and}$$

$$U' = \{u_1(\mathbf{y}_1), u_2(\mathbf{y}_2) : \mathbf{y}_1 + \mathbf{y}_2 = \mathbf{x}_1' + \mathbf{x}_2'\}$$

The upper right-hand boundary of this set is called the *utility possibility frontier*. The utility possibility frontier gives the utility distributions associated with all of the Pareto efficient reallocations of $\mathbf{x}$ and $\mathbf{x}'$. Several cases are depicted in Figure 7.6.

In Figure 7.6(a), the allocation $\mathbf{x}'$ is Pareto preferred to $\mathbf{x}$ since $u_1(\mathbf{x}_1') > u_1(\mathbf{x}_1)$ and $u_2(\mathbf{x}_2') > u_2(\mathbf{x}_2)$. In Figure 7.6 (b), $\mathbf{x}'$ is preferred to $\mathbf{x}$ in the sense of the compensation test: there is some reallocation of $\mathbf{x}'$ that is Pareto preferred to $\mathbf{x}$, even though $\mathbf{x}'$ itself is not Pareto preferred. In Figure 7.6 (c), $\mathbf{x}'$ and $\mathbf{x}$ are simply not comparable—neither the compensation test nor the Pareto test says anything about their relative desirability. In Figure 7.6 (d), we have the most paradoxical situation: here $\mathbf{x}'$ is preferred to $\mathbf{x}$, since $\mathbf{x}''$ is Pareto preferable to $\mathbf{x}$; but *then* $\mathbf{x}$ *is also preferred to* $\mathbf{x}'$ since $\mathbf{x}'''$ is preferred to $\mathbf{x}'$!

Cases (c) and (d) illustrate the main defects of the compensation criterion: it gives no guidance in making comparisons between Pareto efficient allocations, and it can result in paradoxical comparisons.

Nevertheless, the compensation test lies at the basis of much of applied welfare economics. The main problem in applying the compensation criterion is how to use it without resorting to a full-scale survey of the population.

If the projects under consideration are public goods there is not much hope to avoid explicit questioning of the community in order to make social decisions. We have discussed the problems with this type of questioning in Sections 7.1 and 7.2.

If the projects concern private goods, we have a much nicer situation since the current prices of the private goods reflect, in some sense, their marginal value to the individual agents.

Suppose we are currently at a market equilibrium $(\mathbf{x}, \mathbf{p})$ and we are contemplating moving to an allocation $\mathbf{x}'$. Then

PROPOSITION *If* $\mathbf{x}'$ *is preferred to* $\mathbf{x}$ *in the sense of the compensation criterion we must have* $\sum_i \mathbf{p}\cdot\mathbf{x}_i' > \sum_i \mathbf{p}\cdot\mathbf{x}_i$; *i.e., national income measured in current prices is larger at* $\mathbf{x}'$ *than at* $\mathbf{x}$.

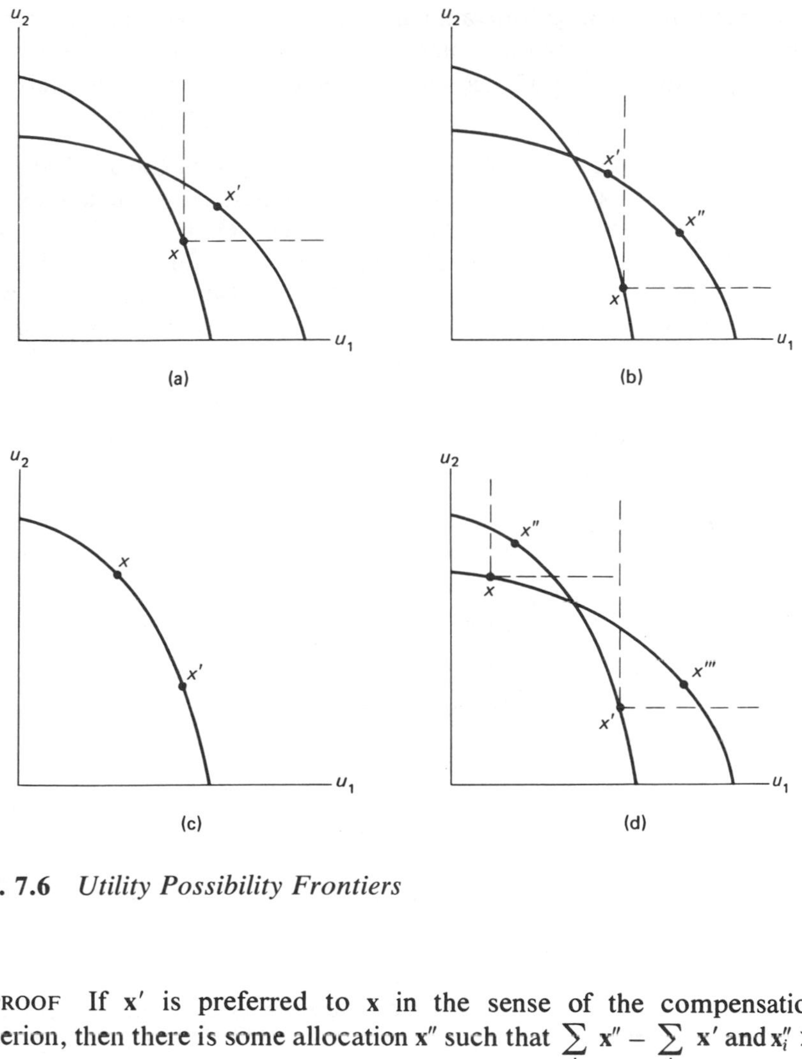

Fig. 7.6 *Utility Possibility Frontiers*

PROOF If $\mathbf{x}'$ is preferred to $\mathbf{x}$ in the sense of the compensation criterion, then there is some allocation $\mathbf{x}''$ such that $\sum_i \mathbf{x}'' - \sum_i \mathbf{x}'$ and $\mathbf{x}_i'' \succ_i \mathbf{x}_i$ for all i. Since $\mathbf{x}$ is a market equilibrium, this means that $\mathbf{p}\cdot\mathbf{x}_i'' > \mathbf{p}\cdot\mathbf{x}_i$ for all i. Summing, we have: $\Sigma\mathbf{p}\cdot\mathbf{x}_i'' > \Sigma\mathbf{p}\cdot\mathbf{x}_i$. But

$$\Sigma\mathbf{p}\cdot\mathbf{x}_i'' = \mathbf{p}\cdot\Sigma\mathbf{x}_i'' = \mathbf{p}\cdot\Sigma\mathbf{x}_i'$$

and this establishes the result. □

This result is nice in the sense that it gives us a one-way test of proposed projects: if national income measured in current prices declines, then the project is certainly not worth doing.

Figure 7.7 makes the proposition geometrically clear. The axes of the graph measure the aggregate amount of two goods available. The current allocation is represented by some aggregate bundle $\mathbf{X} = (X^1, X^2)$ where $X^1 = \sum_i x_i^1$ and $X^2 = \sum_i x_i^2$. (Remember, subscripts are consumers and superscripts are goods.)

We say an aggregate bundle $\mathbf{X}'$ is "socially preferred" to an *allocation* $\mathbf{x}$ if $\mathbf{X}'$ can be distributed among the agents to construct an allocation $\mathbf{x}'$ that is Pareto preferred to $\mathbf{x}$. In other words, the set of socially preferred aggregate bundles is given by $P = \{\Sigma \mathbf{x}_i' : \mathbf{x}_i' \succ_i \mathbf{x}_i \text{ for all } i\}$. When described in this way, the set P should look familiar—it is precisely the same set of bundles we encountered in Section 5.5 during the proof of the second fundamental welfare theorem.

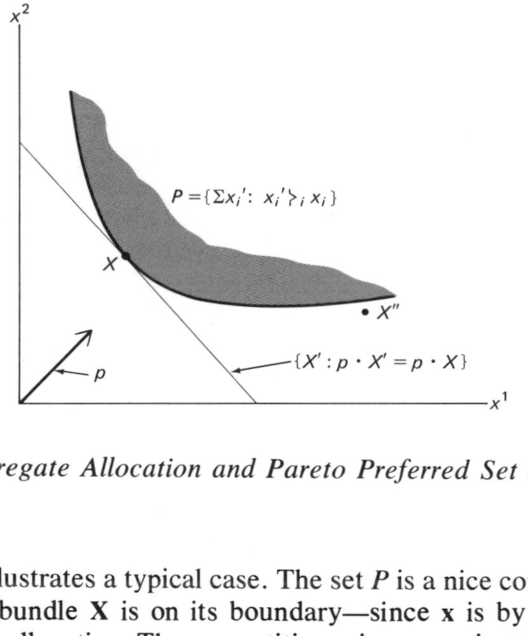

Fig. 7.7 *Aggregate Allocation and Pareto Preferred Set of Aggregate Allocations*

Figure 7.7 illustrates a typical case. The set P is a nice convex set, and the aggregate bundle $\mathbf{X}$ is on its boundary—since $\mathbf{x}$ is by hypothesis a Pareto efficient allocation. The competitive prices $\mathbf{p}$ are just the prices that define the separating hyperplane $\{\mathbf{X}' : \mathbf{p}\cdot\mathbf{X}' = \mathbf{p}\cdot\mathbf{X}\}$ that separates $\mathbf{X}$ from P. From this picture it is easy to see the content of the proposition described earlier. If $\mathbf{x}'$ is preferred to $\mathbf{x}$ in the sense of the compensation criterion then $\mathbf{X}' = \Sigma \mathbf{x}_i'$ must be in P, and hence $\mathbf{p}\cdot\mathbf{X}' > \mathbf{p}\cdot\mathbf{X}$.

We can also see that the converse is not true. The bundle $\mathbf{X}''$ has $\mathbf{p}\cdot\mathbf{X}'' > \mathbf{p}\cdot\mathbf{X}$ but it is not potentially Pareto preferable to $\mathbf{x}$. However, the diagram does suggest an interesting conjecture: if $\mathbf{p}\cdot\mathbf{X}' > \mathbf{p}\cdot\mathbf{X}$ *and* $\mathbf{X}'$ *is close enough to* $\mathbf{X}$, then $\mathbf{X}'$ must be potentially Pareto preferable to $\mathbf{x}$. This seems geometrically clear, and in the following paragraphs we make this conjecture precise.

The argument rests on the fact that, to a first order, changes in utility are proportional to changes in income. This follows from a simple Taylor series expansion:

$$u_i(\mathbf{x}_i') - u_i(\mathbf{x}_i) \approx \mathbf{D}u_i(\mathbf{x}_i)\cdot(\mathbf{x}_i' - \mathbf{x}_i) = \lambda_i \mathbf{p}\cdot(\mathbf{x}_i' - \mathbf{x}_i)$$

It is clear from the above formula that small changes in the bundle $\mathbf{x}_i$ are preferred or not preferred as the change in the value of the bundle is positive or negative.

What we want to show is this: if $\mathbf{p}\cdot\sum_i \mathbf{x}_i' > \mathbf{p}\cdot\sum_i \mathbf{x}_i$ and $|\mathbf{x}_i' - \mathbf{x}_i|$ is small, then it is possible to find a redistribution of $\mathbf{x}'$—call it $\mathbf{x}''$—such that everyone prefers $\mathbf{x}''$ to $\mathbf{x}$.

To show this, we let $\mathbf{X} = \sum_i \mathbf{x}_i$ and $\mathbf{X}' = \sum_i \mathbf{x}_i'$ be the aggregate bundles associated with the two allocations. Then define $\mathbf{x}''$ by:

$$\mathbf{x}_i'' = \mathbf{x}_i + \frac{\mathbf{X}' - \mathbf{X}}{n}$$

Here each agent i is getting $1/n^{\text{th}}$ of the aggregate gain in the movement from $\mathbf{x}$ to $\mathbf{x}'$. Now, according to the above Taylor series expansion

$$\begin{aligned} u_i(\mathbf{x}'') - u_i(\mathbf{x}_i) &\approx \lambda_i\mathbf{p}\cdot\left(\mathbf{x}_i + \frac{\mathbf{X}' - \mathbf{X}}{n} - \mathbf{x}_i\right) \\ &\approx \lambda_i\mathbf{p}\cdot\left(\frac{\mathbf{X}' - \mathbf{X}}{n}\right) \end{aligned}$$

Thus if the right-hand side is positive—national income at the original prices increases—then it must be possible to increase every agent's utility . . . as long as the change in allocation is small enough for the Taylor approximation to be valid.

We can carry this same logic one step further and take a second-order Taylor series approximation.

$$u_i(\mathbf{x}_i') - u_i(\mathbf{x}_i) \approx \lambda_i\mathbf{p}\cdot(\mathbf{x}_i' - \mathbf{x}_i) + \frac{(\mathbf{x}_i' - \mathbf{x}_i)\mathbf{D}^2u_i(\mathbf{x})(\mathbf{x}_i' - \mathbf{x})}{2}$$

Let us simplify this expression by considering a special case where only the allocation of one good changes. In this case we can omit all subscripts and write the Taylor expansion as:

$$u(x') - u(x) \approx \lambda p\,\Delta x + \frac{1}{2}\frac{\partial^2 u(x)}{\partial x^2}(\Delta x)^2$$

We can derive an illuminating interpretation of the last term by using the following fact. The inverse demand curve for the commodity in question must identically satisfy the first-order conditions:

$$\frac{\partial u(x)}{\partial x} \equiv \lambda p(x)$$

Differentiating we have:

$$\frac{\partial^2 u(x)}{\partial x^2} = \lambda \frac{dp(x)}{dx} + p(x) \frac{d\lambda}{dx}$$

In general we would expect that $d\lambda/dx$ would be relatively small—the marginal utility of income should not be very sensitive to the consumption of any one good. If this is true, we can neglect the last term of this expression and substitute into the Taylor expansion to get:

$$u(x') - u(x) \approx \lambda\, p\Delta x + \frac{1}{2}\frac{\partial p(x)}{\partial x}\, \Delta x\, \Delta x$$

The geometrical meaning is made clear in Figure 7.8. The first term $p\Delta x$ is the area of the rectangle while the second term is the area of a triangle with base Δx and height Δp. The *difference* between these two terms is the indicated area—the change in consumer's surplus. (We take the difference since $\partial p(x)/\partial x$ is negative.)

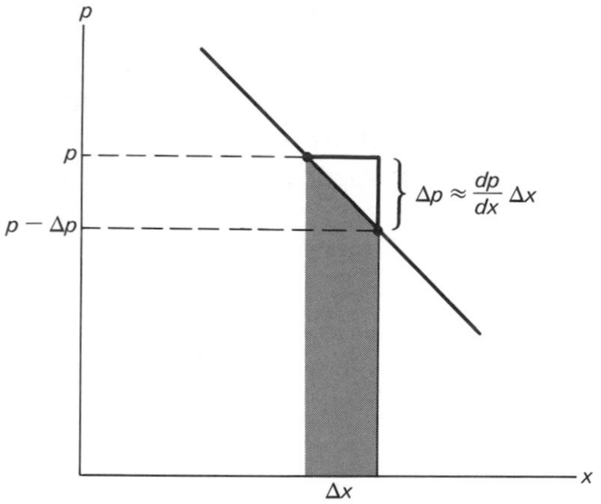

Fig. 7.8 *Consumer's Surplus*

This is precisely in accordance with the results of Section 7.4: changes in utility are approximately proportional to changes in consumers' surplus. (Note that since $dp(x)/dx$ is negative the first-order approximation always overstates the true welfare gain.)

Let us briefly summarize the discussion thus far. The compensation criterion suggests that a reasonable test for whether a project should be undertaken is to ask whether the project represents a potential Pareto improvement on the existing allocation. Given that we accept this logic, we can ask how we can implement such a test in practical terms. We have seen that the market prices give us a natural test: if a project is potentially Pareto preferable it must always increase national income, measured at current prices, and, for small projects, an increase in national income is sufficient to ensure potential Pareto preferability.

We have also seen how one can get a more accurate measure of welfare change by the use of consumers' surplus. However, note that to use the consumers' surplus approach directly we need information on all of the individual's demand functions—and this kind of information is usually difficult to obtain. In some circumstances it is possible to obtain information on demand by different demographic groups, but even this is rare. In practice such niceties are usually neglected and aggregate consumers' surplus is often used to evaluate changes in potential and actual welfare.

As we mentioned earlier in this section, the compensation methodology suffers from the defect that it ignores distributional considerations. An allocation that is potentially Pareto preferred to the current allocation of course has potentially higher welfare. But one might well argue that actual welfare is the relevant criterion.

If one is willing to postulate some welfare function, one can incorporate distributional considerations into a cost-benefit analysis. Let us suppose that we have a linear welfare function:

$$W(\mathbf{u}(\mathbf{x})) = \Sigma a_i u_i(\mathbf{x}_i)$$

As we saw in Section 5.7 the parameters (a_i) are related to the "welfare weights" of individual economic agents. These weights represent the value judgments of the "social planner." Let us suppose we are at a market equilibrium $(\mathbf{x}, \mathbf{p})$ and are considering moving to an allocation $\mathbf{x}'$. Will this movement increase welfare? If $\mathbf{x}'$ is close to $\mathbf{x}$, we can apply a Taylor series expansion to get:

$$W(\mathbf{u}(\mathbf{x}')) - W(\mathbf{u}(\mathbf{x})) \approx \sum_{i=1}^{n} a_i \mathbf{D}\mathbf{u}_i(\mathbf{x}_i)\,(\mathbf{x}_i' - \mathbf{x}_i)$$

Since $(\mathbf{x}, \mathbf{p})$ is a market equilibrium we can rewrite this as:

$$W(\mathbf{u}(\mathbf{x}')) - W(\mathbf{u}(\mathbf{x})) \approx \sum_{i=1}^{n} a_i \lambda_i \mathbf{p} \cdot (\mathbf{x}_i' - \mathbf{x}_i)$$

We see that the welfare test reduces to examining a weighted change of incomes. The weights are related to the value judgments which were originally incorporated into the welfare function.

Suppose as a special case that the original allocation $\mathbf{x}$ were a welfare optimum to begin with. Then the results of Section 5.7 tell us that $\lambda_i = 1/a_i$. In this case we get

$$W(\mathbf{u}(\mathbf{x}')) - W(\mathbf{u}(\mathbf{x})) \approx \sum_{i=1}^{n} \mathbf{p} \cdot (\mathbf{x}_i' - \mathbf{x}_i)$$

The distribution terms drop out—since distribution is already optimal—and we are left with a simple criterion: a small project increases welfare if national income (at the original prices) increases.

This concludes our discussion of welfare measurement. The basic lesson is that prices do indeed serve as a measure of value and can be used to evaluate proposed projects. Of course, in practice many problems of interpretation and measurement arise which tend to obscure this fundamental insight. The references at the end of this chapter discuss some of the problems of cost benefit analysis in considerably more detail.

7.6 OPTIMAL PRICING

Consider the problem facing a public or semipublic agency such as a postal service or a telephone service. Such an agency must determine how to price its products so as to maximize social welfare. If this is the only goal of such an agency, we have seen that prices should be set equal to marginal costs.

Unfortunately, public agencies often have a technology characterized by declining average costs. The two examples mentioned above seem in fact to have technologies involving very large fixed costs and rather small marginal costs. The "price equals marginal cost" rule would undoubtedly result in a negative level of profits. For various reasons, this is socially—and privately—unacceptable.

The question then arises: What would be the optimal pricing policy subject to the constraint that profits equal zero (or some other predetermined level). To answer this question, we make some restrictions on the problem. First of all, we will assume that all consumers are identical, so tion $v(\mathbf{p}, y)$. Second, we will assume income is independent from changes in the price vector, which in this case boils down to assuming that the same goods do not serve as both inputs and outputs.

We let $x_i(\mathbf{p})$ be the consumer demand function for the ith good and let $P(\mathbf{p}) = \Sigma p_i x_i(\mathbf{p}) - \Sigma c_i(x_i(\mathbf{p}))$ be the *monopolist profit function*. Notice that this is different from the profit function discussed in Chapter 1 since it explicitly takes account of the demand behavior of the consumers.

We can now write the maximization problem of the public agency as:

$$\begin{aligned} \max \quad & v(\mathbf{p}, y) \\ \text{s.t.} \quad & P(\mathbf{p}) = 0 \end{aligned}$$

The first-order conditions are:

$$\frac{\partial v(\mathbf{p}^*, y)}{\partial p_i} - t\,\frac{\partial P(\mathbf{p}^*)}{\partial p_i} = 0 \qquad i = 1, \cdots, n$$

Using Roy's identity, we can write this condition as:

$$-x_i(\mathbf{p}, y)\,\frac{\partial v(\mathbf{p}^*, y)}{\partial y} - t\,\frac{\partial P(\mathbf{p}^*)}{\partial p_i} = 0 \qquad i = 1, \cdots, n$$

or

$$\frac{x_i(\mathbf{p}^*, y)}{x_j(\mathbf{p}^*, y)} = \frac{\partial P(\mathbf{p}^*)/\partial p_i}{\partial P(\mathbf{p}^*)/\partial p_j} \qquad \begin{aligned} i &= 1, \cdots, n \\ j &= 1, \cdots, n \end{aligned}$$

This says that the marginal profit yields of changing a price should be proportional to the output levels of the good in question. We can express this condition in a more transparent manner by expanding the derivative of the monopolist's profit function according to its definition. Purely for algebraic simplicity, we will assume that the demand for good i is independent of the price of good j, so that $\partial x_i(\mathbf{p})/\partial p_j = 0$ for $i \neq j$.

We can write the profit function as:

$$P(\mathbf{p}) = \sum_{i=1}^{n} x_i(\mathbf{p})p_i - \sum_{i=1}^{n} c_i(x_i(\mathbf{p}))$$

so that

$$\begin{aligned} \frac{\partial P(\mathbf{p})}{\partial p_i} &= p_i\,\frac{\partial x_i(\mathbf{p})}{\partial p_i} + x_i - \frac{\partial c_i(x_i)}{\partial x_i}\,\frac{\partial x_i(\mathbf{p})}{\partial p_i} \\ &= x_i + \left[p_i - \frac{\partial c_i(x_i)}{\partial x_i}\right]\frac{\partial x_i(\mathbf{p})}{\partial p_i} \end{aligned}$$

We let $\lambda = t/(\partial v(\mathbf{p}^*, y)/\partial y)$ and substitute this into the original first-order conditions:

$$-x_i = \lambda x_i + \lambda\left[p_i - \frac{\partial c_i(x_i)}{\partial x_i}\right]\frac{\partial x_i(\mathbf{p})}{\partial p_i}$$

Rearranging, we get

$$-\frac{(1-\lambda)}{\lambda}\,\frac{x_i}{(\partial x_i(\mathbf{p})/\partial p_i)} = p_i - \frac{\partial c_i(x_i)}{\partial x_i}$$

Divide both sides by p_i and let $\epsilon_i = -\frac{\partial x_i(\mathbf{p})}{\partial p_i}\frac{p_i}{x_i}$ be the own price elasticity of demand. We get:

$$\left(\frac{1+\lambda}{\lambda}\right)\frac{1}{\epsilon_i} = \frac{p_i^* - \frac{\partial c_i(x_i^*)}{\partial x_i}}{p_i^*} \qquad i = 1, \cdots, n$$

This formula says that the percentage deviation of prices from marginal costs should be inversely proportional to the elasticities of demand for the goods in question. This means that goods which have a very small elasticity of demand should sell at a price much larger than marginal cost, and vice versa.

What is the intuition behind this rule? From the viewpoint of social welfare, it is the quantity of each good consumed that is relevant. Goods with small elasticity of demand are relatively insensitive to increases in price; hence, the prices for these goods can be set to be much larger than marginal costs. The prices of goods that are relatively sensitive to price are set much closer to costs. Thus, the distortion from the optimal consumption bundle will be minimized.

Finally, we note that the problem of choosing optimal prices subject to a budget constraint is analogous to the problem of choosing optimal taxes subject to a constraint on tax receipts. The optimal taxation problem can be analyzed by techniques similar to those used in this section. Some references on optimal taxation are given at the end of this chapter.

7.7 *QUASI-LINEAR UTILITY FUNCTIONS*

In Exercise 3.43 we described some special features of the quasi-linear utility function. Recall that this utility function has the form that it is linear in some good and thus can be written as $u(\mathbf{x}) + m$. In this section we explore the consequences of this assumption for equilibrium analysis and welfare analysis.

First, let us consider competitive equilibrium. In what follows we will choose the m good as the numéraire and assign it price 1. In applications this good is often referred to as "money," but this temptation should probably be avoided. It is used only as a unit of account.

Let us first consider the form of the indirect consumer's maximization problem. We have:

$$\begin{aligned} v(\mathbf{p}, y) = \max\ & u(\mathbf{x}) + m \\ \text{s.t. } & \mathbf{px} + m = y \\ & \mathbf{x} \geq 0 \\ & m \geq 0 \end{aligned}$$

Applying the Kuhn-Tucker theorem, we see that there are two interesting classes of solutions. First, we have the case where $m = 0$ and $\mathbf{x} \gg 0$, so that the first-order conditions take the form:

$$\mathbf{D}u(\mathbf{x}) - \lambda \mathbf{p} = 0$$
$$\mathbf{px} = y$$

This is identical to the usual consumer maximization problem. Hence, we find the ordinary sort of demand functions and the ordinary sort of indirect utility function $v(\mathbf{p}, y)$. Let us consider the graph of indirect utility as a function of income—that is, the utility of income curve. In Figure 7.9 we have illustrated a typical shape for this function along with the graph of the line $u = y$.

At the indicated point y^0 the consumer finds that an extra increment of income spent on the x goods gives him less utility than an extra increment spent on the m good—that is, his marginal utility of income is less than 1. Since he can always get a marginal utility of income equal to 1 by consuming the m good, he switches to the m good at this point. Hence, for income greater than y^0, the consumer consumes the $\mathbf{x}$ goods at the level given by $\mathbf{x}(\mathbf{p}, y^0)$ and consumes $m(\mathbf{p}, y) = y - y^0$.

This is why the consumer's demand is independent of the level of his income. Since the marginal utility of consumption of the $\mathbf{x}$ goods declines and the marginal utility of consumption of the m good remains constant, the consumer eventually spends all extra income on the consumption of the m good.

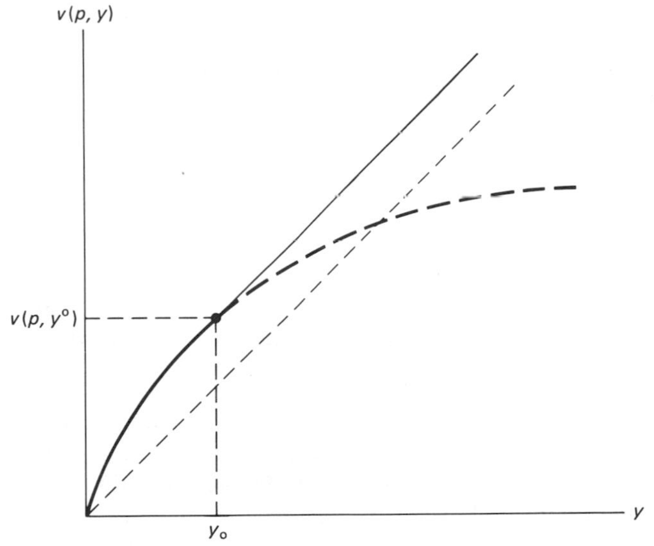

Fig. 7.9 *Utility as a Function of Income*

The indirect utility function takes the form:

$$v(\mathbf{p}, y) = u(\mathbf{x}(\mathbf{p}, y^0)) + y - y^0$$

when y is greater than y^0 and has the usual form for y less than y^0. In most treatments of the constant marginal utility of income situation, we normally assume that the consumption of m is strictly positive so that the above special structure emerges. However, it is sometimes useful to remember that this can only hold true for sufficiently large levels of income.

We have treated the properties of the demand function in an exercise in Chapter 3. Here we briefly summarize the findings:

(1) The substitution matrix is given by $\mathbf{Dx}(\mathbf{p}, \mathbf{y}) = \mathbf{D}^2\mathbf{u}(\mathbf{x}(\mathbf{p}, y))$.
(2) The inverse demand functions are given by $\mathbf{p}(\mathbf{x}) = \mathbf{D}u(\mathbf{x})$.
(3) The direct demand functions are given by $\mathbf{x}(\mathbf{p}) = -\mathbf{D}v(\mathbf{p}, y)$.

Let us now investigate the implications of this special structure for equilibrium analysis. It is straightforward to prove the following theorem:

Theorem Let $(\mathbf{p}, \mathbf{x}, \mathbf{y})$ be a competitive equilibrium. Then $\mathbf{p}$ minimizes the sum of the indirect utility functions. That is, $\mathbf{p}$ solves:

$$\min \sum_{i=1}^{n} [v_i(\mathbf{p}) + \mathbf{pW}_i] + \sum_{j=1}^{m} \pi_j(\mathbf{p})$$

PROOF The first-order conditions for this problem are simply:

$$\sum_{i=1}^{n} (\partial v_i/\partial p_g + W_i^g) + \sum_{j=1}^{m} \partial \pi_j/\partial p_g = 0 \text{ for } g = 1, \cdots, k$$

or

$$\sum_{i=1}^{n} [-x_i^g(\mathbf{p}) + W_i^g] + \sum_{j=1}^{m} y_j^g \text{ for } g = 1, \cdots, k$$

But this is just the condition that demand equals supply. Since both $v_i(\mathbf{p})$ and $\pi_j(\mathbf{p})$ are convex, these conditions are sufficient for the solution to be a global minimum. □

It sometimes seems strange that the equilibrium should be a global minimum of indirect utility; however, for any $\mathbf{p}$ other than the equilibrium price, demand will not equal supply, so the utility the agents *think* they can get (ignoring feasibility) will be greater than the utility they can actually get when such constraints are taken into account.

If $v(\mathbf{p})$ and $\pi(\mathbf{p})$ are strictly convex, then the equilibrium price vector will be unique. Under the usual sort of adjustment mechanism the equilibrium will be stable since the sum of indirect utilities can serve as a Liapunov function.

Let us now impose some special structure on the form of the technology. We will suppose that all of the x goods can be produced from the m good. Hence, we can write the cost function for a given level of production $\mathbf{x}$ as $c(\mathbf{x})$. (This cost function depends on the price of the m good; but we have set that equal to 1, so we omit this factor cost.)

Under this technological structure we can show:

Theorem *Let* $(\mathbf{p}, \mathbf{x}, y)$ *be an equilibrium. Then* $\mathbf{x}$ *maximizes the sum of the direct utility functions minus the cost of production:*

$$\max \sum_{i=1}^{n} u_i(\mathbf{x}_i) - c(\mathbf{x})$$

PROOF Differentiating with respect to x we see that price equals marginal cost for each good and the allocation is feasible. Hence, the allocation satisfies demand price equals supply price for every good, and it is feasible. It is, therefore, a competitive equilibrium. □

This proposition can be clarified by examining Figure 7.10 and 7.11. Consider first Figure 7.10, in which we have a simple supply and demand diagram. Since consumers' surplus analysis is valid in this case, the indirect utility function is given by the area to the left of the demand curve. The profit function is given by the area to the left of the supply curve. At any price *other* than the competitive price, the sum of these two areas will be greater than at the competitive equilibrium.

Now consider Figure 7.11. Since the inverse demand function is given by

$$p(x) = \partial u(x)/\partial x$$

we can integrate this to find:

$$u(x) = \int p(x)dx$$

Just as the supply curve measures marginal cost, the area under the demand curve measures the change in utility in the quasi-linear case.

Thus, at any level of x other than the competitive level, the area under the demand curve and above the supply curve is less than at the competitive level. Hence, this area is maximized at the competitive equilibrium.

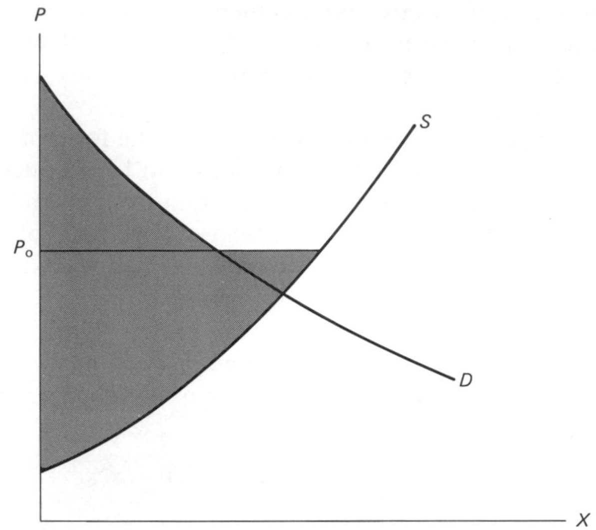

Fig. 7.10 *The Equilibrium Price Minimizes the Sum of the Indirect Utilities*

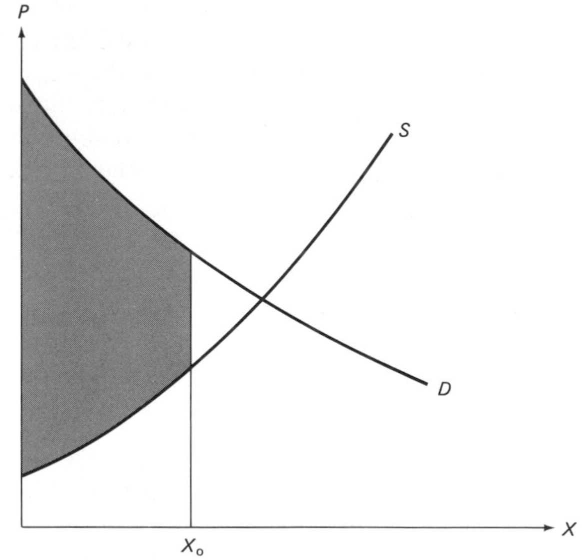

Fig. 7.11 *The Equilibrium Price Maximizes the Sum of Utilities Minus Costs*

Let us now consider welfare analysis. The first and second fundamental welfare theorems work in the usual way, but the set of Pareto efficient points takes on a very particular structure. Figure 7.12 depicts this structure. Here the utility possibilities frontier will be flat for large enough levels of each person's utility. The slope will be -1 since we can transfer utility from one person to another by transferring the m good. After we've taken all of the m good away from one person, his marginal utility of income will then become nonconstant and the utility possibilities frontier will take its usual curved shape.

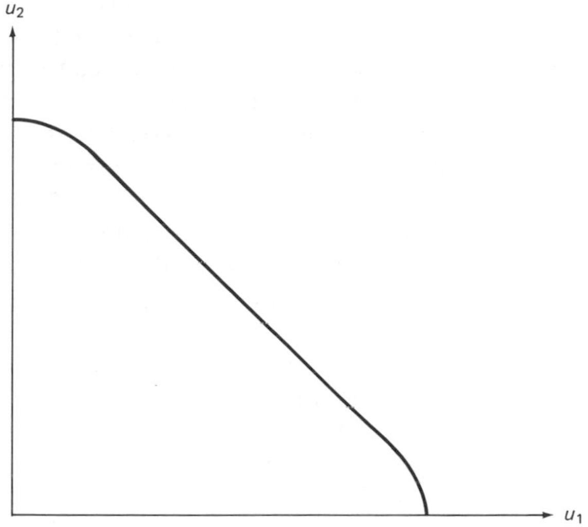

Fig. 7.12 *Utility Possibility Frontier*

Let us now consider the structure of Pareto efficient allocations in terms of commodity bundles held. When each person is holding a positive amount of the m good, we know that he will be consuming some *fixed* bundle $\mathbf{x}(\mathbf{p}, y^0)$. Hence, any transfers of wealth will be converted into the m good demand and will not change the equilibrium prices.

This independence of equilibrium prices from the distribution of wealth also follows quickly from Section 3.15. Since a quasi-linear utility function trivially has the Gorman form, the aggregate demand behavior is consistent with the existence of a "representative consumer," and, hence, aggregate demand behavior will be independent of the distribution of wealth. In fact, many of the special features of the quasi-linear utility function described above carry over to the Gorman case. Some of these generalizations will be examined in the exercises at the end of this chapter.

7.8 FAIR ALLOCATIONS

The welfare economics that we have been analyzing up until now provides a very general approach for examining welfare problems. All value judgments are incorporated into the welfare function, and thus the analysis we have done has been more or less "value free." However, it might be argued that it is of some interest not only to study a general framework in which value judgments may be incorporated but also to study the economic consequences of some specific value judgments. This is the motivation behind the concept of *fair allocations*.

Let us first suppose we are in a situation of pure exchange: we have some fixed bundle of goods, $\mathbf{W}$ in R^k_+, to be divided among n agents. What is a "just" way to divide this bundle of goods? Of course in general the answer to this question will depend on the particular circumstances involved; but in this case, we don't *know* any of the circumstances involved, so we seek a criterion depending only on the information we do have, namely the tastes of the agents involved.

One requirement we will certainly want to impose is that of Pareto efficiency. We would hardly want to divide goods in an inefficient manner. However, as we have seen Pareto efficient allocations still allow for a great variety of distributions. Which of these shall we choose?

Since all the agents are symmetric as far as we are concerned, we would like to have a symmetric division in some sense. A naive notion of symmetry here would be equal division. The problem is that equal division is unlikely to be Pareto efficient. Furthermore, equal division is symmetric "from the outside," as it were, rather than based on a concept of symmetry that depends on the tastes of the individual agents involved.

This notion of "internal symmetry" has led to the idea of an *equitable allocation*.

DEFINITION An allocation $\mathbf{x}$ is equitable if no agent prefers the bundle of any other agent to his own. In symbols, $\mathbf{x}$ is equitable if $\mathbf{x}_i \succsim_i \mathbf{x}_j$ for all i and j.

DEFINITION An allocation $\mathbf{x}$ is fair if it is both equitable and efficient.

An immediate question arises: Are there fair allocations, and, if so, how can they be found? The following simple theorem answers this question:

Theorem *Let* $(\mathbf{x}^*, \mathbf{p}^*)$ *be a Walrasian equilibrium with equal wealth; that is, with* $\mathbf{p}^* \cdot \mathbf{W}_i = \mathbf{p}^* \cdot \mathbf{W}_j$ *for all* i *and* j. *Then* $\mathbf{x}^*$ *is a fair allocation.*

PROOF We have already seen that $\mathbf{x}^*$ must be efficient since it is a Walras equilibrium. Thus we need only show that it is equitable. Assume not. Then there is some agent i that *envies* some agent j; i.e., $\mathbf{x}_i^* <_i \mathbf{x}_j^*$. But if agent i prefers $\mathbf{x}_j^*$, it must cost more than he can afford. But this leads to the following string of inequalities

$$\mathbf{p}\cdot\mathbf{W}_i = \mathbf{p}\cdot\mathbf{x}_i^* < \mathbf{p}\cdot\mathbf{x}_j^* = \mathbf{p}\cdot\mathbf{W}_j$$

which contradict the hypothesis of equal wealth. □

We already know conditions under which Walras equilibria will exist; hence, to ensure the existence of a fair allocation, we need only to divide the initial bundle **W** evenly and allow the agents to trade to such an equilibria.

The success of this approach is gratifying. However, upon reflection, the problem we have solved is rather trivial. Fair division when all agents are symmetric does not seem so difficult; what is hard is deciding what a fair division is when all agents are not fundamentally symmetric.

To be concrete, let us consider a case where agents have different abilities. In particular, let us assume that there is only one kind of labor, q, but agents are endowed with different amounts of ability so that, if agent i works q_i hours, he contributes $a_i q_i$ amount of labor power. Thus agent i has a_i/a_j as much labor power as agent j.

To describe an allocation in this case we need to describe how much each agent consumes of all the goods and how much each agent works. Actually, a morc convenient measure is to describe how much *leisure* (nonlabor) time each person has. If we normalize the total endowment of labor of each consumer to be 1, the consumption bundles will have the form $(x_i, 1 - q_i)$. Given a description of technology available, we can determine the set of feasible allocations, and, given a description of the agents preferences, we can determine the set of Pareto efficient allocations.

What might be an appropriate concept of equity in such circumstances? One idea is to just use the notion we already have and define an allocation $(\mathbf{x}, 1 - \mathbf{q})$ as *equitable* if $(\mathbf{x}_i, 1 - q_i) \succsim_i (\mathbf{x}_j, 1 - q_j)$ for all i and j. Here each agent asks himself: would I prefer to consume what j produces and work as much as j?

The problem with this definition is this: just because I work as much as j doesn't mean that I will produce as much as j. Hence comparisons of this sort may violate a feasibility condition. This problem is far from trivial; in fact, it is possible to find examples where fair allocations do not exist: there may be no feasible, Pareto efficient allocations in a productive economy that are envy free.

What is the problem here? I have suggested that it is due to the nonfeasibility of the envy comparison. Perhaps we should modify the nature of this comparison. Instead of comparing agents' consumption-leisure bundles, we should compare agents' *consumption-output* bundles: then when you claim you envy another agent you are saying that not only would you prefer to consume what he is consuming but you would be willing to produce what he is producing. This can be formalized as follows:

DEFINITION An allocation is *W*-equitable if $(\mathbf{x}_i, 1 - q_i) \succsim_i (\mathbf{x}_j, 1 - (a_j/a_i)\, q_j)$ for all i and j.

This formalizes what we want since $(a_j/a_i)\, q_j$ is how much labor person i would have to engage in to produce as much as person j produces with q_j units of his own labor. Happily, this provides us with an existence theorem:

PROPOSITION *Let* $(\mathbf{x}, 1 - \mathbf{q})$ *be a market equilibrium from* $\left(\frac{\mathbf{W}}{n}, 1\right)$. *Then* $(\mathbf{x}, 1 - \mathbf{q})$ *is* W*-equitable and efficient.*

PROOF First, we apply the standard result to conclude $(\mathbf{x}, 1 - \mathbf{q})$ is efficient. Next we notice that the market equilibrium determines a vector of prices $\mathbf{p}$ and a wage rate r for *labor power*. We can normalize r to equal 1, and we can view each agent's wage r_i as being normalized to equal his ability a_i. We know that the value of an agent's final bundle must equal the value of his endowment, so:

$$(\mathbf{p}, a_j) \cdot (\mathbf{x}_j, 1 - q_j) = (\mathbf{p}, a_j) \cdot \left(\frac{\mathbf{W}}{n}, 1\right)$$
$$\mathbf{p} \cdot \mathbf{x}_j + a_j - a_j q_j = \mathbf{p} \cdot \frac{\mathbf{W}}{n} + a_j$$
$$\mathbf{p} \cdot \mathbf{x}_j - a_j q_j = \mathbf{p} \cdot \frac{\mathbf{W}}{n}$$

Now suppose agent i *W*-envies agent j. Then, since each agent must be maximized in his budget set, the value of j's "bundle" must be greater than the value of i's endowment. This gives:

$$(\mathbf{p}, a_i) \cdot \left(\frac{\mathbf{W}}{n}, 1\right) < (\mathbf{p}, a_i) \cdot \left(\mathbf{x}_j, 1 - \frac{a_j q_j}{a_i}\right)$$
$$\mathbf{p} \cdot \frac{\mathbf{W}}{n} + a_i < \mathbf{p} \cdot \mathbf{x}_j + a_i - a_j q_j$$
$$\mathbf{p} \cdot \frac{\mathbf{W}}{n} < \mathbf{p} \cdot \mathbf{x}_j - a_j q_j$$

But this inequality violates the earlier equality. □

The *W*-fair allocation is rather conservative in a sense, since it makes no correction for the initial distribution of abilities, which is, after all, arbitrary. Pazner and Schmeidler have suggested an alternative concept of distributive justice that we might call an *income-equitable allocation:*

DEFINITION A Walras equilibrium allocation $((\mathbf{x}_i, 1 - q_i))$ is income equitable if $\mathbf{p}\cdot\mathbf{x}_i + w_i(1 - q_i) = \mathbf{p}\cdot\mathbf{x}_j + w_j(1 - q_j)$ for all i and j.

Income equity requires that all agents have the same implicit income when evaluated at the equilibrium prices. Notice that each agent's consumption of leisure is evaluated at his personal wage rate—the wage rate associated with his ability. Will income-fair allocations generally exist? The following argument gives a constructive proof.

Suppose we divide up each agent's endowment of leisure among all the agents, as well as dividing up the physical endowments of the economy evenly. Then each agent will have an identical initial endowment. Suppose we now trade to a Walrasian equilibrium. Agents may sell other agents' labor to whoever wishes to purchase it—firms or the agent in question. In equilibrium it is clear that all agents must hold final bundles of equal value—since the endowments all have equal value.

The income-fair notion completely compensates for initial distribution of ability. At this allocation one might feel that the "able" are exploited by the "unable." Although neither wealth-fair nor income-fair allocations seem completely desirable, they do seem to illustrate clearly the trade-offs and problems concerning distributive justice when abilities differ.

Exercises

7.1 (10) Suppose demand functions have income included endogenously in the form $\mathbf{x}(\mathbf{p}, \mathbf{p}\cdot\mathbf{w})$. Show that the marginal utility of income can never be independent of prices.

7.2 (10) Show that the area above the supply curve equals profits plus rents by using the profit function.

7.3 (10) Suppose preferences are strictly convex and monotonic. Show that, if two agents have identical preferences, they must receive the same bundle at any fair allocation.

7.4 (20) Suppose preferences are strictly convex and monotonic. Show that for a two-person economy every point in the equal division core is fair, but this does not generalize to larger economies.

7.5 (20) Suppose that the indirect utility function is separable so that $v(\mathbf{p}, y)$ can be written as $\phi(\mathbf{p}) + y$. Show that the area under the demand curve gives us an exact measure of the welfare loss due to a price change.

7.6 (20) Suppose that the demand function for good 1 has constant income elasticity. Show that the indirect utility function has the form $v(\mathbf{p}, y) = \phi(\mathbf{p}) + f(y)$ where $\phi(\mathbf{p})$ is related to consumer's surplus. (Hint: Use Roy's identity.)

7.7 (20) Suppose the demand for good 1 has the form $x_1(p, y) = x_1(p, y_0)\, g(y)$. Show that $g(y) = [y/y^0]^n$. (Hint: Use homogeneity.)

7.8 Let individual indirect utility functions have the Gorman form: $v_i(\mathbf{p}, y_i) = a_i(\mathbf{p}) + b(\mathbf{p})y_i$. Show that a competitive equilibrium must minimize the sum of these indirect utility functions.

7.9 Show that if the individual indirect utility functions have the Gorman form, the utility possibility frontier is flat.

Notes

The concept of public good is due to Samuelson (1964). The treatment of consumer's surplus follows that of Willig (1976). The concepts of compensating and equivalent variation and their relationship to consumer's surplus is due to Hicks (1956). The constant income elasticity formula is due to Willig (1976).

The concept of equitable allocations is due to Foley (1967). The concept of fair allocations is due to Schmeidler and Yaari (1971). The difficulty with the existence of fair allocations in the productive case was shown in Pazner and Schmeidler (1974). The concept of wealth-fair allocations is due to Varian (1974). The concept of income-fair allocations is due to Pazner and Schmeidler (1972). For a discussion of the philosophical problem of distributive justice see Varian (1975).

For more on optimal pricing see Baumol and Bradford (1970). For optimal taxation see Diamond and Mirrlees (1971) and Diamond and McFadden (1974).

The discussion of preference revelation here is based on Green, Kohlberg, Laffont (1975). Basic references on preference revelation are Groves and Ledyard (1977), Groves and Ledyard (1976), and the references cited therein.

The material on cost benefit analysis and changes in national income is drawn from Radner (1974). For more material on cost benefit analysis, see Mishan (1971).

References

BAUMOL, W., and BRADFORD, D. 1970. "Optimal Departures from Marginal Cost Pricing." *American Economic Review* 69:265–283.

DIAMOND, P., and MCFADDEN, D. 1974. "Some Uses of the Expenditure Function in Public Finance." *Journal of Public Economics* 3:3–21.

DIAMOND, P., and MIRRLEES, J. 1971. "Optimal Taxation and Public Production, I, II." *American Economic Review*. 61:8–27; 261–278.

FOLEY, D. 1967. "Resource Allocation and the Public Sector." *Yale Economic Essays* 7.

GREEN, J., KOHLBERG, E., and LAFFONT, J. 1975. "Partial Equilibrium Approach to the Free Rider Problem." Harvard Discussion Paper no. 436.

GROVES, T., and LEDYARD, J. 1976. "Some Limitations of Demanded Revealing Processes." Northwestern University Discussion Paper No. 219.

———. 1977. "Optimal Allocation of Public Goods: A Solution to the Free Rider Problem." *Econometrica* 45:783–810.

HICKS, J. 1956. *A Revision of Demand Theory*. London: Oxford University Press.

MISHAN, E. 1971. *Cost Benefit Analysis*. New York: Praeger.

PAZNER, E., and SCHMEIDLER, D. 1974. "A Difficulty in the Concept of Fairness." *Review of Economic Studies* 41:441–443.

———. 1972. "Decentralization, Income Distribution, and the Role of Money in Socialist Economies." Technical Report no. 8, The Foerder Institute for Economic Research, Tel Aviv University.

RADNER, R. 1974. "Notes on the Theory of Cost Benefit Analysis in the Small." Unpublished.

SAMUELSON, P. 1964. "The Pure Theory of Public Expenditure." In *Collected Scientific Papers of Paul A. Samuelson*, ed. J. Stiglitz. Cambridge, Mass.: MIT Press, 1966.

SCHMEIDLER, D., and YAARI, M. 1971. "Fair Allocations." Unpublished.

VARIAN, H. 1974. "Equity, Envy, and Efficiency." *Journal of Economic Theory* 9:63–91.

———. 1975. "Distributive Justice, Welfare Economics and the Theory of Fairness." *Philosophy and Public Affairs* 4:223–247.

WILLIG, R. 1976. "Consumer's Surplus without Apology." *American Economic Review* 66:589–597.

Chapter 8

Topics in the Economics of Information

Until this chapter we have made very little mention of the topic of information. This is not unusual for an economics text; until 1960, virtually no discussion of the economics of information was available in an explicit form. Since that time, however, there has been much significant work in the area.

In this chapter we will survey a few topics in the economics of information. The models described are adapted directly from some recently published papers; the acknowledgements and references are given in the notes at the end of the chapter. Before we turn to these models, let us consider how information might affect the neoclassical theory that we have presented thus far.

A very fundamental concept of economics is the concept of a *good*. We have implicitly assumed that all consumers are aware of what goods are available and in fact what each good *is*. But is this really plausible for all goods? Consider, for example, the case of an automobile. All consumers may agree that a particular automobile is a certain model, or a certain vintage. But we all know that there are considerable quality variations in automobiles within a given model-vintage class. In general, we do not know precisely what the *quality* of the car is: is it a good car for its class, or is it a lemon?

Many other goods have quality variations of a similar sort: there are good and bad workers, good and bad restaurants, good and bad houses, and so on. How such quality variations interact with market institutions is one main theme in the economics of information.

The concept of information was explicitly mentioned once in a previous chapter of this text. In the section entitled "Pure Competition" in Chapter 2, we argued that, if consumers are rational and *well informed* about the prices being charged, it is clear that each firm that produces a positive amount of the good in question must sell it at the same price.

Of course, in reality consumers are not always so well informed. It is rational not to be fully informed because, in general, information is costly.

In order to discover what prices are being charged for a particular good one needs to *search* among various firms. Since it is costly to discover what prices are being charged we might expect to see different prices being charged in equilibrium. This topic, the phenomenon of the cost of information and its implication for market institutions, is the second main theme in the economics of information.

8.1 THE MARKET FOR LEMONS

Let us consider the market for automobiles. Suppose for simplicity that there are only four types of cars: good new cars, bad new cars, good used cars, and bad used cars. A certain proportion of the new cars, say q, are good, and thus $1 - q$ are bad. Everyone agrees that the probability of getting a good new car is q. Let us further suppose that a good used car is a perfect substitute for a good new car and a bad used car is a perfect substitution for a bad new car.

There is no particular problem with the functioning of the *new* car market. All consumers are equally well informed about the quality variations in the market. The commodity "a new car" is really a gamble: "with probability q one gets a good new car and with probability $1 - q$ one gets a bad new car." This was called a lottery in the section on expected utility theory, and we saw there how one could integrate such lotteries into our standard utility theory. Hence, we can determine the demand for such lotteries and the price that consumers are willing to pay for such lotteries. These demands can be coupled with an industry supply curve to determine an equilibrium price for new automobiles.

The market for used cars is somewhat different. After one has owned a car for a while, one learns something about the quality of the automobile. The seller of a used car knows more about its quality than the buyer of a used car. The market for used cars exhibits an *asymmetry of information.*

Since we have assumed new and used cars of given qualities are perfect substitutes, this asymmetry of information is the only significant difference between the new and the used car market. Nevertheless, this difference in information affects the operation of the market in fairly serious ways.

Let us consider the equilibrium price of a used car. Since a buyer cannot tell the difference between a good and a bad car, both good and bad cars must sell for the same price. How does this used car price compare to the new car price? Clearly it must be less. For if new and used cars sold at the same price, then it would pay to buy a new car, see if it were a lemon, and then sell it if it was and buy another new car. If the price of a used car were the same as the price of a new car, there would be zero demand for used cars. We conclude that the equilibrium price of a used car must be *less* than the equilibrium price of a new car—even though the proportion of good used cars is the same as the proportion of good new cars!

Of course, the catch is that the proportion of good used cars *offered for sale* may be smaller than the proportion of good new cars offered for sale. At this point it is useful to be a bit more explicit about the decision to sell a used car. Let us suppose that the supply of used cars depends on both the price of new cars and the price of used cars: $S_u(P_N, P_u)$. We might argue that, if the gap between P_u and P_N is rather small, some consumers might well decide they are better off selling their lemon and buying a new car. Of course, this will cost them $P_N - P_u > 0$. Let us suppose for the moment that this is the only motive for selling a used car. Then the equilibrium prices for new and used cars must equate demand and supply in each market; that is, P_N^* and P_u^* must satisfy:

$$D_N(P_N^*, P_u^*) = S_N(P_N^*)$$

$$D_u(P_N^*, P_u^*) = S_u(P_N^*, P_u^*)$$

Now notice an interesting feature about this equilibrium: the only used cars that will ever be sold will be the bad used cars! Just as bad money drives out good money, the lemons will drive the good cars out of the used car market. In this case, the market system serves as a "self-selection" mechanism—the fact that one offers a used car for sale is sufficient evidence that it is a lemon.

Of course, the reason for this is that we assumed that the only motive for selling a used car was to get rid of a lemon. Let us now suppose that there is an additional motive for selling used cars. To keep things simple, we imagine that each year a certain number of consumers T are transferred overseas and have to sell their cars. Of these cars, on the average qT are good and $(1-q)T$ are lemons. The total number of used cars offered for sale is therefore:

$$S_u(P_N, P_u) + T$$

of which $S_u(P_N, P_u) + (1-q)T$ are lemons and qT are good. In such a case, the demand for used cars will depend on the proportion p that the consumers believe are good cars. In equilibrium, this belief of the consumers should be confirmed by their experience. Thus, the equilibrium conditions will take the form:

$$D_N(P_N^*, P_u^*, p^*) = S_N(P_N^*)$$

$$D_u(P_N^*, P_u^*, p^*) = S_u(P_N^*, P_u^*)$$

$$p^* = \frac{qT}{S_u(P_N^*, P_u^*) + (1-q)T}$$

At the equilibrium we would expect $p^* < q$ so that lemons dominated the used car market and $P_u^* < P_N^*$ so that this was reflected in the price of used cars. Notice also that the equilibrium is inefficient at least as compared to the full information equilibrium. A buyer of a used car would be willing to pay more than P_u^* if he were sure of getting a good one, and the seller of a good used car would definitely like to make such a transaction. But the asymmetry of information rules out such trades.

Of course, lemon phenomena occur in many other models. In insurance markets, the lemon principle goes under the name of "adverse selection." In markets for insurance, the basic asymmetry of information is that the purchasers of insurance may well have a better idea of the relevant risks than does the insurance company. For example, suppose an insurance company wants to offer a policy that insures bicycles against theft. They may examine the theft statistics for bicycles and set a rate that would allow them to break even on the policy. But consider what happens when they offer the policy to the public. The people who live in areas with very high theft rates will buy the insurance while those who live in less dangerous areas will not. Thus, the insurance company will have to revise its rates upward in order to break even.

Of course, in actual insurance policies the insurance company tries to sort individuals so that each pays a premium commensurate with his risk class. But as long as there is some residual asymmetry of information so that the insured knows more about his risk situation than the insurer, we would expect to see adverse selection occur.

8.2 *SIGNALS AND PRICES*

In the lemon market model, agents have no way to acquire the information about the quality of the good in question except by observing the average quality available in the market. In many circumstances one can get an estimate of the quality of a good by observing certain features. In the case of an automobile one can go to a garage and pay a mechanic to examine it and appraise its quality. The mechanic's appraisal provides a *signal* about the car's quality; it will reduce, but not eliminate, the risk of acquiring a lemon.

Let us try to model a market with such signals. Let us think for example of the market for the stock in some company. Suppose that the value of the stock depends on an observable signal s and an unobserved random variable ϵ. For example, s could be the current earnings of the company and ϵ could be all sorts of exogenous random factors. We might as well assume a linear relationship:

$$v = s + \epsilon$$

The expected equilibrium price is just $p = v$, but different observations of the random variable will result in different equilibrium prices. The market demand for the stock in question will depend on its price and the value of the signal that is observed.

Suppose that there are two sorts of consumers in the economy: "informed" consumers observe s, while "uninformed" consumers do not. We can think of the informed consumers as being consumers who take the time to examine the annual report of the company, while uninformed consumers don't bother with such details. We write $X(p, s)$ for the market demand of the informed consumers and $X(p)$ for the market demand of the uninformed consumers. Suppose that t per cent of the market is informed and $1 - t$ per cent is uninformed; let X_s be the supply of the good available.

In equilibrium we would expect the market to clear:

$$tX(p, s) + (1 - t)X(p) = X_s$$

For each value of s observed by the informed consumers we would expect to see a different equilibrium price, $p(s)$. Over time uninformed consumers would come to recognize this relationship between the signal s and the equilibrium price. *Hence, any uninformed consumer can infer the value of s simply by observing the equilibrium price.* Thus, the market itself conveys all the information available about the value of the stock.

Of course, this assumes that the market equilibrium *exists,* an assumption that is far from obvious. Suppose, for example, that it is costly to observe the signal s. Think of this as the cost of taking the time to read the annual report. Suppose that initially no consumers are informed ($t = 0$). Then, if the cost of observing s is small, some consumers at least will want to acquire the information, i.e., to examine the annual report. Thus, $t = 0$ cannot be an equilibrium situation.

On the other hand, if some traders are informed ($0 < t \leqq 1$), the market equilibrium price must reflect their information; hence, one might as well save on the cost of observing the signal and just observe the price instead. Thus, there is no reason for anyone to be informed! In this type of market, no equilibrium value of t will exist.

The problem is that the price itself must convey all the information available—so there is no need to purchase the information. But if no one purchases the information, the price cannot convey it.

Let us suppose instead that we have a situation where the price can convey only imperfect information about the signal. Let us suppose that the supply of the good X_s is in fact random. Then, the equilibrium price may be high because informed traders observe a large value of s, or because the (unobserved) value of X_s is low. In this model the uninformed consumer cannot get complete information about s just by observing p.

We therefore write the equilibrium price as a function of both s and $X_s : p = p(s, X_s)$. We assume this function can be inverted to give $s = s(p, X_s)$. Thus, each consumer can determine the value of the signal from the market price *conditional on the possible values of* X_s.

Since X_s is unobserved consumers do not know what the true value of the good in question is; they only know that, for any given of X_s and p, the value will be:

$$v = s(p, X_s) + \epsilon$$

Suppose now that the uninformed consumers have a probability distribution over the possible values of X_s. Then, they can compute the probability distribution of the value of the good from the above equation. They can determine the expected utility of purchasing various amounts of this good and thereby determine their demand, $X(p)$. The informed consumers observe p and s and maximize their expected utility using the same probability distribution on X_s; this determines their demand, $X(p, s)$.

For each realization of supply the market price is determined by

$$tX(p^*, X_s) + (1 - t)\, X(p^*) = X_s$$

The forecasting function used by the uninformed consumers should be rational in the sense that it predicts the right price given the appropriate values of s and X_s. Hence, we need to require that:

$$p^* = p(s, X_s)$$

Since there are costs to observing the signal s, in equilibrium it must be the case that each agent is just indifferent as to whether he should be informed or uninformed. If no one is informed ($t = 0$), the market price will convey no information so it would pay people to become informed. If everyone is informed, the market price will be very informative so it would pay some people to drop out and just observe the price instead. An equilibrium level of t would be one where if an agent switched from being informed to being uninformed it would make the market price just a trifle more noisy, so that the prices no longer conveyed the amount of information compatible with the equilibrium conditions.

It can be shown that under certain assumptions concerning the cost of acquiring the signal s such an equilibrium will exist. Some agents just observe the price to make their decisions, and some purchase an extra signal. The informed agents do better, but their "profits" just cover the cost of acquiring the signal.

8.3 SIGNALING

In the last section we have seen that the price of a commodity may often reflect much of the relevant information about the value of that commodity. In the models presented there, the signal about the value of the commodity was *exogenously supplied*. In some markets, signals may be endogenous in the sense that they may be supplied by members of the market.

Consider, for example, the labor market. It is often felt that education is a signal that conveys information about the productivity of workers. Thus, the wages that workers are offered will depend on the amount of education that they attain. But the amount of education that workers attain will depend on the wages that are offered. What will the equilibrium situation be in such a model?

Let us consider a simple situation where there are only two types of agents, type 1 and type 2. The type-1 workers are b proportion of the market and the type-2 workers are $1-b$ of the market. Let e_1 and e_2 be the amount of education acquired by each of the two types, at a cost of c_1e_1 and c_2e_2 respectively. For expository purposes we will assume that education does not affect productivity at all, so that the marginal products of each type of worker are constants, a_1 and a_2, and output is just a linear function of employment, $y = a_1l_1 + a_2l_2$.

How will workers decide to invest in education? Clearly, they will compare the costs and benefits of acquiring education. How will firms decide how much to pay workers? We will assume that it is very difficult to observe individual ability. Hence, the payment to a worker is based on the observable signal, namely the worker's education; we will assume firms are competitive enough so that the wage of a group of workers with education e is equal to the average ability of the members of that group.

An allocation will consist of a description of the educational levels achieved by each of the two types of workers and the wages received as a function of the education, $w(e)$. An *equilibrium* allocation is one where no agent finds it in his interest to change what he is doing.

As an example, suppose that $c_2 > c_1 > a_2 > a_1$, that everyone is paid the same wage $w(e) = ba_1 + (1-b)a_2$, and that $e_1 = e_2 = 0$. Then, this is an equilibrium. Let's check the behavior of each of the agents. Does it make sense for any firm to raise its wage? No, because then it would be paying workers more than average marginal product. Would any firm lower its wage? No, because then it would lose all of its workers.

Would a worker of type 2 want to acquire any education? No, he would not because he would still get the same wage and incur some cost. Similarly, the type-1 workers would not want to change. Each agent is satisfied. Here the costs of education are too expensive for any worker to want to acquire education; hence, workers are all identical from the point of view of the firm and are just payed their average marginal product.

Now let's consider a very different type of equilibrium. Suppose $a_2 > a_1$, $c_2 < c_1$ and let e^* be any number satisfying the following inequality:

$$\frac{a_2 - a_1}{c_1} < e^* < \frac{a_2 - a_1}{c_2}$$

Then consider the allocation where $e_1 = 0$, $e_2 = e^*$ and $w(e) = a_1$ for $0 \leqq e < e^*$, $w(e) = a_2$ for $e > e^*$. We claim that this is an equilibrium. Does it make sense for any agent to change his behavior? Consider an agent of type 1; the benefit of acquiring education level e^* is the difference in wages $a_2 - a_1$. The cost of acquiring this education level is $c_1 e^*$. Costs exceed benefits if:

$$c_1 e^* > a_2 - a_1$$

But e^* meets this condition by hypothesis.

Now consider type-2 agents. They certainly would not want to acquire any more education than e^* since that increases their costs but doesn't affect their wages at all. Similarly, they would never want to set e_2 at any value where $0 < e_2 < e^*$, for they could lower their costs to 0 by setting $e_2 = 0$ and this would not change their wages at all. Thus, the choice comes down to setting $e_2 = e^*$ or $e_2 = 0$. The benefits to changing from e^* to 0 are the savings in educational costs, $c_2 e^*$. The costs are the lost wages, $a_2 - a_1$. The costs of changing will exceed the benefits if:

$$c_2 e^* < a_2 - a_1$$

But e^* satisfies this inequality by hypothesis.

Now consider the firms. Since all workers of type 1 find it rational to acquire 0 education, paying these workers a_1 is just paying them their marginal product. Similarly, all workers of type 2 acquire education e^*, so they will just be paid their marginal product, a_2.

Notice an interesting feature of the model—there is a whole continuum of equilibria, one for each value of e^* that satisfies the relevant inequality. Notice further that each signaling equilibrium is wasteful in that the same amount of output is produced as in the no-signaling equilibrium, but agents have to pay for the education in the signaling case. The signals do not affect the total amount of output but only how it is divided among the agents. The signal allows for self-selection by the individuals, but it does not result in any more output being produced. It is rational for each individual to acquire the signal, but it is wasteful from the point of view of society.

There are many similar examples of signaling behavior; Spence (1974) mentions a few:

(1) a firm that offers a guarantee for its product signals about durability;
(2) an individual who chooses an insurance policy signals about his perception of the relevant probability;
(3) an individual who chooses the size of the loan and an interest rate signals about the probability of his default;
(4) workers who choose jobs may signal about their abilities, and so on.

These signaling models have many interesting features. The notes at the end of this chapter list some of the relevant references.

8.4 MORAL HAZARD

In the last section we saw how the presence of signals may result in inefficient allocation of resources. However, the absence of signals may cause problems too. Let us consider a situation where we have a market for insurance. For concreteness, let us think of a market for bicycle insurance. We suppose that all consumers are identical and have the same probability of having their bicycle stolen. This removes the adverse selection phenomenon described in Section 8.1, and allows us to simplify the analysis somewhat.

Let us assume that the probability of having one's bicycle stolen depends to some extent on how careful one is; i.e., whether one parks it in well-lit places, whether one locks it securely, and so on. Now if the insurance company can observe the level of care undertaken, there is no problem. They can choose a rate that allows them to break even on the policy they offer. In Example 3.7 we showed that in such circumstances a risk-averse consumer would insure himself fully against a loss.

Suppose on the other hand that the insurance company cannot observe the level of care exercised by the individual agents. Suppose instead it just sets its policy premiums so as to break even given the historical frequency of bicycle thefts—i.e., it sets its policy rates to be consistent with the historical, pre-insurance level of care. Again, as shown in Example 3.7, the consumer will choose to insure himself fully. But now the problem arises—if the consumer is fully insured, why should he be careful? If he is completely insured against loss now, why should he exercise the same level of care as in the pre-insurance case? Presumably he will not, and the insurance company will find itself losing money.

Of course, what we see happening in real life is that insurance companies offer deductible policies. Thus, consumers cannot be fully insured, and this gives them an incentive to exercise some care. However, it is not at all clear that a deductible policy gives the appropriate incentives to offer some optimal level of care. If care could be observed, there would be no problem: consumers could fully insure themselves against risk at whatever level of care they chose. Since care cannot be observed, consumers end up worse off.

8.5 INFORMATION ABOUT PRICES

We turn now to the second aspect of the economics of information mentioned in the introduction to this chapter. In our discussion of consumer behavior in Chapter 2 we argued that, if consumers were rational and fully informed about the prices being charged in a market, there could be only one price in equilibrium. Here we will relax the full-information hypothesis and consider a model where information about the distribution of prices is costly and hence price dispersion can persist.

We will describe a model of price dispersion due to Salop and Stiglitz. The essential feature of the model is that information about the distribution of prices is costly.

We suppose that there are a large number, L, of consumers. Each consumer is willing to pay u dollars for one unit of some commodity, and no consumer wants to purchase more than one unit of the commodity. If there were only one firm in the market, it would clearly charge the monopoly price u.

However, let us assume that there are potentially n firms in the market charging prices $p_1, p_2, \ldots, p_n$. The consumers are assumed to know what prices are available in the market, but they do not know exactly which stores are charging which prices.

However, they can acquire such information by paying a fixed charge. We can think of this as a kind of "search cost." One interpretation would be that there is a large newspaper published which lists all of the stores and the prices being charged. Each consumer can purchase this paper and study the advertisements to determine the best prices. Alternatively a consumer can forgo "searching" and just choose a store at random. The decision depends on the relationship between the best price being charged, $p_{\min}$, the average price being charged, $\bar{p}$, and the consumer's search cost, c_i. Clearly consumer i will become informed about the prices if

$$p_{\min} + c_i < \bar{p}$$

To simplify the analysis, we will assume that there are only two kinds of consumers, a proportion α with search cost c_1 and a proportion $(1 - \alpha)$ with search cost $c_2 \geqq c_1$.

Turning now to the behavior of firms, we will make the assumption that firms behave as monopolistic competitors; that is, each firm is aware that consumers will respond to its pricing decision, but also each firm neglects the impact of its pricing decision on the other firms' behavior. We will examine equilibrium configurations where each firm is maximizing profits given the demand *curve* of the consumers and given the price *levels* of the other firms. Finally we assume that free entry occurs so that profits are driven to zero and each firm is charging a price equal to its average cost of production. We assume positive fixed costs and increasing marginal costs so that average cost curves are U-shaped.

This completes the description of the model. We turn now to a description of the possible equilibrium configurations.

8.6 EQUILIBRIUM CONFIGURATIONS

Salop and Stiglitz describe the possible equilibria in a series of elegant lemmas. We sketch these arguments below. First we note:

Fact 8.1 There can be at most two distinct prices being charged in equilibrium.

PROOF Suppose to the contrary that there were an equilibrium with three prices being charged, denoted by $p_h > p_m > p_l$. If more than one price is being charged it must be that some consumers find it worthwhile to search (and thus only go to the store charging p_l) while some consumers just choose a store at random. But if some consumers choose a store at random, the number of customers, who come to the store charging p_h must be the same as the number who come to the store charging p_m. But this implies that the profits of the firm charging p_h must be greater than those of the firm charging p_m and this contradicts the assumption that we have a zero profit equilibrium. □

Fact 8.2 If a single price equilibrium obtains it must either be at price equals minimum average cost (the competitive price denoted by p^*) or at price equal to u (the monopoly price).

PROOF Suppose to the contrary that we have an equilibrium configuration where each firm charges some price $\hat{p}$ where $p^* < \hat{p} < u$. There are two cases to consider:

(a) $0 < c_1$. Suppose that a firm considers raising its price to $p' = \hat{p} + \epsilon$. This will raise the average price to $\bar{p}' = \hat{p} + \epsilon/n$ but will leave the minimum price at $p_{\min} = \hat{p}$. Now, a type-1 consumer will find it unprofitable to search if

$$\bar{p} < p_{\min} + c_1$$

or

$$\hat{p} + \epsilon/n < \hat{p} + c_1$$

or

$$\epsilon < nc_1$$

Clearly the firm can choose a price rise $\epsilon > 0$ so that no consumer is induced to search. But this means that it will not lose any customers, and thus its profits will increase, again contradicting the assumption of equilibrium.

(b) $c_1 = 0$. Suppose a firm lowers its price from $\hat{p}$ to $\hat{p} - \epsilon$. Since search costs for the informed group are zero, all of this group will immediately come to his firm. Since an arbitrarily small price cut ϵ results in a finite jump in sales, profits must rise, again contradicting the assumption of equilibrium. □

Now we know that all single-price equilibria must have an equilibrium price which is either the competitive price or the monopolistic price. Under what conditions do each of these occur?

8.7 CLASSIFICATION OF SINGLE-PRICE EQUILIBRIA

First, it is clear that if $c_1 = c_2 = 0$ we must have a competitive equilibrium with each store selling at a price $p^* =$ minimum average cost and selling a quantity $q^* = L/n$. This is the conventional perfect information result of a competitive market. Conversely, the argument presented in part (a) of the proof of Fact 8.2 shows that, if $c_2 \geqq c_1 > 0$, a competitive equilibrium can not obtain. This is because a small price rise by any single firm will not induce any customers to search.

Therefore we consider the case where $c_2 > c_1 = 0$. In this case, a firm which raises its price by any small $\epsilon > 0$ will lose all of its type-1 customers and none of its type-2 customers. It will thus receive a higher revenue on smaller sales, which may raise or lower its profits.

Clearly, if a deviant firm raises its price, it will raise it as high as it can without inducing type-2 customers to search.

This break-even price p_d is given by:

$$p_{\min} + c_2 = \bar{p}$$

which in this case is given by: $p^* + c_2 = p^* + \frac{1}{n}(p_d - p^*)$

or

$$p_d = p^* + nc_2$$

Of course p_d must also be less than u, or else no one will buy the good at all. At the price p_d, the deviant firm will get only its share of the uninformed people and its total sales will be

$$q_d = \frac{(1-\alpha)L}{n}$$

This strategy of raising price above the competitive price will be *unprofitable* if

$$p_d < AC(q_d)$$

or

$$AC\left(\frac{(1-\alpha)L}{n}\right) > \min\,[u,\, p^* + nc_2]$$

This condition may well hold when u and c_2 are small or, most importantly, when α is large; that is, the competitive equilibrium will obtain when a large proportion—but not necessarily all—of the market is well informed. Thus the well-informed consumers exert a beneficial externality on the uninformed consumers—as long as there are enough smart shoppers, the classical competitive forces ensure that all consumers pay the lowest possible price.

A similar sort of analysis can be done to determine conditions under which the monopoly price equilibrium prevails. For large L and large n, the condition boils down to

$$u - p^* \leqq c_1 \leqq c_2$$

This condition is fairly intuitive. If a firm considers lowering its price from u to p^*, the gains from search will be approximately $u - p^*$. As long as this is less than the cost of search, consumers will not find it in their interest to search, and the monopoly price equilibrium will persist.

8.8 TWO-PRICE EQUILIBRIA

In the preceding discussion we have established that we get a single-price equilibrium when:

(1) $c_1 = c_2 = 0$
(2) $AC((1-\alpha)L/n) > \min[u, p^* + nc_2]$
(3) $u - p^* \leqq c_1 \leqq c_2$

Cases (1) and (2) result in the competitive price equilibrium p^* while case (3) gives the monopoly price u. For all other values of the parameters either an equilibrium will not exist or a two-price equilibrium obtains.

Sufficient conditions for existence of a two-price equilibrium are rather delicate; it turns out that existence depends critically on the global behavior of the average cost curve. Salop and Stiglitz analyze the conditions for existence of a two-price equilibrium in the reference cited in the notes at the end of this chapter.

We can however establish *necessary* conditions for a two-price equilibrium; that is, assuming a two-price equilibrium exists we can describe what it looks like. Let us describe a two-price equilibrium by three numbers (β, p_l, p_h) where β is the proportion of firms charging the low price, p_l, and $(1-\beta)$ is the proportion of firms charging the high price, p_h. We can show

Fact 8.3 The low price, p_l, must equal the competitive price p^*.

PROOF The argument is similar to the argument for Fact 8.2. Since we have by hypothesis a two-price equilibrium some proportion of the consumers must be informed. Therefore any firm charging $p > p^*$ could lower its price by a small amount and capture all of the informed customers. □

Fact 8.4 The high price is either the monopoly price or a price that makes the type 2 consumers indifferent between becoming informed or purchasing randomly; that is, $p_h = \min[u, p^* + c_2/(1-\beta)]$

PROOF Suppose that $p_h < p_l + c_2/(1-\beta)$. Rearranging this inequality we have:

$$p_{\min} + c_2 = p^* + c_2 > \beta p^* + (1-\beta)p_h = \bar{p}$$

This implies that type-2 consumers do not find it profitable to engage in search. Thus any firm that raised its price by ϵ would not lose customers, which contradicts profit maximization. □

The above two facts characterize two-price equilibria, assuming that they exist.

The above model of price dispersion is meant only to be indicative of the kinds of phenomena that imperfect differential information may generate. We have seen that in certain cases the classical cases of monopolistic or competitive market structures may emerge, while in other cases we may find markets where several prices are charged. This does seem to have real life counterparts: many retail industries exhibit price dispersion in the form of *sales*. Some consumers read ads and shop wisely to take advantage of sales while other consumers shop randomly. At any one time several prices may prevail: the institution of sales allows stores to discriminate among consumers and attract the smart shoppers during the sales yet still exploit the uninformed consumers during other times.

8.9 SUMMARY

We have surveyed four models in the economics of information. The first three were concerned with *signals* and how signals interacted with prices in the market place. We might describe these three models as describing various aspects of the *supply* of information. The lemon model showed how one may supply information in the very act of attempting to buy or sell a good. The signals and prices model showed how exogenous information about a good might be translated into price information. Finally, the signaling model showed how consumers might choose to supply signals in order to further their own interests.

The fourth model was concerned with the *demand* for information, in the sense that we were concerned about how consumers determine how much to search for low prices and what resulting equilibrium price distributions might be like.

The brief discussions of these models in this chapter have only scratched the surface of this important area. The reader is urged to consult the original sources listed in the notes at the end of the chapter.

Notes

The lemon market model is due to Akerloff (1970). The material on signals and prices was taken from Grossman and Stiglitz (1976). The material on signaling was taken from Spence (1974).

The material on price dispersion was taken from Salop and Stiglitz (1976). Other models of price dispersion can be found in Pratt, Wise, and Zeckhauser (1975) and Rothchild (1973). Lippman and McCall (1976) provide a fairly complete theory of the search literature.

References

AKERLOFF, G. 1970. "The Market for Lemons: Qualitative Uncertainty and the Market Mechanism." *Quarterly Journal of Economics* 84:488–500.

GROSSMAN, S., and STIGLITZ, J. 1976. "Information and Competitive Price Systems." *American Economic Review* 66:246–253.

LIPPMAN, S., and MCCALL, J. 1976. "The Economics of Job Search: A Survey." *Economic Inquiry* 14:155–189.

PRATT, J., WISE, D.; and ZECKHAUSER, R. 1975. "Price Variations in Almost Competitive Markets." Kennedy School of Government Discussion Paper no. 37D. To appear in *Quarterly Journal of Economics*.

ROTHSCHILD, M. 1973. "Models of Market Organization with Imperfect Information: A Survey." *Journal of Political Economy* 81:1,283–1,308.

SALOP, S., and STIGLITZ, J. 1976. "Bargains and Ripoffs." *Review of Economic Studies* 44:493–510.

SPENCE, M. 1974. *Market Signalling*. Cambridge, Mass.: Harvard University Press.

Mathematical Appendix

The main mathematical requirements for this text are calculus and elementary linear algebra. In addition, some multivariate calculus and elementary analysis are used in a few sections. Finally, some special topics concerning convexity, maximization, and so on are used in various places throughout the book.

We will review these basic mathematical topics in this appendix. This is most definitely a *review;* it is not meant to be a self-contained introduction to these topics. For such an introduction one should consult the references listed at the end of this chapter. As in the rest of the text, we will indicate optional advanced material by an M in the margin.

A.1 LINEAR ALGEBRA

We will denote the set of all n-tuples of real numbers by R^n. The set of all n-tuples of *nonnegative* real numbers is denoted by R^n_+. The elements of these sets will be referred to as "*points*" or "*vectors*." Vectors are indicated by boldface type. If $\mathbf{x} = (x_1, x_2, \cdots, x_n)$ is a vector, we will denote its ith component by x_i. We can *add* two vectors by adding their components: $\mathbf{x} + \mathbf{y} = (x_1 + y_1,\ x_2 + y_2, \cdots,\ x_n + y_n)$. We can perform *scalar multiplication* on a vector by multiplying every component by some fixed real number t: $t\mathbf{x} = (tx_1, \cdots,\ tx_n)$. Geometrically, vector addition of $\mathbf{x}$ and $\mathbf{y}$ is done by drawing the vector $\mathbf{x}$ and translating $\mathbf{y}$ to the head of $\mathbf{x}$; scalar multiplication is done by drawing a vector t times as long as the original vector. A vector $\mathbf{x}$ is a *linear combination* of a set of vectors A if $\mathbf{x} = \sum_{\mathbf{y}_i \text{ in } A} t_i \mathbf{y}_i$ for some set of scalars t_i. A set of vectors A is *linearly independent* if there is no nonzero set of scalars (t^i) such that $\Sigma t^i \mathbf{x}^i = 0$ for some set of $\mathbf{x}^i$ in A. An equivalent definition is that no vector in A can be represented as a linear combination of the other vectors in A.

Given two vectors we can form their *dot product:* $\mathbf{x} \cdot \mathbf{y} = \sum_{i=1}^{n} x_i y_i$. We can define the *norm* of $\mathbf{x}$, $|\mathbf{x}|$ as being $|\mathbf{x}| = \sqrt{\mathbf{x} \cdot \mathbf{x}}$. Notice that the norm of $\mathbf{x}$ is just the distance of $\mathbf{x}$ from the origin, or equivalently, the length of the vector $\mathbf{x}$ (apply the Pythagorean theorem.)

There is a very important geometric interpretation of the dot product, illustrated in Figure A.1. We have two vectors $\mathbf{x}$ and $\mathbf{y}$; the dotted line is

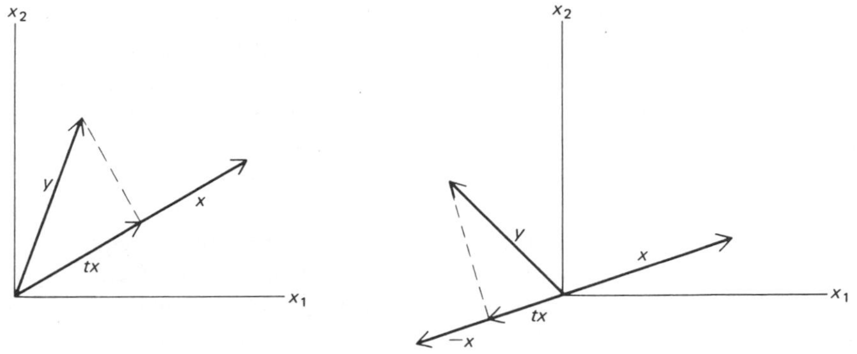

A.1 *The Projection of* **y** *on* **x**

dropped from the head of $\mathbf{y}$ to $\mathbf{x}$ and is perpendicular to $\mathbf{x}$. The vector $\mathbf{z}$ from the tail of $\mathbf{x}$ to the point where the dotted line intersects $\mathbf{x}$ is called the *projection of* $\mathbf{y}$ *on* $\mathbf{x}$. Certainly the projection of $\mathbf{y}$ on $\mathbf{x}$ is a vector of the form $t\mathbf{x}$. Let us calculate t. By the Pythagorean formula,

$$|t\mathbf{x}|^2 + |\mathbf{y} - t\mathbf{x}|^2 = |\mathbf{y}|^2$$

$$t^2\mathbf{x}\cdot\mathbf{x} + (\mathbf{y} - t\mathbf{x})\cdot(\mathbf{y} - t\mathbf{x}) = \mathbf{y}\cdot\mathbf{y}$$

$$t^2\mathbf{x}\cdot\mathbf{x} + \mathbf{y}\cdot\mathbf{y} - 2t\mathbf{x}\cdot\mathbf{y} + t^2\mathbf{x}\cdot\mathbf{x} = \mathbf{y}\cdot\mathbf{y}$$

$$t\mathbf{x}\cdot\mathbf{x} = \mathbf{x}\cdot\mathbf{y}$$

$$t = \frac{\mathbf{x}\cdot\mathbf{y}}{\mathbf{x}\cdot\mathbf{x}}$$

This formula says that if we project $\mathbf{y}$ on $\mathbf{x}$ we get a vector that points in the same direction as $\mathbf{x}$ but is only $\dfrac{\mathbf{x}\cdot\mathbf{y}}{|\mathbf{x}|}$ times as long as $\mathbf{x}$. If $\mathbf{x}\cdot\mathbf{y} = 0$, $\mathbf{x}$ and $\mathbf{y}$ are said to be *orthogonal*. Let θ be the angle between $\mathbf{x}$ and $\mathbf{y}$. Then it is clear from elementary trigonometry that $t|\mathbf{x}| = |\mathbf{y}| \cos\theta$. If we combine this with the other formula for t we get $\mathbf{x}\cdot\mathbf{y} = |\mathbf{x}||\mathbf{y}| \cos\theta$. Hence if $\theta = 90°$, we have $\mathbf{x}\cdot\mathbf{y} = 0$; if θ is greater than $90°$, $\mathbf{x}\cdot\mathbf{y} < 0$, and if θ is smaller than $90°$, $\mathbf{x}\cdot\mathbf{y} > 0$.

We can consider maps between R^n and R^m that send vectors into vectors; we denote such maps by $\mathbf{f}: R^n \to R^m$. A map $\mathbf{f}: R^n \to R^m$ is a *linear function* if $\mathbf{f}(t\mathbf{x} + s\mathbf{y}) = t\mathbf{f}(\mathbf{x}) + s\mathbf{f}(\mathbf{y})$ for all scalars t and s and vectors $\mathbf{x}$ and $\mathbf{y}$. If $\mathbf{f}$ is a linear function and $\mathbf{f}$ goes to R^1, $\mathbf{f}: R^n \to R$, $\mathbf{f}$ is called a *linear functional*. If $\mathbf{p}$ is a linear functional we can represent $\mathbf{p}$ by a vector $\mathbf{p} = (p_1 \cdots p_n)$; in this case $\mathbf{p}(\mathbf{x}) = \mathbf{p} \cdot \mathbf{x} = \sum_{i=1}^{n} p_i x_i$. A set of points $H(\mathbf{p}, a) = \{\mathbf{x} \text{ in } R^n: \mathbf{p} \cdot \mathbf{x} = a\}$ is called a *hyperplane*.

The hyperplane $H(\mathbf{p}, 0)$ consists of all vectors $\mathbf{x}$ that are orthogonal to the vector $\mathbf{p}$. It is not hard to see that it is an $n - 1$ dimensional set. The hyperplanes of the form $H(\mathbf{p}, a)$ are just translations of this basic hyperplane $H(\mathbf{p}, 0)$. Hyperplanes are important in economic analysis since $H(\mathbf{p}, a)$ consists of all vectors $\mathbf{x}$ that have value a at the prices $\mathbf{p}$, that is, all vectors $\mathbf{x}$ such that $\mathbf{p} \cdot \mathbf{x} = a$.

If $\mathbf{A}$ is a linear function $\mathbf{A}: R^n \to R^m$, we can represent $\mathbf{A}$ by an n-by-m matrix $\mathbf{A} = (a_{ij})$. Then $\mathbf{A}(\mathbf{x}) = \mathbf{A}\mathbf{x}$; i.e., to find the image of $\mathbf{x}$ under the map $\mathbf{A}$ we just apply ordinary matrix multiplication. A *symmetric* matrix is one such that $a_{ij} = a_{ji}$ for all i and j.

We will follow a standard sign convention for vectors and write $\mathbf{x} \geqq \mathbf{y}$ if $x_i \geqq y_i$ for all i and $\mathbf{x} \gg \mathbf{y}$ if $x_i > y_i$ for all i.

A.2 DEFINITE AND SEMIDEFINITE MATRICES

Let $\mathbf{A}$ be a square matrix. Then, if we premultiply $\mathbf{A}$ by some vector $\mathbf{x}$ and postmultiply $\mathbf{A}$ by the same vector $\mathbf{x}$, we say we have a *quadratic form*. For example,

$$[x_1 x_2] \begin{bmatrix} a_{11} & a_{12} \\ a_{21} & a_{22} \end{bmatrix} \begin{bmatrix} x_{12} \\ x_{22} \end{bmatrix} = a_{11}x_1^2 + (a_{21} + a_{12})x_1x_2 + a_{22}x_2^2$$

Suppose that $\mathbf{A}$ is an identity matrix. In this case whatever the values of x_1 and x_2, the resulting expression must be nonnegative, and, in fact, it will be strictly positive as long as x_1 and x_2 are not both zero. The identity matrix is an example of a *positive definite matrix*.

DEFINITION A matrix $\mathbf{A}$ is:

(a) positive definite if $\mathbf{xAx} > 0$ for all $\mathbf{x} \neq 0$;
(b) negative definite if $\mathbf{xAx} < 0$ for all $\mathbf{x} \neq 0$;
(c) positive semidefinite if $\mathbf{xAx} \geq 0$ for all $\mathbf{x}$;
(d) negative semidefinite if $\mathbf{xAx} \leq 0$ for all $\mathbf{x}$.

In certain cases we do not want to require that $\mathbf{xAx}$ has a definite sign for *all* values that $\mathbf{x}$ could take on. We will say that $\mathbf{A}$ is *positive definite subject to the constraint* $\mathbf{bx} = 0$ if $\mathbf{xAx} > 0$ for all $\mathbf{x}$ such that $\mathbf{bx} = 0$.

The other definitions extend to the constrained case in a natural manner.

It is often convenient to have an operational criterion to recognize a negative or positive definite matrix. There is a simple necessary condition: if a matrix is positive semidefinite, its diagonal terms must all be nonnegative. The proof is simply to note that if $\mathbf{x} = (1, 0, 0, \cdots, 0)$, then $\mathbf{xAx} = a_{11} \geq 0$. This fact has an obvious generalization to the other three cases described above.

The necessary and sufficient condition takes a more complicated form. The *minor matrices* of a matrix A are those matrices one forms by eliminating any k columns and the same numbered k rows.

The *naturally ordered (or nested) principal minor matrices* of a matrix A are those minor matrices given by:

$$a_{11} \quad \begin{bmatrix} a_{11} & a_{12} \\ a_{21} & a_{22} \end{bmatrix} \quad \begin{bmatrix} a_{11} & a_{12} & a_{13} \\ a_{21} & a_{22} & a_{23} \\ a_{31} & a_{32} & a_{33} \end{bmatrix}$$

The *minor determinants* of a matrix A are just the determinants of the minors, and similarly for the principal minor determinants. It is a common practice to drop the word *determinants* and just refer to the determinants themselves as the minors and principal minors of a matrix.

Suppose now that we are given a matrix $\mathbf{A}$ and a vector $\mathbf{b}$ as above. We can "border" A by the vector $\mathbf{b}$ in the following way:

$$\begin{bmatrix} a_{11} & \cdots & a_{1n} & b_1 \\ \cdot & & & \cdot \\ \cdot & & & \cdot \\ \cdot & & & \cdot \\ a_{n1} & & a_{nn} & b_n \\ b_1 & \cdots & b_n & 0 \end{bmatrix}$$

This matrix is called the *bordered matrix*. The useful generalization of the minor matrices to this case is what is called the *border-preserving principal minors*. They are simply the submatrices formed by deleting the appropriate rows and columns of the matrix A and deleting the *same* numbered elements of the border, but not deleting the border itself. Thus the deletions can only come from rows and columns 1 through n and not from row or column $n + 1$, which is the location of the border.

Now we can state the algebraic criterion for a matrix to be definite subject to a linear constraint:

Theorem A matrix $\mathbf{A}$ is

(a) *positive definite* if and only if the principal minor determinants are all positive;

(b) *negative definite* if and only if the principal minor determinants of order k have sign $(-1)^k$ for $k = 1, \cdots, n$.
(c) *positive definite subject to* $\mathbf{bx} = 0$ if and only if the border-preserving principal minors of the bordered matrix are all negative;
(d) *negative definite subject to* $\mathbf{bx} = 0$ if and only if the border-preserving principal minors of the bordered matrix have sign $(-1)^k$ for $k = 2, \cdots, n$.

This theorem has a corollary that is sometimes useful. In each of the four cases described above it can be shown that if the naturally ordered principal minors have the appropriate property, then *all* of the principal minors will have the relevant property.

A.3 CRAMER'S RULE

Here is a convenient rule for solving linear systems of equations of the form:

$$\begin{bmatrix} a_{11} & \cdots & a_{1n} \\ \cdot & & \cdot \\ \cdot & & \cdot \\ \cdot & & \cdot \\ a_{n1} & \cdots & a_{nn} \end{bmatrix} \cdot \begin{bmatrix} x_1 \\ \cdot \\ \cdot \\ \cdot \\ x_n \end{bmatrix} = \begin{bmatrix} b_1 \\ \cdot \\ \cdot \\ \cdot \\ b_n \end{bmatrix}$$

which we can write more conveniently at $\mathbf{Ax} = \mathbf{b}$.

CRAMER'S RULE To find the component x_i of the solution vector of this system of linear equations, replace the ith column of the matrix A with the column vector $\mathbf{b}$ to form a matrix $\mathbf{A}_i$. Then x_i is simply the determinant of $\mathbf{A}_i$ divided by the determinant of $\mathbf{A}$. That is, $x_i = |\mathbf{A}_i|/|\mathbf{A}|$.

(M) A.4 ANALYSIS

Given a vector $\mathbf{x}$ in R^n and a positive real number e we define an *open ball of radius e at* $\mathbf{x}$ as: $B_e(\mathbf{x}) = \{\mathbf{y} \text{ in } R^n: |\mathbf{y} - \mathbf{x}| < e\}$. A set of points A is called *open* if for every $\mathbf{x}$ in A there is some $B_e(\mathbf{x})$ which is contained in A. If $\mathbf{x}$ is in arbitrary set A and there is an e such that $B_e(\mathbf{x})$ is contained in A, $\mathbf{x}$ is said to be in the *interior of A*. A set A is called *closed* if $R^n \setminus A$ is an open set. ($R^n \setminus A$ is the set which consists of all points in R^n that are not in A.) A set A is called *bounded* if there is some $\mathbf{x}$ and some e such that A is contained in $B_e(\mathbf{x})$. If a set in R^n is both closed and bounded it is called *compact*. A set N is a *neighborhood* of a point $\mathbf{x}$ if $\mathbf{x}$ is in the interior of N.

A sequence in R^n, $(\mathbf{x}^i) = (\mathbf{x}^1, \mathbf{x}^2, \mathbf{x}^3, \ldots)$ is just an infinite set of points in R^n, one point for each positive integer i.

A sequence $(\mathbf{x}^i)$ is said to converge to a point $\mathbf{x}^*$ if for every $e > 0$ there is an integer m such that, for all i greater than m, $\mathbf{x}^i$ is in $B_e(\mathbf{x}^*)$. We sometimes express this by saying that $\mathbf{x}^i$ eventually gets as close to $\mathbf{x}^*$ as we want. We also say $\mathbf{x}^*$ is the limit of $(\mathbf{x}^i)$ and write it as $\lim_{i\to\infty} \mathbf{x}^i = \mathbf{x}^*$. If a sequence converges to some point, we call it a *convergent sequence*.

Fact A.1 *A is a closed set if every convergent sequence in A converges to a point in A.*

Fact A.2 *If A is compact then every sequence in A has a convergent subsequence.*

A function $\mathbf{f}: R^n \to R^m$ is *continuous* at $\mathbf{x}^*$ if for every sequence $(\mathbf{x}^i)$ which converges to x^* we have the sequence $(\mathbf{f}(\mathbf{x}^i))$ converging to $\mathbf{f}(\mathbf{x}^*)$. A function which is continuous at every point in its domain is called a *continuous function*.

A.5 CALCULUS

Calculus is a way of tying linear algebra and analysis together by approximating certain functions by linear transformations. Given a function $f: R \to R$ we define its derivative at a point x^* by the number $\frac{df(x^*)}{dx} = \lim_{t\to 0} \frac{f(x^* + t) - f(x^*)}{t}$ if that limit exists. The derivative $df(x^*)/dx$ is also denoted by $f'(x^*)$. If the derivative of f exists at x^*, we say f is *differentiable* at x^*. We can view $\frac{df(x^*)}{dx}$ as a linear transformation:

$$\frac{df(x^*)}{dx} : R \to R \quad \text{where} \quad \frac{df(x^*)}{dx}(t) = t\,\frac{df(x^*)}{dx}\text{; that is,}$$

to find the image of t under the map $\frac{df(x^*)}{dx}$ we just multiply the number $\frac{df(x^*)}{dx}$ by the number t. The map $f(x^*) + \frac{df(x^*)}{dx}\,t$ is a good approximation to the map f near x^* since $f(x^* + t)$ is approximately $f(x^*) + \frac{df(x^*)}{dx}\,t$; that is,

$$\lim_{t\to 0} \frac{f(x^* + t) - f(x^*) - \frac{df(x^*)}{dx}\,t}{t} = 0$$

In the same way if we are given a map $\mathbf{f}: R^n \to R^m$ we can define its derivative at the vector $\mathbf{x}^*$, $\mathbf{Df}(\mathbf{x}^*)$, as being that linear map from $R^n \to R^m$ that approximates $\mathbf{f}$ close to $\mathbf{x}^*$ in the sense that

$$\lim_{|\mathbf{t}| \to 0} \frac{|\mathbf{f}(\mathbf{x}^* + \mathbf{t}) - \mathbf{f}(\mathbf{x}^*) - \mathbf{Df}(\mathbf{x}^*)\,\mathbf{t}|}{|\mathbf{t}|} = 0$$

We have to use norm signs since both the numerator and the denominator are vectors. The map $\mathbf{f}(\mathbf{x}^*) + \mathbf{Df}(\mathbf{x}^*)$ is a good approximation to f at $\mathbf{x}^*$ in the sense that for small vectors $\mathbf{h}$

$$\mathbf{f}(\mathbf{x}^* + \mathbf{h}) \approx \mathbf{f}(\mathbf{x}^*) + \mathbf{Df}(\mathbf{x}^*) \cdot \mathbf{h}$$

Given a function $f: R^n \to R$ we can also define the partial derivative of f with respect to x_i evaluated at $\mathbf{x}^*$ by holding all components of $\mathbf{x}^*$ fixed except for the ith component and evaluating the above limit as x_i approaches x_i^*. We denote this partial derivative by $\partial f(\mathbf{x}^*)/\partial x_i$.

Since $\mathbf{Df}(\mathbf{x}^*)$ is a linear transformation, we can represent it by a matrix; to determine that representation we only have to determine what the transformation does to a set of n-linearly independent vectors. Thus, if we regard $\mathbf{f}: R^n \to R^m$ as a set of maps $f = (f^1 \cdots f^m)$, we know that $\partial f^j(\mathbf{x}^*)/\partial x_i$ closely approximates the behavior of f^j along the ith coordinate near $\mathbf{x}^*$. Therefore the matrix representation of $\mathbf{Df}(\mathbf{x}^*)$ should just be:

$$\mathbf{Df}(\mathbf{x}^*) = \begin{bmatrix} \dfrac{\partial f^1(\mathbf{x}^*)}{\partial x_1} & \cdots & \dfrac{\partial f^1(\mathbf{x}^*)}{\partial x_n} \\ \vdots & & \vdots \\ \dfrac{\partial f^m(\mathbf{x}^*)}{\partial x_1} & \cdots & \dfrac{\partial f^m(\mathbf{x}^*)}{\partial x_n} \end{bmatrix}$$

The matrix representing $\mathbf{Df}(\mathbf{x}^*)$ is called the *Jacobian matrix* of $\mathbf{f}$ at $\mathbf{x}^*$. We will often work with functions from R^n to R so that $\mathbf{Df}(\mathbf{x}^*)$ will be an n-by-1 matrix, or just a vector.

If there is a linear map that approximates the behavior of $\mathbf{f}$ at $\mathbf{x}$ in the sense just described, $\mathbf{f}$ is said to be *differentiable* at $\mathbf{x}$. If $\mathbf{f}$ is differentiable at every point, $\mathbf{f}$ is called a *differentiable function*.

Sometimes we have a function $f: R^n \times R^m \to R$ of the form $f(\mathbf{x}, \mathbf{y})$ where $\mathbf{x}$ is in R^n and $\mathbf{y}$ is in R^m. A convenient way to denote the derivative of this function with respect to the x variables is $\mathbf{D_x}f(\mathbf{x}^*, \mathbf{y}^*)$. Note that $\mathbf{Df}(\mathbf{x}^*, \mathbf{y}^*) = (\mathbf{D_x}f(\mathbf{x}^*, \mathbf{y}^*), \mathbf{D_y}f(\mathbf{x}^*, \mathbf{y}^*))$ and $\mathbf{D}_{x_i}f(\mathbf{x}^*, \mathbf{y}^*) = \partial f(\mathbf{x}^*, \mathbf{y}^*)/\partial x_i$ for $i = 1, \cdots, n$.

If we have a function $f: R^n \to R$ we can define a new function $\mathbf{f}': R^n \to$

R^n by $\mathbf{f}'(x) = \mathbf{Df}(\mathbf{x})$. This function also has a derivative which we define by

$$\mathbf{D}^2 f(\mathbf{x}) = \mathbf{D}(\mathbf{Df}(\mathbf{x}))$$

$\mathbf{D}^2 f(\mathbf{x})$ can be represented by an n-by-n matrix of second partial derivatives $\left(\frac{\partial^2 f(\mathbf{x})}{\partial x_i \partial x_j}\right)$; this matrix is called the *Hessian* of f at $\mathbf{x}$.

This process can be continued to define third, fourth, and n^{th} derivatives. If *all* derivatives are well defined—that is, if all the appropriate limits exist—the function will be said to be *smooth*. Any continuous function on a compact set can be arbitrarily closely approximated by a smooth function. Hence, we will generally assume the functions that we encounter are smooth, although much weaker assumptions will usually suffice.

Let $f: R^n \rightarrow R$, and let $\mathbf{x}$ and $\mathbf{y}$ be two vectors. Then it can be shown that

$$f(\mathbf{y}) = f(\mathbf{x}) + \mathbf{D}f(\mathbf{z}) \cdot (\mathbf{y} - \mathbf{x})$$

$$f(\mathbf{y}) = f(\mathbf{x}) + \mathbf{D}f(\mathbf{x}) \cdot (\mathbf{y} - \mathbf{x}) + \frac{(\mathbf{y} - \mathbf{x})\mathbf{D}^2 f(\mathbf{w})(\mathbf{y} - \mathbf{x})}{2}$$

where $\mathbf{z}$ and $\mathbf{w}$ are points on the line segment between $\mathbf{x}$ and $\mathbf{y}$. These expressions are called the *Taylor series expansions* of f at $\mathbf{x}$.

If $\mathbf{x}$ and $\mathbf{y}$ are close together and f is a smooth function, then $\mathbf{Df}(\mathbf{y})$ is approximately equal to $\mathbf{Df}(\mathbf{z})$, and $\mathbf{D}^2 f(\mathbf{y})$ is approximately equal to $\mathbf{D}^2 f(\mathbf{w})$. We therefore often write the Taylor expansion as:

$$f(\mathbf{y}) \approx f(\mathbf{x}) + \mathbf{D}f(\mathbf{x}) \cdot (\mathbf{y} - \mathbf{x})$$

$$f(\mathbf{y}) \approx f(\mathbf{x}) + \mathbf{D}f(\mathbf{x}) \cdot (\mathbf{y} - \mathbf{x}) + \frac{(\mathbf{y} - \mathbf{x})\mathbf{D}^2 f(\mathbf{x})(\mathbf{y} - \mathbf{x})}{2}$$

where the symbol $\approx$ stands for the relationship "approximately equal to."

A.6 CONVEXITY

A function $f: R^n \rightarrow R$ is *concave* if $f(t\mathbf{x} + (1-t)\,\mathbf{y}) \geqq tf(\mathbf{x}) + (1-t)f(\mathbf{y})$ for $0 \leqq t \leqq 1$. If f is twice differentiable we have equivalent criteria:

Fact A.3 *The function* f *is concave if* $\mathrm{f}(\mathbf{y}) \leqq \mathrm{f}(\mathbf{x}) + \mathbf{D}f(\mathbf{x})(\mathbf{y} - \mathbf{x})$ *for all* $\mathbf{x}$ *and* $\mathbf{y}$ *in* R^n. *The function* f *is concave if the matrix of second derivatives* $\mathbf{D}^2\mathrm{f}(\mathbf{x})$ *is negative semidefinite at all* $\mathbf{x}$.

The first part of Fact A.3 is geometrically obvious from Figure A.2 below. It says that the graph of a concave function always lies below its tangent line. In higher dimensions, we say that the graph of a concave function always lies below its tangent hyperplane.

The second part of Fact A.3 follows from the first part and a simple Taylor expansion:

$$f(\mathbf{y}) \leqq f(\mathbf{x}) + \mathbf{D}f(\mathbf{x})(\mathbf{y} - \mathbf{x})$$

$$f(\mathbf{x}) + \mathbf{D}f(\mathbf{x})(\mathbf{y} - \mathbf{x}) + 1/2(\mathbf{y} - \mathbf{x})\mathbf{D}^2 f(\mathbf{w})(\mathbf{y} - \mathbf{x}) \leqq f(\mathbf{x}) + \mathbf{D}f(\mathbf{x})(\mathbf{y} - \mathbf{x})$$

so

$$(\mathbf{y} - \mathbf{x})\mathbf{D}^2 f(\mathbf{w})(\mathbf{y} - \mathbf{x}) \leqq 0 \qquad \text{for all } \mathbf{x} \text{ and } \mathbf{y}.$$

But this is just the definition of a negative semidefinite matrix.

A set of points A in R^n is *convex* if $\mathbf{x}$, $\mathbf{y}$ in A implies $t\mathbf{x} + (1 - t)\,\mathbf{y}$ is in A for $0 \leqq t \leqq 1$. It is easy to see that if f is a concave function then $A = \{\mathbf{x}$ in $R^n\!: f(\mathbf{x}) \geqq a\}$ is a convex set. Unfortunately, a set of the form of A may be convex even if f isn't concave. We will say a function $f\!:R^n \rightarrow R$ is *quasi-concave* if $A = \{\mathbf{x}$ in $R^n\!:f(\mathbf{x}) \geqq a\}$ is a convex set. Clearly, every concave function is also quasi-concave. A function f is *quasi-convex* if $-f$ is quasi-concave.

Fact A.4 *If A and B are two convex sets that are disjoint, there exists a linear functional* $\mathbf{p} \neq 0$ *such that* $\mathbf{p}\cdot\mathbf{x} \geqq \mathbf{p}\cdot\mathbf{y}$ *for all* $\mathbf{x}$ *in A and* $\mathbf{y}$ *in B.*

This fact is called the separating hyperplane theorem, since the theorem says that, if A and B are two disjoint convex sets, we can find a hyperplane $H(\mathbf{p}, a)$ that lies between them. See Figure A.3.

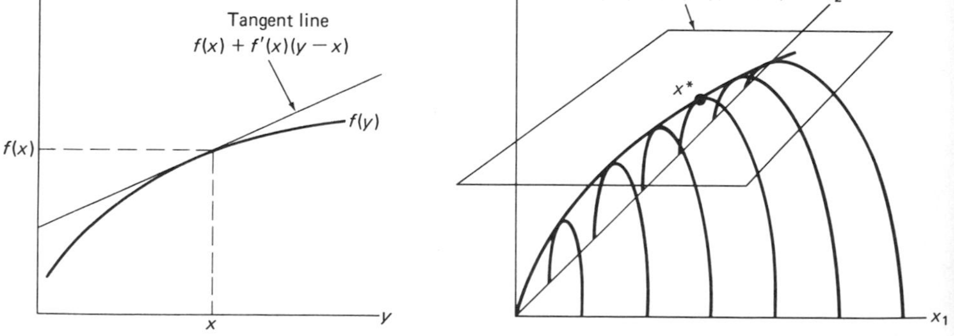

A.2 *A Concave Function*

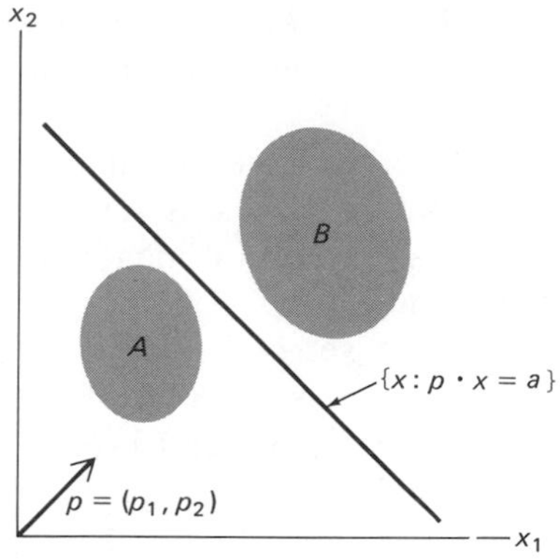

A.3 *A Separating Hyperplane*

Fact A.5 *If $f : A \to R$ is concave, then f is continuous at all $\mathbf{x}$ in the interior of A.*

If a function f is both concave and convex then it is called *affine;* that is, f is affine if

$$f(t\mathbf{x} + (1 - t)\mathbf{y}) = tf(\mathbf{x}) + (1 - t)f(\mathbf{y})$$

If we have an affine function $f : R \to R$ then f can be written as

$$f(x) = ax + b$$

This is true in general but is most easy to prove in the differentiable case. In this situation we have $f''(x) \geqq 0$ and $f''(x) \leqq 0$ since f is both concave and convex. Therefore $f''(x) = 0$ for all x and the result follows immediately.

A.7 THE IMPLICIT FUNCTION THEOREM

Suppose that we have a linear function $\mathbf{A} : R^n \to R^m$ where $m \leqq n$. Suppose that the linear function (matrix) $\mathbf{A}$ has rank k. We know from basic linear algebra that the set of points $N = \{\mathbf{x} \text{ in } R^n : \mathbf{Ax} = 0\}$ forms a linear subspace of R^n. The "fundamental theorem of linear algebra" tells us that the dimension of this subspace is $n - k$. Geometrically speaking, we are saying that the equation $\mathbf{Ax} = 0$ determines an $n - k$ dimensional "linear surface."

The implicit function theorem generalizes these facts to nonlinear functions. Consider a situation where we have a differentiable function $\mathbf{f}: R^n \to R^m$ with $m \leqq n$. Suppose that, at some point $\mathbf{x}^*$, we have

$\mathbf{f}(\mathbf{x}^*) = \mathbf{y}^*$ and the rank of $\mathbf{Df}(\mathbf{x}^*)$ is k. Then, loosely speaking, the implicit function theorem tells us that the set of points where $\mathbf{f}(\mathbf{x}^*) = \mathbf{y}^*$ is *locally* an n-k dimensional "surface."

To make these facts precise, we have to define what we mean by an n-k dimensional surface. For our purposes, a set of points in R^n is an n-k dimensional surface if we can express it locally as the graph of a differentiable function from R^{n-k} to R^n.

Consider, for example, the set of points in R^3 defined by $x_1^2 + x_2^2 + x_3^2 = 1$. Given x_1 and x_2, we can solve for $x_3 = \sqrt{1 - x_1^2 - x_2^2}$ or $x_3 = -\sqrt{1 - x_1^2 - x_2^2}$. Thus, near any point (x_1^*, x_2^*, x_3^*), with $x_3 > 0$, the surface is locally described by $\mathbf{F}: R^2 \to R^3$ $\mathbf{F}(x_1, x_2) = (x_1, x_2, \sqrt{1 - x_1^2 - x_2^2})$.

In this book we will primarily use the implicit function theorem when we have functions $f: R^n \to R$. In this case, the rank of $\mathbf{D}f(\mathbf{x}^*)$ will be 1, as long as some component of $\mathbf{D}f(\mathbf{x}^*)$ is nonzero. Thus, we can say that the set of points $\{\mathbf{x}: f(\mathbf{x}) = f(\mathbf{x}^*)\}$ is locally an n-1 dimensional surface in R^n. More precisely:

Implicit Function Theorem *Suppose the function* $\mathrm{f}: \mathrm{R}^n \to \mathrm{R}$ *is such that* $\mathrm{f}(\mathrm{x}_1^*, \cdots, \mathrm{x}_n^*) = \mathrm{y}^*$ *and that* $\partial \mathrm{f}(\mathrm{x}^*)/\partial \mathrm{x}_n \neq 0$. *Then there is a neighborhood* N *of* $(\mathrm{x}_1^*, \cdots, \mathrm{x}_{n-1}^*)$ *and a neighborhood* $\mathrm{N}_{\mathrm{x}_n^*}$ *of* x_n^* *and a function* $\mathrm{g}: \mathrm{N} \to \mathrm{N}_{\mathrm{x}_n^*}$ *such that* $\mathrm{f}(\mathrm{x}_1, \cdots, \mathrm{x}_{n-1}, \mathrm{g}(\mathrm{x}_1 \cdots \mathrm{x}_{n-1})) \equiv \mathrm{y}^*$ *for all* $(\mathrm{x}_1, \cdots, \mathrm{x}_{n-1})$ *in* N.

Here the map $F: R^{n-1} \to R^n$ that defines the surface $\{\mathbf{x}: f(\mathbf{x}) = y\}$ is just given by $F(x_1 \cdots x_{n-1}) = (x_1, \cdots, x_{n-1}, g(x_1, \cdots, x_{n-1}))$. A surface defined by $\{\mathbf{x}: f(\mathbf{x}) = a\}$ is called a *level set* of the function f and is denoted by $Q(a)$.

The implicit function theorem gives us a very useful construction that we will use several times. Suppose we have a function $f: R^n \to R$ and we consider its *level sets*, $Q(y) = \{\mathbf{x} \text{ in } R^n: f(\mathbf{x}) = y\}$. Given a point $\mathbf{x}^*$ in $Q(y)$, we can ask a question like the following: suppose we let coordinate i change to $x_i^* + \epsilon$. How much more of coordinate j do we need to add to bring us back to $Q(y)$? We are asking here for the rate at which j can be "substituted" for i in order to keep the value of f the same.

According to the implicit function theorem, as long as $\dfrac{\partial f(\mathbf{x}^*)}{\partial x_n} \neq 0$, we can find a function for x_n in terms of $(x_1, \cdots, x_{n-1})$:

$$f(x_1, \cdots, x_{n-1}, g(x_1 \cdots x_{n-1})) \equiv y$$

Differentiating this identity with respect to x_1 gives us:

$$\frac{\partial f(\mathbf{x}^*)}{\partial x_1} + \frac{\partial f(\mathbf{x}^*)}{\partial x_n} \cdot \frac{\partial g(x_1^*, \cdots, x_{n-1}^*)}{\partial x_1} = 0$$

or
$$\frac{\partial g(x_1^*, \cdots, x_{n-1}^*)}{\partial x_1} = -\frac{\dfrac{\partial f(\mathbf{x}^*)}{\partial x_1}}{\dfrac{\partial f(\mathbf{x}^*)}{\partial x_n}}$$

This is an expression for how much we need to change x_n when x_1 changes a little bit in order to keep the value of f the same. (Of course, there is a similar expression for the "rate of substitution" between any pair of coordinates.)

A.8 *GRADIENTS AND TANGENT PLANES*

Suppose we have a function $f: R^n \to R$. The *gradient of f at* $\mathbf{x}^*$, $\mathbf{D}f(\mathbf{x}^*)$, is defined to be a vector whose coordinates are the partial derivatives of f at $\mathbf{x}^*$; that is, $\mathbf{D}f(\mathbf{x}^*) = (\partial f(\mathbf{x}^*)/\partial x_1, \cdots, \partial f(\mathbf{x}^*)/\partial x_n)$.

Notice that the gradient of f at x^* has exactly the same representation as the derivative of f at x^*, $\mathbf{D}f(\mathbf{x}^*)$. However, they are somewhat different: the derivative is a linear functional on R^n; the gradient is a vector in R^n. As it happens, linear functionals can be represented by vectors and the representation of the derivative has the same components as the gradient. We will abuse notation and use the same symbol to represent the gradient as we do to represent the derivative.

There is an important geometric interpretation of the gradient. We can consider all vectors $\mathbf{h}$ of norm 1 and ask ourselves: in which direction is f increasing most rapidly at $\mathbf{x}^*$—i.e., in which direction $\mathbf{h}$ is $\mathbf{D}f(\mathbf{x}^*)\cdot\mathbf{h}$ the biggest?

We can regard $\mathbf{D}f(\mathbf{x}^*)\cdot\mathbf{h}$ as just the dot product of the vector $\mathbf{h}$ with the vector $\mathbf{D}f(\mathbf{x}^*)$. This dot product will clearly be a maximum when $\mathbf{h}$ points in the same direction as $\mathbf{D}f(\mathbf{x}^*)$. Hence the gradient vector points in the direction in which f is increasing most; furthermore, the dot product of the gradient and a vector $\mathbf{h}$ is just the same as the derivative of f in the direction $\mathbf{h}$.

Consider now the surface defined by $Q(a) = \{\mathbf{x} \text{ in } R^n : f(\mathbf{x}) = a\}$. If we are given a point $\mathbf{x}^*$ in this surface—that is, a point $\mathbf{x}^*$ such that $f(\mathbf{x}^*) = a$—it is often convenient to find an expression for the hyperplane that most closely approximates the shape of the surface near $\mathbf{x}^*$. We will call this approximating hyperplane the *tangent hyperplane*. We know that the linear map $f(\mathbf{x}^*) + \mathbf{D}f(\mathbf{x}^*)(\mathbf{x} - \mathbf{x}^*)$ approximates the nonlinear map $f(\mathbf{x})$ near $\mathbf{x}^*$. Hence, the best linear approximation to $\{\mathbf{x}: f(\mathbf{x}) = a\}$, should be $\{\mathbf{x}: f(\mathbf{x}^*) + \mathbf{D}f(\mathbf{x}^*)(\mathbf{x} - \mathbf{x}^*) = a\}$. Since $f(\mathbf{x}^*) = a$, this last set reduces to $\{\mathbf{x}: \mathbf{D}f(\mathbf{x}^*)(\mathbf{x} - \mathbf{x}^*) = 0\}$.

Now notice an important fact: if $\mathbf{x}$ is some vector in the tangent

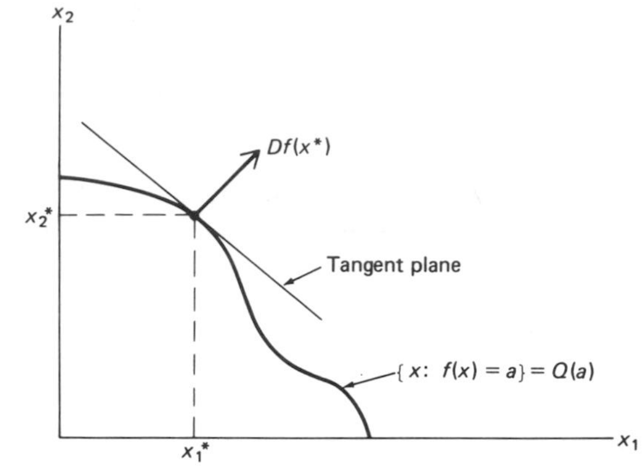

A.4 *Gradients and Tangent Planes*

hyperplane to $Q(a)$ at $\mathbf{x}^*$, then $\mathbf{x} - \mathbf{x}^*$ must be orthogonal to the gradient of f at $\mathbf{x}^*$. This follows directly from the definition of the tangent hyperplane but is also rather intuitive. Along the surface $Q(a)$, the value of the function $f(\mathbf{x})$ is constant. Therefore, the derivative of $f(\mathbf{x})$ in a direction tangent to the surface $Q(a)$ should be zero—since the function is not changing in such directions. (See Figure A.4.)

A.9 MAXIMIZATION

In this section we will give a statement of the basic facts of maximization that are often used in economics; we will also offer intuitive "plausibility arguments" for these statements. The mathematically trained reader may want to consult the more rigorous sources listed in the notes at the end of this appendix for further elaboration of these results.

Let $f: R^n \rightarrow R$, let A be a subset of R^n, and consider the maximization problem:

$$\max \; f(\mathbf{x}) \quad \text{such that } \mathbf{x} \text{ is in } A \qquad \text{MAX1}$$

Fact A.6 *If* f *is continuous and* A *is compact, there is a vector* $\mathbf{x}^*$ *that solves MAX1.*

Suppose we have somehow found a point $\mathbf{x}^*$ that solves MAX1; can we characterize it in any way?

Fact A.7 *If* f *is differentiable at* $\mathbf{x}^*$ *and* $\mathbf{x}^*$ *is in the interior of* A, *then* $\mathbf{Df}(\mathbf{x}^*) = 0$; *in scalar notation,* $\partial f(\mathbf{x}^*)/\partial x_i = 0$ *for* $i = 1, \cdots, n$.

If $\mathbf{D}f(\mathbf{x}^*)$ were not 0, there would be some tiny vector $\mathbf{h}$ such that $\mathbf{x}+\mathbf{h}$ is in A and $\mathbf{D}f(\mathbf{x}^*)\cdot\mathbf{h} > 0$. Since $f(\mathbf{x}^* + \mathbf{h}) \approx f(\mathbf{x}^*) + \mathbf{D}f(\mathbf{x}^*)\mathbf{h}$, this would contradict the assumption that f is maximized.

In many problems we cannot hope that $\mathbf{x}^*$ is in the interior of A. What can we say if it is not?

Let us consider a specialization of the maximization problem where we define A by a system of inequalities: $A = \{\mathbf{x} \text{ in } R^n\text{: } g_i(\mathbf{x}) \leqq 0 \text{ for } i = 1, \cdots, k\}$. Written out, the problem is:

$$\begin{aligned} &\max \quad f(\mathbf{x}) \\ &\text{s.t.} \quad g_i(\mathbf{x}) \leqq 0 \qquad \text{for } i = 1, \cdots, k \end{aligned} \qquad \text{MAX2}$$

The set of points $\{\mathbf{x}\text{: } g_i(\mathbf{x}) \leqq 0 \text{ for } i = 1, \cdots, k\}$ is called the *feasible set*.

The functions g_i for $i = 1, \cdots, k$ are called the *constraints*. If, at a particular $\mathbf{x}^*$, $g_j(\mathbf{x}^*) = 0$, then the jth constraint is said to be *binding;* the set of binding constraints at $\mathbf{x}^*$ is denoted by $I(\mathbf{x}^*)$. If the set of vectors $\{\mathbf{D}g_i(\mathbf{x}^*)\text{: } i \text{ in } I(\mathbf{x}^*)\}$ is linearly independent, then we say *constraint qualification* holds.

Fact A.8 *(Kuhn-Tucker theorem) If* $\mathbf{x}^*$ *solves MAX2 and constraint qualification holds at* $\mathbf{x}^*$, *then* $\mathbf{D}f(\mathbf{x}^*) = \sum_{i \text{ in } I(\mathbf{x}^*)} t_i \mathbf{D}g_i(\mathbf{x}^*)$ *where the* t_i *are nonnegative scalars* (Kuhn-Tucker multipliers). *In scalar notation:*

$$\frac{\partial f(\mathbf{x}^*)}{\partial x_j} = \sum_{i \text{ in } I(\mathbf{x}^*)} t_i \frac{\partial g_i(\mathbf{x}^*)}{\partial x_j} \qquad \text{for } j = 1, \cdots, n.$$

Let us consider the geometric content of this theorem. Suppose we have a two-dimensional maximization problem with one constraint:

$$\begin{aligned} &\max \quad f(x_1, x_2) \\ &\text{s.t.} \quad g(x_1, x_2) \leqq 0 \end{aligned}$$

Let $\mathbf{x}^* = (x_1^*, x_2^*)$ be a solution to this problem. In Figure A.5 we have illustrated the feasible set, $\{\mathbf{x}\text{: } g(\mathbf{x}) \leqq 0\}$, the level set of g at 0, $\{\mathbf{x}\text{: } g(\mathbf{x}) = 0\}$, and the level set of f at $f(\mathbf{x}^*)$. Notice that the gradients $\mathbf{D}f(\mathbf{x}^*)$ and $\mathbf{D}g(\mathbf{x}^*)$ are orthogonal to their respective level sets.

In this case the Kuhn-Tucker theorem asserts that there is some $t \geqq 0$ such that $\mathbf{D}f(\mathbf{x}^*) = t\mathbf{D}g(\mathbf{x}^*)$. Why should this be so?

First we note that the condition implies that $\mathbf{D}f(\mathbf{x}^*)$ must be orthogonal to the level set of the constraint. This is because $\mathbf{D}g(\mathbf{x}^*)$ is always orthogonal to the level set of the constraint, and thus $\mathbf{D}f(\mathbf{x}^*) = t\mathbf{D}g(\mathbf{x}^*)$ must certainly be orthogonal to the level set of the constraint.

But why should $\mathbf{D}f(\mathbf{x}^*)$ be orthogonal to the level set of the constraint? Well, suppose it weren't. Then it would be possible to move along the

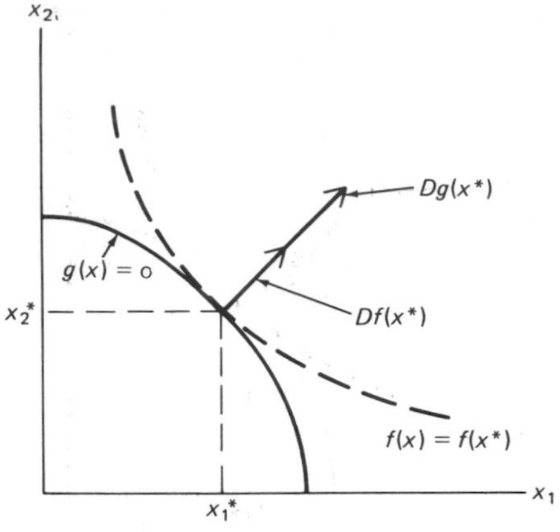

A.5 *The Kuhn-Tucker Theorem with One Constraint*

constraint set a small amount $\mathbf{\Delta x}$ and still have $\mathbf{D}f(\mathbf{x}^*) \cdot \mathbf{\Delta x} > 0$; that is, it would be possible to increase the value of the objective function while staying inside the constraint set—contradicting the fact that $\mathbf{x}^*$ is a constrained optimum.

Now let us consider a two-dimensional problem with two constraints:

$$\begin{aligned} \max \quad & f(x_1, x_2) \\ \text{s.t.} \quad & g_1(x_1, x_2) \leqq 0 \\ & g_2(x_1, x_2) \leqq 0 \end{aligned}$$

Let $\mathbf{x}^* = (x_1^*, x_2^*)$ solve this problem. In Figure A.6 we have illustrated the feasible set, the two constraint sets, and the level set of f at $f(\mathbf{x}^*)$. According to the Kuhn-Tucker theorem, the gradient of f at $\mathbf{x}^*$ should lie in the cone consisting of all nonnegative linear combinations of the gradients of the constraints. Why should this be?

Well, suppose $\mathbf{D}f(\mathbf{x}^*)$ is outside of that cone. Then it would make an acute angle with the level set of one of the constraints. But then, just as before, it would be possible to find some $\mathbf{\Delta x}$ such that $\mathbf{x}^* + \mathbf{\Delta x}$ satisfied both constraints, but $\mathbf{D}f(\mathbf{x}^*) \cdot \mathbf{\Delta x} > 0$. Thus one could increase the value of the objective function and still satisfy the constraints, contradicting the fact that $\mathbf{x}^*$ is a constrained optimum.

It is useful to examine the role that constraint qualification plays in this argument. Figure A.7 shows what can happen if constraint qualification is violated. Here $\mathbf{D}g_1(\mathbf{x}^*)$ and $\mathbf{D}g_2(\mathbf{x}^*)$ are not linearly independent and $\mathbf{D}f(\mathbf{x}^*)$ cannot be expressed in terms of them. However it is clear that this type of situation is rather degenerate and in fact it rarely occurs in applied problems.

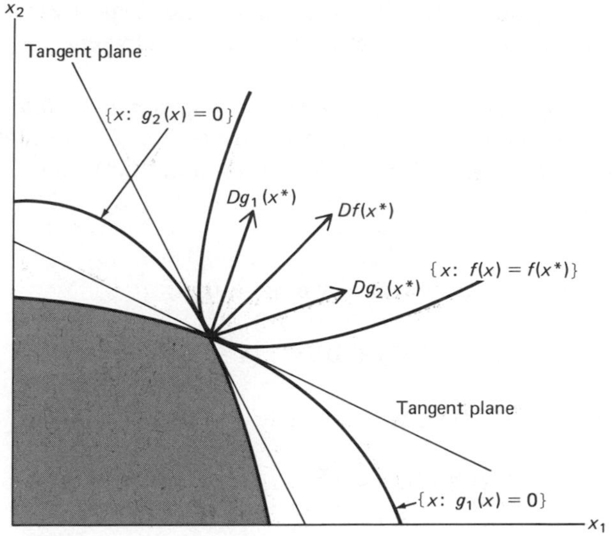

A.6 *The Kuhn-Tucker Theorem with Two Constraints*

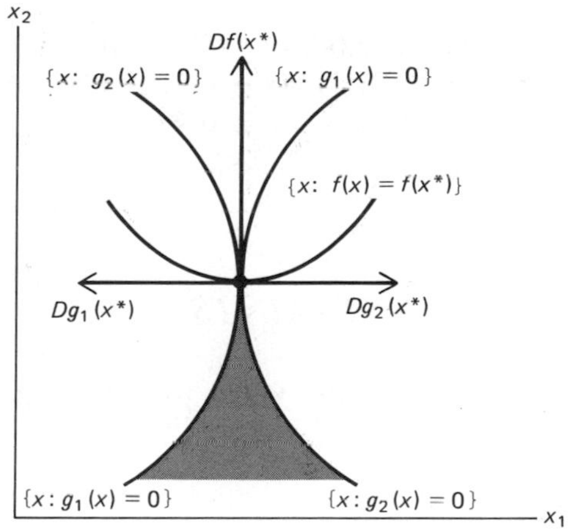

A.7 *Violation of Constraint Qualification*

Sometimes it happens that one or more of the constraints are not binding at $\mathbf{x}^*$. If $g_i(\mathbf{x}^*) < 0$, it can be shown that $t_i = 0$. This gives us the principle of *complementary slackness:* if $g_i(\mathbf{x}^*) < 0$, then $t_i = 0$, and, if $g_i(\mathbf{x}^*) = 0$, then $t_i \geqq 0$.

The first-order conditions in the Kuhn-Tucker theorem are *necessary* conditions: if $\mathbf{x}^*$ solves MAX2, then it must obey the Kuhn-Tucker conditions. In general, the Kuhn-Tucker conditions are not sufficient. However, in one very important case they are sufficient.

Fact A.9 *Suppose that* f *is a concave function and that the* g_i *functions are convex for* $i = 1, \cdots, n$. *Suppose that* $\mathbf{x}^*$ *is a feasible point and that we can find nonnegative numbers* t_i *for* i *in* $I(\mathbf{x}^*)$ *such that* $\mathbf{D}f(\mathbf{x}^*) = \sum_{i \text{ in } I(\mathbf{x}^*)} t_i \mathbf{D}g_i(\mathbf{x}^*)$. *Then* $\mathbf{x}^*$ *solves MAX2.*

PROOF Since $f(\mathbf{x})$ is concave, we have that:

$$f(\mathbf{x}) \leqq f(\mathbf{x}^*) + \mathbf{D}f(\mathbf{x}^*)(\mathbf{x} - \mathbf{x}^*).$$

Since $\mathbf{D}f(\mathbf{x}^*) = \Sigma t_i \mathbf{D}g_i(\mathbf{x}^*)$, we can write this as:

$$f(\mathbf{x}) \leqq f(\mathbf{x}^*) + \sum_{i \text{ in } I(\mathbf{x}^*)} t_i \mathbf{D}g_i(\mathbf{x}^*)(\mathbf{x} - \mathbf{x}^*)$$

Since $g_i(\mathbf{x})$ is convex, we have that:

$$g_i(\mathbf{x}) \geqq g_i(\mathbf{x}^*) + \mathbf{D}g_i(\mathbf{x}^*)(\mathbf{x} - \mathbf{x}^*)$$

Now if $\mathbf{x}$ is a feasible point, $g_i(\mathbf{x}) \leqq g_i(\mathbf{x}^*) = 0$ for all i in $I(\mathbf{x}^*)$. Hence, from the above expression, $\mathbf{D}g_i(\mathbf{x}^*)(\mathbf{x} - \mathbf{x}^*) \leqq 0$ for i in $I(\mathbf{x}^*)$. Using the expression for $f(\mathbf{x})$ and the fact that $t_i \geqq 0$ we find that:

$$f(\mathbf{x}) \leqq f(\mathbf{x}^*). \quad \square$$

A.10 EQUALITY CONSTRAINTS

A special case of MAX2 occurs when we have equality constraints. Then the problem is:

$$\begin{array}{lll} \max & f(\mathbf{x}) & \\ \text{such that} & g_i(\mathbf{x}) = a_i & i = 1, \cdots, k \end{array} \qquad \text{MAX3}$$

In this case, the theorem is slightly different:

Fact A.10 (Lagrange's theorem) *If* $\mathbf{x}^*$ *solves MAX3 and constraint qualification holds then*

$$\mathbf{D}f(\mathbf{x}^*) = \sum_{i=1}^{k} t_i \mathbf{D}g_i(\mathbf{x}^*)$$

where the t_i *are real numbers, positive or negative.*

Geometrically, this means that the gradient of the function f is a linear combination of the gradients of the constraints, but now the weights can be either positive or negative. Consider, for example, the case where $n = 3$ and $k = 2$. Each constraint $g_i(\mathbf{x}) = a_i$ will define a two-dimensional surface in R^3 and their intersection will define a one-dimensional line. At the maximum vector $\mathbf{x}^*$, the gradients of the constraints will be orthogonal to their respective level surfaces and, therefore, orthogonal to the constraint line. Fact A.10 says that, if $f(\mathbf{x}^*)$ is maximized on the constraint line, it must lie in the subspace spanned by the two vectors $\mathbf{D}g_1(\mathbf{x}^*)$ and $\mathbf{D}g_2(\mathbf{x}^*)$. If this were not so, $\mathbf{D}f(\mathbf{x}^*)$ would have a nonzero projection onto the constraint line—but then one could increase the value of f by moving along the line, which violates the hypothesis that f is maximized.

It is worthwhile to sketch an algebraic proof of Fact A.10, if only to illustrate an application of the implicit function theorem. Suppose we have the following problem:

$$\begin{aligned} &\max \quad f(x_1, x_2) \\ &\text{s.t.} \quad g(x_1, x_2) - a = 0 \end{aligned}$$

Suppose $\mathbf{x}^*$ solves the problem. Constraint qualification shows that at least one partial derivative of g does not vanish, so we can find an implicit function defined in a neighborhood of x_1^* such that $g(x_1, x_2(x_1)) \equiv a$. Then consider this problem:

$$\max \quad f(x_1, x_2(x_1))$$

Clearly x_1^* solves this problem, so the derivative of f at x_1^* must vanish:

$$\frac{\partial f(\mathbf{x}^*)}{\partial x_1} + \frac{\partial f(\mathbf{x}^*)}{\partial x_2}\frac{dx_2(x_1^*)}{dx_1} = 0$$

Differentiating the identity defining the function $x_2(x_1)$, we find:

$$\frac{\partial g(\mathbf{x}^*)}{\partial x_1} + \frac{\partial g(\mathbf{x}^*)}{\partial x_2}\frac{dx_2(x_1^*)}{dx_1} = 0$$

or

$$\frac{dx_2(x_1^*)}{dx_1} = -\frac{\dfrac{\partial g(\mathbf{x}^*)}{\partial x_1}}{\dfrac{\partial g(\mathbf{x}^*)}{\partial x_2}}$$

Substituting this into the first-order conditions:

$$\frac{\partial f(\mathbf{x}^*)}{\partial x_1} - \frac{\partial f(\mathbf{x}^*)}{\partial x_2}\cdot\left(\frac{\partial g(\mathbf{x}^*)}{\partial x_1}\bigg/\frac{\partial g(\mathbf{x}^*)}{\partial x_2}\right) = 0$$

or
$$\frac{\partial f(\mathbf{x}^*)/\partial x_1}{\partial f(\mathbf{x}^*)/\partial x_2} = \frac{\partial g(\mathbf{x}^*)/\partial x_1}{\partial g(\mathbf{x}^*)/\partial x_2}$$

This shows $\mathbf{D}f(\mathbf{x}^*) = t\mathbf{D}g(\mathbf{x}^*)$ for some scalar t.

A convenient tool for remembering these first-order conditions is the method of *Lagrange multipliers*. Given a problem:

$$\begin{array}{lll} \max & f(\mathbf{x}) & f: R^n \rightarrow R \\ \text{s.t.} & g_i(\mathbf{x}) = a_i & i = 1, \cdots, k \end{array}$$

we define the Lagrangean function:

$$L: R^{n+k} \rightarrow R \quad \text{by}$$

$$L(\mathbf{x}, \mathbf{t}) = f(\mathbf{x}) - \sum_{i=1}^{k} t_i(g_i(\mathbf{x}) - a_i)$$

Suppose that $\mathbf{x}^*$ is a solution to the maximization problem. Then $DL(\mathbf{x}^*, \mathbf{t}) = 0$. For $\mathbf{D}L(\mathbf{x}^*, \mathbf{t}) = (\mathbf{D}_x L(\mathbf{x}^*, \mathbf{t}), \mathbf{D}_t L(\mathbf{x}^*, \mathbf{t}))$ and

$$\mathbf{D}_x L(\mathbf{x}^*, \mathbf{t}) = \mathbf{D}f(\mathbf{x}^*) - \sum_{i=1}^{k} t_i \mathbf{D}g_i(\mathbf{x}^*) = 0$$

and
$$D_{t_i} L(\mathbf{x}^*, t) = g_i(\mathbf{x}^*) - a_i = 0$$

These are just the first-order conditions described above.

The Lagrangean conditions given above are a very practical way to solve constrained maximization problems. The derivatives with respect to the **x**s give us n equations, and the derivatives with respect to the **t**s give us the k constraints. So all together we have $n + k$ equations and $n + k$ unknown variables. (There are n of the **x**s and k of the **t**s.) Usually we will be able to solve such a system for the optimizing values of the **x**s and the **t**s.

A.11 SECOND-ORDER CONDITIONS

Consider the problem MAX1 again. It is well known that an interior solution to such a problem must obey certain restrictions involving the second derivatives of f at $\mathbf{x}^*$. In particular,

Fact A.11 *If* $\mathbf{x}^*$ *is an interior solution to MAX1, then* $\mathbf{D}^2 f(\mathbf{x}^*)$ *is a negative semidefinite matrix.*

In the one-dimensional case this just says $\partial^2 f(x)/\partial x^2$ is nonpositive. The basic idea behind Fact A.11 comes from looking at a Taylor expansion f at x^*:

$$f(\mathbf{x}^* + \mathbf{h}) \approx f(\mathbf{x}^*) + \mathbf{D}f(\mathbf{x}^*)\mathbf{h} + \frac{\mathbf{h}\mathbf{D}^2 f(\mathbf{x}^*)\mathbf{h}}{2}$$

Using the first-order conditions and the hypothesis of maximization,

$$0 \geqq f(\mathbf{x}^* + \mathbf{h}) - f(\mathbf{x}^*) \approx \frac{\mathbf{h}\mathbf{D}^2 f(\mathbf{x}^*)\mathbf{h}}{2}$$

Since this is true for an arbitrary vector $\mathbf{h}$, Fact A.11 follows.

The second-order conditions for the constrained maximization problem, MAX3, are somewhat more complicated. Recall the basic trick used in deriving the constrained maximization first-order conditions: we used an implicit function to force $\mathbf{x}$ to stay on the constraint surface and then applied the standard first-order conditions. Similarly, we would expect that the right second-order conditions for the constrained maximization problem would be $\mathbf{h}\mathbf{D}^2 f(\mathbf{x}^*)\mathbf{h} \leqq 0$ for any $\mathbf{h}$ that "lies in" the constraint surface. More precisely, we want this condition to hold for any $\mathbf{h}$ that lies in the tangent plane to the constraint surface, and that can be expressed by requiring that $\mathbf{h}$ be orthogonal to all of the gradients of the constraints. Furthermore, the Lagrangean expression $L(\mathbf{x}, \mathbf{t}) = f(\mathbf{x}) - \Sigma t_i g_i(\mathbf{x})$ is identically equal to $f(\mathbf{x})$ on the constraint surface since that is precisely where $g_i(\mathbf{x}) = 0$, $i = 1, \cdots, k$. Putting these observations together provides a motivation for Fact A.12.

Fact A.12 *If* $\mathbf{x}^*$ *solves MAX3, then* $\mathbf{h}\mathbf{D}_{\mathbf{x}}^2 \mathrm{L}(\mathbf{x}^*, \mathbf{t})\mathbf{h} \leqq 0$ *for all* $\mathbf{h}$ *such that* $\mathbf{D}g_i(\mathbf{x}^*)\mathbf{h} = 0$ *for* $\mathrm{i} = 1, \cdots, \mathrm{k}$.

There is another more algebraic way to express this condition when the inequality is strict. Let us define the notation:

$$l_{ij} = \frac{\partial^2 L(\mathbf{x}, \mathbf{t})}{\partial x_i \partial x_j} = \frac{\partial^2 f(\mathbf{x})}{\partial x_i \partial x_j} - \sum_{r=1}^{k} t_r \frac{\partial^2 g_r(\mathbf{x})}{\partial x_i \partial x_j} \qquad \begin{array}{l} i = 1, \cdots, n \\ j = 1, \cdots, n \end{array}$$

$$g_{ih} = \frac{\partial g_i(\mathbf{x})}{\partial x_h} \qquad \begin{array}{l} i = 1, \cdots, k \\ h = 1, \cdots, n \end{array}$$

and let H be the *bordered Hessian* of $L(\mathbf{x}, \mathbf{t})$:

$$H = \begin{bmatrix} D_x^2L(\mathbf{x}, \mathbf{t}) & Dg_1(\mathbf{x}) \cdots Dg_k(\mathbf{x}) \\ Dg_1(\mathbf{x}) & \\ \cdot & \\ \cdot & 0 \\ \cdot & \\ Dg_k(\mathbf{x}) & \end{bmatrix} = \begin{bmatrix} l_{11} & \cdots & l_{1n} & g_{11} & \cdots & g_{k1} \\ & \cdot & & \cdot & & \cdot \\ & \cdot & & \cdot & & \cdot \\ & \cdot & & \cdot & & \cdot \\ l_{11} & & l_{nn} & g_{1n} & \cdots & g_{kn} \\ g_{11} & \cdots & g_{nn} & & & \\ & & & & 0 & \\ g_{k1} & \cdots & g_{kn} & & & \end{bmatrix}$$

Fact A.13 *Suppose constraint qualification holds. Then* $\mathbf{hD^2f(x)h} < 0$ *for* $\mathbf{h} \neq 0$ *satisfying* $\mathbf{Dg_i(x)h} = 0$, $\mathrm{i} = 1, \cdots, \mathrm{k}$ *if and only if* $(-1)^{\mathrm{i}}\mathrm{d_i} > 0$, $\mathrm{i} = \mathrm{k} + 1, \cdots, \mathrm{n}$ *where*

$$\mathrm{d_i} = \det \begin{bmatrix} l_{11} & \cdots & l_{1i} & g_{11} & \cdots & g_{k1} \\ \cdot & & & & & \\ \cdot & & & & & \\ \cdot & & & & & \\ l_{i1} & \cdots & l_{ii} & g_{1i} & \cdots & g_{ki} \\ g_{11} & \cdots & g_{1i} & & & \\ \cdot & & \cdot & & & \\ \cdot & & \cdot & & 0 & \\ \cdot & & & & & \\ g_{k1} & \cdots & g_{ki} & & & \end{bmatrix}$$

The proof of this is a messy expansion of determinants.

In our applications we will typically have only one constraint so that the results of Section A.2 will apply, and we can check to see whether the second-order conditions are satisfied by examining the signs of the principal minors of the bordered Hessian.

A.12 THE THEOREM OF THE MAXIMUM

Consider a parameterized maximization problem of the form:

$$\begin{aligned} \max \quad & f(\mathbf{x}, \mathbf{a}) \\ \text{s.t.} \quad & g_i(\mathbf{x}, \mathbf{a}) \leqq 0 \qquad i = 1, \cdots, k \end{aligned}$$

We let $\mathbf{x}(\mathbf{a})$ be a maximizing choice of $\mathbf{x}$ given $\mathbf{a}$, and we let $M(\mathbf{a}) = f(\mathbf{x}(\mathbf{a}), \mathbf{a})$. It is often useful to know when the functions $M(\mathbf{a})$ and $\mathbf{x}(\mathbf{a})$ are nicely behaved.

Now there is a problem with $\mathbf{x}(\mathbf{a})$ right away: it may not even *be* a function. It is easy to construct examples of maximization problems with nonunique solutions. However, under some special restrictions, we can ensure that the solution to the above problem will be unique.

Fact A.14 *If* f *is strictly concave in* $\mathbf{x}$ *and* g_i *is convex in* $\mathbf{x}$ *for* $i = 1, \cdots, k$, *then, if the above problem has a maximizer* $\mathbf{x}^*$, *it is unique.*

Suppose not. Then let $\mathbf{x}'$ be another optimal choice so that $f(\mathbf{x}^*, \mathbf{a}) = f(\mathbf{x}', \mathbf{a})$. The weighted average $t\mathbf{x}^* + (1-t)\mathbf{x}'$ for $0 < t < 1$ is feasible by the convexity of the constraints and $f(t\mathbf{x}^* + (1-t)\mathbf{x}', \mathbf{a}) > f(\mathbf{x}^*, \mathbf{a})$ by the strict concavity of f. The same sort of proof works if the constraint set is strictly convex, and f is weakly concave.

It is obvious that $M(\mathbf{a})$ is always a function, since there can be only one *maximal* value of $f(\mathbf{x}, \mathbf{a})$ for each choice of $\mathbf{a}$.

Fact A.15 *Suppose* $f(\mathbf{x}, \mathbf{a})$ *and the* $g_i(\mathbf{x}, \mathbf{a})$ *are continuous at* $(\mathbf{x}^*, \mathbf{a}^*)$ *and the range of* f *is compact. Then*

(1) $M(\mathbf{a})$ *is continuous at* $\mathbf{a}^*$.
(2) *If* $\mathbf{x}(\mathbf{a})$ *is a (single-valued) function, it is also continuous at* $\mathbf{a}^*$.

Fact A.15 is often called the *theorem of the maximum.* As a matter of fact, we will often want to assume that $M(\mathbf{a})$ and $\mathbf{x}(\mathbf{a})$ are not only continuous but also differentiable.

If $f(\mathbf{x}, \mathbf{a})$ and $g(\mathbf{x}, \mathbf{a})$ are continuously differentiable functions, then the differentiability of $\mathbf{x}(\mathbf{a})$ and $M(\mathbf{a})$ follows rather quickly from the general version of the implicit function theorem. For the function $\mathbf{x}(\mathbf{a})$ will be determined implicitly by the $n + k$ first-order conditions:

$$\frac{\partial f(\mathbf{x}, \mathbf{a})}{\partial x_i} - \Sigma t_j \frac{\partial g_j(\mathbf{x}, \mathbf{a})}{\partial x_i} = 0 \qquad i = 1, \cdots, n$$

$$g_j(\mathbf{x}, \mathbf{a}) = 0 \qquad j = 1, \cdots, k$$

If the appropriate rank conditions are met, then the implicit function guarantees the existence of a differentiable $\mathbf{x}(\mathbf{a})$. It follows that $M(\mathbf{a}) = f(\mathbf{x}(\mathbf{a}), \mathbf{a})$ will be differentiable.

A.13 THE ENVELOPE THEOREM

Consider a parameterized maximization problem:

$$\max \; f(x, a) \qquad f\colon R^2 \to R$$

For each value of a let $x(a)$ be a maximizing choice of x and let $M(a) = f(x(a), a)$. We are often concerned with examining how $f(x(a), a)$ or

$x(a)$ changes as we change a. These derivatives can be easily evaluated using the chain rule and the first-order conditions.

$$\frac{dM(a)}{da} = \frac{\partial f(x, a)}{\partial x} \cdot \frac{dx(a)}{da} + \frac{\partial f(x(a), a)}{\partial a}$$

Notice that the expression for $dM(a)/da$ has two terms in it. The second term is the direct effect of how changing a changes f holding x fixed at $x(a)$. The first term is the indirect effect of how changing a affects the optimal choice of x and then how this change in x affects the value of f. This expression can be simplified by noticing that, since $x(a)$ is the optimal choice of x for each value of a, we must have $\partial f(x(a), a)/\partial x = 0$. This means that $\frac{dM(a)}{da} = \frac{\partial f(x, a)}{\partial a}$, or *the change in the objective function adjusting x optimally is equal to the change in the objective function when one doesn't adjust x;* that is, the total derivative of $f(x(a), a)$ with respect to a is just equal to the partial derivative of $f(x(a), a)$ with respect to a, evaluated at the optimal choice of x.

To compute the effect of changing a on $x(a)$, we differentiate the first-order conditions:

$$\frac{\partial[\partial f(x(a), a)/\partial x]}{\partial a} \equiv 0$$

$$\frac{\partial^2 f(x(a), a)}{\partial x^2} \cdot \frac{dx(a)}{da} + \frac{\partial^2 f(x(a), a)}{\partial x \partial a} = 0$$

$$\frac{dx(a)}{da} = \frac{-\dfrac{\partial^2 f(x(a), a)}{\partial x \partial a}}{\dfrac{\partial^2 f(x(a), a)}{\partial x^2}}$$

We know that the sign of the denominator is negative by the second-order conditions; therefore the sign of $\frac{dx(a)}{da}$ depends only on the second-order mixed partial appearing in the numerator. This information is often useful in working out problems in comparative statics.

These results can be generalized to constrained maximization problems. Consider the following problem

$$\begin{array}{lll} \max & f(\mathbf{x}, a) & \text{f: } R^n \times R \to R \\ \text{s.t.} & g(\mathbf{x}, a) = 0 & \text{g: } R^n \times R \to R \end{array}$$

Let $L(\mathbf{x}, t, a) = f(\mathbf{x}, a) - tg(\mathbf{x}, a)$ be the associated Lagrangean, let $\mathbf{x}(a)$

be the optimal choice of $\mathbf{x}$ given a, and let $M(a) = f(\mathbf{x}(a), a)$. Then the "envelope theorem" states that:

$$\frac{dM(a)}{da} = \frac{\partial L(\mathbf{x}(a), a)}{\partial a} = \frac{\partial f(\mathbf{x}(a), a)}{\partial a} - t\,\frac{\partial g(\mathbf{x}(a), a)}{\partial a}$$

Again one only has to take account of the change in a and not the associated change in $\mathbf{x}$.

The proof is a simple calculation. By direct differentiation we have:

$$(1) \qquad \frac{dM(a)}{da} = \sum_{i=1}^{n} \frac{\partial f(\mathbf{x}(a), a)}{\partial x_i} \frac{\partial x_i(a)}{\partial a} + \frac{\partial f(\mathbf{x}(a), a)}{\partial a}$$

Since $\mathbf{x}(a)$ is the optimal choice for each a, it must satisfy the first-order conditions:

$$(2) \qquad \frac{\partial f(\mathbf{x}(a), a)}{\partial x_i} = t\,\frac{\partial g(\mathbf{x}(a), a)}{\partial x_i} \qquad i = 1, \cdots, n$$

Furthermore, $\mathbf{x}(a)$ has to identically satisfy the constraint, so that $g(\mathbf{x}(a), a) \equiv 0$. Differentiating this identity:

$$(3) \qquad \sum_{i=1}^{n} \frac{\partial g(\mathbf{x}(a), a)}{\partial x_i} \frac{dx_i(a)}{da} + \frac{\partial g(\mathbf{x}(a), a)}{\partial a} = 0$$

Substituting expressions (2) and (3) into (1) we find:

$$\frac{dM(a)}{da} = \frac{\partial f(\mathbf{x}(a), a)}{\partial a} - t\,\frac{\partial g(\mathbf{x}(a), a)}{\partial a}$$

The envelope theorem gives us a nice interpretation of the Lagrange multipliers described earlier. Recall the problem MAX3:

$$\begin{aligned} M(a) = \max \quad & f(\mathbf{x}) \\ \text{s.t.} \quad & g_i(\mathbf{x}) - a_i = 0 \qquad i = 1, \cdots, k \end{aligned}$$

Then $\dfrac{\partial [g_i(\mathbf{x}) - a_i]}{\partial a_i} = -1$ and $\dfrac{\partial f(\mathbf{x})}{\partial a_i} = 0$. By the envelope theorem $t_i = \dfrac{\partial M(a)}{\partial a_i}$; that is, t_i gives us the marginal increase in f if we relax the ith constraint by a small amount.

A.14 HOMOGENEOUS FUNCTIONS

A function $f: R^n_+ \to R$ is *homogeneous of degree k* if $f(t\mathbf{x}) = t^k f(\mathbf{x})$ for all $t > 0$. In particular, f is *homogeneous of degree 0* if $f(t\mathbf{x}) \equiv f(\mathbf{x})$ and f is *homogeneous of degree 1* if $f(t\mathbf{x}) = tf(\mathbf{x})$.

Suppose we double all the xs in a homogeneous function. The value of a degree-0 function will not change, but the value of a degree-1 function will double.

Fact A.16 *(Euler's law) If* f *is a differentiable function homogeneous of degree* 1, *then* $f(\mathbf{x}) \equiv \sum_{i=1}^{n} \frac{\partial f(\mathbf{x})}{\partial x_i} x_i$.

By way of proof we just note that $f(t\mathbf{x}) \equiv tf(\mathbf{x})$ for all t. Differentiating this identity with respect to t, we get:

$$\sum_{i=1}^{n} \frac{\partial f(t\mathbf{x})}{\partial x_i} x_i = f(\mathbf{x})$$

Setting $t = 1$ gives us the result.

Fact A.17 *If* $f(\mathbf{x})$ *is homogeneous of degree* 1 *then* $\partial f(\mathbf{x})/\partial x_i$ *is homogeneous of degree* 0.

To see this we differentiate the identity $f(t\mathbf{x}) \equiv tf(\mathbf{x})$ with respect to x_i:

$$\frac{\partial f(t\mathbf{x})}{\partial x_i} t = t \frac{\partial f(\mathbf{x})}{\partial x_i}$$

An important implication of Fact A.17 is that the slopes of the level surfaces of a homogeneous function are constant along rays through the origin:

$$\frac{\frac{\partial f(t\mathbf{x})}{\partial x_i}}{\frac{\partial f(t\mathbf{x})}{\partial x_j}} = \frac{\frac{\partial f(\mathbf{x})}{\partial x_i}}{\frac{\partial f(\mathbf{x})}{\partial x_j}}$$

On the other hand there are nonhomogeneous functions that share this property. A function is called *homothetic* if it is a monotonic transform of a homogeneous function. In other words a homothetic function $f(\mathbf{x})$ can be written as $f(\mathbf{x}) = g(h(\mathbf{x}))$ where g is monotonic and h is homogeneous.

A.15 IDENTITIES

An identity is an equation that is true for all values of the relevant variables. An equation, on the other hand, may be true for only certain values of the relevant variables. An identity may hold because of a definition or because of some mathematical truism. For example, the formula

$$x^2 + 2x + 1 = (x + 1)^2$$

is identically true for all values of x. We sometimes use the identity sign $\equiv$ when we want to emphasize that an equality is in fact an identity.

Since an identity holds true for all values of the relevant variables, we can differentiate both sides of the identity and still have an equation that is identically true. In the above example,

$$2x + 2 = 2(x + 1)$$

Similarly, we can integrate both sides of an identity and still have an identity. These statements are definitely not true for formulas that are only equalities.

A.16 PARTIAL DIFFERENTIAL EQUATIONS

A *system of partial differential equations* (PDEs) is a system of equations of the following form:

$$\begin{aligned} \partial f(\mathbf{p})/\partial p_i &= g_i(f(\mathbf{p}), \mathbf{p}) \qquad i = 1, \cdots, n \\ f(\mathbf{q}) &= 0 \end{aligned}$$

The last equation is called the *boundary condition*. (The definition of a partial differential equation can be substantially more general than this, but this definition will do for our purposes.)

A solution to these PDEs is simply a function $f(\mathbf{p})$ that satisfies the equations identically in $\mathbf{p}$. It is not at all obvious that a solution will exist to any given PDE. One necessary condition for a solution comes from the symmetry of cross-derivatives. Since

$$\partial^2 f(\mathbf{p})/\partial p_i \partial p_j = \partial^2 f(\mathbf{p})/\partial p_j \partial p_i$$

we must have

$$\partial g_i(f, \mathbf{p})/\partial f \cdot \partial f/\partial p_j + \partial g_i/\partial p_j = \partial g_j(\mathbf{f}, \mathbf{p})/\partial f \cdot \partial f/\partial p_i + \partial g_j/\partial p_i$$

for all i and j. This type of summetry condition is usually referred to as an *integrability condition*. It turns out that these conditions are not only necessary for a solution to exist, they are also *sufficient* for existence, subject to certain technical restrictions.

Of course, solving for a solution in any particular case may be difficult, but there is one useful and special case that is easy to handle. This is the case where $f(\mathbf{p})$ does not occur explicitly on the righthand side of the above equations. In this case the equations take the form

$$\partial f(\mathbf{p})/\partial p_i = g_i(\mathbf{p}) \qquad i = 1, \cdots, n$$
$$f(\mathbf{q}) = 0$$

We can solve this kind of system by simple integration. Consider, for example, the case where $n = 2$, and assume that the integrability condition $\partial g_1/\partial p_2 = \partial g_2/\partial p_1$ is satisfied. Then the function $f(p_1, p_2)$ that satisfies this system of PDEs is given by:

$$f(p_1, p_2) = \int_{q_1}^{p_1} g_1(t, q_1)dt + \int_{q_2}^{p_2} g_2(p_1, t)dt$$

It is clear that this function satisfies the boundary condition, and simple differentiation shows that $\partial f/\partial p_2 = g_2(p_1, p_2)$. We need only establish that $\partial f/\partial p_1 = g_1(p_1, p_2)$.

Taking the derivative, we find:

$$\partial f(p_1, p_2)/\partial p_1 = g_1(p_1, q_2) + \int_{q_2}^{p_2} \partial g_2(p_1, t)/\partial p_1 \, dt$$

Using the integrability condition:

$$= g_1(p_1, q_2) + \int_{q_2}^{p_2} \partial g_1(p_1, t)/\partial p_2 \, dt$$

But integrating with respect to p_1 and differentiating with respect to p_1 leave us with:

$$= g_1(p_1, q_2) + g_1(p_1, p_2) - g_1(p_1, q_2)$$
$$= g_1(p_1, p_2)$$

which is what we wanted to show. Similar calculations can be done for an arbitrary number of independent variables.

A.17 DYNAMICAL SYSTEMS

The *state* of a system consists of a description of all variables that affect the behavior of the system under consideration. The *state space* of a dynamical system consists of all feasible states. For example, the state space of a particular economic system may consist of all possible price configurations. (Another possibility might be to describe the state space of the economy by all possible price configurations and goods currently held by the agents.)

If we denote the state space by S, we can describe a *dynamical system* on S by a function, $F: S \times R \rightarrow S$. The real line R is interpreted as time, and $F(\mathbf{x}, t)$ is state of the system at time t if it was in state $\mathbf{x}$ at $t = 0$.

Usually the state function is not given explicitly but rather is given implicitly by a differential equation. For example, $\dot{\mathbf{x}}(t) = \mathbf{f}(\mathbf{x}(t))$ is a differential equation that tells how the state of the system changes when the system is in state $\mathbf{x}(t)$. As long as $\mathbf{f}(\mathbf{x})$ is differentiable (or satisfies even weaker conditions), we can show that there is a unique dynamical system defined by $\mathbf{f}$ for each given initial state $\mathbf{x}_0$. Hence, we will often use the terms *system of differential equations* and *dynamical system* interchangeably. A *solution (solution curve, trajectory, orbit)* to a differential equation $\dot{\mathbf{x}} = \mathbf{f}(\mathbf{x})$ is a function $\mathbf{x}: \mathbf{R} \rightarrow \mathbf{R}^n$ such that $\dot{\mathbf{x}}(\mathrm{t}) \equiv \mathbf{f}(\mathbf{x}(\mathrm{t}))$.

An *equilibrium (zero, singularity)* of a dynamical system is a state $\mathbf{x}^*$ in S such that $\mathbf{f}(\mathbf{x}^*) = \mathbf{0}$; equivalently, it is a state $\mathbf{x}^*$ such that $\mathbf{F}(\mathbf{x}^*, t) = \mathbf{x}^*$ for all t. The meaning is clear: if a dynamical system gets into a state $\mathbf{x}^*$, it stays there forever.

Suppose we have a particular dynamical system $\dot{\mathbf{x}} = \mathbf{f}(\mathbf{x})$ and we start at time 0 in some arbitrary state $\mathbf{x}_0$. It is often of interest to know when the state of the system will tend to some equilibrium value $\mathbf{x}^*$. We will say a dynamical system is *globally stable* if $\lim_{t \to \infty} \mathbf{F}(\mathbf{x}, t) = \mathbf{x}^*$ for all initial values $\mathbf{x}$. We note that a globally stable equilibrium must be a unique equilibrium.

There is a very convenient criterion for determining when a dynamical system is globally stable. We will restrict ourselves to a situation where we have (or can choose) the state space, S, to be *compact,* so that we know the system will always stay in a bounded region. Now, suppose we can find a function of the state of the system $V{:}S \rightarrow R$ that has the following two properties:

(1) $V(\mathbf{x})$ reaches its minimum value at $\mathbf{x}^*$;
(2) $\dot{V}(\mathbf{x}(t)) < 0$ for $\mathbf{x}(t) \neq \mathbf{x}^*$; (that is, $\mathbf{D}V(\mathbf{x}) \cdot \dot{\mathbf{x}}(t) < 0$ for $\mathbf{x}(t) \neq \mathbf{x}^*$.)

Such a function is called a *Liapunov function.* We have the following fact:

Fact A.18 *If a dynamical system admits a Liapunov function, its equilibrium* $\mathbf{x}^*$ *is globally stable.*

For some intuition, consider the Figure A.8. We pick a real number c and look at the set of points $V^{-1}(c) = \{\mathbf{x} \text{ in } S\colon V(\mathbf{x}) = c\}$. Since the

Liapunov function is declining over time, we know that once we get inside the region enclosed by $V^{-1}(c)$ we can never get back outside. Hence, given any neighborhood of $\mathbf{x}^*$, we eventually get inside and stay inside of that neighborhood—in other words, the state of the system converges to $\mathbf{x}^*$.

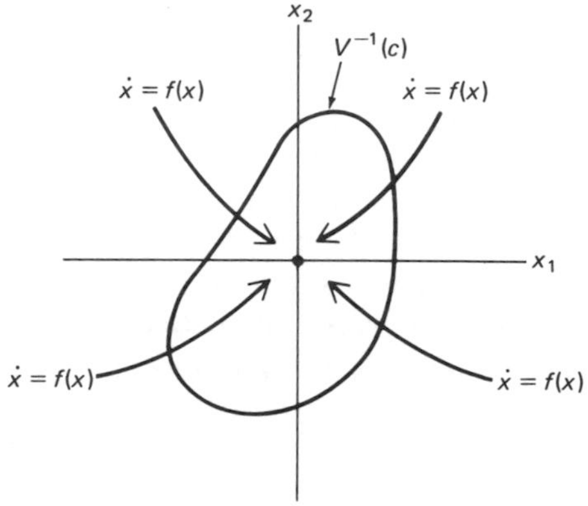

A.8 *Level Set of a Liapunov Function*

Notes

A useful geometrical introduction to linear algebra is Lang (1971). For elementary analysis see, for example, Rosenlicht (1968) and Lang (1968). Berge (1963) covers several topics in topology that are useful in economics and game theory. For calculus, Spivak (1967) and (1965) are quite good. Maximization techniques and some economic applications are covered by Simon (1976). Some other good references on maximization are Dixit (1976), Intriligator (1971), and Varaiya (1972). The complete reference on convexity is Rockafellar (1970). Dynamics are treated in a geometrical manner in Hirsch and Smale (1974). Much of the material in this Appendix is treated in a more complete and rigorous manner by Roberts and Schultz (1973). See Silberberg (1974) for a nice treatment of the envelope theorem and comparative statics.

References

BERGE, C. 1963. *Topological Space*. New York: Macmillan.

DIXIT, A. 1976. *Optimization in Economic Theory*. Oxford, Eng.: Oxford University Press.

HIRSCH, M., and SMALE, S. 1974. *Differential Equations, Dynamical Systems and Linear Algebra*. New York: Academic Press.

INTRILIGATOR, M. 1971. *Mathematical Optimization and Economic Theory*. Englewood Cliffs, N.J.: Prentice-Hall.

LANG, S. 1968. *Analysis I*. Reading, Mass.: Addison-Wesley.

———. *Linear Algebra*. Reading, Mass.: Addison-Wesley, 1971.

ROBERTS, B., and SCHULTZ, D. 1973. *Modern Mathematics and Economic Analysis*. New York: Norton.

ROCKAFELLAR, T. 1970. *Convex Analysis*. Princeton: Princeton University Press.

ROSENLICHT, M. 1968. *Introduction to Analysis*. Glenview, Ill.: Scott, Foresman.

SIMON, C. 1976. "Scalar and Vector Maximization: Calculus Techniques with Economic Applications." In *Studies in Mathematical Economics*, ed. S. Reiter. MAA Studies in Mathematics Series.

SILBERBERG, E. 1974. "A Revision of Comparative Statics Methodology in Economics." *Journal of Economic Theory* 7:159–172.

SPIVAK, M. 1967. *Calculus*. Menlo Park, Calif.: Benjamin.

———. 1965. *Calculus on Manifolds*. Menlo Park, Calif.: Benjamin.

VARAIYA, P. 1972. *Notes on Optimization*. New York: Van Nostrand Reinhold.

Answers and Hints to Selected Exercises

CHAPTER 1

1.1 Apply Kuhn-Tucker.

1.2 Let y^* maximize profits, assume that it doesn't minimize costs and derive a contradiction.

1.3 Follow hint in text.

1.4 You should get $\Delta \mathbf{p} \cdot \Delta \mathbf{y} \geqq 0$.

1.5 (a) What happens when $y \leqq 1$?
(b) $V(y)$ is not closed.
(c) OK; factor demand is difficult.
(d) violates monotonicity.
(e) what happens when $y \geqq 1$?
(f) $-\sqrt{x_1 x_2}$ is a convex function.
(g) OK; $x_1 = 3y$ for $w_1 \leqq w_2 + w_3$, 0 otherwise.

1.6 (a) Not homogeneous.
(b) OK.
(c) OK. Differentiate to get factor demands and eliminate $\sqrt{w_2/w_1}$.
(d) Not homogeneous.
(e) Not concave.
(f) OK.

1.7 (a) Easy.

(b) $$c(\mathbf{w}, y) = w_2 y^2/b \text{ for } \frac{w_1}{a} \geqq \frac{w_2}{b}$$

$$= w_1 y^2/a \text{ for } \frac{w_1}{a} < \frac{w_2}{b}.$$

(c) Use (b).

1.8 homogeneity requires $\alpha + \beta = \gamma + \delta = 0$
symmetry requires $\beta - 1 = \delta \quad \gamma - 1 = \alpha$
positivity of x_1 and x_2 requires $b \geqq 0$, $d \geqq 0$
law demand requires $\alpha \leqq 0$, $\delta \leqq 0$

1.9 Differentiate.
1.10 Try Euler's law.
1.14 Apply envelope theorem.
1.15 Mimic examples 1.9 and 1.21.
1.16 The derivatives of a function that is homogeneous of degree 1 are homogeneous of degree 0.
1.17 Use cross-symmetry of second-order partial derivatives.
1.18 Differentiate.
1.19 $t = \partial c(\mathbf{w}, y)/\partial y$.
1.20 $\pi = p \ln(p/w) - p$ for $\pi \geqq 0$
1.22 This is like a Leontief cost function with y replaced by $y^{1/2}$.

1.23 $$\text{surplus} = \int_{p^0}^{p'} y(p)dp = \int_{p^0}^{p'} \frac{\partial \pi}{\partial p}\, dp = \pi(p') - \pi(p^0)$$

1.24 (b) You have to compare total costs at c to total costs at a, so look at some areas under the marginal cost curves.
1.25 Compute.
1.26 Apply duality.

1.27 $$dy = \Sigma \frac{\partial y}{\partial w_i} \cdot dw_i = -\Sigma \frac{\partial x_i}{\partial p}\, dw_i = -\Sigma \frac{\partial x_i}{\partial y} \frac{\partial y}{\partial p}\, dw_i$$

Since $dy/dp > 0$, we see that if there are no inferior factors, output must decline.

CHAPTER 2

2.1 Use $p(1 + 1/\epsilon) = c'(y)$.
2.2 (d) Since the conditional factor demands do not depend on (w_1, w_2) the isoquants must be L-shaped.
2.3 Draw a graph.
2.4 Use the graph from 2.3.
2.5 Use the graph from 2.3.
2.7 The production of apples cannot go down for the usual reason: supply curves are upward-sloping. The increase in apple production can only arise because some firms switch from producing bananas and coconuts so that output of these goods must decline.
2.8 (a) Consider first the $y = \frac{1}{2}(K + L)$ firms. If $L = 0$, $K = 8$ these firms will produce 4 units apiece just from the fixed factor so in the short run this part of the industry will supply 400 units at an arbitrarily small price. Labor costs are \$2 per unit produced so when $p = 2$, these firms will supply as much as you want.

Now consider the Cobb-Douglas firms with $y = 8^{1/2}L^{1/2}$. Compute the profit-maximizing supply by solving max $p8^{1/2}L^{1/2} - L$ to get $y = 4p$. Finally for $y = \min(K, L)$ firms, if price covers labor costs—$p \geqq 1$—firms will supply 8 units apiece. Put these supply curves together to get an industry supply curve like this:

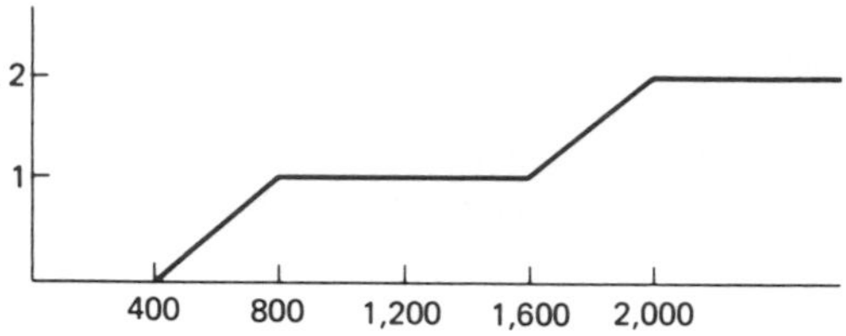

(b) Do this graphically.

2.9 (a) Set w = marginal product of labor to get $L = (24/w)^3$.

(b) Plug labor demand function into production function to get $Q = 36[8(p - .35)]^2$.

(c) Marginal product of capital is
$\frac{18}{4} L^{2/3} K^{-3/4} = \$36$.

(d) At \$36 a day firm will hire $K = 16$ and price will be as in (a).

2.10 (a)

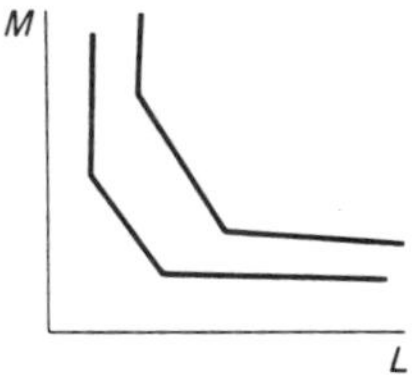

(b) $c(y, w, r) = y \min (2w + r, w + 3r)$.

(c) $p^* = q^* = 40, M^* = 40, L^* = 120$
$p^* = 45, q^* = 20, M^* = 60, L^* = 30$.

(d) $q^* = 80, p^* = 20$
$q^* = 60, p^* = 30$.

2.11 (a) By homogeneity $b = 1 - a$.

(b) $\text{MC} = 2yw_1^a w_2^{1-a}$, $\text{AC} = yw_1^a w_2^{1-a}$.

(c) $y = p/2w_1^a w_2^{1-a}$.

(d) Profits are $p^2/4w_1^a w_2^{1-a}$ which should be at least 10 for firms to produce. Thus

$$S(p) = 0 \quad p \leqq \sqrt{40 w_1^a w_2^{1-a}}$$

$$S(p) = \frac{np}{2w_1^a w_2^{1-a}} \quad \text{if} \quad p \geqq \sqrt{40 w_1^a w_2^b}$$

(e) Presumably firms will enter until $p^2/4w_1^a w_2^{1-a} = 10$.

2.12 None.

2.13 Equilibrium occurs when $r_B(x)/(1 - t) = r_L(x)/(1 - t)$. But this equilibrium is the same as that determined by $r_B(x) = r_L(x)$.

2.14 Monopolistic competition is Nash in that it takes other firms *actions* as given but Stackelberg in that it takes consumers *reactions* as given.

2.15 For firm 1, solve max $(a - b(y_1 + y_2))y_1$ to get $y_1 = (a - by_2)/2b$ and use symmetry to get y_2. Solve to get $y_2 = y_1 = a/3b$.

2.16 (a) $y = p/2$.

(b) $p^* = 2$, $\pi^* = 0$, number of firms = 50.
(c) number of firms = 50, $p^* = 2.02$, $\pi^* = .02$.
(d) $p^* = 2$, $\pi^* = 0$, number of firms = 51.

2.17 (a) $20 - 2y = 2y$ so $y = 5$, $p = 15$.
(b) $\pi = 75 - 26 = 49$.
(c) $20 - y = 2y$ $y = 6.67$, $p = 13.33$, $\pi = 43.43$.

2.18 (a) $y^* = 6$, $p^* = 6$
(b) $y^* = 4$, $p^* = 8$
(c) Compute change in profits.
(d) Compute change in consumers' surplus.

2.19 (a) $y = p/2$.
(b) $Y = 50p$.
(c) $p^* = 2$, $q^* = 100$.
(d) rent = \$100.

2.20 $y_2 = 3a/5b$.

2.22 $p = c/(1 - 1/\epsilon)$.

CHAPTER 3

3.1 Differentiate the budget constraint.

3.3 Follow example in text.

3.4 $\partial u(\mathbf{x})/\partial x_i \leqq \lambda p_i$, $\partial u(\mathbf{x})/\partial x_i = \lambda p_i$ if $x_i > 0$.

3.5 $\partial x_i(\mathbf{p}, \mathbf{p}\cdot\mathbf{w})/\partial p_j = \partial h_i(\mathbf{p}, u)/\partial p_j + (w_j - x_j)\partial x_i(\mathbf{p}, y)/\partial y$.

3.6 Use Slutsky's equation.

3.7 Use a diagram.

3.8 (a) First-order conditions are $1/x_1^2/1/x_2^2 = p_1/p_2$.
Combine with budget constraint to get
$x_1 = y/(p_1 + \sqrt{p_1p_2})$, $x_2 = y/(p_2 + \sqrt{p_1p_2})$.
(b) Plug into utility function.
(c) Invert indirect utility function.
(d) Differentiate the expenditure function.

3.11 Use Slutsky's equation.

3.13 Solve the integrability equation

$$\frac{d\mu}{dt} = at + b\mu + c$$

3.16 Modify the proof used in Example 1.18.
A monotonic transformation of utility cannot affect behavior.

3.17 This is a monotonic transformation of utility, so demand doesn't change at all.

3.18 Since the expenditure function is homogeneous of degree 1, $b = 3/4$.

3.20 Solve the integrability equation $\frac{d\mu}{dp_1} = \frac{1}{p_1}$.

3.21 Use Taylor series to get

$\frac{2}{3}u(w + t) + \frac{1}{3}u(w - t) \approx u(w) + u'(w)(\frac{2}{3} - \frac{1}{3})t > u(w)$

so expected utility of bet is greater than utility of not taking bet, for t small.

3.22 (a) First-order conditions are $\frac{u_1'(x_1)}{p_1} = \frac{u_2'(x_2)}{p_2} = \frac{u_3'(x_3)}{p_3}$.

Since all income is spent, when y increases at least one of the x_i must increase. But if the first-order conditions are to be satisfied then the other x_i's must increase too. There are zero inferior goods.

(b) Since each good is normal, $\partial x_i/\partial p_i < 0$.

(c) Can go either way.

(d) By symmetry of x_2 and x_3 and the fact that each row must have a plus sign

$$\begin{bmatrix} - & + & + \\ + & - & + \\ + & + & - \end{bmatrix}.$$

3.23 Obvious.

3.24 Maximizing the wage bill means

$\max wD(w)$ or $w\frac{dD}{dw} + D(w) = 0.$

Maximizing the wage bill plus unemployment compensation means:

$$\max wD(w) + u(S - D(w))$$

or

$$w\frac{dD(w)}{dw} + D(w) - u\frac{dD}{dw} = 0$$

since $\frac{dD}{dw} < 0$ the result follows.

3.25 Revealed preference.

3.26 Revealed preference.

3.27 Revealed preference.

3.28 Revealed preference.

3.29 Remember $e(\mathbf{p}', u^0)$ is the minimum expenditure required to get utility u^0 at prices $\mathbf{p}'$. Since x^0 gives utility u^0, $e(\mathbf{p}', u^0) \leqq \mathbf{p}' \cdot \mathbf{x}^0$.

3.30 (a) By definition $u(\mathbf{h}(\mathbf{p}, u^0)) \equiv u^0$, so differentiate with respect to p_j.

(b) Use first-order conditions.

(c) Prices are nonnegative numbers.

3.31 Apply 3.16.

3.32 Use Slutsky's equation.

3.33 Show that this solves the differential equation $(\partial x_i(\mathbf{p}, y)/\partial y)(y/x_i) = \eta$.

3.34 By 3.31 $v(\mathbf{p}, y)$ is of form $v(\mathbf{p})y$ so that demand functions have form $x(\mathbf{p})y$.

3.35 $L = u(\mathbf{x}) - \lambda(\mathbf{p} \cdot \mathbf{x} - y)$ so $\partial v(\mathbf{p}, y)/\partial y = \partial L/\partial y = \lambda$.

3.36 $\partial v(\mathbf{p}, y)/\partial p_i = \partial L/\partial p_i = -\lambda x_i$, $\partial L/\partial y = \lambda$.

3.37 $E(a_0 + a_1 y - a_2 y^2) = a_0 + a_1 E(y_1) - a_2^2 E(y^2)$. But $\sigma^2 = E(y^2) - (E(y))^2$.

3.38 The fan's optimal bet is determined by max $p\, ln(w_0 + x) + (1 - p) ln(w_0 - x)$, which leads to the first-order conditions $p/(w_0 + x) = (1 - p)/(w_0 - x)$. Hence observing w_0 and x allows you to calculate p.

3.42 Given a, determine b by the singularity of substitution matrix, $p_1 a + p_2 c = 0$ so $c = -p_1 a/p_2$. By symmetry $b = c$. By singularity $ad - bc = 0$ so this determines d.

3.43 (a) First-order conditions are $\frac{\partial u_i(\mathbf{x})}{\partial x_i} - p_i = 0$ which don't involve y, so $x(\mathbf{p}, y) = x(\mathbf{p})$.

(b) Substitute to get $u(\mathbf{x}(\mathbf{p})) + y$.

(c) Invert indirect utility function.

(d) Differentiate first-order conditions to get

$$\mathbf{D}^2 u(\mathbf{x})\mathbf{D}\mathbf{x}(\mathbf{p}) = \mathbf{I}.$$

3.44 Solve differential equation $u''(x)/u'(x) = r$ to get $u(x) = -e^{rx}$. (Note $r < 0$).

3.45 (ii) $u(x) = x^{r+1}/(r + 1)$.

CHAPTER 4

4.1 For simplicity suppose there were only two factors. Since factor 1 gets payed its marginal product
$w_1 = a_1 x_1^{a_1 - 1} x_2^{1-a_1} = a_1 x_1^{-1}(x_1^{a_1} x_2^{1-a_1}) = a_1 x_1^{-1} y$, or
$w_1 x_1 = a_1 y$ thus $a_1 = w_1 x_1 / y$.

4.2 The short-run demand function for labor.

4.3 for symmetry of $\partial x_i / \partial p_j = \partial x_j / \partial p_i$.

4.4 Estimate production function directly, $y = f(K, L)$.

CHAPTER 5

5.1

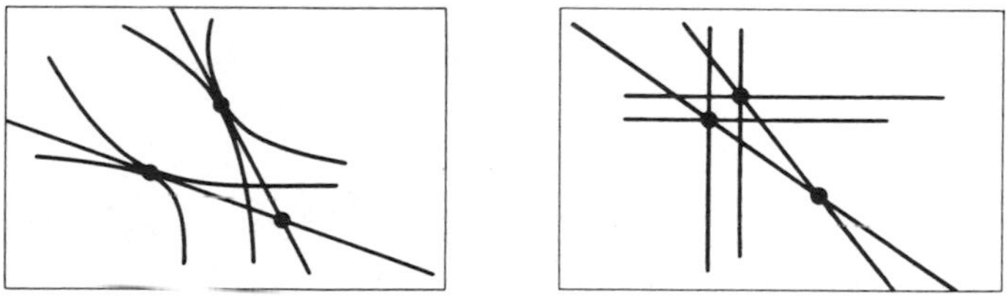

5.2 $\mathbf{x}_i^*$ is not strictly greater than 0.

5.3 Follow outline of proof in text.

5.4 $x_A^1 = ay/p_1 = ap_2/p_1$
$x_B^1 = x_B^2$ so from budget constraint,
$(p_1 + p_2)x_B^1 = p_1$, so $x_B^1 = p_1/(p_1 + p_2)$. Choose $p_1 = 1$
an numeraire and solve $ap_2 + 1/(1 + p_2) = 1$.

5.5 There is no way to make one person better off without hurting someone else.

5.6 $x_1^1 = ay_1/p_1, x_2 = by_2/p_1$ $y_1 = y_2 = p_1 + p_2$.
Solve $x_1^1 + x_2^1 = 2$.

5.7 Use general equilibrium form of Slutsky's equation (Exercise 3.5).

5.11 Note that the application of Walras' law in the proof still works.

CHAPTER 6

6.1 Invert the $G_i(z_i)$ functions.

6.2 Two equilibria must be saddle points, and the third is either totally stable or totally unstable.

6.3 Let $V(\mathbf{p}) = \Sigma k_i p_i - \pi(\mathbf{p})$, then $\partial V/\partial p_i = k_i - x_i(\mathbf{p})$.

6.4
$$\frac{dV(\mathbf{p})}{dt} = -2\mathbf{z}(\mathbf{p})\mathbf{Dz}(\mathbf{p})\dot{\mathbf{p}} = -2\mathbf{z}(\mathbf{p})\mathbf{Dz}(\mathbf{p})[\mathbf{Dz}(\mathbf{p})]^{-1}\mathbf{z}(\mathbf{p})$$
$$= -2\mathbf{z}(\mathbf{p})\cdot\mathbf{z}(\mathbf{p}) < 0.$$

6.5 Let $\mathbf{W}^*$ be any Pareto efficient allocation.

6.6 Since $\mathbf{Dx}(\mathbf{p}) = [\mathbf{D}u(\mathbf{x})]^{-1}$, $\mathbf{Dx}(\mathbf{p})$ is always negative definite so $-\mathbf{Dx}(\mathbf{p})$ has index $+1$.

6.7 (a) Let the price of oil be 1. Then zero profit condition says $p_g 2x - x = 0$ or $p_g = \frac{1}{2}$ and similarly $p_b = \frac{1}{3}$.

(b) Both demands are Cobb-Douglas so

$$x_1^g = \frac{.4 \times 10}{\frac{1}{2}} = 8 \qquad x_1^b = \frac{.6 \times 10}{\frac{1}{3}} = 18$$

$$x_2^g = \frac{.5 \times 10}{\frac{1}{2}} = 10 \qquad x_2^b = \frac{.5 \times 10}{\frac{1}{3}} = 15.$$

(c) To make 18 guns, you need 9 barrels of oil. To make 33 butters you need 11 barrels of oil.

6.8 Let $\mathbf{x}$ minimize costs at $\mathbf{w}$ and let $\mathbf{x}'$ minimize costs at $\mathbf{w}'$. Then $\mathbf{w}'\cdot\mathbf{x}' \geqq \mathbf{w}\cdot\mathbf{x}' \geqq \mathbf{w}\cdot\mathbf{x}$. If (i) holds then the second inequality is strict; if (ii) holds then the first inequality is strict.

6.9 The core is just the initial endowment point.

CHAPTER 7

7.1 The first-order conditions are $\dfrac{\partial u(\mathbf{x}(\mathbf{p}, \mathbf{p}\cdot\mathbf{w}))}{\partial x_i} = \lambda_i p_i$. If p_i doubles, the left hand stays the same so λ must halve.

7.2 Supply curve is $y_i = \partial\pi(p)/\partial p_i$ so the area above the supply curve is

$$\pi(p^*) - \pi(p^0) = p^*y^* - c_v(y^*) - F - (p^0\cdot 0 - c_v(0) - F)$$
$$= p^*y^* - c_v(y^*) - F + F.$$

7.3 Otherwise one would envy the other.

7.4 Suppose not so that $\mathbf{x}_2 >_1 \mathbf{x}_1$ and $\mathbf{x}_1 \gtrsim_1 \mathbf{w}_1$. By convexity $\mathbf{w}_1 = \frac{1}{2}(\mathbf{x}_2 + \mathbf{x}_1) >_1 \mathbf{w}_1$.

7.5 The demand curve is $x_1(\mathbf{p}) = -\partial\phi/\partial p_1$ so area between p_1^1 and p_1^0 is $\phi(\mathbf{p}^0) - \phi(\mathbf{p}^1)$.

7.6 $\phi(\mathbf{p}) = \int_{p_1}^{\infty} x_1(\mathbf{p}, y_0) dp_1 \qquad f(y) = y_0^{\eta} \int_0^y y^{-\eta}\, dy$

so

$$x_1 = \frac{-\partial v/\partial p_1}{\partial v/\partial y} = \frac{x_1(\mathbf{p}, y_0)}{y_0^{\eta} y^{-\eta}} = x_1(\mathbf{p}) \left[\frac{y}{y_0}\right]^{\eta} \text{ as required.}$$

7.7 Use Euler's law, and rearrange to get income elasticity equal to term involving only prices.

Index